Programming Windows Azure

Sriram Krishnan

O'REILLY®

Beijing · Cambridge · Farnham · Köln · Sebastopol · Taipei · Tokyo

Programming Windows Azure

by Sriram Krishnan

Copyright © 2010 Sriram Krishnan. All rights reserved.
Printed in the United States of America.

Published by O'Reilly Media, Inc., 1005 Gravenstein Highway North, Sebastopol, CA 95472.

O'Reilly books may be purchased for educational, business, or sales promotional use. Online editions are also available for most titles (*http://my.safaribooksonline.com*). For more information, contact our corporate/institutional sales department: 800-998-9938 or *corporate@oreilly.com*.

Editors:	Mike Hendrickson and Laurel R.T. Ruma	**Indexer:**	John Bickelhaupt
Production Editor:	Loranah Dimant	**Cover Designer:**	Karen Montgomery
Copyeditor:	Audrey Doyle	**Interior Designer:**	David Futato
Proofreader:	Stacie Arellano	**Illustrator:**	Robert Romano

Printing History:

May 2010:	First Edition.

RepKover.™ This book uses RepKover™, a durable and flexible lay-flat binding.

ISBN: 978-0-596-80197-7

[M]

1273082445

This book is dedicated to my parents. None of this would have been possible without them.

Table of Contents

Preface xiii

1. Cloud Computing 1
   Understanding Cloud Computing   1
      History of Cloud Computing   2
      Understanding the Characteristics of Cloud Computing   7
      Understanding Cloud Services   8
   The Windows Azure Platform   9
      Azure AppFabric   9
      SQL Azure   10
   Windows Azure   10
      Understanding the Origins of Windows Azure   10
      Understanding Windows Azure Features   12
      Virtualization   13
      The Fabric Controller   15
      Storage   16
   When Not to Use the Cloud   18
      Service Availability   18
      Custom Infrastructure Requirements   19
      Security, Confidentiality, and Audits   19
      Capacity Planning and Limits   20
      Unpredictable Performance   20
      Migration and Interoperability   21
   Summary   21

2. Under the Hood 23
   Inside the Cloud   23
   The Data Centers   25
      Security   26
      Compliance   26
   The Hypervisor   27

Hypervisor Architecture   28

Hypercalls and Enlightenments   30

Windows Azure Hypervisor Architecture   30

Windows Azure Hypervisor Features   33

The Fabric   34

The Fabric Controller   35

Coding and Modeling   37

Provisioning and Deployment   40

Management and Monitoring   41

Summary   42

3. Your First Cloud App **43**

Signing Up for Windows Azure   43

The Windows Azure Tool Set   44

Getting and Installing the Tools   44

Satisfying the Prerequisites   44

Getting to Know the SDK and Tools   46

Understanding the Development Fabric   47

Development Storage   49

Developing Your First Cloud Application   50

Writing the Code   50

Packing the Code for the Dev Fabric   52

Running the Code in the Dev Fabric   54

Running the Code in the Cloud   55

Using the Visual Studio Tools   62

Summary   65

4. Service Model **67**

Understanding Windows Azure Roles   67

Role Instances   69

Role Size   71

Service Definition and Configuration   72

Service Definition   73

Service Configuration   74

Introducing the Service Runtime API   75

Accessing Configuration Settings   78

Understanding Endpoints   78

Understanding Inter-Role Communication   80

Subscribing to Changes   83

Looking at Worker Roles in Depth   84

Creating Worker Roles   84

Understanding the Worker Role Life Cycle   85

Understanding Worker Role Patterns   86

Summary   87

5. **Managing Your Service** **89**
   Common Themes Across Windows Azure Services   89
   Windows Azure Developer Portal   90
   Service Management API   91
      Operations   92
      API Authentication   92
      Creating an X.509 Certificate   93
      Uploading the X.509 Certificate   95
      Making API Requests   96
      Using Csmanage   99
   Dealing with Upgrades   102
      In-Place Upgrade   102
      VIP Swap   104
   Summary   105

6. **Native and Non-.NET Code** **107**
   The Windows Azure Sandbox   107
      Hypervisor and Standard User Privileges   107
      Windows Azure Partial Trust   108
      Full Trust and Native Code   109
   Peeking Under the Hood with a Command Shell   109
      Building the Command Shell Proxy   110
      Enabling Native Code Execution   113
      Running the Command Proxy   114
   Running Non-.NET Languages   117
   Understanding FastCGI and PHP   117
      What Is FastCGI?   118
      FastCGI on Windows Azure   119
      PHP on Windows Azure   120
   "Gotchas" with Running Native Code   125
   Summary   126

7. **Storage Fundamentals** **127**
   Accepting the New Storage System   128
   Windows Azure Storage Characteristics   129
      Lots and Lots of Space   129
      Distribution   129
      Scalability   129
      Replication   130
      Consistency   130
      RESTful HTTP APIs   131

Geodistribution	131
Pay for Play	131
Windows Azure Storage Services	131
Blob Storage	132
Queue Storage	132
Table Storage	132
SQL Azure	133
Getting Started with a Storage Account	133
Signing Up for a Storage Account	133
Picking a Geographic Location	135
Affinity Groups	136
Pricing	137
Working with the REST API	138
Understanding the RESTful API Resources	139
HTTP Requests and Responses	140
Building a Storage Client	142
Understanding Authentication and Request Signing	147
Using the Signing Algorithm	148
Creating and Uploading Stuff	151
Using the SDK and Development Storage	153
Installation and Prerequisites	153
Using Cloud Drive	154
Using the Development Storage	155
Summary	156
8. Blobs	**157**
Understanding the Blob Service	157
Using Blobs	158
Pricing	160
Data Model	160
Usage Considerations	162
Requests Could Fail	162
Changes Are Reflected Instantly	163
Compressed Content	164
Using the Blob Storage API	164
Using the Storage Client Library	165
Using Containers	167
Understanding Names and URIs	167
Creating a Container	168
Using an Access Policy	172
Listing Containers	174
Using Metadata	175
Deleting Containers	176

Using Blobs   176
   Names and Paths   177
   Creating and Deleting a Block Blob   178
   Compressed Content   181
   Reading Blobs   184
   Conditional Reads   185
   Listing, Filtering, and Searching for Blobs   187
   Copying Blob   193
Understanding Block Blobs   193
   Using Blocks   194
   PUT Block   195
   Block ID   195
   Put BlockList   195
Understanding Page Blobs   196
   Pages   197
Windows Azure XDrive   198
   XDrive Internals   199
CDN Access and Custom Domain Names   199
   Using Custom Domains   200
Summary   202

9. Queues **203**
Understanding the Value of Queues   204
   Decoupling Components   206
   Scaling Out   207
   Load Leveling   208
Windows Azure Queue Overview   208
   Architecture and Data Model   208
   The Life of a Message   209
   Queue Usage Considerations   211
Understanding Queue Operations   212
   Creating a Queue   213
   Using Queue Metadata   214
   Counting Queue Messages   216
   Listing Queues   216
   Deleting Queues   218
Understanding Message Operations   219
   Enqueuing a Message   219
   Understanding Message TTL   220
   Peeking at a Message   220
   Getting Messages   222
   Deleting Messages   223
   Deleting and Using PopReceipts   224

Summary   224

10. Tables **225**
  Windows Azure Table Overview   226
    Core Concepts   226
    Azure Tables Versus Traditional Databases   229
  ADO.NET Data Services Primer   231
    Exposing Data Services   232
    Consuming Data Services   236
  Table Operations   239
    Creating Tables   239
    Creating Entities   243
    Querying Data   244
    Using Partitioning   248
    Understanding Pagination   255
    Updating Entities   256
    Deleting Tables   258
    Deleting Entities   258
  Summary   260

11. Common Storage Tasks **261**
  Exploring Full-Text Search   261
    Understanding Full-Text Search   261
    Indexing   262
    Building an FTS Engine on Azure   267
  Modeling Data   281
    One-to-Many   281
    Many-to-Many   284
  Making Things Fast   286
    Secondary Indexes   286
    Entity Group Transactions   290
  Utilizing Concurrent Updates   291
  Summary   293

12. Building a Secure Backup System **295**
  Developing a Secure Backup System   296
  Understanding Security   297
  Protecting Data in Motion   298
  Protecting Data at Rest   304
    Understanding the Basics of Cryptography   305
    Determining the Encryption Technique   307
    Generating Keys   308
    Compressing Backup Data   311

    Encrypting Data   313
    Decrypting Data   317
    Signing and Validating Data   317
    Putting the Cryptography Together   319
    Uploading Efficiently Using Blocks   321
  Usage   324
  Summary   325

13. SQL Azure **327**
  Creating and Using a SQL Azure Database   328
    Creating a Database   328
    Adding Firewall Rules   330
    Using SQL Server Management Studio   331
    Using ADO.NET   334
  Differences Between SQL Azure and SQL Server   334
    Resource Restrictions   334
    Language/Feature Differences   335
  Tips and Tricks   335
  Summary   336

Index **337**

Preface

I hate the term *the cloud*. I really do. In a surprisingly short period of time, I've seen the term twisted out of shape and become a marketing buzzword and applied to every bit of technology one can conjure up. I have no doubt that in a few years, the term *the cloud* will be relegated to the same giant dustbin for bad technology branding that the likes of *SOA* and *XML-based web services* are now relegated to. Underneath all that marketing fluff, though, is the evolution of an interesting trend. Call it *the cloud* or *Something-as-a-Service*—it doesn't matter. The idea that you can harness computing and storage horsepower as a service is powerful and is here to stay.

As a builder of things, I love technology that frees up obstacles and lets me focus on what I want to do: create. The cloud does just that. Whether you're a startup or a huge Fortune 500 company with private jets, the cloud lets you focus on building things instead of having to worry about procuring hardware or maintaining a storage area network (SAN) somewhere. Someday, we'll all look back and laugh at the times when trying to run a website with reasonable traffic and storage needs meant waiting a few months for new hardware to show up.

My involvement with this book started in early 2009. Windows Azure had just come on the market and other cloud offerings such as Amazon Web Services and Google's App Engine had been out for some time. I saw a lot of people trying to grapple with what exactly the cloud was, and try to cut through all the marketing jargon and hype. That was no easy feat, let me assure you. I also saw people trying to wrap their heads around Windows Azure. What exactly is it? How do I write code for it? How do I get started? How do I do all those things I need to do to run my app? I hope to answer those questions in this book.

One of the problems about putting anything in print is that it will inevitably be outdated. I have no illusions that this book will be any different. As Windows Azure morphs over time in response to customer needs and industry trends, APIs will change. Features will be added and removed. To that end, this book tries to focus on the "why" more than the "how" or the "what." I'm a great believer that once you know the "why," the "how" and the "what" are easy to wrap your head around. Throughout this book, I've tried to explain why features act in a certain way or why certain features don't exist.

The actual API or class names might have changed by the time you read this book. Thanks to the power of web search, the right answer is never far away.

This book is split into two halves. The first half digs into how Windows Azure works and how to host application code on it. The second half digs into the storage services offered by Windows Azure and how to store data in it. The two halves are quite independent and if you choose, you can read one and skip the other. The nice thing about Windows Azure is that it offers a buffet of services. Like any buffet, you can pick and choose what you want to consume. Want to host code on Windows Azure and host data on the same platform? That's perfect. Want to use the Windows Azure blob service but want to host code in your own machines? That's just as good, too.

Throughout this book, you'll find tiny anecdotes and stories strewn around. Several times, they are only tangentially relevant to the actual technology being discussed. I'm a big fan of books that try to be witty and conversational while being educational at the same time. I don't know whether this book succeeds in that goal. But when you see the umpteenth Star Trek reference, you'll at least understand why it is in there.

How This Book Is Organized

The chapters in this book are organized as follows:

Chapter 1, *Cloud Computing*
: This chapter provides an overview of the cloud and the Windows Azure platform. It gives you a small peek at all the individual components as well as a taste of what coding on the platform looks like.

Chapter 2, *Under the Hood*
: In this chapter, you dive under the hood of Windows Azure and see how the platform works on the inside. The inner workings of the Windows Azure hypervisor and fabric controller are looked at in detail.

Chapter 3, *Your First Cloud App*
: It is time to get your hands dirty and write some code. This chapter gets you started with the Windows Azure SDK and tool set and walks you through developing and deploying your first application on Windows Azure.

Chapter 4, *Service Model*
: In this chapter, you see how to build more advanced services. Core Windows Azure concepts such as service definition and configuration, web roles, worker roles, and inter-role communication are dealt with in detail.

Chapter 5, *Managing Your Service*
: A key part of Windows Azure is managing your service after you have finished writing the code. In this chapter, you see the various service management options provided by Windows Azure. The service management API is looked at in detail.

Chapter 6, *Native and Non-.NET Code*

In this chapter, you learn how to run applications on Windows Azure that are not written in .NET. This could involve writing applications in C/C++ or running other runtimes such as PHP or Ruby.

Chapter 7, *Storage Fundamentals*

Chapter 7 kicks off the storage part of the book. This chapter delves into the basics of the Windows Azure storage services and provides a short overview of the various services offered. The REST API behind the storage services is looked at in detail.

Chapter 8, *Blobs*

This chapter looks at the blobs service offered by Windows Azure. It delves into how to use the blobs API, different types of blobs, and how to use them in common scenarios.

Chapter 9, *Queues*

In this chapter, you learn about the queue service offered by Windows Azure. You see how to use queues in your services, and how to put messages in a queue and take them out.

Chapter 10, *Tables*

A key part of Windows Azure is the ability to store massive amounts of structured data and be able to query it efficiently. The table service offered by Windows Azure is a great option to do just that. This chapter delves into tables—how to efficiently partition, query, and update your data.

Chapter 11, *Common Storage Tasks*

In this chapter, you learn how to perform tasks that you are used to on other systems but may require some work on the cloud. This chapter looks at building full-text search on top of the Windows Azure table service and wraps up by looking at common modeling and performance issues.

Chapter 12, *Building a Secure Backup System*

This chapter happens to be one of my favorites in the book. It walks through the building of a secure backup system, built completely on open source tools and libraries. Along the way, it looks at various security, cryptography, and performance issues while designing applications with the cloud.

Chapter 13, *SQL Azure*

This chapter delves into Microsoft's RDBMS in the cloud: SQL Azure. You see how you can use your SQL Server skill set on Windows Azure and how to port your existing database code to SQL Azure.

Conventions Used in This Book

The following typographical conventions are used in this book:

Italic

>   Indicates new terms, URLs, email addresses, filenames, and file extensions

`Constant width`

>   Used for program listings, as well as within paragraphs to refer to program elements such as variable or function names, databases, data types, environment variables, statements, and keywords

`Constant width bold`

>   Used to highlight significant portions of code, and to show commands or other text that should be typed literally by the user

`Constant width italic`

>   Shows text that should be replaced with user-supplied values or by values determined by context

 This icon signifies a tip, suggestion, or general note.

 This icon signifies a warning or caution.

Using Code Examples

This book is here to help you get your job done. In general, you may use the code in this book in your programs and documentation. You do not need to contact us for permission unless you're reproducing a significant portion of the code. For example, writing a program that uses several chunks of code from this book does not require permission. Selling or distributing a CD-ROM of examples from O'Reilly books does require permission. Answering a question by citing this book and quoting example code does not require permission. Incorporating a significant amount of example code from this book into your product's documentation does require permission.

We appreciate, but do not require, attribution. An attribution usually includes the title, author, publisher, and ISBN. For example: "*Programming Windows Azure* by Sriram Krishnan. Copyright 2010 Sriram Krishnan, 978-0-596-80197-7."

If you feel your use of code examples falls outside fair use or the permission given here, feel free to contact us at *permissions@oreilly.com*.

How to Contact Us

Please address comments and questions concerning this book to the publisher:

O'Reilly Media, Inc.
1005 Gravenstein Highway North
Sebastopol, CA 95472
800-998-9938 (in the United States or Canada)
707-829-0515 (international or local)
707-829-0104 (fax)

We have a web page for this book, where we list errata, examples, and any additional information. You can access this page at:

http://oreilly.com/catalog/9780596801977

To comment or ask technical questions about this book, send email to:

bookquestions@oreilly.com

For more information about our books, conferences, Resource Centers, and the O'Reilly Network, see our website at:

http://oreilly.com

Safari® Books Online

Safari Books Online is an on-demand digital library that lets you easily search over 7,500 technology and creative reference books and videos to find the answers you need quickly.

With a subscription, you can read any page and watch any video from our library online. Read books on your cell phone and mobile devices. Access new titles before they are available for print, and get exclusive access to manuscripts in development and post feedback for the authors. Copy and paste code samples, organize your favorites, download chapters, bookmark key sections, create notes, print out pages, and benefit from tons of other time-saving features.

O'Reilly Media has uploaded this book to the Safari Books Online service. To have full digital access to this book and others on similar topics from O'Reilly and other publishers, sign up for free at *http://my.safaribooksonline.com*.

Acknowledgments

First, I would like to thank the single most important person responsible for the creation of this book: my fiancée, Aarthi. In fact, I want to use this section to somehow apologize for what I made her go through. Not only did she put up with me agonizing over unwritten chapters and being unavailable pretty much every evening and weekend for more than a year, but she also proofread all chapters and corrected an uncountable number of mistakes. She did all of this while making sure I didn't kill myself through the process and essentially taking care of me for more than a year. I promise to never put her through anything like this ever again. Aarthi, I love you and I'm sorry.

This book is dedicated to my parents. This book, my career, and pretty much everything I do today is directly because of them.

Speaking of my career and work, I have a ton of people to thank in and around the Microsoft community. I wouldn't even be at Microsoft if it weren't for people like Janakiram MSV, Paramesh Vaidyanathan, and S. Somasegar. At Microsoft, I've had the benefit of having several friends and mentors who have made sure I didn't get myself fired. In particular, I'd like to mention Barry Bond, who apart from being one of the smartest engineers I've seen and my mentor for several years was also kind enough to review several chapters in this book.

The entire Windows Azure team was of great support to me while I wrote this book. Chief among them was my boss, Vikram Bhambri. I still don't know how he puts up with me every day and hasn't fired me yet. Several people on the Windows Azure team helped me by answering questions and reviewing content. I'd like to thank Manuvir Das, David Lemphers, Steve Marx, Sumit Mehrotra, Mohit Srivastava, and Zhe Yang. Brad Calder and Hoi Vo read early sections of the book and provided feedback. Their early encouragement was of great help. Aleks Gershaft went to a lot of trouble to review my content at the very end and pointed out dozens of minor details. The storage chapters are a great deal better thanks to his efforts. One of the biggest reasons for me joining the Windows Azure team was the chance to work with Dave Cutler. He continues to be an inspiration every single day.

In the O'Reilly world, I've been lucky to work with some great people. Brian Jepson was my first editor and he helped me tremendously. He knows exactly how to deal with the fragile ego of a first-time writer. Laurel Ruma and Mike Hendrickson helped me throughout the process and saw this book out the door. This book is a lot better for their efforts. It couldn't have been easy dealing with me. I'll miss all our arguments.

An army of technical editors went through early versions of my content and helped me improve it: Ben Day, Johnny Halife, Brian Peek, Janakiram MSV, Michael Stiefel, and Chris Williams. They kept me on my toes and made me think really hard about my content. Any flaws in this book are despite their best efforts and are directly due to my stubbornness.

Finally, I'd like to thank you, dear reader. Almost every single time I sat down to write, I would think to myself: "Will the people buying this book think they got value for their money?" I sincerely hope that you do.

Contact me at *mail@sriramkrishnan.com* anytime to tell me what you thought about the book or just to yell at me for some obscure Monty Python reference you didn't get. Sorry about that.

Writing this book was a life-changing experience for me. I hope you have fun reading it and using Windows Azure!

## CHAPTER 1

Cloud Computing

If you drive from the airport in San Jose, California, down Interstate 180 South, chances are you'll spot a sign for a seedy strip joint called the Pink Poodle. The story of Microsoft's cloud computing platform starts in 2006 with an eclectic set of people and this most unlikely of locations. Before I tell that story, we'll examine what cloud computing actually *is*, where it came from, and why it matters to you.

Imagine if tap water didn't exist. Every household would need to dig a well. Doing so would be a pain. Wells are expensive to build, and expensive to maintain. You wouldn't be able get a large quantity of water quickly if you needed it—at least not without upgrading your pump. And if you no longer needed the well, there would be no store to return it to, and no way to recoup your capital investment. If you vacated the house, or the proper plumbing were installed in your house, you would have invested in a well you don't need.

Tap water fixes all of that. Someone else spends the money and builds the right plumbing and infrastructure. They manage it, and ensure that the water is clean and always available. You pay only for what you use. You can always get more if you want it.

That, in a nutshell, is what *cloud computing* is all about. It is data center resources delivered like tap water. It is always on, and you pay only for what you use.

This chapter takes a detailed look at the concepts behind cloud computing, and shows you how Windows Azure utilizes cloud computing.

Understanding Cloud Computing

Microsoft describes Windows Azure as an "operating system for the cloud." But what exactly is the "cloud" and, more importantly, what exactly is cloud computing?

At its core, *cloud computing* is the realization of the long-held dream of *utility computing*. The "cloud" is a metaphor for the Internet, derived from a common representation in computer network drawings showing the Internet as a cloud. Utility computing is a concept that entails having access to computing resources, and paying for the use of those resources on a metered basis, similar to paying for common utilities such as water, electricity, and telephone service.

History of Cloud Computing

Before diving into particulars, let's first take a look at where cloud computing came from. The history of cloud computing includes utilization of the concept in a variety of environments, including the following:

- Time-sharing systems
- Mainframe computing systems
- Transactional computing systems
- Grid computing systems

Time-sharing systems

Cloud computing has its origins in the 1960s. Time-sharing systems were the first to offer a shared resource to the programmer. Before time-sharing systems, programmers typed in code using punch cards or tape, and submitted the cards or tape to a machine that executed jobs synchronously, one after another. This was massively inefficient, since the computer was subjected to a lot of idle time.

Bob Bemer, an IBM computer scientist, proposed the idea of time sharing as part of an article in *Automatic Control Magazine*. Time sharing took advantage of the time the processor spent waiting for I/O, and allocated these slices of time to other users. Since multiple users were dealt with at the same time, these systems were required to maintain the state of each user and each program, and to switch between them quickly. Though today's machines accomplish this effortlessly, it took some time before computers had the speed and size in core memory to support this new approach.

The first real project to implement a time-sharing system was begun by John McCarthy on an IBM 704 mainframe. The system that this led to, the *Compatible Time Sharing System* (CTSS), had the rudimentary elements of several technologies that today are taken for granted: text formatting, interuser messaging, as well as a rudimentary shell and scripting ability.

 John McCarthy later became famous as the father of LISP and modern artificial intelligence. CTSS led to Multics, which inspired Unix.

Tymshare was an innovative company in this space. Started in 1964, Tymshare sold computer time and software packages to users. It had two SDS/XDS 940 mainframes that could be accessed via dial-up connections. In the late 1960s, Tymshare started using remote sites with minicomputers (known as *nodes*) running its own software called the *Supervisor*. In this, Tymshare created the ancestor of modern networked systems.

 The product created by Tymshare, Tymnet, still exists today. After a series of takeovers and mergers, Tymshare is now owned by Verizon.

These efforts marked the beginning of the central idea of cloud computing: sharing a single computing resource that is intelligently allocated among users.

At its peak, there were dozens of vendors (including IBM and General Electric). Organizations opened time-sharing accounts to get access to computing resources on a pay-per-usage model, and for overflow situations when they didn't have enough internal capacity to meet demand. These vendors competed in uptime, price, and the platform they ran on. They started offering applications and database management systems (DBMSs) on a pay-for-play model, as well. They eventually went out of fashion with the rise of the personal computer.

Mainframe computing

Though nearly outdated today, mainframe computing innovated several of the ideas you see in cloud computing. These large, monolithic systems were characterized by high computation speed, redundancy built into their internal systems, and generally delivering high reliability and availability. Mainframe systems were also early innovators of a technology that has resurged over the past few years: virtualization.

IBM dominates the mainframe market. One of its most famous model series was the IBM System/360 (S/360). This project, infamous for its appearance in the book *The Mythical Man Month: Essays on Software Engineering* by Fred Brooks (Addison-Wesley), also brought virtualization to the mainstream.

The CP/CMS operating system on the S/360 could create multiple independent virtual machines. This was possible because of hardware assistance from the S/260, which had two modes of instructions: the normal *problem state* and a special *supervisor state*. The supervisor state instructions would cause a hardware exception that the operating system could then handle. Its fundamental principles were similar to modern-day hardware assistance such as AMD-V (Pacifica) and Intel VT-X (Vanderpool).

Mainframe usage dwindled because several of the technologies once found only on mainframes started showing up on increasingly smaller computers. Mainframe computing and cloud computing are similar in the idea that you have a centralized resource (in the case of cloud computing, a data center) that is too expensive for most companies to buy and maintain, but is affordable to lease or rent resources from. Data centers represent investments that only a few companies can make, and smaller companies rent resources from the companies that can afford them.

Transactional computing

Transactional systems are the underpinning of most modern services. The technology behind transactional systems is instrumental in modern cloud services. Transactional systems allow processing to be split into individual, indivisible operations called *transactions*. Each transaction is atomic—it either succeeds as a whole or fails as a whole. Transactions are a fundamental part of every modern database system.

The history of transactional processing systems has been intertwined with that of database systems. The 1960s, 1970s, and 1980s were a hotbed for database system research. By the late 1960s, database systems were coming into the mainstream. The COBOL committee formed a task group to define a standard database language. Relational theory was formalized in the 1970s starting with E.F. Codd's seminal paper, and this led to SQL being standardized in the 1980s. In 1983, Oracle launched version 3 of its nascent database product, the first version of its database system to support a rudimentary form of transactions.

While database systems were emerging, several significant innovations were happening in the transaction processing space. One of the first few systems with transaction processing capabilities was IBM's *Information Management System* (IMS).

 IMS has a fascinating history. After President John F. Kennedy's push for a mission to the moon, North America Rockwell won the bid to launch the first spacecraft to the moon. The company needed an automated system to manage large bills of materials for the construction, and contracted with IBM for this system in 1966. IBM put together a small team, and legendary IBM engineer Vern Watts joined the effort. The system that IBM designed was eventually renamed IMS.

IMS was a joint hierarchical database and information management system with transaction processing capabilities. It had several of the features now taken for granted in modern systems: Atomicity, Consistency, Isolation, Durability (ACID) support; device independence; and so on. Somewhat surprisingly, IMS has stayed strong over the ages, and is still in widespread use.

IBM also contributed another important project to transaction processing: System R. System R was the first SQL implementation that provided good transaction processing performance. System R performed breakthrough work in several important areas: query optimization, locking systems, transaction isolation, storing the system catalog in a relational form inside the database itself, and so on.

Tandem Computers was an early manufacturer of transaction processing systems. Tandem systems used redundant processors and designs to provide failover. Tandem's flagship product, the NonStop series of systems, was marketed for its high uptime.

Tandem was also famous for its informal culture and for nurturing several employees who would go on to become famous in their own right. The most famous of these was Jim Gray, who, among several other achievements, literally wrote the book on transaction processing.

Tandem's systems ran a custom operating system called Guardian. This operating system was the first to incorporate several techniques that are present in most modern distributed systems. The machine consisted of several processors, many of which executed in lock-step, and communicated over high-speed data buses (which also had redundancy built in). *Process pairs* were used to failover operations if execution on one processor halted for any reason. After a series of takeovers, Tandem is now a part of Hewlett-Packard. Tandem's NonStop line of products is still used, with support for modern technologies such as Java.

The fundamental design behind these systems—that is, fault tolerance, failover, two-phase commit, resource managers, Paxos (a fault-tolerance protocol for distributed systems), redundancy, the lessons culled from trying to implement distributed transactions—forms the bedrock of modern cloud computing systems, and has shaped their design to a large extent.

Grid computing

The term *grid computing* originated in the 1990s, and referred to making computers accessible in a manner similar to a power grid. This sounds a lot like cloud computing, and reflects the overlap between the two, with some companies even using the terms interchangeably. One of the better definitions of the difference between the two has been offered by Rick Wolski of the Eucalyptus project. He notes that grid computing is about users making few, but very large, requests. Only a few of these allocations can be serviced at any given time, and others must be queued. Cloud computing, on the other hand, is about lots of small allocation requests, with allocations happening in real time.

If you want to read more about Wolski's distinction between grid computing and cloud computing, see *http://blog.rightscale.com/2008/07/07/ cloud-computing-vs-grid-computing/*.

The most famous grid computing project is SETI@home. At SETI, employees search for extraterrestrial intelligence. The SETI@home project splits data collected from telescopes into small chunks that are then downloaded into volunteer machines. The software installed on these machines scans through the radio telescope data looking for telltale signs of alien life. The project has logged some astonishing numbers—more than 5 million participants and more than 2 million years of aggregate computing time logged.

Several frameworks and products have evolved around grid computing. The Globus toolkit is an open source toolkit for grid computing built by the Globus Alliance. It allows you to build a computing grid based on commodity hardware, and then submit jobs to be processed on the grid. It has several pluggable job schedulers, both open source and proprietary. Globus is used extensively by the scientific community. CERN will be using Globus to process data from tests of the Large Hadron Collider in Geneva.

Microsoft jumped into this space with the launch of Windows High Performance Computing (HPC) Server in September 2008. Windows HPC Server provides a cluster environment, management and monitoring tools, and a job scheduler, among several other features. Figure 1-1 shows the Windows HPC management interface. Most importantly, it integrates with Windows Deployment Services, and it can deploy operating system images to set up the cluster. Later in this chapter, you'll learn about how the Windows Azure *fabric controller* works, and you'll see similar elements in its design.

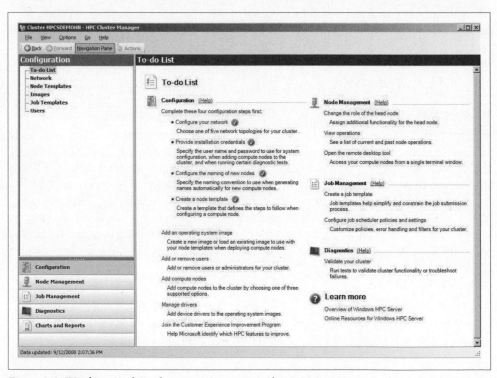

Figure 1-1. Windows High Performance Computing Cluster Manager

The cloud allows you to run workloads similar to a grid. When you have data that must be processed you spin up the required number of machines, split the data across the machines in any number of ways, and aggregate the results together. Throughout this book, you'll see several technologies that have roots in modern grid and distributed computing.

Understanding the Characteristics of Cloud Computing

A modern cloud computing platform (of which, as you will see later in this chapter, Windows Azure is one) typically incorporates the following characteristics:

The illusion of infinite resources
> Cloud computing platforms provide the illusion of infinite computing and storage resources. (Note that this description includes the word *illusion* because there will always be some limits, albeit large, that you must keep in mind.) As a user, you are not required to do the kind of capacity planning and provisioning that may be necessary to deploy your own individual storage and computing infrastructure. You can depend on the companies you are dealing with to own several large data centers spread around the world, and you can tap into those resources on an as-needed basis.

Scale on demand
> All cloud platforms allow you to add resources on demand, rather than going through a lengthy sales-and-provisioning process. Instead of having to wait weeks for someone to deliver new servers to your data center, you typically must wait only minutes to get new resources assigned. This is a really good thing in terms of the cost and time required to provision resources, but it also means your application must be designed to scale along with the underlying hardware provided by your cloud computing supplier.

Pay-for-play
> Cloud computing platforms typically don't require any upfront investment, reservation, or major setup fees. You pay only for the software and hardware you use. This, along with the scaling capacity of cloud platforms, means you won't incur huge capital expenditure (*capex*) costs upfront. All cloud platforms let you move away from capex spending and into operating expenditure (*opex*) spending. In layman's terms, this converts a fixed cost for estimated usage upfront to a variable cost where you pay only for what you use.

High availability and an SLA
> If you choose to depend on someone else to run your business, you must be assured that you won't be subjected to frequent outages. Most cloud providers have a *Service Level Agreement* (SLA) that guarantees a level of uptime, and includes a refund mechanism if the SLA isn't met. Windows Azure provides an SLA for both its storage and its hosting pieces.

Geographically distributed data centers
> When serving customers around the globe, it is critical to have data centers in multiple geographic locations. Reasons for this requirement include legal/regulatory concerns, geopolitical considerations, load balancing, network latency, edge caching, and so on.

In short, cloud computing is like water or electricity. It is always on when you need it, and you pay only for what you use.

In reality, cloud computing providers today have some way to go before they meet the "several 9s" (99.99% and beyond uptime) availability provided by utility companies (gas, water, electricity) or telecom companies.

Understanding Cloud Services

Cloud computing platforms can be differentiated by the kind of services they offer. You might hear these referred to as one of the following:

Infrastructure-as-a-Service (IaaS)
> This refers to services that provide lower levels of the stack. They typically provide basic hardware as a service—things such as virtual machines, load-balancer settings, and network attached storage. Amazon Web Services (AWS) and GoGrid fall into this category

Platform-as-a-service (PaaS)
> Providers such as Windows Azure and Google App Engine (GAE) provide a *platform* that users write to. In this case, the term *platform* refers to something that abstracts away the lower levels of the stack. This application runs in a specialized environment. This environment is sometimes restricted—running as a low-privilege process, with restrictions on writing to the local disk and so on. Platform providers also provide abstractions around services (such as email, distributed caches, structured storage), and provide bindings for various languages. In the case of GAE, users write code in a subset of Python, which executes inside a custom hosting environment in Google's data centers.

In Windows Azure, you typically write applications in .NET, but you can also call native code, write code using other languages and runtimes such as Python/PHP/Ruby/Java, and, in general, run most code that can run on Windows.

Software-as-a-Service (SaaS)
> The canonical example of this model is Salesforce.com. Here, specific provided applications can be accessed from anywhere. Instead of hosting applications such as Customer Relationship Management (CRM), Enterprise Resource Planning (ERP), and Human Resources (HR) on-site, companies can outsource these applications. These are higher-level services that we won't address in much detail this book.

In reality, cloud services overlap these categories, and it is difficult to pin any one of them down into a single category.

The Windows Azure Platform

The Windows Azure Platform stack consists of a few distinct pieces, one of which (Windows Azure) is examined in detail throughout this book. However, before beginning to examine Windows Azure, you should know what the other pieces do, and how they fit in.

The Windows Azure Platform is a group of cloud technologies to be used by applications running in Microsoft's data centers, on-premises and on various devices. The first question people have when seeing its architecture is "Do I need to run my application on Windows Azure to take advantage of the services on top?" The answer is "no." You can access Azure AppFabric services and SQL Azure, as well as the other pieces from your own data center or the box under your desk, if you choose to.

This is not represented by a typical technology stack diagram—the pieces on the top don't necessarily run on the pieces on the bottom, and you'll find that the technology powering these pieces is quite different. For example, the authentication mechanism used in SQL Azure is different from the one used in Windows Azure. A diagram showing the Windows Azure platform merely shows Microsoft's vision in the cloud space. Some of these products are nascent, and you'll see them converge over time.

Now, let's take a look at some of the major pieces.

Azure AppFabric

Azure AppFabric services provide typical infrastructure services required by both on-premises and cloud applications. These services act at a higher level of the "stack" than Windows Azure (which you'll learn about shortly). Most of these services can be accessed through a public HTTP REST API, and hence can be used by applications running on Windows Azure, as well as your applications running outside Microsoft's data centers. However, because of networking latencies, accessing these services from Windows Azure might be faster because they are often hosted in the same data centers. Since this is a distinct piece from the rest of the Windows Azure platform, we will not cover it in this book.

Following are the components of the Windows Azure AppFabric platform:

Service Bus
> Hooking up services that live in different networks is tricky. There are several issues to work through: firewalls, network hardware, and so on. The Service Bus component of Windows Azure AppFabric is meant to deal with this problem. It allows applications to expose Windows Communication Foundation (WCF) endpoints that can be accessed from "outside" (that is, from another application not running inside the same location). Applications can expose service endpoints as public HTTP URLs that can be accessed from anywhere. The platform takes care of such challenges as network address translation, reliably getting data across, and so on.

Access Control
> This service lets you use federated authentication for your service based on a claims-based, RESTful model. It also integrates with Active Directory Federation Services, letting you integrate with enterprise/on-premises applications.

SQL Azure

In essence, SQL Azure is SQL Server hosted in the cloud. It provides relational database features, but does it on a platform that is scalable, highly available, and load-balanced. Most importantly, unlike SQL Server, it is provided on a pay-as-you-go model, so there are no capital fees upfront (such as for hardware and licensing).

As you'll see shortly, there are several similarities between SQL Azure and the table services provided by Windows Azure. They both are scalable, reliable services hosted in Microsoft data centers. They both support a pay-for-usage model. The fundamental differences come down to what each system was designed to do.

Windows Azure tables were designed to provide low-cost, highly scalable storage. They don't have any relational database features—you won't find foreign keys or joins or even SQL. SQL Azure, on the other hand, was designed to provide these features. We will examine these differences in more detail later in this book in the discussions about storage.

Windows Azure

Windows Azure is Microsoft's platform for running applications in the cloud. You get on-demand computing and storage to host, scale, and manage web applications through Microsoft data centers. Unlike other versions of Windows, Windows Azure doesn't run on any one machine—it is distributed across thousands of machines. There will never be a DVD of Windows Azure that you can pop in and install on your machine.

Before looking at the individual features and components that make up Windows Azure, let's examine how Microsoft got to this point, and some of the thinking behind the product.

Understanding the Origins of Windows Azure

The seeds for Windows Azure were sown in a 2005 memo from Ray Ozzie, Microsoft's then-new Chief Software Architect, who had just taken over from Bill Gates. In that memo, Ozzie described the transformation of software from the kind you installed on your system via a CD to the kind you accessed through a web browser. It was a call to action for Microsoft to embrace the services world. Among other things, Ozzie called for a services platform. Several teams at Microsoft had been running successful services, but these lessons hadn't been transformed into actual bits that internal teams or external customers could use.

If you want to read the Ozzie memo, you can find it at *http://www.script ing.com/disruption/ozzie/TheInternetServicesDisruptio.htm*.

In 2006, Amitabh Srivastava, a long-time veteran at Microsoft, was in charge of fixing the engineering processes in Windows. As Windows Vista drew close to launch, Srivastava met Ozzie and agreed to lead a new project to explore a services platform. Srivastava quickly convinced some key people to join him. Arguably, the most important of these was Dave Cutler, the father of Windows NT and Virtual Memory System (VMS). Cutler is a legendary figure in computing, and a near-mythical figure at Microsoft, known for his coding and design skills as well as his fearsome personality. Convincing Cutler to come out of semiretirement to join the new team was a jolt in the arm.

During this period, the nascent team made several trips to all of Microsoft's major online services to see how they ran things, and to get a feel for what problems they faced. It was during one such trip to California to see Hotmail that Cutler suggested (in jest) that they name their new project "Pink Poodle" after a strip joint they spotted on the drive from the San Jose airport. A variant of this name, "Red Dog," was suggested by another team member, and was quickly adopted as the codename for the project they were working on.

After looking at several internal and external teams, they found similar problems across them all. They found that everyone was spending a lot of time managing the machines/ virtual machines they owned, and that these machines were inefficiently utilized in the first place. They found that there was little sharing of resources, and that there was no shared platform or standard toolset that worked for everyone. They also found several good tools, code, and ideas that they could reuse.

The growing team started building out the various components that made up Red Dog: a new hypervisor (software that manages and runs virtual machines), a "fabric" controller (a distributed system to manage machines and applications), a distributed storage system, and, like every other Microsoft platform, compelling developer tools. They realized that they were exploring solutions that would solve problems for everyone outside Microsoft, as well as inside, and switched to shaping this into a product that Microsoft's customers could use. Working in a startup-like fashion, they did things that weren't normally done at Microsoft, and broke some rules along the way (such as turning a nearby building into a small data center, and stealing power from the buildings around it).

 You can read more about this adventure at *http://www.wired.com/tech biz/people/magazine/16-12/ff_ozzie?currentPage=1*.

Red Dog, now renamed Windows Azure, was officially unveiled along with the rest of the Azure stack during the Professional Developers Conference in Los Angeles on October 27, 2008.

Understanding Windows Azure Features

As shown in Figure 1-2, when you use Windows Azure you get the following key features:

Service hosting

You can build services that are then hosted by Windows Azure. *Services* here refers to any generic server-side application—be it a website, a computation service to crunch massive amounts of data, or any generic server-side application. Note that, in the current release of Windows Azure, there are limits to what kind of code is allowed and not allowed. For example, code that requires administrative privileges on the machine is not allowed.

Service management

In a traditional environment, you must deal with diverse operational tasks—everything from dealing with application updates, to monitoring the application, to replacing failed hardware. In a traditional environment, there are a variety of tools to help you do this. In the Microsoft ecosystem outside of Azure, you might use the capabilities built into Windows Server and products such as Systems Center. In the non-Microsoft world, you might be using tools such as Capistrano for deployment and projects such as Ganglia for monitoring. Windows Azure's fabric controller brings this "in-house" and deals with this automatically for you. It monitors your services, deals with hardware and software failures, and handles operating system and application upgrades seamlessly.

Storage

Windows Azure provides scalable storage in which you can store data. Three key services are provided: binary large object (*blob*) storage (for storing raw data), semistructured tables, and a queue service. All services have an HTTP API on top of them that you can use to access the services from any language, and from outside Microsoft's data centers as well. The data stored in these services is also replicated multiple times to protect from internal hardware or software failure. Storage (like computation) is based on a consumption model where you pay only for what you use.

Windows Server

If you're wondering whether your code is going to look different because it is running in the cloud, or whether you're going to have to learn a new framework, the answer is "no." You'll still be writing code that runs on Windows Server. The .NET Framework (3.5 SP1, as of this writing) is installed by default on all machines, and your typical ASP.NET code will work. If you choose to, you can use FastCGI support to run any framework that supports FastCGI (such as PHP, Ruby on Rails,

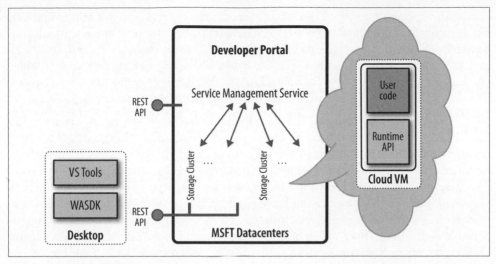

Figure 1-2. Windows Azure overview

Python, and so on). If you have existing native code or binaries, you can run that as well.

Development tools

Like every major Microsoft platform, Windows Azure has a bunch of tools to make developing on it easier. Windows Azure has an API that you can use for logging and error reporting, as well as mechanisms to read and update service configuration files. There's also an SDK that enables you to deploy your applications to a cloud simulator, as well as Visual Studio extensions.

Virtualization

At the bottom of the Windows Azure stack, you'll find a lot of machines in Microsoft data centers. These are state-of-the-art data centers with efficient power usage, beefy bandwidth, and cooling systems. Even the most efficient facilities still possess a lot of room for overhead and waste when it comes to utilization of resources. Since the biggest source of data center cost is power, this is typically measured in performance/watts/dollars. What causes that number to go up?

 As of this writing, Windows Azure is hosted in six locations spread across the United States, Europe, and Asia.

If you run services on the "bare metal" (directly on a physical machine), you soon run into a number of challenges as far as utilization is concerned. If a service is using a machine and is experiencing low traffic while another service is experiencing high traffic, there is no easy way to move hardware from one service to the other. This is a big reason you see services from large organizations experience outages under heavy traffic, even though they have excess capacity in other areas in their data centers—they don't have a mechanism to shift workloads easily. The other big challenge with running on the bare metal is that you are limited to running one service per box. You cannot host multiple services, since it is difficult to offer guarantees for resources and security.

As an answer to these problems, the industry has been shifting to a virtualized model. In essence, *hardware virtualization* lets you partition a single physical machine into many virtual machines. If you use VMware Fusion, Parallels Desktop, Sun's VirtualBox, or Microsoft Virtual PC, you're already using virtualization, albeit the desktop flavor. The *hypervisor* is a piece of software that runs in the lower parts of the system and lets the *host* hardware be shared by multiple *guest* operating systems. As far as the guest operating systems and the software running on them are concerned, there is no discernible difference. There are several popular server virtualization products on the market, including VMware's product, Xen (which Amazon uses in its cloud services), and Microsoft's Windows Hyper-V.

Windows Azure has its own hypervisor built from scratch and optimized for cloud services. In practice this means that, since Microsoft controls the specific hardware in its data centers, this hypervisor can make use of specific hardware enhancements that a generic hypervisor targeted at a wide range of hardware (and a heterogeneous environment) cannot. This hypervisor is efficient, has a small footprint, and is tightly integrated with the kernel of the operating system running on top of it. This leads to performance close to what you'd see from running on the bare metal.

 In case you are wondering whether you can use this hypervisor in your data center, you'll be happy to hear that several innovations from this will be incorporated into future editions of Hyper-V.

Each hypervisor manages several virtual operating systems. All of these run a Windows Server 2008–compatible operating system. In reality, you won't see any difference between running on normal Windows Server 2008 and these machines—the only differences are some optimizations for the specific hypervisor they're running on. This Windows Server 2008 image has the .NET Framework (3.5 SP1, as of this writing) installed on it.

Running on a hypervisor provides Windows Azure with a lot of freedom. For example, no lengthy operating system installation is required. To run your application, Windows Azure can just copy over an image of the operating system, a Virtual Hard Disk (VHD) containing your application-specific binaries. You simply boot the machine from the image using a new boot-from-VHD feature. If you have, say, a new operating system patch, no problem. Windows Azure just patches the image, copies it to the target

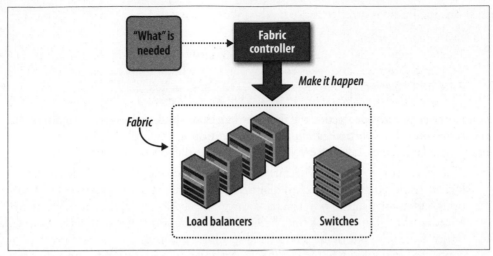

Figure 1-3. What the fabric does

machine, and boots. *Voilà!* You have a patched machine in a matter of minutes, if not seconds.

You can write applications just as you did before, and in almost all cases, you can simply ignore the fact that you're not running on native hardware.

The Fabric Controller

Imagine that you're describing your service architecture to a colleague. You probably walk up to the whiteboard and draw some boxes to refer to your individual machines, and sketch in some arrows. In the real world, you spend a lot of time implementing this diagram. You first set up some machines on which you install your bits. You deploy the various pieces of software to the right machines. You set up various networking settings: firewalls, virtual LANs, load balancers, and so on. You also set up monitoring systems to be alerted when a node goes down.

In a nutshell, Azure's *fabric controller* (see Figure 1-3) automates all of this for you. Azure's fabric controller is a piece of highly available, distributed software that runs across all of Windows Azure's nodes, and monitors the state of every node. You tell it what you want by specifying your *service model* (effectively, a declarative version of the whiteboard diagram used to describe your architecture to a colleague), and the fabric controller automates the details. It finds the right hardware, sets up your bits, and applies the right network settings. It also monitors your application and the hardware so that, in case of a crash, your application can be restarted on either the same node or a different node.

In short, the fabric controller performs the following key tasks:

Hardware management

The fabric controller manages the low-level hardware in the data center. It provisions and monitors, and takes corrective actions when things go wrong. The hardware it manages ranges from nodes to TOR/L2 switches, load balancers, routers, and other network elements. When the fabric controller detects a problem, it tries to perform corrective actions. If that isn't possible, it takes the hardware out of the pool and gets a human operator to investigate it.

Service modeling

The fabric controller maps declarative service specifications (the written down, logical version of the whiteboard diagrams mentioned at the beginning of this section) and maps them to physical hardware. This is *the* key task performed by the fabric controller. If you grok this, you grok the fabric controller. The service model outlines the topology of the service, and specifies the various roles and how they're connected, right down to the last precise granular detail. The fabric controller can then maintain this model. For example, if you specify that you have three frontend nodes talking to a backend node through a specific port, the fabric controller can ensure that the topology always holds up. In case of a failure, it deploys the right binaries on a new node, and brings the service model back to its correct state. Later in this book, you'll learn in detail how the fabric controller works, and how your application can take advantage of this.

Operating system management

The fabric controller takes care of patching the operating systems that run on these nodes, and does so in a manner that lets your service stay up.

Service life cycle

The fabric controller also automates various parts of the service life cycle—things such as updates and configuration changes. You can partition your application into sections (*update domains* and *fault domains*), and the fabric controller updates only one domain at a time, ensuring that your service stays up. If you're pushing new configuration changes, it brings down one section of your machines and updates them, then moves on to the next set, and so on, ensuring that your service stays up throughout.

Storage

If you think of Windows Azure as being similar to an operating system, the storage services are analogous to its filesystem. Normal storage solutions don't always work very well in a highly scalable, scale-out (rather than scale-up) cloud environment. This is what pushed Google to develop systems such as BigTable and Google File System, and Amazon to develop Dynamo and to later offer S3 and SimpleDb.

Windows Azure offers three key data services: blobs, tables, and queues. All of these services are highly scalable, distributed, and reliable. In each case, multiple copies of the data are made, and several processes are in place to ensure that you don't lose your data.

All of the services detailed here are available over HTTP through a simple REST API, and can be accessed from outside Microsoft's data centers as well. Like everything else in Azure, you pay only for what you use and what you store.

 Unlike some other distributed storage systems, *none* of Windows Azure's storage services are *eventually consistent*. This means that when you do a write, it is instantly visible to all subsequent readers. Eventually, consistency is typically used to boost performance, but is more difficult to code against than consistent APIs (since you cannot rely on reading what you just wrote). Azure's storage services allow for *optimistic concurrency* support to give you increased performance if you don't care about having the exact right data (for example, logs, analytics, and so on).

Blob storage

The blob storage service provides a simple interface for storing named files along with metadata. Files can be up to 1 TB in size, and there is almost no limit to the number you can store or the total storage available to you. You can also chop uploads into smaller sections, which makes uploading large files much easier.

Here is some sample Python code to give you a taste of how you'd access a blob using the API. This uses the unofficial library from *http://github.com/sriramk/winazurestorage/*. (We will explore the official .NET client in detail later in this book.)

```
blobs = BlobStorage(HOST,ACCOUNT,SECRET_KEY)
blobs.create_container("testcontainer", False)
    blobs.put_blob("testcontainer","test","Hello World!" )
```

Queue service

The queue service provides reliable storage and delivery of messages for your application. You'll typically use it to hook up the various components of your application, and not have to build your own messaging system. You can send an unlimited number of messages, and you are guaranteed reliable delivery. You can also control the lifetime of the message. You can decide exactly when you're finished processing the message and remove it from the queue. Since this service is available over the public HTTP API, you can use it for applications running on your own premises as well.

Table storage

The table storage service is arguably the most interesting of all the storage services. Almost every application needs some form of structured storage. Traditionally, this is through a relational database management system (RDBMS) such as Oracle, SQL Server, MySQL, and the like. Google was the first company to build a large, distributed, structured storage system that focused on scale-out, low cost, and high performance: BigTable. In doing this, Google was also willing to give up some relational capabilities—SQL support, foreign keys, joins, and everything that goes with it—and denormalize its data. Systems such as Facebook's Cassandra and Amazon's SimpleDb follow the same principles.

The Windows Azure table storage service provides the same kind of capability. You can create massively scalable tables (billions of rows, and it scales along with traffic). The data in these tables is replicated to ensure that no data is lost in the case of hardware failure. Data is stored in the form of *entities*, each of which has a set of *properties*. This is similar to (but not the same as) a database table and column. You control how the data is partitioned using `PartitionKey`s and `RowKey`s. By partitioning across as many machines as possible, you help query performance.

You may be wondering what language you use to query this service. If you're in the .NET world, you can write Language Integrated Query (LINQ) code, and your code will look similar to LINQ queries you'd write against other data stores. If you're coding in Python or Ruby or some other non-.NET environment, you have an HTTP API where you can encode simple queries. If you're familiar with ADO.NET Data Services (previously called Astoria), you'll be happy to hear that this is just a normal ADO.NET Data Service API.

If you're intimidated by all this, don't be. Moving to a new storage system can be daunting, and you'll find that there are several tools and familiar APIs to help you along the way. You also have the option to use familiar SQL Server support if you are willing to forego some of the features you get with the table storage service.

When Not to Use the Cloud

You may be surprised to see a section talking about the pitfalls of cloud computing in this chapter. To be sure, some problems exist with all cloud computing platforms today, and Windows Azure is no exception. This section helps you carefully determine whether you can live with these problems. More often than not, you can. If you find that cloud computing isn't your cup of tea, there is nothing wrong with that; traditional hosting isn't going away anytime soon.

Note that the following discussion applies to every cloud computing platform in existence today, and is by no means unique to Windows Azure.

Service Availability

Outages happen. As a user, you expect a service to always be running. But the truth is that the current state of cloud providers (or any sort of hosting providers, for that matter) doesn't give the level of availability offered by a power utility or a telecom company. Can you live with outages? That depends on several factors, including some possible mitigation strategies:

- Do you know how frequently your existing infrastructure has outages? In most cases, this is probably a much higher number than what you'll see with cloud computing providers.
- You can use multiple cloud computing providers as a backup strategy in case of an outage.
- You can host core business functions on-premises and use the cloud for excess capacity. Or you can run a small on-premises infrastructure and fall back to that in case of an outage.

Outages aren't caused only by software issues. DDoS attacks are another critical problem, and attacks from large botnets are still difficult to defend against, regardless of what kind of provider you're hosted on.

Custom Infrastructure Requirements

Several users have custom hardware needs. Some users may need high-end GPUs for heavy graphics processing, while others need high-speed interconnects for high-performance computing and aren't satisfied with gigabit Ethernet. High-end storage area networks (SANs) and special RAID configurations are popular requests. Cloud computing thrives on homogeneous data center environments running mostly commodity hardware. It is this aspect that drives the cost of these services down. In such an environment, it is difficult to have custom hardware. Having said that, it is only a matter of time before providers of cloud computing start rolling out some specialized hardware to satisfy the more common requests.

Security, Confidentiality, and Audits

This is probably the biggest showstopper with cloud computing adoption today. With on-premises hardware, you have complete control over your hardware and processes—where the data center is located, who touches the hardware, what security processes are in place, and so on. With cloud computing, you must outsource these critical steps to a third party, and that can be hard to swallow for the following reasons:

- You might need data in a specific physical location for legal and regulatory reasons. For example, several firms cannot store data for European customers outside Europe. Other firms cannot take data outside the United States. Some don't want their data in specific countries for legal reasons, with China and the United States leading the list. With cloud computing, you must carefully inspect where your provider hosts the data centers.
- There are several standards with which you may need to comply. The Health Insurance Portability and Accountability Act (HIPAA), the Sarbanes-Oxley Act

(SOX), and Payment Card Industry (PCI) Data Security Standards are some of the popular ones. Most cloud computing providers are not compliant. Some are in the process of being audited, while some standards may never be supported. You must examine your cloud computing provider's policy. With some standards, it may be possible to comply by encrypting data before placing it in the cloud. Health services use this approach today on Amazon S3 and Windows Azure storage to maintain compliance.

- You must ensure that you're following security best practices when inside the cloud—setting the right network settings, using Secure Sockets Layer (SSL) whenever possible, and so on. For the storage services, you must keep the keys safe, and regenerate them periodically.

At the end of the day, the cloud is not inherently less secure than your own infrastructure. It mostly comes down to a trust issue: do you trust the provider to maintain your business-critical data in a responsible manner?

Capacity Planning and Limits

The idea that you don't have to do capacity planning in the cloud is a myth. You still must plan for usage, or you might wind up getting stuck with a huge bill. For example, when hit by a Slashdot effect, you may not want to scale your application beyond a particular point, and you may be willing to live with a degraded experience. Unfortunately, optimizing your applications to cost less on the cloud is a topic that is not well understood, primarily because of the nascent nature of this space—the years of understanding that have gone into planning traditional systems just haven't been experienced with cloud computing.

With cloud computing, the decision to use up more capacity need not rest with the chief investment officer. It could rest with the developer, or someone quite low in the food chain. This raises a lot of unanswered questions regarding how companies should plan for usage.

Though there are no good answers today, one good book on the best practices in this space is *The Art of Capacity Planning (http://oreilly.com/catalog/9780596518585/)* by John Allspaw from Flickr (O'Reilly).

Unpredictable Performance

All cloud computing providers have SLA-backed guarantees on the performance you can get. However, there are no good benchmarks or measurement tools today. You might find that your performance is what was promised most of the time, but once in a while, you might see some variance. Since you're running on a shared infrastructure, this is unavoidable. The customer hosted on the switch next to yours might experience a sudden burst in traffic and have a knock-on effect. On the other hand, this is what you'll experience in most collocation sites, too.

A favorite anecdote in this regard is of a critical business service that was collocated in the same data center as a component from *World of Warcraft* (WoW). Whenever WoW did a major update, the data center's bandwidth got swamped, and the business service started seeing outages. Now, that's a problem that's hard to plan for (and explain to your customers)!

Migration and Interoperability

There are two kinds of migrations that you should care about. One is from traditional on-premises systems to the cloud, and the other is from one cloud provider to another.

For migrating on-premises systems to the cloud, you'll often find yourself needing to rewrite/modify parts of your application. Though platforms such as Windows Azure try to make it as seamless as possible to port applications, there are some inherent differences, and you'll need to make at least some small changes.

Migrating from one cloud provider to another is much more complicated. There is a lack of standards, even de facto ones, in this space. Most APIs are incompatible, and you'll have to hand-roll some custom scripts/code to migrate. In some cases, migration may not be possible at all.

All of this raises questions about lock-in. You must examine how you can get to your data. In the case of Windows Azure, you can always get to your data over HTTP and publicly documented protocols. If you decide to stop using Windows Azure one day, you can pull your data out of the system and put it elsewhere. The same goes for code.

Since these are early days for cloud computing, the tools and thinking around interoperability are early, too. Several efforts related to interoperability standards are spinning up to tackle this problem.

Summary

Very few technologies can claim to be the "Next Big Thing" because their advantages are so obvious. Cloud computing can legitimately claim to be one of them. However, the basic principles and technology behind the cloud have existed for decades. Like Yogi Berra said, "It is like déjà vu all over again."

This chapter provided a lot of text with very little code. In Chapter 3, you'll get to crank open the editor and do some coding!

## CHAPTER 2

Under the Hood

As you wade through the details of a new platform, you may feel like you are fighting a battle without understanding the battlefield. It is critical to know the internals of any platform and how it works. Whether you are building a better-performing application, or trying to understand why you're seeing a weird error message, knowing how things look under the hood can mean the difference between winning and losing the battle.

Even if it isn't useful, peeking under the hood of a complex system is always fun and educational. This chapter provides just that sort of glimpse inside Windows Azure to help you to understand how this new platform works.

Inside the Cloud

Windows Azure is a complex, multitiered platform. It combines hardware and software, split across many layers and many geographic locations. In this complexity, it is easy to get confused. *How does your code run? Which operating system is it running on? How is your code protected? How does Windows Azure work?* The best way to answer these important questions is to walk through the Windows Azure "stack."

Windows Azure is best visualized through an "onion skin" diagram such as the one in Figure 2-1. This chapter examines all the lower layers of that diagram in detail, starting from the innermost ring (the hardware) and working outward.

The actual hardware appears at the innermost "ring." Microsoft operates several data centers around the world, and Windows Azure runs on some of these data centers. Each machine runs a custom *hypervisor* optimized and tuned for the data center, as well as for the specific hardware that runs these machines.

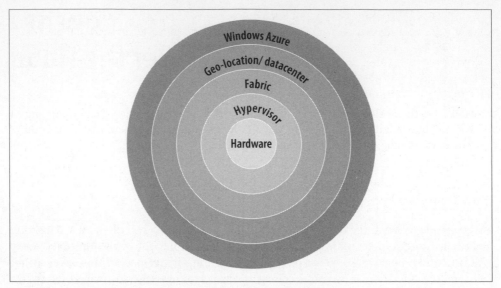

Figure 2-1. Windows Azure onion

 This hypervisor really doesn't have an "official" name. You'll often hear it referred to as the Windows Azure hypervisor, which is the reference that will be used here for the sake of simplicity. The important thing to remember is that this is not the same as Hyper-V, the hypervisor that ships with Windows Server 2008. Later in this chapter, you'll learn more about the differences between the two.

These machines are grouped and managed by a massive distributed software application called *the fabric*. The fabric manages hardware, the operating systems on the machines, and the applications running on the machines. These applications can include everything from the services Windows Azure offers (such as blob, queue, and table storage) to your own code.

There are several of these fabrics in different geographic locations. When you deploy your application, or when you create a storage account, you can choose at which of these locations you want to host it.

Let's dig into each of these concepts in a bit more detail.

Is Windows Azure a "Cloud Operating System"?

You often hear of Windows Azure being described as a "cloud operating system," or as an "operating system for the cloud." Though this is a useful analogy for a nontechnical audience, it often confuses developers who wonder whether there is a new operating system on the loose in Microsoft's data centers.

The key thing to remember here is that this is a stretched analogy. If you look at an operating system, one of its core tasks is to abstract away the hardware from the

---

applications that run on it. Instead of having to worry about the specifics of the hardware, you can write code to a generic API, and let the operating system manage the hardware for you. Windows Azure is an "operating system for the cloud" in a similar sense, because it abstracts away the hardware in the data center. Just as a good desktop operating system abstracts away physical memory and hardware specifics, Windows Azure tries to abstract away the physical aspects of the data center.

However, the analogy ends there. Windows Azure in itself is not a "real operating system" like Windows or Linux or Mac OS X. The operating system that your code winds up running on is just Windows Server 2008.

The Data Centers

Data centers are where all the action is as far as Windows Azure is concerned. Windows Azure physically runs in several of Microsoft's data centers around the world. Like all other major companies building and running data centers, Microsoft likes to keep certain information about them close to the vest, so this section may seem light on details in some areas.

Microsoft built its first data center in September 1989. It was located in the heart of the Microsoft campus in Redmond, Washington, and was a far cry from the modern data centers that power Microsoft's online services today.

The first data centers were similar to the ones you've probably seen in many offices. They had cables running under raised floors, some enhanced security, and environmental controls, but they weren't meant to run services at the massive scale required today. Microsoft has even built several mega data centers around the world over the past few years.

Microsoft doesn't reveal the exact number of data centers—the only official comment to this point has been that the number is between "10 and 100." Also, Microsoft doesn't talk about the exact location of all its data centers. Note that these are Microsoft data centers used for a wide variety of purposes, and not necessarily for running Windows Azure.

Each of these data centers is massive in scale, but at the same time is built to be environmentally friendly. For example, the one in Quincy is approximately 500,000 square feet in area, with critical power of 27 megawatts. That's a lot of juice. However, all power is from a hydroelectric source. Similarly, the one in San Antonio uses recycled water for cooling.

How does Microsoft decide where to build these data centers? Picking locations for data centers is a difficult task, and is almost an art in itself. Think of it as buying a house, albeit one that you can't easily sell. Just as you would scope out the neighborhood, look for the nearest grocery store, and think about the daily commute, any company spending hundreds of millions of dollars building a new data center must also worry about several factors.

Microsoft uses a "heat map" of more than 35 different criteria when picking a location. The criteria include close proximity to an ample power source (for obvious reasons), fiber-optic networks, a large pool of skilled labor, affordable energy rates, tax considerations, and several other factors. Most of these factors are highly stable over time, but once in a while, they change and cause a ripple effect in services that run on these data centers.

As an example of how things can fluctuate over time, during the time it was in CTP mode, Windows Azure itself was forced to change when a geolocation was removed because of local tax law changes.

Security

As you might expect, security is very tight in these data centers. Let's look at two specific aspects of data center security.

This discussion is quite limited in scope, and touches only lightly on some of the protection mechanisms. A complete look at the security controls in place in Windows Azure would be voluminous and beyond the scope of this book.

Physical security
> Each data center has several layers of physical security with increasing controls through each perimeter. Access is restricted, and only essential personnel are authorized to manage customer applications and services. To keep the "baddies" out, as well as to detect intrusions, a wide array of security devices are in use, including cameras, biometrics, card readers, and so on.

Network security
> Network protection comes from a wide collection of network devices, including load balancers, specialized hardware firewalls, and intrusion prevention devices. Applications and services are split into segmented virtual local area networks (VLANs) to ensure that traffic doesn't cross application boundaries. Additional controls are also in place to lessen the impact of distributed denial of service (DDoS) attacks.

Compliance

Compliance is a hot topic in cloud computing, especially for those looking to move enterprise applications to the cloud. Microsoft's data centers are periodically audited to ensure that they are in compliance with Payment Card Industry (PCI) Data Security

Standards, Sarbanes-Oxley (SOX), Health Insurance Portability and Accountability Act (HIPAA), and several other hard-to-pronounce standards.

However, note that this is compliance as far as the data centers go. As of this writing, Microsoft hasn't made any public comment regarding which standards Windows Azure is compliant with. This is one area where users should expect future statements and clarification.

The Hypervisor

With all of the machines in these data centers, the next obvious question concerns how an operating system actually runs on these machines. The default option would be to install Windows Server 2008 directly on these machines and run them. This is, in fact, how most people run Microsoft software in their data centers today, and indeed is how Microsoft runs several of its services in its data centers.

 Microsoft doesn't reveal how many machines it uses to run Windows Azure. The exact hardware used in Microsoft data centers also has not been specified, but as with most modern data center deployments, it is safe to assume that it is fairly homogeneous. When managing thousands of machines, you want as much uniformity as you can get away with.

However, there are two key problems with this approach:

Sharing resources
Henry Ford once said, "Any customer can have a car painted any color, as long as it is black." Running operating systems directly on the hardware means the same holds true for machine size. Every application gets to use the same type of machine in the data center. However, if you have beefy, eight-core machines with tens of gigabytes of RAM, and several users each have tiny websites with no traffic, it makes little sense to give each user his own machine (and make the user pay for the entire machine).

Migrating workloads
You cannot move applications and workloads around easily. If Website A were experiencing low traffic and Website B suddenly goes viral and is taking a pounding, you cannot quickly take A's machines and give them to B. You would need to wipe A's machines to get rid of any custom installation and changes A might have performed, install Windows again, and then install B on top of it.

The industry solution to these (and several other) problems with running different workloads in the data center is to use *virtualization*. This refers to the capability to run several *guest operating systems* simultaneously on the same machine under a *host operating system*. Each operating system sees an entire machine (typically called a *virtual machine*), and is unaware of the existence of the other operating systems. These virtual machines share the resources of the underlying hardware, and also run in a sandbox to ensure that they can't access resources they're not supposed to, or affect any of the other operating systems running on the machine.

How Is Virtualization Different from What Operating Systems Do Today?

In general, *virtualization* refers to abstracting away some hardware resource. Most modern operating systems have a degree of virtualization built in. Different processes on the same machine all see the same amount of RAM, and can't get at virtual memory from another process. Multiple disks might be bound together under a RAID configuration and appear as one logical disk. However, this isolation isn't sufficient for today's cloud computing needs.

For example, some providers try to work around the problem of sharing resources by running multiple services/websites on the same machine, and using operating system user accounts/access control lists (ACLs) to isolate one service from another. However, this frequently proves insufficient. One website could consume 100% of the CPU and starve other websites on the machine, or use up all the bandwidth on the network interface. The best way to fix that is to use one of the virtualization techniques described in this chapter.

Hypervisor Architecture

To create several virtual machines on one physical machine, a thin piece of low-level system software called the *hypervisor* or *Virtual Machine Monitor* (*VMM*) is used. The hypervisor is responsible for fair allocation of resources between the various virtual machines. It schedules CPU time and I/O requests, and provides for isolation between the various virtual machines.

To perform these tasks efficiently, the hypervisor relies on hardware support. Since this is a relatively new development in the x86/x64 hardware world, each vendor has its own twist on how this support works. Both Intel and AMD developed extensions to their x86/x64 processor line. Though they are incompatible, fortunately for you (and for all the developers building hypervisors) they both work using similar concepts. To understand how they work, let's first look a bit deeper at certain parts of how x86/x64 code is executed on your machine.

A typical x86/x64 processor has four *privilege levels* called *Rings*, with Ring 0 being the most powerful and Ring 3 being the most restricted. In general, code executing in Ring N has access to all the same functionality as code executing in Ring $0..N$. All modern operating systems follow a model where the operating system kernel (the core or heart of the operating system) runs in Ring 0, and all user-mode applications run in Ring 3.

Most operating systems don't use Ring 1 or Ring 2 because other architectures/chipsets didn't support anything other than two modes of operation.

For example, in Windows, *ntoskrnl.exe* (the "System" task in Task Manager) runs in Ring 0, along with all drivers, and all user code and applications run in Ring 3. When code running in Ring 3 wants to perform a privileged operation (such as changing its page table mapping, or mucking around with I/O devices directly), it would execute the `sysenter` x86 instruction to transition from user mode to kernel mode, where the kernel would execute the privileged operation on behalf of the user-mode process.

This, of course, describes the execution of a normal operating system. Where does the hypervisor run if Ring 0 is the most-privileged level and all kernels expect to run there? This is the problem Intel and AMD solved with their extensions. They added a new privilege level called "Root mode" (better known as "Ring –1"). By adding an entirely new privilege level, all guest operating systems can execute unmodified as they used to in Rings 0 and 3.

 This description may not be completely accurate. Some virtualization products used to move the guest operating systems into Ring 1 (which isn't used for any other purpose) and trap any privileged instruction in Ring 0. This has issues, though. There are several x86 instructions and architecture quirks that the VMM can't intercept running in this mode. For example, the instruction `HLT` immediately causes a general-protection fault. This is typically worked around by modifying the guest operating system kernel to call through to the VMM in this case.

How does all this work? Let's say the guest operating system kernel is merrily executing away. By default, most x86 instructions don't require special privileges, so everything is executing as normal. All of a sudden, the guest kernel tries to perform a privileged operation, such as direct access to an I/O port. Since there are several guest operating systems executing in a data center, you must ensure that one doesn't trample over another operating system's page table. This sounds like a job for the hypervisor!

The processor recognizes that this is a privileged instruction and transitions from the guest operating system to the hypervisor, and the hypervisor executes some privileged code for the operation. Since the hypervisor has knowledge of all guest operating systems on the machine, it can ensure fairness and security. Once the hypervisor is finished, it returns control to the guest kernel, which continues along its merry path.

Hypercalls and Enlightenments

You now know how an unmodified operating system runs on the hypervisor. However, let's say the operating system's creators knew beforehand that their operating system might be run on a hypervisor. Could they take advantage of that somehow?

As you might have guessed from the fact that the question was asked, yes, they can. Guest operating systems can communicate with the hypervisor they run on using a mechanism called *hypercalls*. The relationship between guest operating systems and a hypervisor is roughly analogous to a normal user-mode process and the kernel. Just as a process can call an API to get the kernel to do something, the guest operating system kernel can invoke a hypercall that will result in code executing on the hypervisor.

An *enlightened kernel* is one that uses these hypercalls to notify and work along with the hypervisor to improve performance. (The "enlightening" here refers to the knowledge the guest operating system kernel has of the hypervisor underneath it.) A canonical example of enlightenment is that of a long busy-wait spin loop. Typically, the processor would sit in a tight loop waiting for the spin lock to be released. If the spin lock code notifies the hypervisor with a hypercall, the hypervisor can schedule another virtual processor to execute, instead of wasting resources on the tight loop. Because of optimizations such as these, enlightened kernels can greatly outperform unenlightened kernels in several scenarios.

Windows Azure Hypervisor Architecture

What you have learned thus far is relevant to all the hypervisors on the market today. Let's now look at one of them specifically: the Windows Azure Hypervisor. Sometime in 2006/2007, a team led by Dave Cutler (the father of Windows NT) started work on a new hypervisor meant to be optimized for the data center. This hypervisor was designed with the following three principles in mind:

Fast
> The Windows Azure hypervisor has been designed to be as efficient as possible. A lot of this is achieved through good old-fashioned, low-level optimizations, as well as pushing workloads onto hardware whenever possible. Since Windows Azure controls the hardware in its data centers, it can rely on the presence of hardware features, unlike generic hypervisors designed for a broader market.

Small
> The hypervisor is built to be lean and mean, and doesn't include any features that are not directly relevant to the cloud. Smaller code not only means better performance, but also means less code to fix or update.

Tightly integrated with the kernel
> Earlier, you learned how enlightened operating systems that integrate tightly with the hypervisor running underneath them can achieve better performance than unenlightened operating systems. In Windows Azure, the kernel of the operating

system that runs on the hypervisor is tightly optimized for the hypervisor, and contains several enlightenments.

Are the Windows Azure Hypervisor and Hyper-V the Same?

With Windows Server 2008, Microsoft launched a hypervisor called Hyper-V. There is often confusion about the differences between Hyper-V and the Windows Azure hypervisor, and some books/articles often assume they're the same.

In reality, both are different and are built for different purposes. Hyper-V ships as a part of Windows, and is meant to run on a broad variety of hardware for a broad variety of purposes. The Windows Azure hypervisor runs only on Microsoft data centers, and is optimized specifically for the hardware that Windows Azure runs on.

As you might expect with two similar products from the same company, there is sharing of code and design. In the future, new features from the Windows Azure hypervisor will make their way into Hyper-V, and vice versa, where applicable.

Figure 2-2 shows the architecture of the Windows Azure hypervisor. Those familiar with Hyper-V will recognize many elements right away.

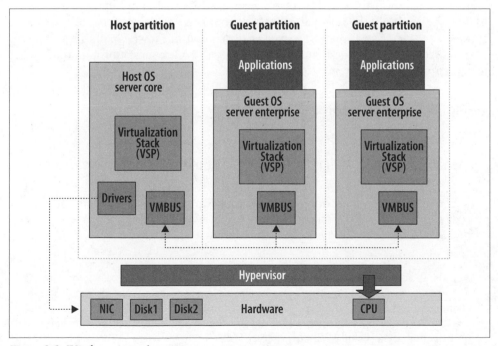

Figure 2-2. Windows Azure hypervisor

The hypervisor divides the system into multiple virtual machines or *partitions*. User applications go into *guest partitions*, each of which runs a guest operating system instance. A guest partition has visibility only over its own address space, but doesn't have direct access to the hardware, and can't see, manage, or modify other partitions.

When the system boots (the boot process for Windows Azure is covered a bit later), the booting instance is designated as the *root* or the *host partition*. This partition is special in several ways. The root partition has full access to I/O ports, physical memory, and the raw hardware. It also performs one critical function: it is used to perform all hardware device access using standard Windows device drivers.

This might sound slightly surprising. Why doesn't the hypervisor deal with devices itself using its own device drivers? Indeed, this is the model used by other hypervisors in the industry. However, in the Windows Azure hypervisor (and in Hyper-V), all hardware device I/O initiated in a child partition is intercepted by the hypervisor, and is routed into the host partition where the I/O is performed by hardware device drivers using normal Windows device drivers. This lets the Windows Azure hypervisor (and Hyper-V) run on a wide array of hardware (since Windows enjoys good driver support), and doesn't force hardware vendors to write new device drivers.

This "routing" of I/O requests happens over a high-speed, high-bandwidth pathway called the *Virtual Machine Bus* (VMBus). A typical guest operating system, without enlightenments, could naively perform many discrete hardware accesses for a single logical operation. This would involve several transitions between the guest and the hypervisor, and into the host partition. To avoid this problem, each guest operating system on Windows Azure has a special *virtualization stack*, which takes over the role of device drivers in the guest, and directly forwards I/O requests through the VMBus to the host operating system.

Using this mechanism, several "chatty" calls are consolidated into a few "chunky" calls, greatly improving performance.

What Operating System Does Your Code Run Under on Windows Azure?

Even with all this discussion about operating system enlightenments and integration with the hypervisor, most developers only really care about what environment their code runs in (the guest operating system). The answer to that is simple. Applications run on Windows Server 2008 x64 Enterprise Edition.

Well, almost.

Microsoft calls it a "Windows Server 2008-compatible" operating system, which refers to the fact that it is Windows Server in almost every respect—except the low-level changes to optimize for the hypervisor. However, applications are abstracted several layers away from these changes, and shouldn't notice anything different from running on a normal, plain-vanilla Windows Server machine.

Windows Azure Hypervisor Features

The Windows Azure hypervisor includes a few features that were built specifically for the cloud. Because some of these are obviously useful for Hyper-V, you might see them make their way into future versions of Hyper-V, or even Windows itself.

Performance features

As mentioned, the hypervisor takes advantage of the homogeneous hardware environment to get better performance. One performance feature (with quite an unexciting name) is worth calling out: *Second Level Address Translation* (SLAT).

 SLAT for Azure is the same as AMD's Nested Page Table support, or Intel's Extended Page Table support.

One of the functions of the hypervisor is the capability to translate the guest's physical address to the system's physical address. This was typically done in the hypervisor by using something called *shadow page tables*. Every guest had a mirror of its page tables created that kept information about the physical location of guest memory. Every time a guest operating system changed its page table mapping, these shadow page tables had to be updated as well. This constant updating consumed CPU cycles and added to performance overhead.

Newer processors (such as the one used in Windows Azure's hardware) allow some of this work to be done by the hardware itself. Using SLAT, a new identifier is added to the Translation Lookaside Buffer (TLB) cache on the processor. (TLB is a low-level CPU cache that speeds up virtual address-to-physical address translation.) This allows identification of which guest virtual machine the TLB entry came from. Because the mapping is now stored in hardware, this greatly reduces the work the hypervisor must perform, and removes the need to update shadow page tables.

One side benefit of using SLAT is the support for large pages. SLAT supports page sizes of 2 MB and 1 GB. Larger page sizes bring a host of performance benefits, since they can reduce the number of cache misses and deal with memory in larger "chunks."

Apart from memory improvements, the scheduler was tweaked to be tuned for data center workloads. For example, scenarios involving ASP.NET and IIS were specifically tested and optimized for. The scheduler was also improved to be more predictable and fairer, and to deal with heavy I/O requests. Apart from this, improvements were made to reduce the number of intercepts into the hypervisor, as well as add enlightenments into the guest operating systems to make spin locks perform better.

Image-based deployment

Whenever there is an update, hotfix, or any other change, it could be a complicated task to roll out the change across thousands of machines. The risk of the installation failing on some of the machines and leading to these machines being in an unknown state is too high—anyone who has had to administer a large server environment can attest to this. To avoid these issues, the Windows Azure hypervisor uses an *image-based deployment model*.

Operating systems are never installed on Windows Azure. An operating system image is constructed offline. This image is really just a Virtual Hard Disk (VHD). Whenever there is a patch or an update, this image is updated. Separate images are constructed for the root and for the guest partitions and different flavors are offered for different services on Windows Azure. Instead of having to install an operating system on thousands of machines, Windows Azure simply boots this VHD directly. This *boot-from-VHD* feature doesn't exist in Windows Server 2008, but was later incorporated into Windows 7.

Rolling out a new patch becomes a simple process of using XCOPY to create a new VHD, pointing the bootloader at it, and then rebooting the machine into the new updated operating system. This saves a lot of time spent with installation and configuration, and avoids the errors that inevitably occur when using update/upgrade scripts and setup.

After discovering a bit about the hypervisor, you might be asking some or all of the following questions:

- How does the machine know which image to pull down, and how does it get started at the first boot?
- What happens when a new machine comes to life in the Windows Azure data center?
- What does the boot process look like?
- How does user application code wind up on the machines?

To understand the answers to these questions, you must first understand one of the most important components of Windows Azure: the fabric controller.

The Fabric

Consider how the operating system and programming frameworks abstract over memory. Instead of having to deal with individual RAM cells, the operating system and your programming platform provide several abstractions on top:

- With *raw physical memory*, programmers can allocate memory and deal with memory addresses, rather than individual memory cells.

- With *virtual memory* and *paging*, developers can ignore the actual physical memory limits on the machine, and not worry about trampling over memory used by other processes in the system.
- With *garbage collection*, programmers don't have to worry about allocating or freeing memory, since that is done automatically for them.
- With the *hot-adding of RAM*, use of modern operating systems may allow for the addition of extra memory on-the-fly without having to shut down the machine.

Now, consider how computers are managed in a typical infrastructure setup. Machines are usually referred to and named individually. Adding and removing machines often means some changes to code, or at least to configuration. At a minimum, some network configuration changes will be needed. Relocating applications and data machines is a tedious, error-prone task, and is typically avoided as much as possible.

The Azure *fabric* tries to do to hardware what virtual memory/paging/garbage collection does to memory: provide useful abstractions. This would allow programmers to move from describing "how" they want things done to a model where programmers describe "what" they want done—and the system does it for them.

The fabric itself is a massive, distributed application that runs across all of Windows Azure's machines. Instead of having to deal with thousands of machines individually, other parts of Windows Azure (and the users of Windows Azure) can treat the entire set of machines as one common resource managed by the fabric.

The Fabric Controller

Though fabric code is running on all machines in the Windows Azure world, almost all the heavy lifting is done by a small core set of machines known as the *fabric controller*. The fabric controller is often called "the brain" of Windows Azure, and for good reason: it controls the operation of all the other machines, as well as the services running on them.

The fabric controller is responsible for the following key tasks:

- The fabric controller "owns" all the data center hardware. This ranges from normal machines on racks to load balancers, switches, and so on. The fabric controller knows the state of each of them, and can detect failures on them (at which time, a human being is notified if the failure can't be fixed programmatically). Just as a normal operating system has drivers to deal with video cards, sound cards, and so on, the fabric controller has "drivers" that encode the knowledge of dealing with specific types of hardware. When new types of hardware must be brought online, a new driver is written to give the fabric controller knowledge of how to work with that hardware.

- The fabric controller makes provisioning decisions. The fabric controller's inventory of machines is dynamic, and can be added to/removed easily. We will discuss how these provisioning decisions are made a bit later in this chapter.
- The fabric controller maintains the health of all the services. It monitors the services and tries to take corrective action upon detection of a failure. It also deals with upgrades and configuration changes to services.

As you can imagine, a failure in the fabric controller can be bad for overall system health. To help ensure reliability, the fabric controller is built as a set of five to seven machines, each with a *replica*, as shown in Figure 2-3. All replicas share state with a Paxos-based replication system.

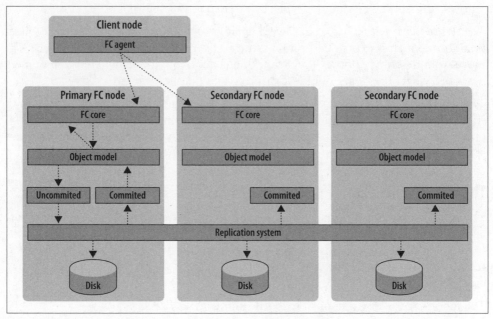

Figure 2-3. Fabric controller nodes and replication

 Paxos is a distributed consensus algorithm, typically used to share some form of state between a distributed set of machines. See *http://en.wiki pedia.org/wiki/Paxos_algorithm* for more on Paxos.

At any time, a *primary* machine is responsible for executing all key tasks. Any changes in state to the primary are automatically replicated to all the nodes in the fabric controller cluster. If the primary goes down, a new primary is picked up seamlessly from one of the other nodes. Even in the unlikely case that all five to seven replicas go down, all user services will still continue to run until the fabric controller can be brought up.

An outage involving all five to seven replicas is only theoretical. Because of the way the replicas are spread out in the data center, and how the code in the fabric controller is written, the chances of this actually happening are very remote.

The state on these replicas is quite valuable, since it contains knowledge of the running services. To avoid or recover from corruption, the state on each replica is checkpointed regularly. This helps to prevent code or operator errors.

How does the fabric controller get upgraded, changed, and configured? In the Windows Azure world, anything that needs to get upgraded goes through a fabric controller. So, in the case of the fabric controller, it is itself managed by another fabric controller called the *utility fabric controller*.

To understand the workings of the fabric and the fabric controller, let's walk through the life cycle of a service, from the time code is written on a developer's machine to the time it is running in a machine in a data center.

Coding and Modeling

In the Windows Azure world, you *model* your service and produce a *service model* with such things as worker roles, web roles, service configuration, and so on. These are all nothing more than ways to define the topology of your service.

To better understand a service model, consider how a website or service's architecture typically gets described in a 1:1 setting. You start scribbling on a whiteboard or paper. You draw boxes to refer to the various machines or logical components that make up your service. You draw arrows between the boxes to denote how these machines talk to each other, and you might annotate these arrows with the protocols and ports used.

Now, consider the effort it takes to actually get that diagram working. A build gets generated containing the binaries for the various parts of your service, your SQL database scripts, and whatever else your service needs. Getting the right parts of the build installed and configured on the right machines usually involves some voodoo. Everything from off-the-shelf tools to homegrown scripts is used to copy bits over and set them up. If you're lucky, you won't have to do any network changes, and your scripts are written in such a way that they are resilient to changes in machine names and environments. In essence, it is a lot of hard work to get from your code to that whiteboard diagram.

That is exactly what the service model does for you.

In Windows Azure, each service (from the simplest "Hello World" website to the most complex services) has an associated service model. This service model is just a giant XML file that contains the same elements that your whiteboard diagram does. However, it describes them using well-defined elements such as roles, endpoints, configuration settings, and so on. The service model defines what roles your service contains, what HTTP or HTTPS endpoints they listen on, what specific configuration settings you expect, and so on.

Once this service model has been defined, the fabric controller can basically automate what you had to do manually: copy bits to the right machine, perform the right networking configuration, and so on. Moreover, the fabric controller maintains that service model. If some part of the model fails (such as a machine going down), it takes corrective action, brings up a new machine, and configures the new machine with the right binaries and network settings so that your service model is restored.

The key advantage of having such a model is that it defines "what" you want as opposed to "how" it should be done. The service model only specifies the final configuration, and it is up to the fabric controller to map that to a set of procedural actions.

For example, if the service model specifies a simple ASP.NET website with a single *.aspx* page, configured to listen on *http://foo.cloudapp.net*, the fabric controller transforms them into a set of procedural actions such as "bring up virtual machine," "copy bits to Machine *X*," "configure load balancer," "provision DNS," and so on. Specifying things in a model-driven manner not only is easier and less error-prone, but also frees up the fabric controller to optimize tasks and parallelize execution of various such tasks across the system.

Service configuration files and service models

You might be wondering how to generate one of these service models yourself. Generating one of these service models directly is a complex process, and the generated service models are quite gnarly beasts.

Instead of forcing users to deal directly with the complexity of creating service models, Windows Azure ships with a few service model *templates* that users can use. The web role, the worker role, and the CGI role are all examples of these templates. When you build a package, the CSPack tool uses your code and your service configuration to generate service models for your applications based on these templates.

What Does a Service Model File Look Like?

As discussed, the *.cspkgx* file generated by the build process is just a fancy *.zip* file. If you extract the contents of the *.zip* file, you can find the actual service model for your application in the *ServiceDefinition.rd* file. Note that this file is useful to look at only as a curiosity—it is complex and undocumented, changes from release to release, and should never be modified directly. In a sense, think of it as the raw output that the platform "executes."

Following is a snippet from *ServiceDefinition.rd* for the Hello Fabric sample that ships with the SDK. You can see how elements from the service definition and configuration files show up here:

```
<componentports>
    <inPort name="HttpIn" protocol="http">
        <inToChannel>
            <lBChannelMoniker
name="/HelloFabric/HelloFabricGroup/FELoadBalancerHttp
In" />
        </inToChannel>
    </inPort>
</componentports>
<settings>
    <aCS name="WebRole:BannerText" defaultValue="">
        <maps>
            <mapMoniker
name="/HelloFabric/HelloFabricGroup/MapWebRole:BannerTe
xt"
/>
        </maps>
    </aCS>
... (more XML follows)
```

Along with the service model, each service also gets configuration values as part of a service configuration file. This is the processed form of the configuration values defined in the *ServiceConfiguration.cscfg* and *ServiceConfiguration.csdef* files. These are simple name/value pairs, and their usage is up to your imagination. They're used for everything from storing credentials to storing trivial application-specific properties.

Before wrapping up the discussion on service models, there are two final concepts worth covering: *update domains* and *fault domains*.

Update domains

Consider how you update a multimachine service. You typically update one component first (say, the database or the web frontends). You then walk through the rest of the components in some specific order.

Update domains let you achieve the same in the service model. You can partition your service into a number of update domains. When you want to upgrade your service, the fabric controller will walk through each update domain in turn, and will start with a new one only when the previous update domain has been completed. Update domains are also used in updates initiated by Windows Azure. When a new operating system image must be rolled out, each service is upgraded, update domain by update domain.

Fault domain

A *fault domain* is a way of splitting up your service so that it is spread out across the data center. No two critical resources are present within the same fault domain. Suppose that all your web roles are within the same rack in the data center, and the switch connected to the rack bursts into flames (a very unlikely scenario, but play along here). You would instantly see downtime as the fabric controller tries to bring up your web roles elsewhere.

Instead, if you split your web roles into fault domains, the fabric controller will spread them out across the data center so that, even if there's a physical failure in one part of the data center (on one rack, one floor, and so on), your other virtual machines still have a chance of continuing to run. Unfortunately, as of this writing, there is no manual way to specify how your service should be partitioned into fault domains, and you must rely on Windows Azure to pick fault domains for you. This might be a feature exposed in a future release.

The complete service model, along with the configuration settings and your application binaries, make up the package that you upload to Windows Azure. The trio has all the information required by the fabric to deploy, run, and manage your application.

Provisioning and Deployment

Once the package reaches the fabric controller (that is, the *.cspkgx* file is uploaded), the fabric controller first tries to find a home for the various role instances that make up the service. This is essentially a constraint-solving problem—the service model expresses constraints such as the number of role instances, the fault domains required, the local disk and machine size required, and so on. The fabric controller looks across its machine pool and finds the right set of nodes to act as homes for these role instances, based on these constraints.

Once it has made up its mind on the location where these role instances will live, the fabric controller starts the process of getting the bits onto the machine and getting the service running. This is done in tandem with network hardware and the hypervisor running on these machines.

How this is accomplished behind the scenes is fairly interesting. Following is a brief synopsis:

1. In the beginning, all servers have nothing on them, and the fabric controller powers them on programmatically.

2. Each server is configured to boot from the network using normal Preboot Execution Environment (PXE) requests. (PXE is a standard mechanism to boot computers using a network interface.) It downloads a small operating system image called the *maintenance OS* and boots into it. (That name is a bit of a misnomer, since it actually doesn't do any "maintenance" per se; rather, it bootstraps the machine and is the first bit of fabric code that runs on the target node.) All communication with the maintenance OS is through a fabric *agent* that lives on the maintenance OS.

3. The maintenance OS talks to the fabric controller. After some secure handshaking, it sets up the host partition. Remember that of the various partitions on the hypervisor, the host/root partition is special and has the capability to directly talk to the hardware.

4. The maintenance OS pulls down a VHD with the operating system for the host partition. Currently, this is based on Windows Server Core, the lightweight, minimal, stripped-down version of Windows Server 2008. The maintenance OS restarts the machine to boot into the host OS. This is done using a "boot-from-VHD" feature, which, as mentioned previously, is now available as a part of Windows 7.

5. When the host partition/virtual machine starts up, it has an agent that can talk to the fabric controller as well. The fabric controller tells the agent how many guest partitions to set up, and what VHDs to download. These are cached so that this download must happen only the first time.

6. For each guest partition, there's a *base VHD* that contains the operating system, and a *differencing disk* that contains any changes to disk. This is a standard practice used with virtual machines that lets you destroy the differencing disk to get back to the pristine base VHD state. In the case of Windows Azure, resetting a guest virtual machine to its original state is as simple as deleting the differencing disk. These guest VHDs contain a version of Windows Server 2008 Enterprise with modifications to integrate with the Windows Azure hypervisor.

7. Once the guest virtual machine is up and running, the specified role instance's files are copied onto the machine. Depending on the kind of role, different actions are taken. For example, a web role is launched in an *http.sys*-based web hosting environment, while a worker role is launched similar to a normal program. Currently, there is a strict enforcement of one role instance to one virtual machine. This helps ensure that the virtual machine is an isolation boundary both from a security and a resource utilization perspective.

8. The fabric controller repeats this process for each role instance in the service model. Typically, only the last step must be performed, because most machines would have had the initial bootstrapping done already.

9. The fabric controller programs the load balancer and other network hardware to route traffic from the external address assigned to the service (say, for example, *foo.cloudapp.net*) to the individual role instances. The role instances are placed behind a load balancer, which performs a simple round-robin algorithm to route traffic between the instances. Once the right networking routes are in place, traffic from the outside world flows to and from the role instances.

Note how there's no installation in these steps. With everything relying on an XCOPY model, the chances of misconfigured or failed installations are lowered dramatically.

Management and Monitoring

The fabric controller maintains information about every role instance in the form of a state machine. Every role instance has a *goal state* that it must get to, and the fabric controller tries to keep moving the role instance along to the goal state. This is important to note, because this forms a key part of how the fabric controller implements some critical functions in Windows Azure.

Whenever any part of the service must be upgraded, the fabric controller walks the service, update domain by update domain. Updates don't have to be initiated by the user alone—operating system updates (security patches, fixes, and so on) are rolled out periodically using the same mechanism.

Monitoring uses the same goal state features as well. The fabric controller monitors the health of all roles and quickly detects when a role dies. A role can also inform the fabric controller that it is unhealthy.

When the fabric controller learns that a particular role is unhealthy, it updates its internal state machine and tries to push the role back to its goal state. This could range from restarting the role, to taking specific corrective action.

The fabric controller also monitors the health of the nodes in the data center. If the fabric controller detects that the node is offline (for example, because of not hearing from the agent on the machine), the fabric controller migrates all role instances on the machine to a new node. This new node is picked based on the constraints in the service model. For example, if the role instance in a failed node was part of a separate fault domain, the new role instance will be placed on a node in the same fault domain as well. The fabric controller then fixes up the network settings to restore the service model to bring the service back to its original state.

Summary

Frankly, you'll rarely be exposed to any of the details covered in this chapter. However, knowing how the system works underneath will help you understand how the various pieces of Windows Azure fit together.

For example, when you see a `FabricInternalError` in the portal, you can now guess at what is going on. Whether you're creating a new deployment using the management API, or optimizing your application for the hypervisor, knowing how the fabric controller and the Windows Azure hypervisor work their magic provides you a distinct advantage when programming in the world of Windows Azure.

## CHAPTER 3

Your First Cloud App

In Douglas Adams' seminal work *The Hitchhiker's Guide to the Galaxy* (Pan Books), the title refers to a fictional electronic guidebook that serves as the repository for all knowledge and wisdom. If you were off on an interstellar adventure, this would be the book you would want by your side at all times. However, since the device itself looked insanely complicated to operate, and partly because intergalactic adventures tend to get scary at times, the book had the words "DON'T PANIC" written in large, friendly letters on the back cover, always in uppercase.

In this chapter, you'll start building applications on Windows Azure. You'll begin by downloading the SDK, exploring it, peeking around its corners, and getting a basic application running inside a Microsoft data center somewhere. Windows Azure is a vast, sprawling platform, and exploring it can look a bit daunting at first. But rest assured that it is all familiar Microsoft technology, with standard, easy-to-use APIs and friendly developer tools. So, in the immortal words of Douglas Adams, "DON'T PANIC."

Signing Up for Windows Azure

The Windows Azure Developer Portal is a one-stop shop for all your service management and Windows Azure needs. The portal contains everything from all the projects/ storage accounts underneath your account, to links to billing information. To sign up, head to *http://windows.azure.com*. You'll be asked to create an account by signing in with your Live ID credentials and providing billing information. The entire account-creation process is quick and painless.

You'll be using the portal throughout this book: for creating new hosted services and storage services, uploading new deployments to the cloud, managing your code and data once it is in the cloud, and other administrative functions.

The Windows Azure Tool Set

What kinds of tools do you need to work with Windows Azure? First, to run code, you need tools to package your application into a format that Windows Azure can understand and run. For storing data on Windows Azure, you will probably need some tools to help you import/export/view data. Importantly, you'll probably need some tools to help you develop all this on your local development machine.

Remember that services hosted in Windows Azure are all about running existing code inside Windows in a Microsoft data center—Windows Azure is not a new programming language or programming framework. Most of the work in running code is in packaging your application correctly and ensuring that it works in the cloud. When it comes to hosting applications, almost all the new concepts that Windows Azure introduces deal with how your application is packaged. There are very little (to no) new language features or fundamentally different programming idioms. The idea is to let you run as much of your current code as possible.

 Doing anything on the cloud costs money, albeit in small incremental amounts. Doing as much development as possible locally can save you quite a bit.

Getting and Installing the Tools

You can use the following two primary tools to develop for Windows Azure:

- Windows Azure Software Development Kit (SDK)
- Windows Azure Tools for Visual Studio (which is bundled with the SDK as well)

The Windows Azure SDK is a free download that contains CSPack (used for packaging your applications), the Development Fabric, and other essential tools needed for building applications for Windows Azure. (You'll learn what these tools do later in this chapter.) The SDK typically has a new version released every few months. You can find a link to the latest SDK download at *http://www.microsoft.com/azure*.

The Windows Azure Tools for Visual Studio (referred to simply as the "Visual Studio tools" throughout this book) are bundled with the SDK and plug into Visual Studio to make development against the SDK easier. The biggest add-on that the Visual Studio tools provide is a set of Visual Studio project templates, as well as the ability to debug locally.

Satisfying the Prerequisites

Before installing the SDK and the Visual Studio tools, you must ensure that you have installed several prerequisites on your machine. You must have at least Windows Vista SP1 and .NET Framework 3.5 SP1 installed. IIS 7 with ASP.NET is required to run your

---

cloud services on your local machine, and Windows Communication Foundation (WCF) HTTP Activation must be turned on. The SDK installs a mock version of the storage services in the cloud meant for local development. You'll need SQL Server (either the full-blown version or the Express edition) installed to make that work.

Installing these prerequisites separately can be a hassle. One easy way to install all of them with one tool is through the Microsoft Web Platform installer, available from *http://www.microsoft.com/web*. Figure 3-1 shows the Web Platform installer with the Windows Azure tools (an early version) set to be installed. Note how the necessary dependencies are detected and installed.

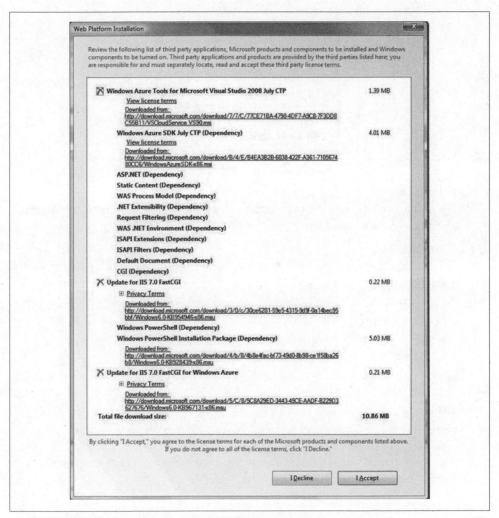

Figure 3-1. Web Platform installer with the Windows Azure tools

To get the Windows Azure tools download to show up in the Web Platform installer, go to the Options dialog and select the Developer Tools checkbox.

Getting to Know the SDK and Tools

If everything installed correctly, you should see a variety of new items in your Start menu, as shown in Figure 3-2. (Note that this figure is reproduced from an early build of the software, and you'll almost surely see a different icon.)

Figure 3-2. SDK and Visual Studio tools in the Start menu

To make it easier to use the tools that come with the SDK as this discussion progresses, let's take a brief look at what you get when you install the SDK:

Documentation

Like all good SDKs, you get the latest documentation corresponding to the release. Apart from the *.chm* files, there are *readme* files scattered throughout the samples.

 The documentation is mirrored on the MSDN website, and you're probably better off looking at the online versions because any changes/additions are instantly reflected there.

CSPack

This is arguably the most important binary shipping in the SDK. *Cspack.exe* enables you to package up your application into a format that Windows Azure can understand and run. Whether you call this binary directly, or whether it is called for you by a tool (such as Visual Studio), this is what you use to package up your services.

You'll see a lot of tools/file extensions starting with the letters *CS* in Windows Azure. The letters stand for "Cloud Service." The actual acronym to use was picked close to the date of Windows Azure's initial launch, and there was a bit of discussion on the exact extension to use. One contender was the letters *UC* (for "Utility Computing"), which you can find in other parts of early SDKs.

Development Fabric and Development Storage

These provide a simulated version of Windows Azure to help you develop code on your own machine, and test it before deploying against the actual cloud. We examine both of these in greater detail later in this chapter.

Samples

The SDK ships with the obligatory samples, as well as some useful tools masquerading as samples. You'll learn how to use some of these tools throughout the book.

As of this writing, some of these samples were being moved out of the SDK and onto *http://code.msdn.microsoft.com/windowsazure samples*. If you can't find some of the samples referenced, check that URL.

An easy way to access all the tools that come with the SDK is through the *setenv.cmd* batch file in the *bin* folder of the SDK. This can also be accessed through the Windows Azure SDK Command Prompt option on the Start menu. This brings all the right folders into your environment PATH, and sets up some environment variables required for these tools to work.

Project templates and debugging

Though it is possible to fully complete your development without Visual Studio at all, you'll save yourself a ton of effort by using the integrated support for the SDK in Visual Studio. The biggest value-adds in Visual Studio are the presence of project templates corresponding to the different ways in which you can package your application, as well as debugging support for you to locally debug your application.

Understanding the Development Fabric

When you're developing for an environment that is very different from your desktop computer, it really helps to have a local simulator/emulator/mock interface to help you develop. For example, most mobile platforms include a simulator that runs on normal machines and attempts to simulate a mobile phone with high fidelity. ASP.NET developers are familiar with Cassini, the local development web server that ships with Visual Studio. The same need for a local simulator holds true for the cloud as well.

On the actual cloud, your code runs on different virtual and physical machines. Since launching a virtual machine on a normal physical (development) machine requires a lot of overhead, the Development Fabric (Dev Fabric) launches different processes instead. For every virtual machine you'll see launched in the cloud, the Dev Fabric launches a local process called *RdRoleHost.exe* to host your application. Since these are just normal processes, you can attach a debugger to them, and perform typical debugging tasks (such as setting breakpoints, inspecting and changing values, stepping through code, and so on). In fact, this is how the Visual Studio extensions provide debugging support; they attach to the processes launched by the Dev Fabric.

Figure 3-3 shows the Dev Fabric providing a simulation of the Windows Azure fabric on a local machine. In short, the Dev Fabric enables a developer to build, debug, and test code locally before deploying to the actual cloud.

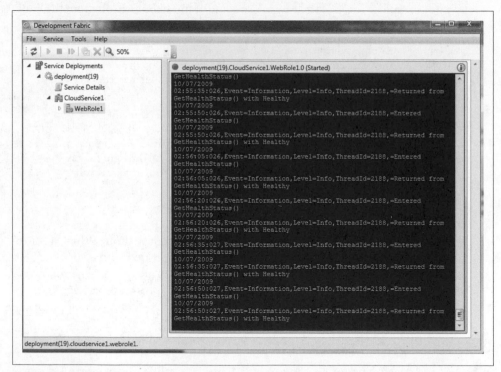

Figure 3-3. Running a Dev Fabric instance

You can launch the Dev Fabric from the Start menu item installed by the SDK, or through the CSRun tool (which you'll learn about shortly). The Dev Fabric is rarely launched directly; most developers simply use the integrated Visual Studio support, and have Visual Studio launch it for them.

Differentiating between the cloud and the Dev Fabric

Though the Dev Fabric tries to provide as accurate a simulation of the cloud as possible, there are some fundamental differences between running code on your local machine and running code on the cloud. Following are some "gotchas" that sometimes trip up developers when they find that code works on the cloud but does not work on the Dev Fabric (or vice versa):

- The Dev Fabric uses processes to simulate virtual machines. If your package is configured to run on five different virtual machines, it'll run on five different processes on your local machine. This can lead to some quirky performance differences. For example, a misbehaving process can affect other processes locally, but a misbehaving virtual machine will not.

- The Dev Fabric doesn't check for code that can't run on the cloud, nor does it ensure that you don't use something that doesn't exist on the cloud. For example, if you try to use a registry key/file/COM component that exists on your local machine, it'll work on the Dev Fabric, but will fail on the cloud if it doesn't exist there as well.

- The Dev Fabric runs on the same architecture as your local machine's operating system. If you have an x86 operating system, the Dev Fabric will run in x86 mode. However, in the actual cloud, all code is 64-bit, so you might run into issues moving from x86 to x64. This difference becomes critical when running native binaries.

- Since the Dev Fabric is running on your local machine, network performance is very different from what you'll experience in the cloud. This difference is especially noticeable when talking to other Windows Azure services (such as the Windows Azure storage services). When your code is running in the cloud, network latency is reduced because of other services being in the same data center. When your code is running on your local machine, it takes longer to access storage services in a Microsoft data center. Note that, in the case of storage, you can use the Development Storage (which you'll learn about shortly) on your local machine.

- You shouldn't use the Dev Fabric to get an accurate sense of performance. Since the Dev Fabric is just another process on your local machine, performance will vary based on your machine's hardware. Unless your machine is a 1:1 match to the virtual machine in the cloud in terms of resources (highly unlikely), you'll notice a significant difference in performance.

Development Storage

While the Dev Fabric simulates the Windows Azure fabric and is used for hosting code, the Development Storage (Dev Storage) part of the SDK is used to simulate the Windows Azure storage services—blobs, tables, and queues. It does this by using a local SQL Server instance as a backing store, and providing a local running instance of the Windows Azure blobs, tables, and queues.

You'll learn more about the storage services and the Dev Storage in Chapter 7.

Developing Your First Cloud Application

With a basic understanding of the available tool set, now is a good time to write and run your first cloud application. In the grand tradition of programming books, your first application will somehow display the text "Hello World!" on your screen.

For this first application, you will create a simple website—in fact, possibly the simplest website that can be created in HTML. You'll run that website locally in the Dev Fabric and then move it to the cloud. In the cloud, you will first run it in a staging environment, and then have it show up in its final production environment. This site will have no backend processing—no database access, no access to the Windows Azure storage services, none of that. In fact, this site won't even contain any .NET code/native code execution. You will simply be hosting plain HTML web pages.

For your first application, you will be exclusively using the command-line tools that ship with the SDK. This will familiarize you with the steps required to write and run code. For the remainder of this book, you'll be using the Visual Studio extensions to automate all of these steps for you. Using the command-line tools included with Visual Studio enables you to see what is happening under the covers. Think of this as the difference between manually invoking *csc.exe* to compile some C# code, and building the same from within Visual Studio.

Writing the Code

As mentioned, you will create a simple website that contains a solitary HTML page that displays only the text "Hello World!" Since this is just pure HTML, no server-side code is being executed. However, Windows Azure will be doing the heavy lifting in terms of hosting the site, and it is a short step from doing plain HTML to running ASP.NET code (which you'll see in the next sample).

Let's start by creating a directory to hold your code. In this example, let's call it *htmlwebsite*, as shown here:

```
D:\>mkdir htmlwebsite
D:\>cd htmlwebsite
D:\htmlwebsite>
```

 Although you can certainly replace *htmlwebsite* with whatever you feel like, remember to replace all references to the directory name in the commands you'll be running later on.

This directory will be the root of your website—the equivalent to *inetpub/wwwroot* in IIS, or the root of your ASP.NET application. Any content you put in here will "hang" off the root URL of your website.

Let's now create the contents of the website. Create a new file called *index.html* in the *htmlwebsite* directory with the contents shown in Example 3-1. (Since this is just a normal HTML page, you can put any valid HTML content you want in here.)

Example 3-1. Über-complex web page

```
<html>
<body>
Hello World!
</body>
</html>
```

To get Windows Azure to run this trivial site, you must provide two pieces of metadata: the *service definition* and the *service configuration*. These are stored in two XML files called *ServiceDefinition.csdef* and *ServiceConfiguration.cscfg*, respectively.

Remember that Windows Azure can host any type of code, and provides a ton of configurable knobs/settings for you to tweak. The service definition defines what kind of code your website/service is made of. This is specified when building your service, and can't be changed dynamically when your application is running. The service configuration contains tweakable settings (the most important one being the number of virtual machines your code will use). These settings can be changed on-the-fly without having to rebuild and redeploy your application.

So, let's create two files called *ServiceDefinition.csdef* and *ServiceConfiguration.cscfg* with the contents of Examples 3-2 and 3-3, respectively.

Example 3-2. Sample ServiceDefinition.csdef

```
<?xml version="1.0" encoding="utf-8"?>
<ServiceDefinition name="CloudService1"
 xmlns=
"http://schemas.microsoft.com/ServiceHosting/2008/10/ServiceDefinition">
  <WebRole name="WebRole1" enableNativeCodeExecution="false">
    <InputEndpoints>
      <InputEndpoint name="HttpIn" protocol="http" port="80" />
    </InputEndpoints>
    <ConfigurationSettings />
  </WebRole>
</ServiceDefinition>
```

Example 3-3. Sample ServiceConfiguration.cscfg

```
<?xml version="1.0"?>
<ServiceConfiguration serviceName="CloudService1"
 xmlns=
"http://schemas.microsoft.com/ServiceHosting/2008/10/ServiceConfiguration">
  <Role name="WebRole1">
    <Instances count="1" />
```

```
    <ConfigurationSettings />
  </Role>
</ServiceConfiguration>
```

Chapter 4 provides more information on these, so it's not important here to delve into the details of what each element does. In short, the service definition defines a new "web role" called WebRole1. Chapter 4 provides more on what "roles" are and the different types of roles. For now, simply be aware that a *web role* is how web applications/sites are packaged and run on Windows Azure. The service configuration file specifies that WebRole1 should have one (1) instance, meaning that the code will run on one virtual machine in the cloud.

Packing the Code for the Dev Fabric

You now have all the code you need to run the service on Windows Azure. However, to run applications on Windows Azure (either the production fabric or in the Dev Fabric), you must package the applications in a special format. This lays out your application binaries in a specific folder structure, and generates some files used internally by Windows Azure. Once deployed to the cloud, the Windows Azure fabric opens up this package and runs your code by copying it to the right number of virtual machines, and makes the necessary configuration changes.

You use the *cspack.exe* tool (or CSPack) that ships with the SDK to perform the packaging. (You can find it in the SDK's *bin* directory.) In this case, you first pack the code to run in the Dev Fabric. The command you use to package the application for the cloud is slightly different.

 For the cloud, CSPack performs an additional step of zipping all the files and folders into one single file that the Windows Azure fabric extracts. Without this, you would have to upload each file individually to Windows Azure. On the local machine, this step is skipped because the Dev Fabric can just be pointed to the files and folders.

Run the command shown in Example 3-4 from the directory above *htmlwebsite* (which contains the *index.html* web page). This will "package" your application code and service definition file into a Windows Azure-understandable format in a directory named *output*.

Example 3-4. Packing the sample application for the Dev Fabric

```
D:\>cspack htmlwebsite\ServiceDefinition.csdef
        /role:WebRole1;htmlwebsite /out:output /copyonly
Windows(R) Azure(TM) Packaging Tool version 1.0.0.0
for Microsoft(R) .NET Framework 3.5
Copyright (c) Microsoft Corporation. All rights reserved.

D:\>
```

This command takes a service definition file, a /role parameter (specifying the role's name), and its directory, as well as an output location. The /copyonly parameter is specific to the Dev Fabric—it specifies that it should copy the files over, instead of zipping them together. You leave out this parameter when packing for the cloud. If the command executed successfully, you should have an *output* folder with the structure shown in Figure 3-4.

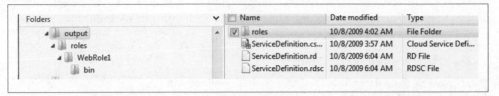

Figure 3-4. CSPack's output

Looking at all the files and folders (shown in Example 3-5), you see that this folder essentially contains the files you typed up, as well as some auto-generated files (*ServiceDefinition.rd*, *ServiceDefinition.rdsc*, *ucruntime.dll*) that the Windows Azure fabric uses to run your code.

Example 3-5. Listing of output directory's contents

```
D:\>dir /s output
 Volume in drive D has no label.
 Volume Serial Number is 34DA-B4F3
 Directory of D:\output
10/08/2009  04:02 AM    <DIR>          .
10/08/2009  04:02 AM    <DIR>          ..
10/08/2009  04:02 AM    <DIR>          roles
10/08/2009  03:57 AM               489 ServiceDefinition.csdef
10/08/2009  04:02 AM             3,866 ServiceDefinition.rd
10/08/2009  04:02 AM               374 ServiceDefinition.rdsc
               3 File(s)          4,729 bytes
 Directory of D:\output\roles
10/08/2009  04:02 AM    <DIR>          .
10/08/2009  04:02 AM    <DIR>          ..
10/08/2009  04:02 AM    <DIR>          WebRole1
               0 File(s)              0 bytes
 Directory of D:\output\roles\WebRole1
10/08/2009  04:02 AM    <DIR>          .
10/08/2009  04:02 AM    <DIR>          ..
10/08/2009  04:02 AM    <DIR>          bin
10/08/2009  03:54 AM               109 index.html
10/08/2009  03:57 AM               276 ServiceConfiguration.cscfg
10/08/2009  03:57 AM               489 ServiceDefinition.csdef
               3 File(s)            874 bytes
 Directory of D:\output\roles\WebRole1\bin
10/08/2009  04:02 AM    <DIR>          .
10/08/2009  04:02 AM    <DIR>          ..
07/07/2009  09:11 PM            18,288 ucruntime.dll
               1 File(s)         18,288 bytes
```

```
Total Files Listed:
        7 File(s)           23,891 bytes
       11 Dir(s)   19,353,911,296 bytes free
```

Running the Code in the Dev Fabric

The final step in creating your first application is to run the packaged application in the Dev Fabric. To do that, run the command shown in Example 3-6. This uses another utility that ships with the SDK, CSRun, to point to the output files and to launch the Dev Fabric with your specified configuration.

Example 3-6. Launching the Dev Fabric

```
D:\>csrun /run:output;htmlwebsite/ServiceConfiguration.cscfg
Windows(R) Azure(TM) Desktop Execution Tool version 1.0.0.0
for Microsoft(R) .NET Framework 3.5
Copyright (c) Microsoft Corporation. All rights reserved.
Created deployment(21)
Started deployment(21)
Deployment input endpoint HttpIn of role WebRole1 at http://127.0.0.1:81/
```

The Dev Fabric acts not only as a simulation of the Windows Azure fabric, but also as a local web server. In this case, as the last line of the command output indicates, it has launched your site at the local URL *http://127.0.0.1:81*. Since your web page was called *index.html*, navigate to *http://127.0.0.1:81/index.html* in any web browser. You should see something similar to Figure 3-5.

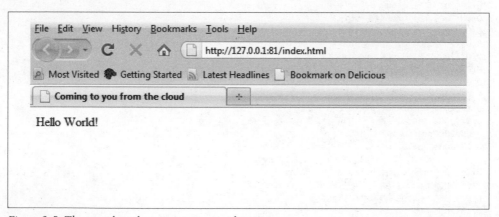

Figure 3-5. The sample web page running in a browser

 The Dev Fabric's web server isn't configured to redirect requests from *http://127.0.0.1:81* to *http://127.0.0.1:81/index.html*. However, when you are writing ASP.NET code, redirecting to the default page is done automatically for you.

You now have your first web page running in the Windows Azure Dev Fabric. Since this is essentially a simulation of the cloud, it is a short step from running on the Dev Fabric to running on the actual Windows Azure fabric.

You can click on the Dev Fabric icon in the system tray/notification area to launch the Dev Fabric UI. This shows you what services you have running, as well as health data from each of your roles and instances. For example, in Figure 3-6, you can see that one `WebRole` is running and that the Dev Fabric's health checks on it are returning a healthy response.

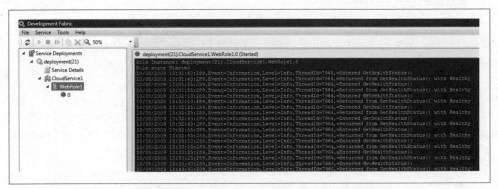

Figure 3-6. Running the Dev Fabric with our "Hello World" website

 Note the little green icon on the left of the screen in Figure 3-6 with the number "0" after it. This denotes the number of running role instances. In the actual cloud, this will correspond to running virtual machines. You can change the number of role instances in the *ServiceConfiguration.cscfg* file. It is much faster to launch a few dozen role instances in the Dev Fabric (since they are just instances of the *RdRoleHost.exe* process) than it is to spin them up in the actual Windows Azure fabric. It's also cheaper!

Running the Code in the Cloud

Now that you have your code up and running in the Dev Fabric, let's get it running in the actual Windows Azure cloud.

Packaging code for the cloud

You have seen how to use CSPack to package code to run in the Dev Fabric. Packaging for the cloud is the same process, except that the output files and folders are zipped together, and then optionally encrypted. This encryption ensures that only the Windows Azure fabric can crack open the package.

To create a package for upload, you call CSPack again, but without the /copyonly argument. You can call the output package anything you want, but the Windows Azure convention is to tag a *.cspkg* extension to it. Example 3-7 shows the command you need to run.

Example 3-7. Packaging for the cloud

```
D:\>cspack htmlwebsite\ServiceDefinition.csdef
        /role:WebRole1;htmlwebsite /out:package.cspkg
Windows(R) Azure(TM) Desktop Execution Tool version 1.0.0.0
for Microsoft(R) .NET Framework 3.5
Copyright (c) Microsoft Corporation. All rights reserved.
```

You should now have a file called *package.cspkg* in your current directory. This is the package you must upload to the cloud to run your service.

Creating a new hosted service project

The Developer Portal is also where you create *projects*, which are either hosted services (that let you run code) or storage accounts (that let you store data in Windows Azure storage).

 Be careful not to confuse Windows Azure "projects" with Visual Studio "projects," which are two different things.

Log in to the Developer Portal. Click the New Service link appearing in the top right. The portal displays the different kinds of projects available to you, as shown in Figure 3-7. Click Hosted Services.

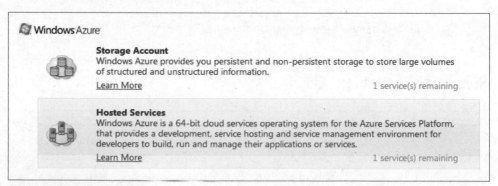

Figure 3-7. Choice of projects

A *hosted service project* is essentially a container for running your package in the cloud. Apart from just running your package, it also provides a public URL from which to access your web roles, and provides the ability to upload two packages—one as a *staging* version that is used for testing, and one as a *production* version that your users will see. It also provides the ability to deploy upgrades and manage your code. You'll learn how to manage your service in Chapter 5.

 In the world of Windows Azure, anything that runs on the Windows Azure fabric is generally called a "service." This is different from the definition of a "service" used by other parts of the Microsoft ecosystem, where the only "services" are "web services."

After you click Hosted Services, a new project wizard kicks in. The first step is to enter a label and description for your new hosted service. This is for your use only, so you can go crazy and enter anything you want here. Figure 3-8 shows this screen with some conservative choices for Service Label and Service Description. Once you have entered the information, click Next.

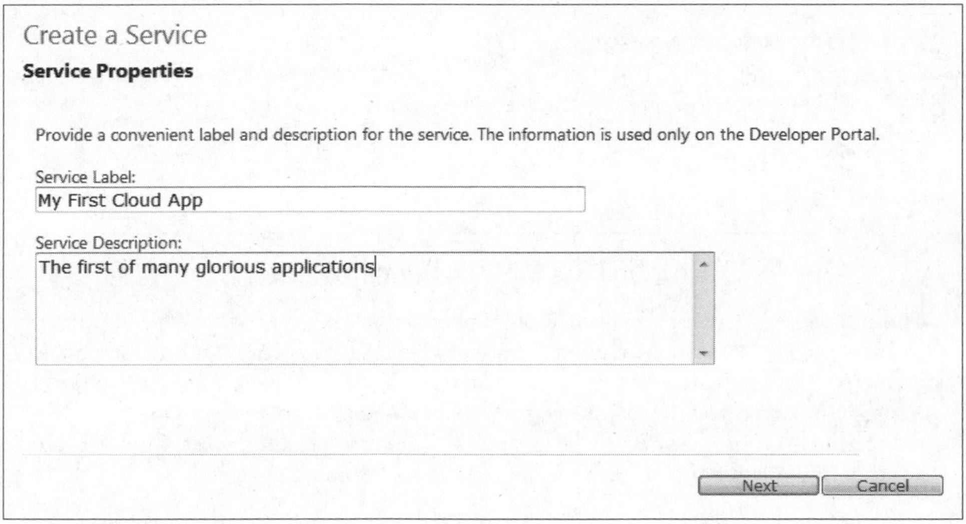

Create a Service
Service Properties

Provide a convenient label and description for the service. The information is used only on the Developer Portal.

Service Label:
My First Cloud App

Service Description:
The first of many glorious applications

[Next] [Cancel]

Figure 3-8. Entering service properties

The next step is arguably the most important when creating a new hosted service project. On the next screen shown in Figure 3-9, you pick the service name/URL for your website. This service name must be globally unique across Windows Azure. It is used all across Windows Azure, so pick carefully.

Most important of all, the service name determines at which URL the website will run. The service name is prepended to the domain *cloudapp.net*, and this URL is used for accessing your service. Note in Figure 3-9 that *booksample* appears as the service name, which in turn means the service's final URL will be *http://booksample.cloudapp.net*.

Select a name for your hosted service. This name must be globally unique.

Service Name: http:// booksample .cloudapp.net [Check Availability]

booksample is available.

Hosted Service Affinity Group

Does this service need to be hosted in the same region as some of your other hosted services or storage accounts?

○ No, this service is not related to any of my other hosted services or storage accounts and does not need to be stored in the same region.
Region: [USA - Anywhere ▼]

○ Yes, this service is related to some of my other hosted services or storage accounts and needs to be stored in the same region.
○ Use existing Affinity Group: [▼]
Region:

○ Create a new Affinity Group: [ ]
Region: [USA - Anywhere ▼]

[Previous] [Create] [Cancel]

Figure 3-9. Picking a service name/URL

 Since service names are unique, you must use some other service name for this step in creating a new hosted services project.

How Do I Use My Own Domain Name?

The *cloudapp.net* URL provides a well-known, stable endpoint with which you can access your service. However, most of us would want to use our own domain names for our websites instead of *<someurl>.cloudapp.net*. To make your website on Windows Azure show up on your domain (say, *www.example.com*), you set up a DNS CNAME redirection from your domain name to *<yourservicename>.cloudapp.net*. CNAMEs are a standard domain name feature available with most domain registrars.

The screen shown in Figure 3-9 also enables you to pick where your code will be hosted. Windows Azure is present in a few geographic locations at launch, and this list is constantly being expanded as Microsoft builds out infrastructure. You typically want to host your services as close to your end users as possible for the best network performance.

You can also choose to host your services as part of an *affinity group*, which will place your hosted services close to the Windows Azure storage data that it uses. Let's ignore this option for now. You'll learn more about affinity groups when we examine the Windows Azure storage services in Chapter 7.

Once you've picked a service name and location, click Create. This will allocate a new hosted service project for you with which you can upload your packages and run them.

Uploading packages

Consider how new builds of a website are deployed in your current environment, or, for that matter, anywhere in the noncloud world. Typically, the build goes first to a staging/testing/preproduction environment where the build is tested. When everything looks good, the build is deployed to the final production environment and goes live.

Windows Azure offers you the same two environments. They're called *deployment slots*, and there are two of them: *staging* (where you deploy your build if you want to test it before it goes live) and *production* (where the build goes live). Each slot can contain its own package, and each runs separately on its own URL. The production slot runs at the *servicename.cloudapp.net* URL you picked out, while the staging slot runs at a randomly picked URL of the form *<some-guid>.cloudapp.net*.

Figure 3-10 shows the two slots represented as two molded cubes on the portal.

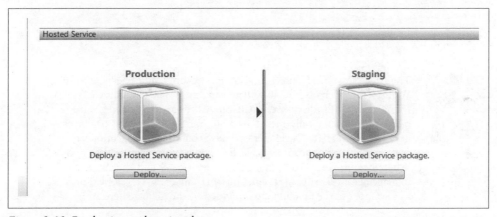

Figure 3-10. Production and staging slots

You'll learn more about how these slots work and how you can switch between the two in Chapter 5. For the rest of this example, let's ignore the staging slot and upload the build directly to production. This is acceptable for a "Hello World" example and trivial applications, but it is almost always a good practice to test your code on staging first.

To upload a package to the production deployment slot, click the Deploy button underneath the production cube to bring up the screen shown in Figure 3-11. This is where you upload the *package.cspkg* file you created earlier. Click the Browse button to locate and select the package you created earlier.

My First Cloud App
Production Deployment

Application Package

○ Upload a file from your local storage ○ Use a file from an Azure Storage account
Select a file:

`package.cspkg`   [Browse]

Configuration Settings

○ Upload a file from your local storage ○ Use a file from an Azure Storage account
Select a file:

`ServiceConfiguration.cscfg`   [Browse]

Service Deployment Name

Choose a label for this deployment: `testdeployment`

[Deploy]   [Cancel]

Figure 3-11. Upload package

 The screen shown in Figure 3-11 also supports uploading packages from Windows Azure blob storage. When using the Windows Azure Service Management API (discussed in Chapter 5), uploading packages from blob storage is the only mechanism supported. Uploading packages manually through the Developer Portal is great for test applications, but real production applications typically have a build process that publishes their packages to Windows Azure storage, and then uses the management API to deploy them. You can think of the Developer Portal as a wrapper to the functionality provided by the management API.

Every package upload also must have an associated configuration file. This is the *ServiceConfiguration.cscfg* file you created earlier. This specifies application settings for your service, and, as mentioned earlier, can be changed on-the-fly without having to go through the deployment rigmarole all over again. Most importantly, it controls the number of virtual machines (or role instances, in Windows Azure terminology) your service will use. Under the Configuration Settings portion of this page, browse to the *ServiceConfiguration.cscfg* file you created earlier and select it.

The final step is to pick a deployment label to uniquely identify the deployment. This can be any text you like (*testdeployment* has been used in Figure 3-11), but it typically contains a build number or some versioning information.

Click Deploy to kick off the process. You should see a wait cursor and a progress bar as your package gets deployed to the Windows Azure fabric.

You learned about how Windows Azure works under the hood in Chapter 2. Essentially, when you click Deploy, the Windows Azure fabric kicks in and starts deploying the package. The fabric controller finds unused virtual machines on which to place the website, copies a new operating system image over onto the virtual machines, and copies the package files over. It modifies network settings to make requests to your *cloudapp.net* URL resolve to the IP address of the virtual machine on which your code has been placed.

The final step to run your code is to click the Run button, as shown in Figure 3-12. This causes the fabric controller to go to the virtual machine(s) on which your code has been placed, and launch the application. Depending on the complexity of your application and the number of virtual machines you use, this can take anywhere from a few seconds to a few minutes.

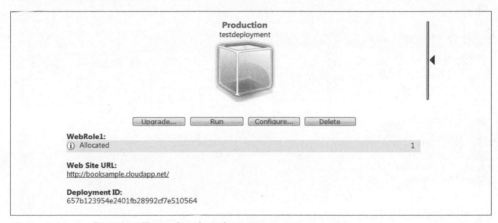

Figure 3-12. Deployment allocated and ready to run

At this point, your code is up and running. Head on over to your *cloudapp.net* URL (which is *booksample.cloudapp.net* in the example shown here) in a web browser. You should see the text "Hello World!" as shown in Figure 3-13.

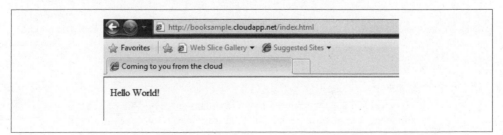

Figure 3-13. Website running in the cloud

Congratulations! You've successfully launched code in Windows Azure.

Using the Visual Studio Tools

Just as Visual Studio wraps around the C# or Visual Basic compilers to provide an integrated experience with the IDE, the Visual Studio extensions wrap around CSPack and the Dev Fabric to provide an integrated experience with Windows Azure. This also provides an additional important feature that is difficult to reach with just the command-line tools alone: debugging support.

The following discussion assumes that you've finished installing the SDK and the Visual Studio tools. If you haven't, follow the instructions presented earlier in this chapter on where to get the right bits and how to install them.

Let's start by opening Visual Studio and selecting File→New→Project. Select the Cloud Service template on the list, as shown in Figure 3-14.

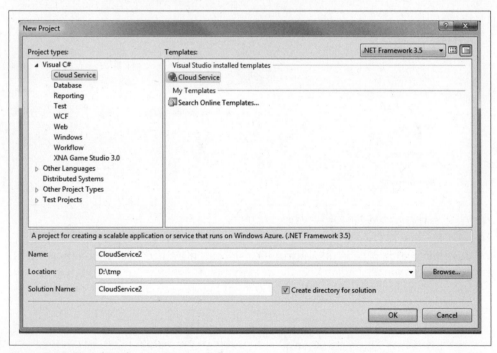

Figure 3-14. Visual Studio New Project dialog

 You can also use the Cloud Service template as a good way to check whether the SDK and tools installed cleanly. If you don't see the Cloud Service template, it means something failed in the installation process.

A *cloud service* solution contains only the service definition and service configuration files for your service. It doesn't contain (by default) the actual roles that make up your service. As mentioned earlier, Chapter 4 provides more information on roles. For now, you simply should be aware that you can add roles to your cloud service project in two ways:

- Using the New Cloud Service Project dialog, which pops up when you create a new cloud service solution, as shown in Figure 3-15. This dialog shows you a list of role types available for adding to your project. This list is frequently expanded, so you may see more items on this list with newer builds of the SDK.
- Using the Visual Studio Solution Explorer later in the development cycle to add them to your solution.

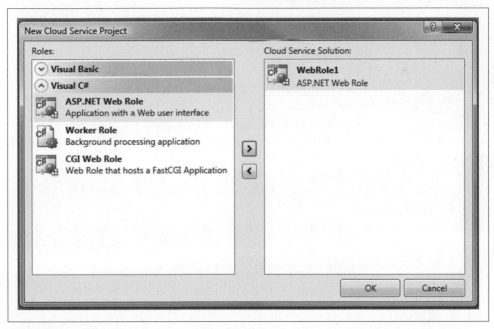

Figure 3-15. Adding roles to your Visual Studio solution

Since you are creating a simple website, let's add an ASP.NET Web Role to your project by clicking that option, as shown on the right side of the dialog shown in Figure 3-15.

At this time, Visual Studio generates a cloud service solution, a web role project, and some default files for you. Your Solution Explorer should look similar to Figure 3-16. The Cloud Service project is a container for your service definition and service configuration files. You should have default *ServiceDefinition.csdef* and *ServiceConfiguration.cscfg* files generated for you. These files automatically reference the WebRole1 project and are set to use one virtual machine.

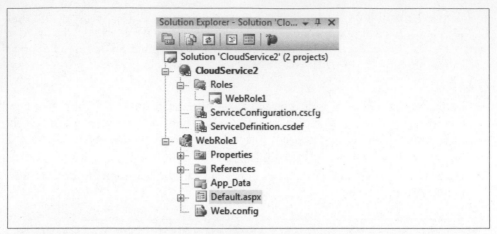

Figure 3-16. Default web role project created by Visual Studio

The WebRole1 project itself is just an ASP.NET web application project under the covers. It is identical to a typical ASP.NET project in almost all ways. However, instead of hooking up with the ASP.NET development server, Cloud Service projects are automatically run in the Dev Fabric.

At this point, you can press F5 to build and launch your empty website. Visual Studio will build your website, call CSPack to package it for the Dev Fabric, and then launch the Dev Fabric. Most importantly, it will attach a debugger to the Dev Fabric so that normal Visual Studio debugging functions "just work." You can set a breakpoint, step through code, inspect local variables, and do everything that you would normally do while debugging an ASP.NET website.

Finally, you can package your service for Windows Azure by right-clicking on the Cloud Service node in the Solution Explorer and selecting Publish, as shown in Figure 3-17.

 Note that *Publish* happens to be a widely used term inside Visual Studio. Also note that selecting Build→Publish invokes a completely different and unrelated menu.

Clicking Publish will call CSPack and create a *.cspkg* file and a *.cscfg* file for uploading to Windows Azure. You can then upload this to the cloud using the Developer Portal, or through the Windows Azure Service Management API.

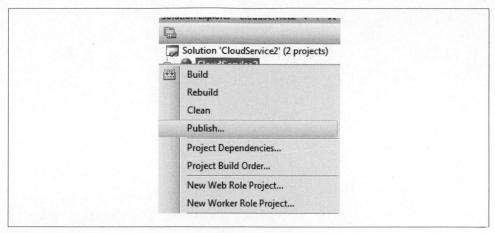

Figure 3-17. Packaging our project using CSPack

Summary

The Windows Azure SDK and associated tools help you build, debug, and package your code to run it in the cloud. Windows Azure doesn't bring many new concepts to the table in terms of code or frameworks. It tries really hard to use existing Microsoft technologies. There might be a few new terms involved (such as *cloud service*, *roles*, and *deployments*), but under the covers, it is all familiar ASP.NET code (in the case of web roles) running on Windows.

## CHAPTER 4

Service Model

Chapter 3 examined how to get your first service running on Windows Azure. You briefly saw how to create a web role, service definition, and configuration files. Roles that are composed using the service definition file are used to create complex services on Windows Azure. In this chapter, you'll see what roles are, and how to compose them to model your service. You'll also see how to use the various features offered by the service definition and configuration files to build complex services on Windows Azure.

Understanding Windows Azure Roles

In Chapter 2, you had a brief peek at how the service model helps you model your service; similar to how you might draw out your service architecture on a whiteboard. Let's go back to that analogy for a second.

Consider a service architecture such as the one shown in Figure 4-1. When you draw it out on the whiteboard, you typically show the different "types" of boxes you use, and if you have a small number, the individual boxes themselves. For example, you might have a few "web frontend" boxes that host your web server, a few "DB" boxes hosting your database, and so on.

Each of these "types" typically has the same kind of code/software/bits running on that machine. All your web frontends typically have the same web frontend code, all your database machines have the same database software installed (with different partitions of data), and all your backend mail servers probably run the same mail transfer agent. This similarity is deliberate. If you want an extra web frontend, you add one more machine with the right bits, and twiddle with the load balancer to bring the new machine into rotation.

Windows Azure takes this informal grouping of machines that most applications do and formalizes it into something called *roles*. A Windows Azure role roughly corresponds to a "type" of box. However, each role is tweaked for a special purpose. There's

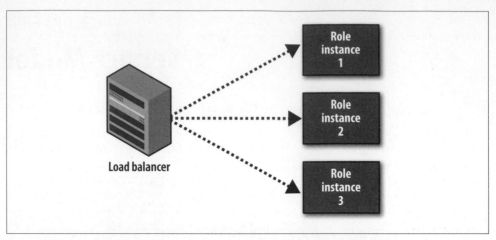

Figure 4-1. Load balancer and roles

a *web role* that contains your website and frontend code. There's a *worker role* suited to background jobs and long-running transactions.

Taking these core web and worker roles, Visual Studio offers a few *role templates* that customizes them for specific scenarios such as hosting a Windows Communication Foundation (WCF) service or a FastCGI application. Table 4-1 lists the roles and role templates offered by Windows Azure and what each of them is suited for. You'll see web and worker roles explored in detail later in this chapter.

Table 4-1. Windows Azure role and role template types

Role type	Description
Web role	This is analogous to an ASP.NET website hosted in IIS (which is, in fact, exactly how Windows Azure hosts your code, as you saw in Chapter 2). This is your go-to option for hosting websites, web services, and anything that needs to speak HTTP, and can run on the IIS/ASP.NET stack.
Worker role	A worker role in Windows Azure fulfills the same role a long-running Windows service/cron job/ console application would do in the server world. You get to write the equivalent of an `int main()` that Windows Azure will call for you. You can put absolutely any code you want in it. If you can't fit your code in any of the other role types, you can probably find a way to fit it here. This is used for everything, including background jobs, asynchronous processing, hosting application servers written in non-.NET languages such as Java, or even databases such as MySQL.
CGI web role (web role)	Windows Azure offers direct support to host languages and runtimes that support the FastCGI protocol. The `CGI Role` template makes it easier for you. You'll see how this FastCGI support works in Chapter 6. Though this is offered as a first-class role type in Visual Studio, under the covers it is just a web role with the CGI option turned on.
WCF service role (web role)	This is another customized version of the web role targeted at hosting WCF Services. Under the covers, this is just a web role with some Visual Studio magic to make it easier to write a WCF service.

Though each role is targeted at a specific scenario, each can be modified to fit a variety of scenarios. For example, the worker role can act as a web server by listening on port

80. The web role can launch a process to perform some long-running activity. You'll have to resort to tactics such as this to run code that isn't natively part of the Microsoft stack. For example, to run Tomcat (the popular Java application server), you must modify the worker role to listen on the correct ports.

How Do Roles Fit in with the Windows Azure Service Model?

You might be wondering how these roles fit in with the Windows Azure fabric and service model described in Chapter 2. Service models in their current form in Windows Azure are difficult to construct by hand. The "roles" are, in reality, prepackaged service models. For example, a web role is a service model component that specifies that the code should be hosted inside IIS, should listen on port 80, and other magic bits to make normal websites work.

You get a few pregenerated service models with the SDK: one that has the web role alone, one that has the worker role alone, and one that contains both web and worker roles in various combinations.

In the future, Windows Azure will have the capability to construct more advanced service models directly.

Role Instances

Let's consider the boxes and arrows on the whiteboard. When you draw out your architecture, you probably have more than one "type" of box. Any site or service with serious usage is probably going to need more than one web frontend. Just like the "type" of box corresponds to a role in Windows Azure, the actual box corresponds to a *role instance*.

Note the use of the terms *type* and *instance*. The similarity to the same terms as used in object-oriented programming (OOP) is deliberate. A role is similar to a class/type in that it specifies the blueprint. However, the actual code runs in a role instance, which is analogous to an instantiated object.

Also note that there is a strict limitation of one role instance per virtual machine; there is no concept of multiple roles on the virtual machine. If you want to host more than one role on the same virtual machine, you'll need to pack the code together into a single web role or worker role, and distribute the work yourself.

Role instances and the load balancer

In the boxes-and-diagrams version, how incoming traffic is routed to your machines completely depends on your network setup. Your infrastructure could have a mass of virtual local area networks (VLANs), software and hardware load balancers, and various other networking magic.

In Windows Azure, the relationship between role instances and incoming traffic is simple. As shown earlier in Figure 4-1, all role instances for a role are behind a load balancer. The load balancer distributes traffic in a strict round-robin fashion to each role instance. For example, if you have three web role instances, each will get one-third of the incoming traffic. This even distribution is maintained when the number of instances changes.

How does traffic directed toward *foo.cloudapp.net* end up at a web role instance? A request to a **.cloudapp.net* URL is redirected through DNS toward a *virtual IP address* (*VIP*) in a Microsoft data center that your service owns. This VIP is the external face for your service, and the load balancer has the knowledge to route traffic hitting this VIP to the various role instances.

Each of these role instances has its own special IP address that is accessible only inside the data center. This is often called a *direct IP address* (*DIP*). Though you can't get at these DIPs from outside the data center, these are useful when you want roles to communicate with each other. Later in this chapter, you'll see the API that lets you discover what these IP addresses are used for with the other role instances in your service.

Controlling the number of instances

The number of role instances that your service uses is specified in the service configuration (that is, the *ServiceConfiguration.cscfg* file). Under each `Role` element, you should find an `Instances` element that takes a `count` parameter. That directly controls the number of role instances your service uses. Since this is part of the service configuration (and not the definition), this can be updated separately, and doesn't require rebuilding/redeploying your package.

Example 4-1 shows a sample service configuration with one instance. You can specify the instance count separately for each role in your service.

Example 4-1. Sample service configuration

```
<?xml version="1.0"?>
<ServiceConfiguration serviceName="CloudService1"
 xmlns=
"http://schemas.microsoft.com/ServiceHosting/2008/10/ServiceConfiguration">
  <Role name="WebRole1">
    <Instances count="1" />
    <ConfigurationSettings />
  </Role>
</ServiceConfiguration>
```

Note that all instances in your role are identical. Later in this chapter, you'll see how to have roles on different virtual machine sizes. It is currently not possible to have role instances of the same role with different sizes.

Today, there is a direct mapping between the number of role instances and the number of virtual machines. If you ask for three role instances, you'll get three virtual machines. This also factors into how your application gets billed. Remember that one of the resources for which you are billed is the number of virtual machine hours used. Every running role instance consumes one virtual machine hour every hour. If you have three role instances, that is three virtual machine hours every hour. Keep this in mind when changing the instance count, because a typo could wind up as an expensive mistake!

Though changing the number of role instances is simple in the service configuration, it can take longer to update in the cloud than other service configuration changes. The reason behind this is that changing the instance count (or, to be specific, adding new instances) means that new machines must be found to run your code. Depending on the current state of the machine, some cleanup may be required before your code can be run on the new machines. Take this into account when making large changes to instance counts.

Role Size

In Chapter 2, you learned how the Windows Azure hypervisor takes a single beefy machine and chops it up into smaller virtual machine sizes. What if you don't want a small virtual machine? What if you want half the machine, or the entire machine itself?

Though this wasn't available as part of the initial Windows Azure release, the ability to specify the size of the virtual machine was added in late 2009. To be specific, you get to choose how many "slices" of the machine you want combined. Each size has a different billing rate. As always, consult the Windows Azure website for up-to-date information on the latest billing rates.

To specify the size for your role, use the `vmsize` attribute in the service definition file. Since this is a service definition attribute, you cannot change this dynamically without reuploading your package, or doing a service upgrade.

Example 4-2 shows a sample configuration file with the virtual machine size set to "extra large" (the largest virtual machine size available). As of this writing, there are four virtual machine sizes, ranging from `Small` to `ExtraLarge`.

Example 4-2. Virtual machine size

```
<?xml version="1.0" encoding="utf-8"?>
<ServiceDefinition name="Test"
 xmlns=
"http://schemas.microsoft.com/ServiceHosting/2008/10/ServiceDefinition">
  <WorkerRole name="Test"  vmsize ="ExtraLarge">
    <ConfigurationSettings/>
  </WorkerRole>
</ServiceDefinition>
```

Table 4-2 lists all the virtual machine sizes and their equivalent configuration if they were real machines. This is meant to act as a rule of thumb to give you an idea of the kind of performance you can expect. As you go from small to large, you get a bigger slice of the CPU, RAM, and hard disk, as well as I/O benefits. However, you should do performance and load testing with your target workload before picking the virtual machine size on which you want to run your code.

Table 4-2. Virtual machine reference sizes

Virtual machine size	Reference machine specifications
Small	One core, 1.75 GB RAM, 225 GB disk space
Medium	Two cores, 3.5 GB RAM, 490 GB disk space
Large	Four cores, 7.0 GB RAM, 1,000 GB disk space
ExtraLarge	Eight cores, 14 GB RAM, 2,040 GB disk space

 With the billing differences between virtual machine sizes, you can test out various interesting configurations to see what works the cheapest. This is especially true if your service doesn't scale strictly linearly as you add more role instances. For example, a bigger virtual machine size might work out to be cheaper than having multiple role instances while delivering equivalent performance, or vice versa. Experiment with different sizes and numbers of instances to determine how your service performs, and find the cheapest option that works for you.

Service Definition and Configuration

Before digging into the web and worker roles, let's look at two important files that you have touched a couple of times now: *ServiceDefinition.csdef* and *ServiceConfiguration.cscfg*. Using these files, you control everything from how much disk space your application can access, to what ports your service can listen on.

You'll be modifying these files often when building services to be hosted on Windows Azure. The best way to modify these files is through the Visual Studio tool set, since it not only provides IntelliSense and shows you what all the options can be, but also does some basic checking for syntax errors. It is much quicker to catch errors through Visual Studio than it is to deal with an error when uploading a service configuration file through the Developer Portal, or through the management API.

Figure 4-2 shows Visual Studio's Solution Explorer with the *ServiceConfiguration.cscfg* and *ServiceDefinition.csdef* files for the Thumbnails sample that ships with the SDK.

Though both of these files are closely related, they serve very different purposes, and are used quite differently. The single most important difference between the two files is that the definition file (*ServiceDefinition.csdef*) cannot be changed without rebuilding

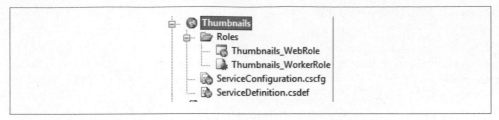

Figure 4-2. ServiceConfiguration and ServiceDefinition files in Visual Studio

and reuploading the entire package, whereas the configuration file (*ServiceConfiguration.cscfg*) can be quickly changed for a running service.

Service Definition

The *service definition* is everything that goes into *ServiceDefinition.cscfg*. You'll need to modify this file fewer times than the service configuration when using the Visual Studio tools because large portions are auto-generated for you. This essentially acts as a simplified service model for your service. It lays out a few critical components of your service:

- The various roles used by your service.
- Options for these roles (virtual machine size, whether native code execution is supported).
- Input endpoints for these roles (what ports the roles can listen on). You'll see how to use this in detail a bit later.
- Local disk storage that the role will need.
- Configuration settings that the role will use (though not the values themselves, which come in the configuration file).

Example 4-3 shows a sample service definition file. This example is taken from the `Thumbnails` sample which ships with the SDK. When building a package, the CSPack tool uses this file to generate a Windows Azure service model that the fabric can understand, and that has the right roles, endpoints, and settings. When the fabric sees the service model file, it programs the network settings and configures the virtual machine accordingly (see Chapter 2 for the gory details).

Example 4-3. Sample service definition

```
<?xml version="1.0" encoding="utf-8"?>
<ServiceDefinition name="Thumbnails" xmlns=
"http://schemas.microsoft.com/ServiceHosting/2008/10/ServiceDefinition">
  <WorkerRole name="Thumbnails_WorkerRole"  vmsize ="ExtraLarge">
    <ConfigurationSettings>
      <Setting name="DataConnectionString" />
      <Setting name="DiagnosticsConnectionString" />
    </ConfigurationSettings>
  </WorkerRole>
```

```
    <WebRole name="Thumbnails_WebRole" >
      <InputEndpoints>
        <!-- Must use port 80 for http and port 443 for
             https when running in the cloud -->
        <InputEndpoint name="HttpIn" protocol="http" port="80" />
      </InputEndpoints>
      <ConfigurationSettings>
        <Setting name="DataConnectionString" />
        <Setting name="DiagnosticsConnectionString" />
      </ConfigurationSettings>
    </WebRole>
</ServiceDefinition>
```

Don't worry if this seems like a load of mumbo-jumbo at the moment. To effectively use the elements defined in the service definition file, you must use the Windows Azure Service Runtime API, which is discussed shortly. At that time, usage of these individual elements will be a lot clearer.

Service Configuration

The service configuration file (*ServiceConfiguration.cscfg*) goes hand in hand with the service definition file. There is one important difference, though: the configuration file can be updated without having to stop a running service. In fact, there are several ways in which you can update a running service without downtime in Windows Azure, and updating the configuration file is a key component.

The service configuration file contains two key elements:

Number of role instances (or virtual machines) used by that particular role
> Note that the size of these virtual machines is configured in the service definition file. This element is critical because this is what you'll be changing when you want to add more virtual machines to your service to help your service scale.

Values for settings
> The service definition file defines the names of the settings, but the actual values go in the configuration file, and can be read using the Windows Azure Service Hosting API. This is where you'll place everything from your storage account name and endpoints, to logging settings, to anything that you need tweaked at runtime.

Example 4-4 shows a sample service configuration file. In this example taken from the Thumbnails sample, you can see a web role and a worker role, with one role instance count each. You also see both have two configuration settings called DataConnection String and DiagnosticConnectionString. Later in this chapter, you'll see how to use the Service Runtime API to read the values of these settings.

Example 4-4. Sample service configuration file

```
<?xml version="1.0"?>
<ServiceConfiguration serviceName="Thumbnails"
 xmlns="http://schemas.microsoft.com/ServiceHosting/2008/10/ServiceConfiguration">
```

```
  <Role name="Thumbnails_WorkerRole">
    <Instances count="1" />
    <ConfigurationSettings>
      <Setting name="DataConnectionString"
        value="UseDevelopmentStorage=true" />

      <Setting name="DiagnosticsConnectionString"
value="UseDevelopmentStorage=true" />
    </ConfigurationSettings>
  </Role>
  <Role name="Thumbnails_WebRole">
    <Instances count="1" />
    <ConfigurationSettings>
      <Setting name="DataConnectionString" value="UseDevelopmentStorage=true" />
      <Setting name="DiagnosticsConnectionString"
value="UseDevelopmentStorage=true" />
    </ConfigurationSettings>
  </Role>
</ServiceConfiguration>
```

Since the service configuration can be changed at runtime, this is a good spot for placing several settings that you would want to change without bringing down your service. Here are some tips to effectively use your service configuration file:

- Place your storage account name and credentials in your configuration file. This makes it easy to change which storage account your service talks to. This also lets you change your credentials and make your service use new credentials without having to bring down your service.

- Place all logging options in your configuration file. Make it so that, by switching flags in your configuration on or off, you control what gets logged, and how.

- Have different configuration files for staging, production, and any other test environments you're using. This makes it easy to go from staging to production by just updating your configuration file.

Introducing the Service Runtime API

In Chapter 2, you saw how the Windows Azure fabric launches and hosts your application code, be it a web role or a worker role. Earlier in this chapter, you saw how the service definition and configuration files let you control various aspects of your service. This leads to some obvious questions. How do you interact with this environment set up for you by the Windows Azure fabric? How do you read settings from the configuration file? How do you know what your endpoints are? How do you know when the configuration is being updated?

As you might guess, the answer is the Service Runtime API. This API is meant for code that runs inside the cloud. It is meant to be included as a part of your web and worker roles. It lets you access, manipulate, and respond to the ambient environment in which your code runs.

The Service Runtime API is at times referred to as the *Service Hosting API* by some blogs. Both refer to the same thing. This is not to be confused with the *Service Management API*. See the sidebar, "How Is This Different from the Service Management API?" on page 76 for more on the difference between the two.

The API itself can be accessed in one of two ways. For managed code, the SDK ships with an assembly called *Microsoft.WindowsAzure.ServiceRuntime.dll*, which is automatically referenced when you create a new cloud service project using Visual Studio (Figure 4-3). For native code, header and library files ship with the SDK that let you call into the Service Runtime API using C. Both the native and managed libraries have equivalent functionality, and it is easy to translate code from one to the other, since they use the same concepts. In the interest of keeping things simple, this chapter covers only the managed API.

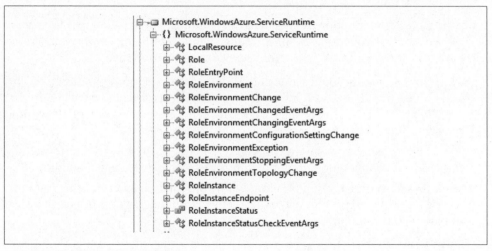

Figure 4-3. Service Runtime API's types

How Is This Different from the Service Management API?

In Chapter 5, you'll see a different API called the Windows Azure Service Management API. Though it is meant for a completely different purpose, there is some overlap between the Service Runtime API and the Service Management API in terms of information you can get at.

Here's a simple mental model to distinguish the two. The Service Runtime API that is covered in this chapter is meant to be run "inside" the cloud. It gives code already running in Windows Azure the right hooks to interact with the environment around it. The Service Management API is meant to be run "outside" the cloud. You can use it to manipulate your running services from outside.

To use the Service Runtime API, add a reference in your projects to *Microsoft.Win-dowsAzure.ServiceRuntime.dll*. If you're using the Visual Studio tools, you're in luck, since it is one of the three assemblies added automatically by default, as shown in Figure 4-4. Bring in the namespace `Microsoft.WindowsAzure.ServiceRuntime` to use it in your code.

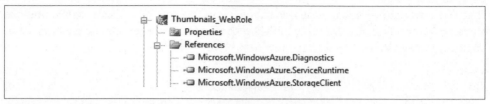

Figure 4-4. Automatic project references, including the service runtime

The most common use of the Service Runtime API is to access information about your service and your roles:

- It enables you to access the latest value of your configuration settings as defined in the service definition and service configuration files. When you update your configuration for your running service, the API will ensure that the latest configuration value is returned.
- It is also used to access the topology of your service—what roles are running, how many instances each role has, and so on.
- In the case of worker roles, it is tightly bound to the role's life cycle.

`Microsoft.WindowsAzure.ServiceRuntime.RoleEnvironment` is the important type to look at here.

Table 4-3 shows a short list of interesting methods and properties on that type, which you'll be using frequently.

Table 4-3. RoleEnvironment properties/methods/events

Property/method/event on RoleEnvironment	Description
`GetConfigurationSettingValue(string)`	Lets you access configuration settings and the latest value from *ServiceConfiguration.cscfg*.
`GetLocalResource(string)`	Gets the path to a "local resource"—essentially a writable hard disk space on the virtual machine you're in.
`RequestRecycle()`	Recycles the role instance.
`DeploymentId`	A unique ID assigned to your running service. You'll be using this when using the Windows Azure logging system.
`Roles`	A collection of all the roles of your running service and their instances.
`Changed, Changing, StatusCheck, Stopping`	Events you can hook to get notified of various points in the role's life cycle.

Now that you've had a quick peek at the Service Runtime API, let's see it in action.

Accessing Configuration Settings

Earlier in this chapter, you saw how to define configuration settings in *ServiceDefinition.csdef* and assign them values in *ServiceConfiguration.cscfg*. During that discussion, one critical piece was left out: how to read the values assigned and use them in your code. The answer lies in the `GetConfigurationSettingValue` method of the `RoleEnvironment` type.

Consider the two values defined in Examples 4-3 and 4-4. To read the values of the settings `DataConnectionString` and `DiagnosticsConnectionString`, you would call `RoleEnvironment.GetConfigurationSettingValue("DataConnectionString")` and `RoleEnvironment.GetConfigurationSettingValue("DiagnosticsConnectionString")`, respectively.

Understanding Endpoints

By default, web roles can be configured to listen on port 80 and port 443, while worker roles don't listen on any port. However, it is often necessary to make worker roles listen on a port. If you want to host an FTP server, an SMTP/POP server, a database server, or any other non-HTTP server, you'll probably need your server to listen on other ports as well.

Using a combination of the service definition and the Service Runtime API, you can make your service listen on any TCP port and handle traffic, either from the Internet or from other roles.

 As of this writing, Windows Azure does not support worker roles dealing with UDP traffic. For example, you cannot host DNS servers on Windows Azure, or any other protocol that needs UDP.

At this point, you may be wondering why you should go to all this trouble. Why can't an application listen on any port without having to declare it in the service definition? And why is the Service Runtime API involved in this at all?

The answer to these questions is twofold. The first part of the answer concerns security. Windows Azure tries to lock down open ports as much as possible—opening only the ports that your application uses is a good security practice. The second part of the answer concerns the fact that Windows Azure sometimes maps external ports to different internal ports because of the way its networking capabilities are implemented. For example, though your service is listening on port 80 on the Internet, inside the virtual machine it will be listening on an arbitrary, random port number. The load balancer translates traffic between port 80 and your various role instances.

To understand this in detail, let's look at a sample time server that must listen on a TCP port. Figure 4-5 shows a hypothetical service, *MyServer.exe*, listening on port 13 (which happens to be the port used by time servers). In the figure, there are two role instances of the worker role hosting the time server. This means the load balancer will split traffic between the two equally.

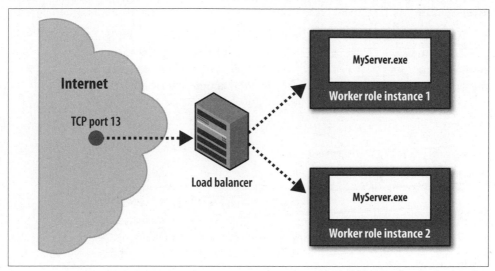

Figure 4-5. Worker role listening on external endpoint

To make *MyServer.exe* listen on port 13, you must do two things. The first is to declare in your service definition file the port it is going to listen on (13, in this case) and assign it an *endpoint name*. You'll use this endpoint name later in your code. This can be any string, as long as it is unique among all the endpoints you declare. (Your server can listen on as many TCP ports as it chooses.)

Example 4-5 shows the service definition file for *MyServer.exe*. It declares the service will listen on port 13 and the endpoint name is set to DayTimeIn. The protocol is set to tcp (the other options for protocol are http and https, which will set up your worker role as a web server).

Example 4-5. Declaring an endpoint in the service definition

```
<WorkerRole name="WorkerRole" enableNativeCodeExecution="true">
  <Endpoints>
    <!-- This is an external endpoint that allows a
         role to listen on external communication, this
         could be TCP, HTTP or HTTPS -->
    <InputEndpoint name="DayTimeIn" port="13" protocol="tcp" />
  </Endpoints>
</WorkerRole>
```

Now that an endpoint has been declared, Windows Azure will allow your traffic on port 13 to reach your role's instances. However, there is one final issue to deal with.

Since Windows Azure can sometimes map external ports to random internal ports, your code needs a way to "know" which port to listen on. This can be a source of confusion—if you create a socket and listen on port 13, you won't receive any traffic because you're not listening on the correct internal port to which the load balancer is sending traffic.

To determine the right port to listen on, you must use the Service Runtime API. Specifically, you use the `RoleEnvironment.CurrentRoleInstance.InstanceEndpoints` collection. This contains all the endpoints you declared in your service definition, along with the port they're mapped to inside the virtual machine.

Example 4-6 shows code that uses the Service Runtime API to retrieve the correct port and endpoint on which to listen. It then creates a socket and binds to that endpoint.

Example 4-6. Listening on the correct port

```
RoleInstanceEndpoint dayTimeIn =
    RoleEnvironment.CurrentRoleInstance.InstanceEndpoints["DayTimeIn"];

IPEndPoint endpoint = dayTimeIn.IPEndpoint;

//Create socket for time server using correct port and address
// The load balancer will map network traffic coming in on port 13 to
// this socket

Socket sock = new Socket(endpoint.AddressFamily, SocketType.Stream,
          ProtocolType.Tcp);
sock.Bind(endpoint);
sock.Listen(1000);

//At this point, the socket will receive traffic sent to port 13
// on the service's address. The percentage of traffic it receives
// depends on the total number of role instances.
```

Understanding Inter-Role Communication

One important use of declaring endpoints is to enable communication between the various roles of your service. When the Windows Azure fabric spins up your role instances, each role instance gets an internal IP address (the DIP) that is accessible only from within the data center. However, you can't get to this IP address even if you're within the same service. Windows Azure locks down firewall and network settings for all ports by default.

Windows Azure sets up networking within the data center so that only role instances belonging to your own service can access other role instances from your service. Several layers protect applications that run on Windows Azure from one another, and the way the network is set up is one of them.

To open up a port, you must declare an endpoint in your service definition. Isn't this the same as opening up an endpoint to the Internet, like you did previously? Very close.

The difference between declaring an endpoint that anyone on the Internet can access and opening up a port for inter-role communication comes down to the load balancer. When declaring an `InputEndpoint` in your service definition like you did earlier in this chapter, you get to pick a port on the load balancer that maps to an arbitrary port inside the virtual machine. When you declare an `InternalEndpoint` (which is the XML element used in a service definition for inter-role communication), you don't get to pick the port. The reason is that, when talking directly between role instances, there is no reason to go through the load balancer. Hence, you directly connect to the randomly assigned port on each role instance. To find out what these ports are, you use the Service Runtime API.

Figure 4-6 shows you how a web role can connect using inter-role endpoints to two worker role endpoints. Note the lack of a load balancer in the figure. Making this architecture work is simple, and requires two things: declaring the endpoint and connecting to the right port and IP address.

Let's walk through both steps. The first step is to modify your service definition and an `InternalEndpoint` element, as shown in Example 4-7. This is similar to the `InputEnd point` element you used earlier in this chapter, except that you don't specify the port.

Example 4-7. Inter-role endpoint

```
<WorkerRole name="MyWorkerRole" enableNativeCodeExecution="true">
  <Endpoints>
    <!-- Defines an internal endpoint for inter-role communication
      that can be used to communicate between worker
      or Web role instances -->
    <InternalEndpoint name="InternalEndpoint1" protocol="tcp" />
  </Endpoints>
</WorkerRole>
```

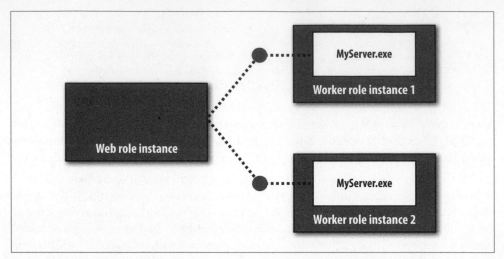

Figure 4-6. Inter-role communication

When your worker role starts, ensure that it listens on the correct port. The code to do this is the same as what was shown in Example 4-6.

Finally, you just need to discover the IP addresses and ports, and then connect to them. To do that, enumerate the `RoleEnvironment.Roles` collection to find your role, and then loop through each instance, as shown in Example 4-8. Once you have an IP address and a port, you can write any common networking code to connect to that role instance.

Example 4-8. Finding the right inter-role endpoint

```
foreach (var instance in RoleEnvironment.Roles["MyWorkerRole"].Instances)
{
    RoleInstanceEndPoint endpoint =
        instance.InstanceEndpoints["InternalEndpoint1"];

    IPEndPoint ipAndPort = endpoint.IPEndpoint;

    // ipAndPort contains the IP address and port. You can use it with
    // any type from the System.Net classes to connect.

}
```

 Though all the examples in this chapter show .NET code, it is easy to integrate this API with code not written for Windows Azure. For example, one common scenario is to run MySQL on Windows Azure. Since MySQL can't call the Service Runtime API directly, a wrapper is written that calls the Service Runtime API, calls the right port to listen on, and then calls the MySQL executable, passing the port as a parameter. Of course, whether you can do this depends on whether the software you're working with has configurable ports.

Subscribing to Changes

When your service runs on Windows Azure, it is running in a highly dynamic environment. Things change all the time: the configuration gets updated, role instances go down and come up, and role instances could disappear or be added.

The Service Runtime API provides a mechanism to *subscribe* to updates about your service. Let's look at some common updates and how to get notified when they happen. All changes can be "hooked" using the `RoleEnvironment.Changing` and `RoleEnvironment.Changed` events. The argument, `RoleEnvironmentChangedEventArgs`, contains the actual changes.

The most common form of updates occurs when you add or remove role instances. When you have inter-role communication as shown earlier, it is important to be notified of these changes, since you must connect to new instances when they come up. To get access to the role instances being added, you must poke through the `RoleEnvironmentChangedEventArgs` and look for `RoleEnvironmentTopologyChanges`. Example 4-9 shows how to access the new instances when they are added to your service.

Example 4-9. Topology changes

```
RoleEnvironment.Changed += delegate(object sender,
    RoleEnvironmentChangedEventArgs e)
{
    foreach (var change in e.Changes)
    {
        var topoChange = change as RoleEnvironmentTopologyChange;
        // Return new value
        if (topoChange != null)
        {
            // Name of role that experienced a change in instance count
            string role = topoChange.RoleName;
            // Get the new instances
            var instances =
                RoleEnvironment.Roles[role].Instances;
        }
    }
};
```

Another common set of changes is when configuration settings are updated. Example 4-10 shows how to use the same event handler to look for new configuration settings.

Example 4-10. Configuration change

```
RoleEnvironment.Changed +=
    delegate(object sender, RoleEnvironmentChangedEventArgs e)
{
    foreach (var change in e.Changes)
    {
        var configChange =
            change as RoleEnvironmentConfigurationSettingChange;
```

```
        if (configChange != null)
        {
            // This gets you new value for configuration setting
            RoleEnvironment.GetConfigurationSettingValue(
                configChange.ConfigurationSettingName);
        }
    }
};
```

Looking at Worker Roles in Depth

Web roles are fairly straightforward—they are essentially ASP.NET websites hosted in IIS. As such, they should be familiar to anyone well versed in ASP.NET development. All common ASP.NET metaphors—from *web.config* files to providers to HTTP modules and handlers—should "just work" with web roles.

Worker roles are a different story. Though the concept is simple, their implementation is unique to Windows Azure. Let's dig into what a worker role is and how to use it.

A worker role is the Swiss Army knife of the Windows Azure world. It is a way to package any arbitrary code—be it something as simple as creating thumbnails, to something as complex as entire database servers. The concept is simple: Windows Azure calls a well-defined entry point in your code, and runs it as long as you want. Why is this so useful?

With a web role, your code must fit a particular mold: it must be able to serve HTTP content. With a worker role, you have no such limitation. As long as you don't return from the entry point method, you can do anything you want. You could do something simple, such as pull messages from a queue (typically, a Windows Azure storage queue, something you'll see later in this book). In fact, this is the canonical example of how worker roles are used. Or you could do something different, such as launching a long-running transaction, or even launching an external process containing an entire application. In fact, this is the recommended way to run other applications from non-.NET languages. There is little that can't be squeezed into the worker role model.

Creating Worker Roles

Creating a worker role is simple using the Visual Studio tools. Figure 4-7 shows how to add a new worker role to your project using the new cloud service dialog (you can add one to an existing solution, too, if you prefer). This will generate a new Visual Studio project for you, along with the correct entries in *ServiceDefinition.csdef*.

A worker role project is very similar to a normal .NET class library project, except that it is expected to have a class inheriting from `RoleEntryPoint` and to implement a few methods. When your worker role code is run, the assembly is loaded and run inside a 64-bit hosting process.

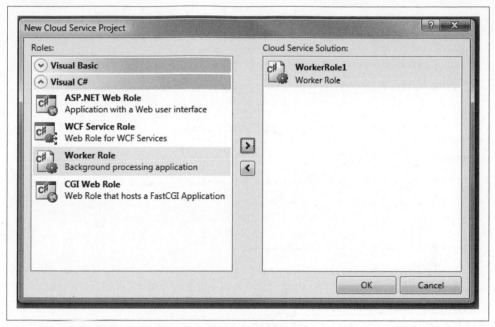

Figure 4-7. Creating a worker role using the Visual Studio tools

Understanding the Worker Role Life Cycle

To understand the life of a worker role, let's look at the boilerplate code that Visual Studio generates for you. Example 4-11 shows the code. The key things to notice are the various methods.

Example 4-11. Worker role boilerplate code

```
public class WorkerRole : RoleEntryPoint
{
    public override void Run()
    {
        // This is a sample worker implementation. Replace with your logic.
        Trace.WriteLine("WorkerRole1 entry point called", "Information");

        while (true)
        {
            Thread.Sleep(10000);
            Trace.WriteLine("Working", "Information");
        }
    }

    public override bool OnStart()
    {
        DiagnosticMonitor.Start("DiagnosticsConnectionString");

        // Restart the role upon all configuration changes
        // Note: To customize the handling of configuration changes,
```

```
        // remove this line and register custom event handlers instead.
        // See the MSDN topic on "Managing Configuration Changes"
        // for further details
        // (http://go.microsoft.com/fwlink/?LinkId=166357).
        RoleEnvironment.Changing += RoleEnvironmentChanging;

        return base.OnStart();
    }

    private void RoleEnvironmentChanging(object sender,
RoleEnvironmentChangingEventArgs e)
    {
        if (e.Changes.Any
    (change => change is RoleEnvironmentConfigurationSettingChange))
            e.Cancel = true;
    }
}
```

Let's walk through the life of a worker role:

1. When Windows Azure launches your worker role code, it calls the `OnStart` method. This is where you get to do any initialization, and return control when you're finished.

2. The `Run` method is where all the work happens. This is where the core logic of your worker role goes. This can be anything from just sleeping for an arbitrary period of time (as was done in Example 4-11), to processing messages off a queue, to launching an external process. Anything goes.

3. You have other event handlers for other events in the worker role life cycle. The `RoleEnvironmentChanging` event handler lets you deal with networking topology changes, configuration changes, and any other role environment changes as you saw earlier. The code inside the event handler can choose to either restart the role when it sees a change, or say, "This change is trivial—I can deal with it and I don't need a restart."

Understanding Worker Role Patterns

Though worker roles can be used in a wide variety of ways, you'll typically find their usage falls into one of a few very common patterns.

Queue-based, asynchronous processing

The queue-based, asynchronous processing model is shown in Figure 4-8. Here, worker roles sit in a loop and process messages of a queue. Any queue implementation can be used, but since this is Windows Azure, it is common to use the Windows Azure Storage queue service. Typically, a web role will insert messages into the queue—be it images that need thumbnails, videos that need transcoding, long-running transactions, or any job that can be done asynchronously. Since you want your frontend web roles to be as

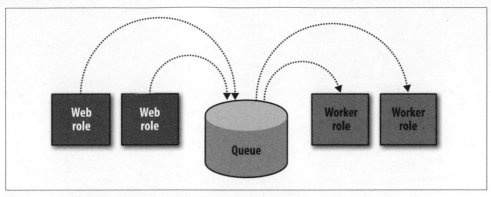

Figure 4-8. Queue-based worker roles

responsive as possible, the idea here is to defer all expensive transactions/work by inserting work items into a queue, and having them performed in a worker role.

There are several advantages to having such an architecture. Chief among them is the fact that your web role and worker roles are asynchronously coupled, so you can scale/add instances/remove instances to one of them without affecting the other. You can also upgrade one of them without affecting the other, or incurring service downtime.

Caching layer

More complex services have multiple layers. For example, it is common to have a frontend layer consisting of web roles, and a caching layer consisting of a distributed cache system (such as memcached), with the two sets of roles talking to each other through inter-role communication.

Summary

Worker roles are the jack-of-all-trades of the Windows Azure world. For almost any application you can think of that needs to run on Windows Azure, there is probably a way to squeeze it into a worker role. Get creative in the use of worker roles, and you can wield a wide range of flexibility.

## CHAPTER 5

Managing Your Service

So far, you've seen how to write code for your application and get it running in the cloud. That's just one part of the puzzle. The work involved with any application extends far beyond just writing code and developing new features. It involves monitoring, diagnosing failures, debugging bugs, and, when you have a fix or when you have new features, upgrading to a new build. And all of this takes place while trying to ensure that your service stays up and running. This can be quite a juggling act, and often gets ignored when people talk about cloud development.

In this chapter, you'll see how you can manage your applications in Windows Azure. You'll see how you can use the Windows Azure Developer Portal, or use the Service Management API, to manipulate your services. You'll see how to create, run, suspend, delete, and change deployments on-the-fly. You'll also see how to precisely control your upgrades to ensure that your service runs on new bits without experiencing downtime.

Common Themes Across Windows Azure Services

Before digging into what the manageability options are, it is useful to have a good mental model of how a well-run service on Windows Azure is *supposed* to behave. You'll see the following themes come up over and over again with features across Windows Azure, the idea being to push services into adopting a few best practices:

Services run constantly
> One pervasive idea across all of Windows Azure is that applications/services run constantly. Remember that common page you see on websites that says, "We are currently upgrading our systems"? That is something that should rarely occur, and preferably, should never occur. This makes upgrades tricky.

Multiple versions of a service can run at any given time
> One common mistake developers make is to assume that only one version of the service is running at any given point in time. However, the moment the application grows in scale, that assumption goes out the window. You'll have multiple versions

running at the same time: the current version and the new version to which you're trying to upgrade. You might have a test version pointing to production data, or a preproduction version waiting in the wings to take over. Your service must be resilient to this, and it must deal with concurrency/sharing issues that might arise.

Parts of your service might fail

Any well-written/architected service needs to deal with failures. Be it components misbehaving or botched upgrades, your code and processes must handle Murphy's Law.

You'll be using two primary tools to manipulate your services: the Developer Portal and the Service Management API.

Windows Azure Developer Portal

You already saw the Windows Azure Developer Portal (or "portal") in action earlier in this book. In short, this is the website that lives at *http://windows.azure.com*, and this is what you used to upload a "Hello World" package back in Chapter 3. Figure 5-1 shows the portal in action with its distinctive jello cube representing a running deployment.

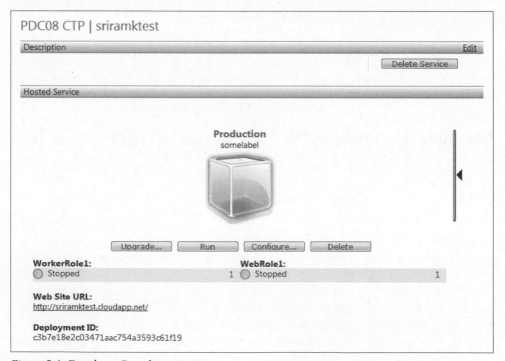

Figure 5-1. Developer Portal in action

The portal is your one-stop shop for everything management-related on Windows Azure. From creating hosted services or storage accounts to deploying new packages, changing configurations, or upgrading deployments, the portal does it all. If you're playing with Windows Azure, or you are early in the development phase, the portal should suffice as far as all your needs go.

However, at the end of the day, the portal is a website. You can't automatically deploy builds, write code to scale up and scale down your service, use tools and utilities, or reap any of the benefits that an API provides. And that is exactly what the Windows Azure Service Management API provides.

Service Management API

You can access the service management capabilities and perform day-to-day tasks (creating, deleting, and updating stuff) through the Service Management API. This RESTful HTTP API can be accessed from both inside and outside Microsoft data centers. Unlike the Windows Azure storage APIs that you'll see later in the book, this API is free to use.

 The "free" part comes with a caveat. Any misbehaving/malicious usage could get throttled.

The Service Management API and the storage APIs form the two major REST API families in Windows Azure. However, there's one major difference between the two. While the storage APIs are targeted at every Windows Azure developer and will show up in almost all Windows Azure applications, the Service Management API is meant primarily for toolmakers. Your day-to-day interaction with this API will be to use tools built on top of it.

In light of that, this chapter will only lightly touch on the REST API URIs and protocol that make up the Service Management API, and will focus more on the tools you can use with it.

 To see detailed descriptions of the Service Management API protocol, check out the official documentation at *http://msdn.microsoft.com/en -us/library/ee460799.aspx*.

Operations

The API offers a subset of the functions you can perform on the Developer Portal. You'll find that almost all day-to-day functions can be performed using the API (or, to be specific, tools built on top of the API), and you'll rarely (if ever) need to visit the Developer Portal.

Following are some of the operations supported by the API:

- Listing all hosted services, storage services, and affinity groups.
- Creating new deployments and deleting existing deployments.
- Viewing properties for an individual deployment (including the ability to drill into each role instance in the deployment and see what state it is in).
- Running or stopping existing deployments.
- Swapping deployments.
- In-place upgrading of existing deployments to new versions. This further splits into performing a manual rolling upgrade and an automated upgrade. You'll see how this works a bit later in this chapter.
- Viewing and regenerating storage credentials.

The API doesn't support all the functionality the portal does. Operations such as creating a new hosted or storage service, getting at billing data, and enabling Content Delivery Network (CDN) access, all require using the portal.

API Authentication

The first step in using the API is to figure out how to authenticate against it and call it. All calls to the Service Management API must be authenticated. Since all of the operations/data exposed by the Service Management API deal directly with your services and their states, you want to ensure that only you (and people you authorize) have access to them. Hence, unlike the storage APIs, no anonymous requests are allowed.

Authentication in the Service Management API is built on Secure Sockets Layer (SSL) client authentication. You are no doubt familiar with SSL. When you visit any URL with an https:// prefix (with a lock icon in a modern web browser), that's SSL in action. This is typically used to identify the server to you (the client). However, SSL can also be used to authenticate in the other direction—the client to the server. This is called *client authentication*, and it is supported by all web browsers, web servers, and operating system stacks.

Client authentication requires a *client certificate* in X.509 format. X.509 is an industry-defined format for SSL certificates. X.509 and client authentication can be used in myriad ways, with all sorts of extensions. X.509 certificates themselves are considered by many developers to be complex and difficult to use. Thankfully, the API limits itself to using X.509 certificates in the simplest way possible, and shields you from most of this complexity.

 If you're curious about X.509 and SSL client authentication, Wikipedia has good articles that go into great detail on both topics:

- *http://en.wikipedia.org/wiki/X.509*
- *http://en.wikipedia.org/wiki/Transport_Layer_Security#Client-au thenticated_TLS_handshake*

Creating an X.509 Certificate

At this point, you may wonder what an X.509 certificate really is. For the purposes of this chapter, you can think of an X.509 certificate as something that contains a public-private key pair. You generate the public-private key pair when you create the certificate (typically using RSA). The private key portion is sensitive data, and should be protected (in Windows, through the certificate store). The public key portion can be widely distributed.

Let's create our very own certificate. Dozens of tools are available for creating X.509 certificates. On Windows, if you have IIS installed, go into the Server Certificates section and select "Create Self-Signed certificate." Another handy way is to use the following command line, which uses the *makecert.exe* tool to create your very own self-signed certificate creatively titled "Preconfigured Cert":

```
makecert -r -pe -a sha1 -n "CN=Preconfigured Cert"
-ss My -len 2048
-sp "Microsoft Enhanced RSA and AES Cryptographic Provider" -sy 24
preconfig.cer
```

This cryptic command line generates a self-signed certificate, containing a 2,048-bit key pair, signed using the RSA algorithm, and outputs the public portion of the certificate to a file named *preconfig.cer*. This file contains nonsensitive data, and can be freely shared. In fact, this is the file you'll be uploading to Windows Azure.

At the same time, the `-ss My` parameter installs the private key portion of the certificate into your certificate store. Figure 5-2 shows the certificate in the certificate store.

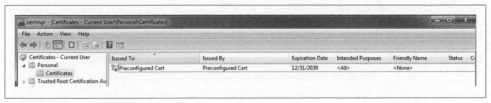

Figure 5-2. Certificate Manager

If you're not on Windows, the OpenSSL set of tools has great support for certificates. You can create your self-signed certificate with the following command:

```
openssl req -nw -newkey rsa:2048 -days 365 -nodes
-x509 -keyout preconfig.pem  -out preconfig.pem
```

Note that the output file is PEM-encoded by default. You'll need to use OpenSSL's conversion capabilities to convert it into the *.cer* format that Windows Azure accepts.

If you double-click on the certificate in the certificate store, you can inspect the properties of the certificate. One property is of interest: the Thumbprint. Figure 5-3 shows the Thumbprint highlighted for this particular certificate. You'll be using this Thumbprint later to identify which certificate you want to use with the tools that work with the API.

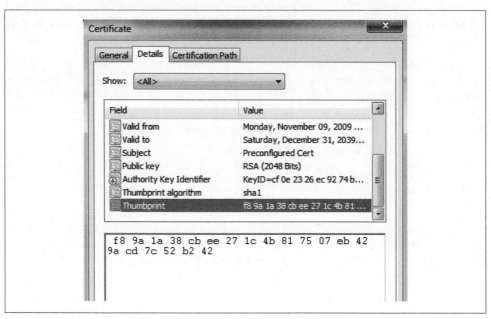

Figure 5-3. Certificate properties

 This private key portion of your certificate contains very sensitive data. If someone else gets it, she can impersonate you, and do anything you can with the API. When transporting the certificate between machines (typically by exporting it to a *.pfx* file), be sure to set a strong password.

Uploading the X.509 Certificate

The next step is to upload the *.cer* file through the Windows Azure Developer Portal. This lets Windows Azure know that it can trust that particular private-public key combination for your account. To do this, go to the Account tab in the Developer Portal, as shown in Figure 5-4. This contains your *subscription ID* (which is your unique user ID on Windows Azure) and has a Manage My API Certificates link. Clicking on that link takes you to the API Certificates tab.

API Certificates

You can upload several certificates that provide you with the required authentication agair Service Management API.

 Manage My API Certificates

Affinity Groups

You can create multiple affinity groups for your hosted services and storage accounts. You you have already created, and delete the affinity groups that no longer contain any memb

  Manage My Affinity Groups

Support Information

Subscription ID: BD38CFDF-C191-4B09-B299-F706985CE348

Figure 5-4. Account tab with subscription ID

 The word *subscription* can be a bit confusing, since in this context it originates from a financial use of the term, not a technical one. Specifically, it refers to the billing relationship you have with Microsoft (with your credit card, your MSDN subscription, your free preview, etc.). If you have multiple such accounts set up, you have multiple subscriptions. A "subscription ID" uniquely identifies your account in such a case.

The API Certificates tab (shown in Figure 5-5) enables you to manage the certificates with which you wish to authenticate. You can have up to five certificates at any time. Typically, this is used to create certificates for different purposes and tools. At any time, you can delete a certificate to revoke access for that particular certificate.

Now, upload the *preconfig.cer* file you created. You should see it appear in the API listing. Note that the Thumbprint displayed here is the same Thumbprint you saw in Figure 5-3.

At this point, you're good to go with making requests against the API.

Figure 5-5. API Certificates listing

Making API Requests

API requests are simply HTTP calls against a specified URI under *management.core.windows.net*. For example, to list all the hosted services underneath your account, you would need to make an authenticated request to *https://management.core.windows.net/<subscription-id>/services/hostedservices*.

Example 5-1 shows a sample program to access the Windows Azure Service Management API. This is a simple console application that accesses the Service Management API and retrieves the list of hosted services.

Example 5-1. Sample API access

```
using System;
using System.Linq;
using System.Xml.Linq;
using System.Text;
using System.Security.Cryptography.X509Certificates;
using System.Net;
using System.IO;

namespace apidemo
{
    class Program
    {
        static void Main(string[] args)
        {
            // Make request to URL under correct subscription-id
            // The long GUID is my subscription ID - you need to replace
            // that with yours to make this code work
            var req = (HttpWebRequest)WebRequest.Create(
        "https://management.core.windows.net/BD38CFDF-C191-4B09-B299-
F706985CE348/services/hostedservices");

            //Target right version of the API
            req.Headers.Add("x-ms-version:2009-10-01");
```

```
//Load the certificate created using makecert earlier
req.ClientCertificates.Add(
 X509Certificate2.CreateFromCertFile("D:/preconfig.cer"));

//Read content and use XElement to pretty print it to the
//console
var respStream = req.GetResponse().GetResponseStream();

var xml = new StreamReader(respStream).ReadToEnd();

Console.WriteLine(XElement.Parse(xml));

Console.Read();

        }
    }
}
```

The program starts by constructing the right URL to make an HTTP request to the API. Note that this code sample uses my subscription ID (the long GUID in the middle of the URI); you would want to replace it with your subscription ID. The API mandates that all calls specify which version of the API the client expects. Only one version is out there currently, so the code adds the `x-ms-version` header set to the right version date.

At this point, you have an HTTPS request with the correct URI and the correct headers. The last missing piece is the certificate. The code attaches the X.509 certificate you created earlier. Note that although the code points to the *.cer* file, the Windows crypto APIs will look up the associated private key from the certificate store. Finally, the code makes the request and prints out the XML returned.

If everything worked, you should see output similar to Example 5-2. Note the little bit of XML with the service name `sriramktest`. This is essentially listing the same service displayed in the Developer Portal back in Figure 5-1.

Example 5-2. Sample hosted services listing

```
<HostedServices xmlns=http://schemas.microsoft.com/windowsazure
 xmlns:i="http://www.w3.org/2001/XMLSchema-instance">
  <HostedService>
    <Url>https://management.core.windows.net/BD38CFDF-C191-4B09-B299-
F706985CE348/services/hostedservices/sriramktest</Url>
    <ServiceName>sriramktest</ServiceName>
  </HostedService>
</HostedServices>
```

By playing with the URIs that the code hits, you can dig into your services. For example, to get detailed information on `sriramktest`, you must switch the URI in Example 5-1 to the following: *https://management.core.windows.net/BD38CFDF-C191-4B09-B299-F706985CE348/services/hostedservices/sriramktest?embed-detail=true* (again, using your subscription ID and your service's name). This returns the following XML:

```xml
<HostedService xmlns=http://schemas.microsoft.com/windowsazure
 xmlns:i="http://www.w3.org/2001/XMLSchema-instance">
  <Url>https://management.core.windows.net/BD38CFDF-C191-4B09-B299-
F706985CE348/services/hostedservices/sriramktest</Url>
  <ServiceName>sriramktest</ServiceName>
  <HostedServiceProperties>
    <Description />
    <Label>c3JpcmFta3Rlc3Q=</Label>
  </HostedServiceProperties>
  <Deployments>
    <Deployment>
      <Name>testdemodeployment</Name>
      <DeploymentSlot>Production</DeploymentSlot>
      <PrivateID>c3b7e18e2c03471aac754a3593c61f19</PrivateID>
      <Status>Suspended</Status>
      <Label>c29tZWxxhYmVs</Label>
      <Url>http://sriramktest.cloudapp.net/</Url>
      <Configuration>...dGlvbj4=</Configuration>
      <RoleInstanceList>
        <RoleInstance>
          <RoleName>WorkerRole1</RoleName>
          <InstanceName>WorkerRole1_IN_0</InstanceName>
          <InstanceStatus>Stopped</InstanceStatus>
        </RoleInstance>
        <RoleInstance>
          <RoleName>WebRole1</RoleName>
          <InstanceName>WebRole1_IN_0</InstanceName>
          <InstanceStatus>Stopped</InstanceStatus>
        </RoleInstance>
      </RoleInstanceList>
      <UpgradeDomainCount>1</UpgradeDomainCount>
    </Deployment>
  </Deployments>
</HostedService>
```

Note how this XML reflects detailed information on my service. Apart from returning the name, its label, and its ID, it also returns all the roles contained within, their instances, and each instance's status. This is your one-stop shop for all the status information you need on your services.

Now, here's a bait-and-switch tactic. You'll almost never write code such as this. Of course, if you're a tool developer, you can write your own library. But in almost all cases, you're better off using the sample client library available at *http://code.msdn.microsoft.com/windowsazuresamples*. This provides a friendly .NET wrapper to use over the API.

For most of us, though, our primary interest is not in building tools with the API, but rather to use it for our day-to-day management tasks. For that, you should pick out one of the many tools that build on top of the API. Arguably, the most important such tool is csmanage.

Using Csmanage

The file *csmanage.exe* is a command-line tool that wraps on top of the Service Management API to provide you with a command-line interface to Windows Azure. It ships as a free sample, or as a sample with source. If you're planning to use the Service Management API, you'll probably wind up becoming very familiar with csmanage.

 Binaries and code are available at *http://code.msdn.microsoft.com/win dowsazuresamples*.

After downloading csmanage and unzipping its contents, the first thing you must do is to configure it with the certificate it should use, and with your subscription ID. To do that, open *csmanage.exe.config* in the directory you extracted to. You'll see place-holders for `SubscriptionID` and `CertificateThumbprint`. Fill in these placeholders with your subscription ID and the Thumbprint of the certificate you created and uploaded. You can get the Thumbprint either from the Windows Certificate Manager (Figure 5-3) or from the Windows Azure portal (Figure 5-5). Example 5-3 shows a sample *csmanage.exe.config* file using the same subscription ID and certificate used in the examples so far.

Example 5-3. Sample csmanage.exe.config file

```
<?xml version="1.0" encoding="utf-8" ?>
<configuration>
  <system.serviceModel>
    <bindings>
      <webHttpBinding>
        <binding name="WindowsAzureServiceManagement_WebHttpBinding"
 closeTimeout="00:01:00"
                  openTimeout="00:01:00" receiveTimeout="00:10:00"
 sendTimeout="00:01:00">
               <readerQuotas maxStringContentLength="1048576"
 maxBytesPerRead="131072" />
             <security mode="Transport">
             <transport clientCredentialType="Certificate" />
           </security>
         </binding>
       </webHttpBinding>
    </bindings>
    <client>
      <endpoint name="WindowsAzureEndPoint"
                address="https://management.core.windows.net"
                binding="webHttpBinding"
 bindingConfiguration="WindowsAzureServiceManagement_WebHttpBinding"
                contract=
 "Microsoft.Samples.WindowsAzure.ServiceManagement.IServiceManagement" />
    </client>
  </system.serviceModel>
```

```
<appSettings>
  <add key="CheckServerCertificate" value="true"/>
  <!-- Insert your subscriptionId as shown by the Windows Azure
       developer portal -->
  <add key="SubscriptionId"
       value="BD38CFDF-C191-4B09-B299-F706985CE348"/>
  <!-- Insert your certificate thumbprint without spaces -->
  <add key="CertificateThumbprint"
         value="F89A1A38CBEE271C4B817507EB429ACD7C52B242"/>
</appSettings>
</configuration>
```

Once configured, csmanage is simple to use. Enter **csmanage /?** to get a listing of all the commands supported. All *csmanage.exe* operations have a 1:1 mapping to the underlying API they call, so it provides a great way to learn how the API works as well.

Let's start by using csmanage to do the same thing that Example 5-1 did: listing hosted services. Example 5-4 shows how this is done with the formatted output.

Example 5-4. Csmanage listing hosted services

```
D:\csmanage>csmanage /list-hosted-services
Using certificate: CN=Preconfigured Cert
Listing HostedServices
HostedServiceList contains 1 item(s).
HostedService Name:sriramktest
HostedService
     Url:https://management.core.windows.net/BD38CFDF-C191-4B09-B299-
F706985CE348/services/hostedservices/sriramktest
Operation ID: 4279aa416ba84eda9cf6c0d9a0ba076e
HTTP Status Code: OK
StatusDescription: OK
```

Apart from formatting the data structures returned by the API, csmanage also shows you the operation ID of the API call. In the case of an error, or for troubleshooting issues, you'll need to tell the Microsoft Support staff this ID to find out what went wrong.

Let's do something more complex now. Creating a new deployment is arguably the most important operation supported by the API, and probably the most complex as well. Example 5-5 shows how to create a new deployment and upload a package to staging. The code has been reformatted slightly to help with readability.

Example 5-5. Creating a new deployment with csmanage

```
D:\csmanage>csmanage /create-deployment
/hosted-service:sriramktest
/name:mydeployment
/slot:staging
/label:somelabel
/package:http://sriramk.blob.core.windows.net/packages/webnworker.cspkg /config:D:\
\webnworker\bin\Debug\Publish\ServiceConfiguration.cscfg
```

```
Using certificate: CN=Preconfigured Cert
Creating Deployment... Name: mydeployment, Label: somelabel
Operation ID: 47bc156f14a94180aa737887aa1c09a1
HTTP Status Code: Accepted
StatusDescription: Accepted
Waiting for async operation to complete:
..............Done
Operation Status=Succeeded
```

Note the csmanage parameters highlighted in Figure 5-5. Apart from the name, label, and slot (**staging** or **production**), csmanage must be told which configuration to use, and which package to use. There's one big difference between the API and the Developer Portal shown here. The API requires that any package be uploaded to Windows Azure blob storage first, whereas the portal can accept packages directly from your local filesystem.

At this point, if you go to the Developer Portal, you should see the package in the **staging** slot. However, it isn't running. Let's fix that by using csmanage again. Example 5-6 shows how.

Example 5-6. Running a deployment using csmanage

```
D:\ \csmanage>csmanage /update-deployment /status:running
/slot:staging /hosted-service:sriramktest
Using certificate: CN=Preconfigured Cert
Updating DeploymentStatus
Operation ID: af111bddb6ea4effb2cd03ac4e10c11a
HTTP Status Code: Accepted
StatusDescription: Accepted
Waiting for async operation to complete:
..............Done
Operation Status=Succeeded
```

Now you have a running deployment in the cloud without using the Windows Azure Developer Portal at all. Csmanage is a handy little tool, and you can imagine using it by invoking it from build scripts, tools, and toy applications that must deploy to the cloud.

Calling the API from Cygwin/OS X/Linux

If you're not calling the API from the Windows world, you have some extra work to do. As of this writing, there are no csmanage-like tools available. However, since the API is just REST-based, it is simple to script common open source tools.

First, export your certificate to a *.pfx* file from the certificate store. You can use the OpenSSL family of tools to convert the *.pfx* file to a PEM file, which plays better with the non-Windows world:

```
$ openssl pkcs12 -in preconfig.pfx -out preconfig.pem
-nodes
Enter Import Password:
MAC verified OK
```

After this, calling an API is just a question of making the right HTTP request. A widely used tool for constructing HTTP requests is curl. Following is a sample curl command to list hosted services:

```
$ curl -H "x-ms-version:2009-10-01" -E preconfig.pem
 https://management.core.windows.net/BD38CFDF-C191-
4B09-
B299- F706985CE348/services/hostedservices
```

Dealing with Upgrades

One of the trickiest parts of dealing with a running service is upgrades. The technology industry is strewn with horror stories of things going terribly wrong when upgrading a service. To be clear, upgrades with Windows Azure aren't somehow magically going to be easier—the issues are fundamental to any service. However, Windows Azure does give you a set of tools to manage your upgrades, and to deal with issues when an upgrade gets botched for some reason.

In-Place Upgrade

The easiest way to upgrade your service is through the *in-place upgrade mechanism*. (This is a new addition to Windows Azure and is preferred over VIP Swap, which is discussed later in this chapter.) Essentially, you get to point to a new package, and Windows Azure upgrades your service.

The Windows Azure fabric highly optimizes how this upgrade is rolled out. In Chapter 4, you saw *upgrade domains* for the first time. These are the subdivisions into which your services are partitioned, and are used at upgrade time. When the Windows Azure fabric rolls out an upgrade, it walks through your service, upgrade domain by upgrade domain. Instead of taking down all your virtual machines at once, it takes down the virtual machines in the first upgrade domain, and finishes the upgrade there before moving on to the second. You can configure the number of upgrade domains your service is partitioned into by using the `upgradeDomainCount` attribute in your *Service-Definition.csdef* file.

Figure 5-6 shows the Developer Portal page for upgrading your service. The key parts to look at are the places where you are asked to fill in the package and the configuration file.

Figure 5-6 also shows off a couple of other options when doing an in-place upgrade:

Automatic versus manual upgrade
> Instead of having the Windows Azure fabric walk the upgrade domains automatically, you can make it pause after every upgrade domain, and wait until you give the go-ahead. This is a great way to ensure that your upgrade is progressing smoothly, and enabling you to hit the reset switch if things go bad. This is especially

```
Upgrade Mode
    ⦿Automatic Upgrade: All upgrade domains will be upgraded in sequence.
    ○Manual Upgrade: You can walk through each upgrade domain manually and retry a service upgrade.

Application Package

    ⦿Upload a file from your local storage○Use a file from an Azure Storage account
    Select a file:
    [                                              ] [ Browse... ]

Configuration Settings
    ⦿Upload a file from your local storage○Use a file from an Azure Storage account
    Select a file:
    [                                              ] [ Browse... ]

Service Deployment Name
    Choose a label for this deployment: [                    ]

Service Upgrade
    Do you want to upgrade the whole service?
        ○Yes, I want to upgrade the whole service. all the web and worker roles will be upgraded in this
        deployment.
        ⦿No I only want to upgrade the selected role specificed below in this deployment.
            [ WorkerRole1                        ▼ ]
```

Figure 5-6. Upgrade options

handy if your service is quite large. The Windows Azure team uses this mechanism
internally to upgrade most of its services.

Upgrading specific roles

Let's say you just finished deploying your fancy new service, and then you realize
that one of your pages has a typographical error in it. It doesn't make sense to roll
out an upgrade that takes down your worker roles just to update some HTML on
a web role. Your worker roles could be in the middle of processing some long-
running transaction, and interrupting them could mean losing valuable work. An
in-place upgrade lets you pick which of your roles you want upgraded. In the Developer Portal, this is done through the combo box at the bottom of Figure 5-6.

If you're using the API and not the portal, look at the UpgradeDeployment API. You'll
see a 1:1 mapping between what the API lets you do and what the portal lets you do.
For users of csmanage, `upgrade-deployment` and `walk-upgrade-domain` are the parameters that let you perform an in-place upgrade.

One limitation of an in-place upgrade is that the new package should have the same service definition as the current version. If you're making changes, you should be looking at VIP Swap.

VIP Swap

If you've used Windows Azure anytime since its first preview launch, you're probably familiar with the picture shown in Figure 5-7. As discussed earlier in this book, this lets you "swap" the endpoint of your staging deployment with that of your production deployment. If you're using the Developer Portal, you click the "swap" icon, as shown in Figure 5-7. After a couple of minutes, Windows Azure will finish "swapping" the endpoints, and your staging deployment will now run at your designated *.cloudapp.net address.

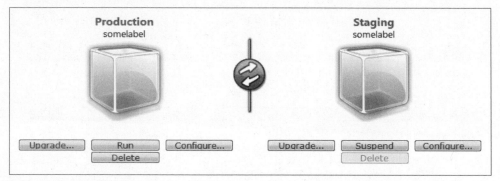

Figure 5-7. VIP Swap

 The "VIP" in "VIP Swap" refers to "Virtual IP Address," which is the term Windows Azure uses for your *.cloudapp.net endpoint.

Though you should be using an in-place upgrade for all your upgrade needs, there is one specific scenario in which you absolutely have to use VIP Swap. That's when you change your service architecture. Adding/removing roles and changing endpoints all constitute a change in the service model. In such cases, you should first bring up a staging deployment (which is as close in shape and scale to your production deployment as possible) before swapping.

Summary

In this chapter, you saw how Windows Azure provides you with some tools to help you manage your services. However, these tools are just building blocks. The really interesting functionality emerges when you start putting these features together.

For example, one common use of the Service Management API is to automatically scale up or scale down the service based on the load the service is seeing. You don't even have to write a lot of this code yourself. With several community and third-party offerings, a lot of code is available for you to use and reuse to automatically manage your services.

## CHAPTER 6

Native and Non-.NET Code

When Windows Azure was initially released all of the program code executed inside a .NET sandbox, with no possibility of escape. This ruled out not only any non-.NET DLLs, but also any non-.NET environments. You couldn't write Python or Ruby or Java code.

As part of the MIX release in March 2008, all of this changed. Windows Azure now exposes an option to enable users to run any code on the platform, with .NET now being only one option among many. Obviously, this opens up a wealth of possibilities, many of them explored in this chapter.

The Windows Azure Sandbox

You might be wondering why you have to do anything special to run native code at all. After all, .NET has good support for interoperating with native code—from P/Invoke to COM Interop. However, those mechanisms don't work out of the box on Windows Azure because of the sandbox in which your code runs.

Hypervisor and Standard User Privileges

All user code in Windows Azure runs on the Windows Azure hypervisor. Also, any code that runs in Windows Azure runs under the context of a "standard user" (as opposed to a "user with administrative privileges").

This distinction is important, because this is something that cannot be opted out of, regardless of whether you're running native or managed code. Actions that require administrative-level privileges on the machine (such as installing drivers, or changing system binaries or protected parts of the registry) will fail.

You should always ensure that your code doesn't require administrative privileges. One common "gotcha" is that the Dev Fabric runs under the context of your user account on your local machine. If you're the local administrator on your machine (as most of us are), your code will seem to execute fine, but will fail in the cloud. To avoid these issues, consider using a low-privileged account to test your code locally.

Windows Azure Partial Trust

By default, all managed code on Windows Azure runs on a restricted trust level called *Windows Azure partial trust*. Because the user account is not an administrator on the virtual machine, this adds even further restrictions than those imposed by Windows. This trust level is enforced by .NET's *Code Access Security* (*CAS*) support.

Users familiar with CAS might recognize this as being very similar to the "medium trust" level in .NET. Access is granted only to certain resources and operations. Table 6-1 shows some of the key resources and operations, and their restrictions on access. In general, your code is allowed only to connect to external IP addresses over TCP, and is limited to accessing files and folders only in its "local store," as opposed to any location on the system. Any libraries that your code uses must either work in partial trust or be specially marked with an "allow partially trusted callers" attribute.

Table 6-1. Windows Azure partial trust restrictions

Permission	State	Details
AspNetHosting	Level	Medium
DnsPermission	Unrestricted	Permitted
EnvironmentPermission	Unrestricted/Read/Write	TEMP; TMP
FileIOPermission	Read	App directory, any named local store
	Write	Any named local store
RegistryPermission	Unrestricted	Denied
SocketPermission	Connect	External sites only over TCP
	Accept	Denied
WebPermission	Connect	External sites only

Why run code in such a restrictive environment by default? The idea is to be secure by default. If your web application gets compromised in some way, the attacker is limited in the amount of damage he can do. For example, a malicious attacker couldn't modify any of your ASP.NET pages on disk by default, or change any of the system binaries.

However, the downside of such a restrictive environment is that it is, well, restrictive. Several useful libraries (such as those used for accessing the registry, or accessing a well-known file location) don't work in such an environment for trivial reasons. Even some of Microsoft's own frameworks don't work in this environment because they don't have the "partially trusted caller" attribute set.

Full Trust and Native Code

For the first several months after the launch of Windows Azure, the partial trust environment was the only one available to users. As a part of the March 2009 MIX release, Windows Azure added a key option: the ability to run code under *full trust*, instead of the partial trust environment described previously. "Full trust" here refers to the least-restrictive permission level allowed by .NET CAS. Running under full trust means the code has access to anything the Windows user account it is running under has access to.

Specifying that a role should have full trust privileges is easy. Add an `enableNativeCo deExecution` (yes, the name is a bit of a mismatch) attribute in the service definition file with its value set to `true`, as shown in Example 6-1.

Example 6-1. Full-trust privileges for a role

```
<?xml version="1.0" encoding="utf-8"?>

<ServiceDefinition name="HelloWorldService"
xmlns="http://schemas.microsoft.com/ServiceHosting/2008/10/ServiceDefinition">

  <WebRole name="WebRole" enableNativeCodeExecution="true">
    <InputEndpoints>
      <InputEndpoint name="HttpIn" protocol="http" port="80" />
    </InputEndpoints>
  </WebRole>
</ServiceDefinition>
```

The name `enableNativeCodeExecution` hints at the possibilities that get opened up with this option set. Running code under full trust means managed code can not only P/Invoke to native code, but also launch other native processes. This last bit of functionality is important, and it is often used to support additional languages/environments on Windows Azure.

Peeking Under the Hood with a Command Shell

As described earlier, full trust/native code execution support can be used to launch other processes. This little bit of functionality can be useful in several ways. Here's one particularly useful way that can be a lifesaver when troubleshooting issues.

One of the current downsides with running in Windows Azure is that you don't get the usual set of tools to peek inside a Windows machine. You currently can't use remote desktop, nor can you log in to the box and run a command shell.

Or can you?

Remember from Chapter 2 that all application code is run inside a standard Windows Server 2008 operating system. All the familiar command-line tools are present inside already. The trick is how to get to them.

Setting up a remote command-line session using standard Windows tools such as *psexec* or *remote.exe* isn't possible, since all role instances are behind a load balancer. These tools are not available, except when you have a session open with the "server'" portion, and that isn't possible when every request could be directed to a different virtual machine. Also, none of these tools tunnel over HTTP, which is the port opened by default on Windows Azure.

To work around these limitations, let's write some code that will act as a frontend to the Windows command shell—*cmd.exe*. The idea here is simple. A web role will be augmented with some simple UI to input commands and see command output. Whenever a user enters a new command, the web role passes the command to a new instance of *cmd.exe*, executes it, and returns the output. The output is captured, and then displayed on a web page, making the website into a command-shell-proxy-thingamajig-whatchamacallit (that's my official name for it).

The magic that will make all this work is the `enableNativeCodeExecution` flag. Without that flag, code running in the cloud won't be able to perform full-trust actions such as launching a new process. With that flag set, the restriction no longer exists, and code can launch native processes whenever it feels like it. Note that any process will still run under the context/user account of the web role. Although native code can be run, that code will still not have any administrator-level access to the machine.

 Since this is just a sample, there will be no authentication or security built in. However, the danger of leaving this running can't be overstated. Any malicious user who gets his hands on this can essentially do anything on your virtual machine that your code can. This is a sure recipe for disaster. *Do not run this code in production without some form of protection.*

Building the Command Shell Proxy

Let's start by creating a blank `CloudService` and adding a web role to it. In this sample, let's call the cloud service `NativeCodeCmd`. (You can obviously choose any name for it.) The Solution Explorer should look similar to Figure 6-1.

Users will need a place to type in commands and see the output of their commands. This calls for some UI. In this case, the UI is going to be quite Spartan (and downright ugly), but functional. There'll be one text box to type in commands, and then one more text box to show output. To keep things simple, let's use the ASP.NET controls that come out of the box.

Change the markup inside the `body` tag in *Default.aspx* to match the code shown in Example 6-2.

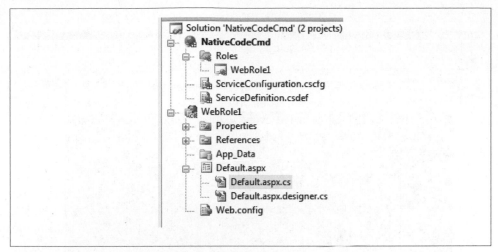

Figure 6-1. Our native code command shell processor

Example 6-2. Two text boxes and a button

```
<body>
    <form id="form1" runat="server">
    <div>
        Command: <asp:Textbox  id="txtCmd" runat="server" />
        <asp:Button id="btnRun" runat="server" OnClick="btnRun_Click"
         Text="Run" /> <br/><br/>

        Output:
        <asp:Textbox
 TextMode="MultiLine" style="color:white;background-color:black;"
 id="txtOutput"              runat="server" Height="413px" Width="890px" />

    </div>
    </form>
</body>
```

This is quite a simple ASP.NET markup. There are three different UI elements here: a text box named txtCmd to accept commands, a multiline text box named txtOutput to show command output, and a button called btnRun to run the command. btnRun has an event handler defined to call the btnRun_Click method when pressed. When you run it by pressing F5, the Dev Fabric should launch it, and your default browser should open to something similar to what is shown in Figure 6-2.

This is not exactly a showcase of website design and aesthetics, is it? Feel free to play with the design and make it less painful on the eyes.

This doesn't do anything yet, so let's make it useful. The Windows command shell *cmd.exe* has a /c parameter that enables you to pass commands as startup arguments to it. *Cmd.exe* will execute the command and print the results to standard output (stdout). To make this command proxy work, the button click handler must spin up

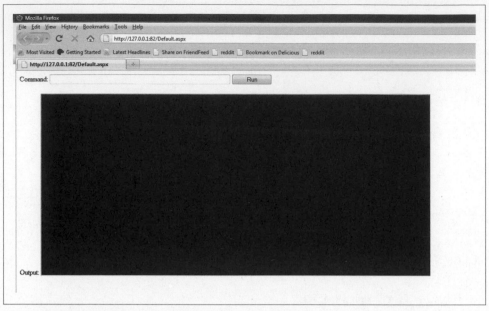

Figure 6-2. Blank screen

cmd.exe with the /c parameter, pass the right command in, and redirect standard output to the text box. Example 6-3 shows the code to do this.

Example 6-3. Launching cmd.exe and capturing stdout

```
protected void btnRun_Click(object sender, EventArgs e)
{

    var newProc = new System.Diagnostics.Process();

    // Fill in new process object's startinfo
    // cmd.exe will always exist in the path. Pass in
    // the /c parameter followed by the contents of the
    // txtCmd text box. Redirect standard output
    newProc.StartInfo.FileName = "cmd.exe";
    newProc.StartInfo.Arguments = "/c" + txtCmd.Text;
    newProc.StartInfo.UseShellExecute = false;
    newProc.StartInfo.RedirectStandardOutput = true;
    newProc.EnableRaisingEvents = false;

    newProc.Start();

    // Capture standard output and append it to the multiline
    // text box
    txtOutput.Text += newProc.StandardOutput.ReadToEnd()+"\r\n";

    newProc.Close();

}
```

The code shown in Example 6-3 uses the `System.Diagnostics.Process` class to spin up a new instance of *cmd.exe*, pass arguments, and read the output of the process before closing it.

Press F5 to run the website under the Dev Fabric. Type in a command (say, **dir**) and press Enter. Instead of a listing of files, the output is a security exception, as shown in Figure 6-3.

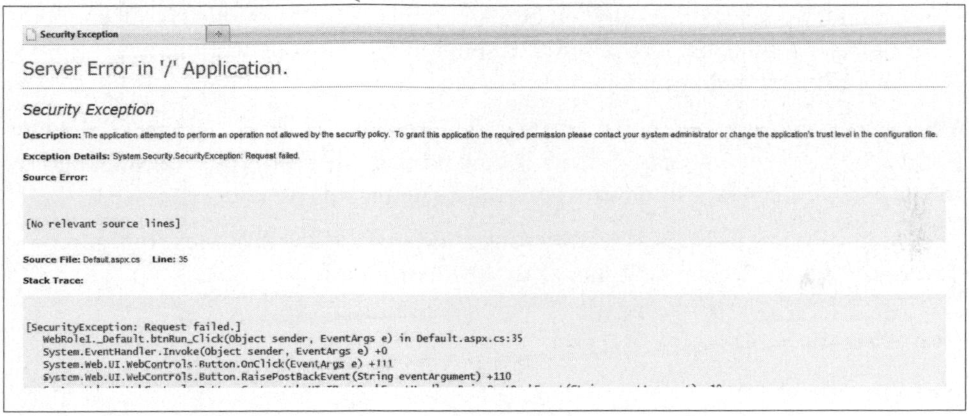

Figure 6-3. Security exception when launching a process

Why is that? Remember that, on the sandbox, managed code in Windows Azure runs in medium trust by default, which blocks creation of processes programmatically. To do this, the security chains must be loosened by enabling full trust/native code execution.

Enabling Native Code Execution

Enabling native code execution is easy. Open *ServiceDefinition.csdef* and modify the code as shown in Example 6-4. Only one change needs to be made: set `enableNative CodeExecution` to `true`.

Example 6-4. Native code-enabled service definition

```xml
<?xml version="1.0" encoding="utf-8"?>
<ServiceDefinition name="NativeCodeCmd" xmlns=
"http://schemas.microsoft.com/ServiceHosting/2008/10/ServiceDefinition">
  <WebRole name="WebRole1" enableNativeCodeExecution="true">
    <InputEndpoints>
      <InputEndpoint name="HttpIn" protocol="http" port="80" />
    </InputEndpoints>
    <ConfigurationSettings />
  </WebRole>
</ServiceDefinition>
```

This attribute tells the Windows Azure fabric that this specific role instance should be launched differently. When launched, all role instances are placed in a specific kind of hosting environment. This flag changes the hosting environment to run the application in full trust, rather than the Windows Azure trust sandbox.

Running the Command Proxy

Build the package and deploy it to the cloud just like with any normal cloud service. (See Chapter 3 for a walkthrough on how to do this.) Hit the public HTTP endpoint. Your browser should load the minimal UI built in the previous section. But the difference here is that any command now runs inside the virtual machine.

You now have the equivalent of a command line inside a virtual machine in Windows Azure. At this point, you can run any command that will work on Windows, and see its output. This can be a lifesaver when you are debugging an issue.

Let's start by doing a simple directory listing. Type **dir** in the input text box and press Enter. You should see a listing similar to the following:

```
 Volume in drive E has no label.
 Volume Serial Number is 1695-ED26

 Directory of E:\

09/11/2009  12:37 PM    <DIR>          bin
09/11/2009  12:33 PM               932 Default.aspx
09/11/2009  05:33 AM             1,048 e8364df2-0cea-4b1c-ad3f-df9446281643.csman
09/11/2009  12:43 PM                 0 fde6446adf8d4566a4972d17a8085223.0.cssx.tag
09/11/2009  12:13 PM             7,913 Web.config
09/11/2009  05:33 AM               491 [Content_Types].xml
09/11/2009  12:37 PM    <DIR>          _rels
               5 File(s)         10,384 bytes
               2 Dir(s)  1,038,286,848 bytes free
```

This tells you a few things about how your application is deployed inside the virtual machine. As you can see, your *.cspkg* package is extracted into the root of the *E:* partition, and your application is run from there. You can also try looking at the other partitions on the virtual machine, but some partitions/directories are locked down by an access control list (ACL), so the actual data you can get at is quite limited.

Another interesting command to run to "poke" around the environment is **set** to see all the environment variables, as shown in the following code snippet. As you can see, this returns a large number of environment variables:

```
ALLUSERSPROFILE=D:\ProgramData
APPDATA=D:\Users\9bb5edca-9aa1-4337-8df4-6667534b68a2\AppData\Roaming
APP_POOL_ID={8ED53209-8C24-459B-A2E3-300449E9F4DF}
CommonProgramFiles=D:\Program Files\Common Files
CommonProgramFiles(x86)=D:\Program Files (x86)\Common Files
COMPUTERNAME=RD00155D30217E
ComSpec=D:\windows\system32\cmd.exe
Coverage=D:\ProgramData\coverage
```

```
DFSTRACINGON=FALSE
FP_NO_HOST_CHECK=NO
LOCALAPPDATA=D:\Users\9bb5edca-9aa1-4337-8df4-6667534b68a2\AppData\Local
NUMBER_OF_PROCESSORS=1
OS=Windows_NT
PATHEXT=.COM;.EXE;.BAT;.CMD;.VBS;.VBE;.JS;.JSE;.WSF;.WSH;.MSC
PROCESSOR_ARCHITECTURE=AMD64
PROCESSOR_IDENTIFIER=AMD64 Family 16 Model 2 Stepping 3, AuthenticAMD
PROCESSOR_LEVEL=16
PROCESSOR_REVISION=0203
ProgramData=D:\ProgramData
ProgramFiles=D:\Program Files
ProgramFiles(x86)=D:\Program Files (x86)
PROMPT=$P$G
PUBLIC=D:\Users\Public
SystemDrive=D:
SystemRoot=D:\windows
USERDOMAIN=CIS
USERNAME=9bb5edca-9aa1-4337-8df4-6667534b68a2
USERPROFILE=D:\Users\9bb5edca-9aa1-4337-8df4-6667534b68a2
windir=D:\windows
RdRoleRoot=E:\
RoleRoot=E:
RdRoleId=fde6446adf8d4566a4972d17a8085223.WebRole1_IN_0
TEMP=C:\Resources\temp\fde6446adf8d4566a4972d17a8085223.WebRole1\RoleTemp
TMP=C:\Resources\temp\fde6446adf8d4566a4972d17a8085223.WebRole1\RoleTemp
PATH=D:\windows\system32;D:\windows;D:\windows\System32\Wbem;
D:\windows\System32\WindowsPowerShell\v1.0\;
D:\Packages\Runtime\WebRole1_IN_0\x64;D:\Packages\Runtime\WebRole1_IN_0\x86
```

 This listing changes often, so what you see will surely be different.

These variables let you glean several bits of interesting information. You can see that your code runs under username 9bb5edca-9aa1-4337-8df4-6667534b68a2 under the domain CIS. You can see that there is a specially created *TEMP* folder to which the role actually has write access. You can also see that the code is running on an AMD 64-bit processor.

The two most useful groups of commands to use while you are debugging issues are those that let you inspect processes and the network. For the former, a useful built-in command is tasklist, which lets you view running processes, along with some basic statistics on all of them. It is handy for taking a quick look at your virtual machine and spotting a process that is leaking memory (a common scenario when spawning badly written native code processes).

Here's the output from running tasklist on a virtual machine. Note the number of processes with the prefix Rd that denotes their heritage from the Red Dog project, which you will recall from Chapter 1. Remember that these are deep implementation details of the machine, and you should never depend on them. In fact, you'll probably see a dramatically different set of processes from the ones you see in the following example:

```
Image Name                     PID    Session#    Mem Usage
==========================   ========  ===========  =============
System Idle Process             0         0           24 K
System                          4         0        3,904 K
smss.exe                      392         0          988 K
csrss.exe                     456         0        4,612 K
csrss.exe                     496         1        4,676 K
wininit.exe                   504         0        4,732 K
winlogon.exe                  532         1        5,592 K
services.exe                  580         0        6,196 K
lsass.exe                     592         0       11,044 K
lsm.exe                       600         0        5,856 K
svchost.exe                   776         0        6,704 K
svchost.exe                   848         0        6,700 K
svchost.exe                   944         0       19,348 K
svchost.exe                   300         0        9,036 K
svchost.exe                   412         0        6,900 K
svchost.exe                   428         0       30,560 K
SLsvc.exe                     436         0       11,720 K
svchost.exe                   816         0        9,876 K
svchost.exe                   644         0       13,088 K
vmicsvc.exe                  1148         0        4,472 K
vmicsvc.exe                  1168         0        4,640 K
BlobStorageProxy.exe         1196         0        5,016 K
osdiag.exe                   1236         0        6,168 K
svchost.exe                  1256         0        6,248 K
svchost.exe                  1308         0        3,364 K
svchost.exe                  1368         0       14,172 K
svchost.exe                  1388         0        5,772 K
svchost.exe                  1404         0        4,736 K
LogonUI.exe                  1832         1       15,760 K
rdagent.exe                  1756         0       15,796 K
msdtc.exe                    2248         0        7,956 K
RDMonitorAgent.exe           2572         0        7,376 K
RdRoleHost.exe               1956         0       64,036 K
cmd.exe                      2772         0        2,072 K
tasklist.exe                 2112         0        5,540 K
WmiPrvSE.exe                 1508         0        7,108 K
```

For networking-related troubleshooting, use the `netstat` command to see the current open ports on the machine. This can be useful for debugging when there is a conflict caused by a port already being in use. The reason you don't see the familiar 80 and 443 ports is because external requests don't directly flow to these role instances. Recall that all requests go to a load balancer, which then farms the request to the correct role instance. As a part of that process, these requests get mapped to a different port as well:

```
Active Connections

  Proto  Local Address           Foreign Address         State
  TCP    10.113.114.77:16001     vlan424:34341           TIME_WAIT
  TCP    10.113.114.77:16001     vlan424:35601           TIME_WAIT
```

```
TCP   10.113.114.77:16001   vlan424:36864          TIME_WAIT
TCP   10.113.114.77:16001   vlan424:38124          TIME_WAIT
TCP   10.113.114.77:16001   vlan424:39391          TIME_WAIT
TCP   10.113.114.77:16001   vlan424:40651          TIME_WAIT
TCP   10.113.114.77:16001   vlan424:41920          TIME_WAIT
TCP   10.113.114.77:16001   vlan424:43180          TIME_WAIT
TCP   10.113.114.77:16001   vlan424:33799          TIME_WAIT
TCP   10.113.114.77:16001   vlan424:35066          TIME_WAIT
TCP   10.113.114.77:16001   vlan424:36326          TIME_WAIT
TCP   10.113.114.77:16001   vlan424:37589          TIME_WAIT
TCP   10.113.114.77:16001   vlan424:38849          TIME_WAIT
TCP   10.113.114.77:16001   vlan424:58243          TIME_WAIT
TCP   10.113.114.77:16001   vlan424:59503          TIME_WAIT
TCP   10.113.114.77:16001   vlan424:60771          TIME_WAIT
TCP   10.113.114.77:20000   c-67-170-0-208:24712   CLOSE_WAIT
TCP   10.113.114.77:20000   c-67-170-0-208:24714   ESTABLISHED
TCP   10.113.114.77:52917   co1-bc1-sn52:microsoft-ds  SYN_SENT
TCP   10.113.114.77:52918   co1-bc1-sn52:netbios-ssn   SYN_SENT
```

Running Non-.NET Languages

Every code sample up to this point in this chapter has been run on .NET. However, with the native code execution support described previously, it is now possible to run non-.NET code as well. How does that work?

Let's look at how most languages are run on Windows. .NET is slightly unique in that it creates a special executable that "knows" how to load the .NET runtime and execute the Microsoft Intermediate Language (MSIL) inside. However, most other languages must have a process launched to execute compiled bytecode or interpret a script. For example, to run Python code, the Python interpreter (*python.exe*) must be launched. To run Ruby code, the Ruby interpreter (*ruby.exe*) must be launched.

Running languages and runtimes other than .NET on Windows Azure is a simple matter of launching the right interpreter/execution binary, and then passing the code to be executed to it. The tricky part is to ensure that the binary is copied correctly (remember that no installation is possible), and that it has all its dependencies present in the correct location.

Let's now take a look at not only how to run code from a non-.NET language, but also how to have it respond to web requests from IIS.

Understanding FastCGI and PHP

One way to run other languages/virtual machines is by invoking a native process. However, what happens if you write web application code using Java/PHP/Python/Ruby/<insert-programming-language-here>? How can they be made to listen to incoming web requests and respond to them?

One perfectly legitimate mechanism is to make the process listen on port 80. (Chapter 4 describes how to make roles listen on arbitrary TCP ports.) However, this would involve bundling a web server somehow with your role. Since there is already a full-fledged web server on the virtual machine (that is, IIS), is there a way to use that somehow and integrate it with your runtime of choice?

This is where FastCGI comes in.

What Is FastCGI?

In the early days of the Web, most web servers used *Common Gateway Interface* (CGI) programs to execute code on incoming requests, and return a response to the user. Web servers would create a new process (typically Perl, or sometimes a shell), send it the incoming request through standard input, and read the results from the process's standard output.

However, launching a process on every request was a big drag on performance. Not only was creating a new process a heavyweight operation (and more so on Windows, since NT has a different model for process creation than what Unix has), but having hundreds of these processes hanging around executing code would play havoc with memory usage.

Web server developers knew this, of course. Two different solutions evolved to deal with the issue of heavyweight CGI processes.

The first is what has been referred to as the *in-process module*. This is the model followed by IIS with its ISAPI filters or its modules in IIS7. This is also the model behind `mod_perl`/ `mod_php` and several other popular open source Apache modules. Here, the web server process loads a library into its address space that "knows" how to execute code. This library typically implements an API specific to that web server (the IIS plug-in API, the Apache module API, and so on). When a request comes in, the web server calls this library and executes the request. Since the library lives within the server process, there is no expensive process setup/tear-down or communication to worry about.

The source of the speed is also the source of a few problems. Each web server typically has its own API, so these modules must be rewritten multiple times. Since the module lives within the server process, it can do whatever the server process does. A security exploit within one of these libraries can take over the web server. More importantly, a crash in the module will take down the web server as well.

FastCGI is an alternative to this model. In FastCGI, instead of the web server loading a module in-process, the web server communicates to a special FastCGI process. This FastCGI process hosts the language runtime. Since it is a different process, any crashes or security vulnerabilities don't affect the web server process. The FastCGI process is *long-lived* (that is, it isn't restarted for each connection), so there is none of the process setup/tear-down overhead experienced with CGI. Best of all, FastCGI is an open standard supported by all major web servers, so a wide variety of language implementations support it.

FastCGI on Windows Azure

Windows Azure uses the FastCGI support in IIS to enable users to "hook up" any language that supports FastCGI. Since this reuses the stock IIS implementation, any FastCGI implementation that works on a normal Windows machine with IIS will work with Windows Azure as well.

Let's look at a few details.

Enabling FastCGI mode

Turning on FastCGI support in Windows Azure requires following these steps:

1. Since all FastCGI implementations on IIS must execute native code (to interface with IIS), you must first enable Windows Azure to run native code. You do this using the `enableNativeCodeExecution` service configuration element shown earlier in this chapter. When developing against the Dev Fabric, you must install FastCGI support. You can install FastCGI support for IIS by clicking the CGI button (yes, this controls both CGI and FastCGI) in the familiar "Turn Windows features on or off" dialog, as shown in Figure 6-4. This dialog is accessible from the Control Panel.

2. If you're developing using the Dev Fabric on Windows Vista and you don't have SP2 installed, you must install a hotfix from *http://support.microsoft.com/kb/967131*. This is rolled into Windows Vista SP2 and Windows 7, so you don't have anything to install on those environments. In the cloud, this hotfix is installed for you by default, so again, you have nothing to do.

3. The next step is to point Windows Azure to the actual binary to launch. This binary must implement the FastCGI protocol and interface with IIS. This is done by including a *Web.roleconfig* in the root of your project and adding a `fastCgi` element within it, as shown in the following code snippet. Note that the binary and all its dependencies must be packaged with your application.

   ```
   <?xml version="1.0" encoding="utf-8" ?>
   <configuration>
     <system.webServer>
       <fastCgi>
         <application fullPath="%RoleRoot%\fast-cgi-binary.exe" />
       </fastCgi>
     </system.webServer>
   </configuration>
   ```

4. The final step is to tell IIS which file types to map to the FastCGI binary specified previously. In the following code snippet (which goes into *web.config*, not *.roleconfig*), the handler maps the *.fastcgi* extension to the FastCGI binary specified in step 3:

```
<configuration>
  <system.webServer>
    <handlers>
      <add name="My FastCGI implementation"
           path="*.fastcgi"
           verb="*"
           modules="FastCgiModule"
           scriptProcessor="%RoleRoot%\fast-cgi-binary.exe"
           resourceType="Unspecified" />
    </handlers>
  </system.webServer>
</configuration>
```

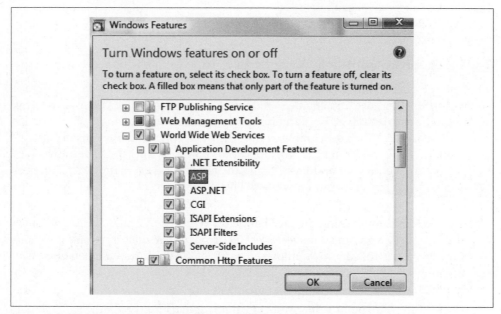

Figure 6-4. Enabling FastCGI support for local development

When this service runs, Windows Azure will launch *fast-cgi-binary.exe* to deal with FastCGI requests. IIS intercepts individual web requests to any path with a *.fastcgi* extension, and sends them over to the running *fast-cgi-binary.exe* instance to deal with.

PHP on Windows Azure

Let's use the FastCGI mechanism just described to run PHP code on Windows Azure. PHP ships with a FastCGI implementation for Windows and IIS, which can be reused on Windows Azure. Don't worry if you're unfamiliar with PHP; there's literally only one line of PHP code in this examination, and this technique can be reused with any FastCGI-compatible installation.

Let's start by creating a new blank cloud service as outlined in previous chapters. To this blank service, you must add a web role to act as a container of sorts for the PHP

FastCGI binary. One option is to create a blank web role, manually add a *Web.roleconfig*, and make the other necessary changes.

An easier method is to use the `CGI Web Role` template that ships with the right configuration files added by default, as well as template comments in all the right places. Pick the `CGI Web Role` project to add to your solution, as shown in Figure 6-5. This should give you a project named `WebCgiRole1` with some placeholder configuration files.

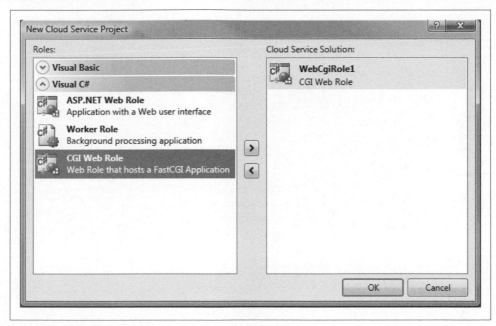

Figure 6-5. Selecting the CGI Web Role project

Finding and adding a PHP FastCGI implementation

Running PHP in Windows Azure wouldn't be possible without a PHP implementation, would it? Go to *http://www.php.net/downloads.php* and download the latest nonthread-safe version for Windows. Get the *.zip* version instead of the installer. As of this writing, all stable versions were x86 only. However, this doesn't affect their running in the x64 virtual machines in Windows Azure, since they get launched under the Windows Wow64 emulation mode by default.

The next step is to package this PHP implementation with your role. Extract the contents of the *.zip* file (*php-5.3.0-Win32-VC9-x86.zip*, in this case) to a *php* subfolder under your web role's root. In Visual Studio, ensure that all the files have their Build Action set to Content. Your Solution Explorer should look like Figure 6-6 at this point.

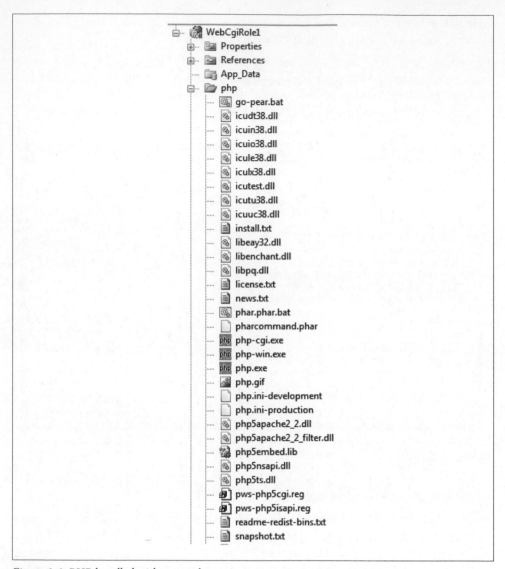

Figure 6-6. PHP bundled with your role

Hooking up the PHP support

You need to change some configuration options to ensure that Windows Azure knows how to map *.php* file extensions to the PHP binaries just added.

The first step is to ensure that native code can be run as a part of your service. You can do this by changing `enableNativeCodeExecution` to `true` in *ServiceConfiguration.csdef*, as shown in Example 6-5.

Example 6-5. Enabling native code for our PHP support

```xml
<?xml version="1.0" encoding="utf-8"?>
<ServiceDefinition name="PHPAzure"
xmlns="http://schemas.microsoft.com/ServiceHosting/2008/10/ServiceDefinition">
  <WebRole name="WebCgiRole1" enableNativeCodeExecution="true">
    <InputEndpoints>
      <!-- Must use port 80 for http and port 443
for https when running in the cloud -->
      <InputEndpoint name="HttpIn" protocol="http" port="80" />
    </InputEndpoints>
    <ConfigurationSettings />
  </WebRole>
</ServiceDefinition>
```

Next, you must tell Windows Azure to launch *php-cgi.exe* (which is the PHP FastCGI implementation, despite its name) along with your role. That change must happen inside *Web.roleconfig*, which is a Windows Azure-specific configuration file that specifies the location of the FastCGI binary. By default, its contents look like Example 6-6.

Example 6-6. Default Web.roleconfig

```xml
<?xml version="1.0"?>

<configuration>
  <system.webServer>
    <fastCgi>
      <!-- Set the "Enable Full Trust" property to true
           on the corresponding
           Web Role in the Cloud Service project.
      -->

      <!-- Define the fastCgi application here. The application must be located
           under the role root folder or subfolder. The handler is defined in
           the Web.config file.

           Ensure that all of the handler binaries have their
         "Build Action" Solution
           Explorer file property set to "Content".

      <application fullPath="%RoleRoot%\cgi-handler.exe"
        arguments="arg1 arg2 ..." />
      -->
    </fastCgi>
  </system.webServer>

</configuration>
```

Remember that the PHP installation was placed under the *php* folder. Using that and the special `%RoleRoot%` defined by all Windows Azure virtual machines, you can point to the PHP binary in your *Web.roleconfig* file, as shown in Example 6-7.

Example 6-7. Pointing to our PHP FastCGI installation

```xml
<?xml version="1.0"?>

<configuration>
  <system.webServer>
    <fastCgi>
      <application fullPath="%RoleRoot%\php\php-cgi.exe" />
    </fastCgi>
  </system.webServer>

</configuration>
```

The final configuration step is to tell IIS that any request ending with a *.php* extension gets redirected to the PHP FastCGI process. To do that, change the *web.config* file and add the code in Example 6-8 under `system.webServer/handlers`. You can add it any-where among the list of handlers already present.

*Example 6-8. Changing *.php request routing*

```xml
<!--Under the 'handlers' section in 'system.webServer' -->

<add name="FastGGI Handler"
         verb="*"
         path="*.php"
         scriptProcessor="%RoleRoot%\php\php-cgi.exe"
         modules="FastCgiModule"
         resourceType="Unspecified" />
```

Writing and running PHP

To try out the PHP support, create a new text file in your project called *test.php*. Add the line shown in Example 6-9 to it. `phpinfo` is a standard, diagnostic PHP function that displays some output about the PHP installation. This is commonly used to try out PHP installation, and to ensure that everything's working right.

Example 6-9. Test.php

```php
<?php phpinfo(); ?>
```

And that's it! At this point, building and running this package should show you a screen similar to Figure 6-7 when you hit *test.php* in your web browser. The particular text differs from machine to machine. Figure 6-7 shows `phpinfo`'s output running on a Windows Azure virtual machine.

At this point, you can write any PHP code you want and run it on Windows Azure. Though PHP's support itself is rock-solid, some of the extensions that ship with it don't play very well with the normal user process included in Windows Azure, so be sure that you test thoroughly.

PHP Version 5.3.0

System	Windows NT RD00155D3021C1 6.0 build 6002 (Windows Server 2008 Enterprise Edition Service Pack 2) i586
Build Date	Jun 29 2009 21:52:31
Compiler	MSVC9 (Visual C++ 2008)
Architecture	x86
Configure Command	cscript /nologo configure.js "--enable-snapshot-build" "--disable-isapi" "--enable-debug-pack" "--with-pdo-oci=D:\php-sdk\oracle\instantclient10\sdk,shared" "--with-oci8=D:\php-sdk\oracle\instantclient10\sdk,shared" "--with-oci8-11g=D:\php-sdk\oracle\instantclient11\sdk,shared" "--with-enchant=shared"
Server API	CGI/FastCGI
Virtual Directory Support	enabled

Figure 6-7. PHP code running in the cloud

If you're using PHP with Windows Azure storage, look at the code from *http://phpazure* *.codeplex.com/*, which implements support for Windows Azure blobs, tables, and queues from inside PHP.

"Gotchas" with Running Native Code

When developing applications that use the native code techniques described in this chapter, be aware of the following common mistakes:

- Remember that the Dev Fabric runs under your credentials on your local machine. If your operating system is 32-bit, the Dev Fabric will run in 32-bit mode. However, in the cloud, all 32-bit processes will be run in Wow64 mode, which can be different in subtle ways. Moreover, a 64-bit process cannot load a 32-bit DLL. One common mistake is to P/Invoke a 32-bit DLL and to upload the DLL to the cloud. Though it'll work in the Dev Fabric running in 32-bit mode, it will fail in the cloud.

- In the cloud, all code is run under a restricted user account. Any operations requiring administrative privileges will fail. Common operations such as launching *msiexec* or registering a COM component currently won't work inside the Windows Azure virtual machine.

Summary

The ability to launch arbitrary processes can be a great blunt hammer to make a lot of scenarios work on Windows Azure that are not supported out of the box. However, with great power comes great responsibility, and frequent headaches. Test your application on the cloud, and ensure that your native code behaves the way you expect it to.

## CHAPTER 7

Storage Fundamentals

I'm a big fan of all things *Star Trek*. I was a big fan of *TOS* ("The Original Series," for all you non-Trekkies), which was the original television series from the 1960s. My evenings were filled with the Prime Directive, about Klingons and Vulcans and Romulans and transporters and phasers and aliens in bad rubber costumes. The captain of the U.S.S. Enterprise, James T. Kirk, was a swashbuckling space cowboy who preferred to shoot phasers first and ask questions later. Several episodes ended in a fistfight with Kirk duking it out with some bad guy. It was also common for Kirk to jump into bed with a beautiful female alien in every episode; something I always thought would drive exobiologists in the twenty-fourth century crazy.

One fine day, I ran out of *TOS* episodes. The television channel advertised that it would be broadcasting a new show starting the following week: *Star Trek: The Next Generation* (*TNG* from now on). I instantly hated it. Instead of the bold, aggressive Kirk, we had Picard (played by Patrick Stewart), who was much happier to negotiate than fire phasers. Thankfully, he never jumped into bed with any alien woman. Instead of a dynamic relationship with a Vulcan first officer and a cranky doctor, Picard had a bland android and a personality-deprived first officer. I was not happy...for a while. Over time, the show grew on me. Pretty soon, I loved *TNG* much more than I had ever loved *TOS*. I loved the characters and the twentieth century relevance of the storylines. Most of all, I loved Picard, and imagined that I would follow him into battle anywhere.

Over the course of the following chapters, you might feel like a *TOS* fan who has to suddenly endure one of Picard's monologues. The systems used in Azure are quite different from the ones you might be used to and have a lot of experience with. However, just like *TNG* and *TOS*, they're set in the same surroundings and they work on similar principles. Azure's blob storage can be made to look like the filesystems you have used. The queue system is similar (in principle) to popular messaging systems. And the table service is similar in some aspects to your favorite relational database management system (RDBMS).

But the similarities end after a point, and you'll run into the fact that these are fundamentally different services. The queue service can take any number of messages, but it lacks features found in Microsoft Message Queuing (MSMQ). The table service can store and query billions of rows, but you cannot enforce relational constraints. Like moving from Kirk to Picard, it can take awhile to get used to the new features and limitations of these cloud storage services.

This chapter begins by looking at the different storage services and the basic features they offer. You'll learn how you can create an account and specify where it should be geographically located. Each storage service has a REST API against which you'll be writing code.

Before digging into the details of each storage service, it is important to know how the REST API works, and how it authenticates you. After you become familiar with the different storage systems and their features, this chapter examines how these REST APIs work, and how you can build a sample client library to work with them.

Accepting the New Storage System

Developers are used to working with filesystems, databases, and queuing systems (such as MSMQ). These have served developers well for a long time, so why introduce a new model? Why isn't Windows Azure storage just MSMQ on a really beefy server, or SQL Server on some high-end hardware? Why should developers be forced to change?

One perfectly valid response is that you don't have to move to Azure's new model unless you need the specific benefits offered by the cloud. For small applications with low scalability requirements, a shared filesystem backed by a beefy hard disk works just fine. However, scaling such a filesystem to a larger scale is very difficult. When faced with similar issues for the large sites and services they run, companies such as Google, Amazon, and Microsoft quickly discovered that some of these traditional mechanisms don't scale very well—technically or financially.

Windows Azure storage (like other competing cloud storage systems) takes a different approach. Instead of having to predict how much storage you will need, you can pay as you go, and the storage system will scale with your needs. Instead of high-end hardware, it uses distributed software design techniques to provide scalability and reliability.

There are some trade-offs, however, as a consequence of using this distributed software design, and as a result of providing other features. One of these trade-offs is caused by the fact that familiar abstractions and technologies (that is, files and MSMQ) don't translate well to the cloud and highly scalable applications. Instead, you have new concepts to deal with: blobs, queues, Windows Azure tables, and SQL Azure. Though you must rewrite code (or make use of wrappers that make these Windows Azure concepts look like plain old files or MSMQ queues) and become familiar with new concepts, in return you get data storage that is highly scalable and reliable.

Windows Azure Storage Characteristics

The next few chapters of this book examine the various storage services and the features they offer. However, all these storage services share some common aspects. They're all based on a common strata, and they all share code and architecture. Let's take a look at some of the common characteristics across all the Windows Azure storage services.

Lots and Lots of Space

All the storage services can take huge amounts of data. People have been known to store billions of rows in one table in the table service, and to store terabytes of data in the blob service. However, there is not an infinite amount of space available, since Microsoft owns only so many disks. But this is not a limit that you or anyone else will hit.

You could draw a parallel to IPv6, which was designed as a replacement for the current system of IP addresses, IPv4. The fact is that IPv4 is running out of IP addresses to hand out—the limit is 4.3 billion, and the number of available IP addresses is quickly diminishing. IPv6 has a finite number of addresses as well, but the limit will never be reached, since that finite number is incredibly large: 3.4×10^{38}, or 3.4 followed by 38 zeros!

The same holds true for these storage services. You need not worry about running out of space on a file share, negotiating with vendors, or racking up new disks. You pay only for what you use, and you can be sure that you'll always have more space if you need it. Note that this represents the total data you can store. There are limits on how large an individual blob or a table entity/row can be, but not on the number of blobs or the number of rows you can have.

Distribution

All the storage services are massively distributed. This means that, instead of having a few huge machines serving out your data, your data is spread out over several smaller machines. These smaller machines do have higher rates of failure than specialized storage infrastructure such as storage area networks (SANs), but Windows Azure storage deals with failure through software. It implements various distributed software techniques to ensure that it stays available and reliable in the presence of failures in one or more of the machines on which it runs.

Scalability

All the storage services are scalable. However, *scalable* is a loaded, often abused word. In this context, it means your performance should stay the same, regardless of the amount of data you have. (This statement comes with some caveats, of course. When you learn about the table service, you'll see how you can influence performance through partitioning.) More importantly, performance stays the same when load increases. If your site shows up on the home page of Slashdot or Digg or Reddit, Windows Azure does magic behind the scenes to ensure that the time taken to serve requests stays the same. Commodity machines can take only so much load, because there are multiple mechanisms at play—from making multiple copies to having multiple levels of hot data caching.

Replication

All data is replicated multiple times. In case of a hardware failure or data corruption in any of the replicas, there are always more copies from which to recover data. This happens under the covers, so you don't need to worry about this explicitly.

Consistency

Several distributed storage services are *eventually consistent*, which means that when an operation is performed, it may take some time (usually a few seconds) for the data you retrieve to reflect those changes. Eventual consistency usually means better scalability and performance: if you don't need to make changes on several nodes, you have better availability. The downside is that it makes writing code a lot trickier, because it's possible to have a write operation followed by a read that doesn't see the results of the write you just performed.

Don't misinterpret this description—eventual consistency is great in specialized scenarios. For example, Amazon's shopping cart service is a canonical example of an eventually consistent application. The underlying store it writes to (Dynamo) is a state-of-the-art distributed storage system. It lets Amazon choose between insert/add performance and not retrieving the latest version of the data. It doesn't reflect changes instantly, but by not having to do so, it gives Amazon the ability to add items to shopping carts almost instantly, and more importantly, to never miss an item added.

Amazon decided that not losing shopping cart items was very important and worth the trade-off of a minuscule percentage of users' shopping carts not seeming to have all items at all times. For more information, read Amazon's paper on the topic at *http://s3.amazonaws.com/AllTh ingsDistributed/sosp/amazon-dynamo-sosp2007.pdf*.

Windows Azure storage is not eventually consistent; it is *instantly/strongly consistent*. This means that when you do an update or a delete, the changes are instantly visible to all future API calls. The team decided to do this since they felt that eventual consistency would make writing code against the storage services quite tricky, and more important, they could achieve very good performance without needing this. While full database-style transactions aren't available, a limited form is available where you can batch calls to one partition. Application code must ensure consistency across partitions, and across different storage account calls.

RESTful HTTP APIs

All the storage services are exposed through a RESTful HTTP API. You'll learn about the building blocks of these APIs later in this chapter. All APIs can be accessed from both inside and outside Microsoft data centers. This is a *big* deal. This means that you could host your website or service in your current data center, and pick and choose what service you want to use. For example, you could use only blob storage, or use only the queue service, instead of having to host your code inside Windows Azure as well. This is similar to how several websites use Amazon's S3 service. For example, Twitter runs code in its own infrastructure, but uses S3 to store profile images.

Another advantage of having open RESTful APIs is that it is trivial to build a client library in any language/platform. Microsoft ships one in .NET, but there are bindings in Python, Ruby, and Erlang, just to name a few. Later in this chapter, you will learn how to build a rudimentary library to illustrate the fundamental concepts, but in most of the storage code, you'll be using the official Microsoft client library. If you want to implement your own library in a different language/environment, just follow along through the sample in this chapter, and you should find it easy to follow the same steps in your chosen environment.

Geodistribution

When you create your storage account, you can pick in which geographical location you want your data to reside. This is great for not only ensuring that your data is close to your code or your customers, but also spreading your data out geographically. You don't want a natural disaster in one region to take out your only copy of some valuable data.

Pay for Play

With Windows Azure storage, like the rest of Windows Azure, you pay only for the storage you currently use, and for bandwidth transferring data in and out of the system.

Windows Azure Storage Services

Windows Azure offers four key data services: blobs, tables, queues, and a database. All these services share the characteristics described in the previous section. Let's take a brief look at three of the four services, as well as a glance at SQL Azure.

Blob Storage

The blob storage service provides a simple interface for storing named files along with metadata. You can store unstructured data up to several hundred gigabytes in size. Blobs are stored together in a *container*, which is roughly analogous to a directory in a normal filesystem. Each blob and container has a unique URL, and blobs can be created, deleted, updated, and accessed through the REST API.

Containers are also used to set permissions and access control policy. Set a container to be publicly accessible and any blobs under that container can be accessed by anyone over the public Internet. Since everything works over HTTP, this access can be as simple as typing the blob's URL in a web browser. Under the covers, all blob data is replicated multiple times to ensure that no data loss occurs in case of hardware failure. Moreover, the system scales automatically when under load, so even if your blobs are being heavily accessed, you won't see a drop in performance.

Blobs are also the underlying storage mechanism for a feature called Windows Azure XDrives. These are NTFS volumes in the cloud that are backed by blob storage. This lets you use normal filesystem access code, which in turn writes to blob storage underneath.

You'll learn more about blob storage in Chapter 8.

Queue Storage

Queues provide reliable storage and delivery of messages for your application. At a high level, they are similar in concept to MSMQ, IBM's WebSphere MQ, or other queuing systems. However, the actual implementation is different from MSMQ, and the two technologies have different APIs.

Queues are typically used to compose different parts of an application. Applications can enqueue an unlimited number of messages, and can be guaranteed that the messages are delivered at least once. Like the other Windows Azure storage services, the queue service is accessed using a REST API, and can be accessed from the public Internet.

You'll learn more about queue storage in Chapter 9.

Table Storage

Table storage enables you to store massive amounts of structured data cheaply and efficiently, and query over the tables. This is used in the same way relational databases are used, but table storage differs significantly from traditional RDBMSs. Data is stored in the form of *entities*, each with a set of *properties*. However, there is no fixed schema for each table. Every row/entity can have a different set or number of properties.

Application developers have precise control over how this data is partitioned physically using *partition keys*. Picking the right partition key is critical, since the selection also affects query performance. Speaking of queries, you can't query table storage with SQL since it isn't a relational store. Instead, you can use an ADO.NET Data Services REST interface (or write LINQ code using the .NET wrapper) to perform queries against your entities. Querying support is not as rich as SQL—you have access to a limited subset of query operators.

In return for giving up some of the power of SQL, you get almost unlimited scale. Several applications routinely write millions of entities every day to their tables. There are no indexes to tune or database administration to perform—the system takes care of optimizing queries and other storage operations.

You'll learn more about table storage in Chapter 10.

SQL Azure

While Windows Azure table storage is optimized for cheap and highly scalable storage, SQL Azure is focused more on bringing SQL Server to the cloud. With SQL Azure, you can work against a SQL Server database with your normal tools and code, except that the actual database is running in Microsoft's data centers. Chapter 13 discusses how to pick between using SQL Azure and Windows Azure tables.

As mentioned, the following chapters dig into each of these services in depth. In the remainder of this chapter, you'll learn how to get started with a storage account, and how the REST API access to these storage services looks. You'll also learn about some common tools that you can use to help develop code and manage these services.

Getting Started with a Storage Account

Setting up a storage account is relatively simple, but there are a few details you should be aware of, as explained in the following discussions.

Signing Up for a Storage Account

The first steps before writing any code are to sign up for and create a storage account (also known as a *project*). You can sign up for an account at *http://windows.azure .com*. For more on creating an account and the Developer Portal, see the discussion in Chapter 3.

To create a storage account, you log in to your Windows Azure account, create a new project, and click Storage Account. From there, you specify a unique name, an optional description, and some other information.

You must also pick a geolocation. Shortly, you will learn what this choice means, and how to pick a good location for your data. Note that this decision is binding, so if you really care about where your data is placed, you should read the section "Picking a Geographic Location" on page 135 before you lock in a selection. If you're building a toy application, the default should work for you.

Once you have entered this information, you should see a screen similar to Figure 7-1 that confirms you have created an account. This screen also shows you the API access keys needed to work with the new account you've created.

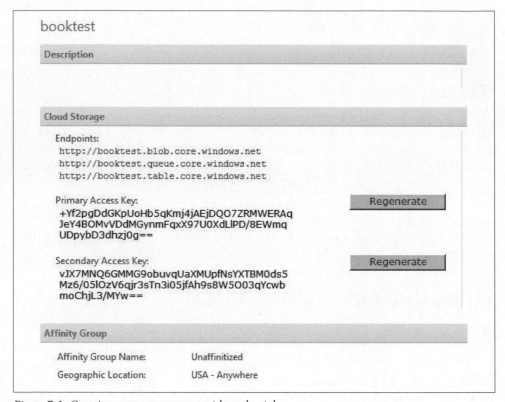

Figure 7-1. Creating a storage account with credentials

 Don't worry if you don't see the same web page as the one shown in Figure 7-1. The UI around the Developer Portal in Windows Azure is constantly being modified.

Note the fields for Primary Access Key and Secondary Access Key in Figure 7-1. These keys are the way into your storage kingdom, so guard them safely. If your firm has management policies for passwords and other secrets, use them. These keys are used to sign all requests to the storage services. If an attacker gets access to either of these, the attacker can use them to perform any operation that you can. Not only can an attacker get access to your data, but also any operation the attacker performs will be charged to your account.

 In terms of functionality, the primary and secondary keys are exactly the same. They have equal powers, and vary just in what they're called in the UI.

One good practice is to periodically regenerate the keys. Doing so immediately invalidates the old key and creates a new one with which you must update your application. (Note that the keys shown in the figure have been regenerated for security reasons.) This brings us to why there are two keys in the first place.

You typically include the primary key in your service configuration file. In case your primary key is compromised, you could easily toggle a switch in your configuration (or have your code try the second key automatically if the first one fails to authenticate) and start using the secondary key while you regenerate the primary key. Remember that configuration updates can be applied without downtime using either an in-place upgrade or a normal upgrade mechanism. Since this can be done quickly without a redeploy/recompile, this helps you to react quickly to key compromises.

Another piece of information to note in Figure 7-1 is the URLs at which your storage accounts reside. You'll be using them in your code (or configuration files), so make a note of them. Finally, there is a bit at the bottom about where your account is located. You'll learn more about this in the following discussion about geodistribution.

Picking a Geographic Location

When you create your account, you have a choice of placing your account within a couple of geographic locations. As of this writing, there are locations in the United States, Europe, and Asia, but Microsoft plans to add more locations over time.

You want to do this for a few reasons. First, you want your data to be as close to your customers as possible. If you know a lot of your customers are from California, it makes sense to place your data in the South Central United States. As Microsoft expands its Windows Azure presence globally, you'll find big performance wins by placing data in the same geographic region as the users of your service.

Second, you may want your data to be inside or outside specific countries for legal/ regulatory reasons. For example, you may want to specify that your data should be hosted within the European Union by choosing North Europe or Anywhere Europe to comply with the European Union's privacy laws.

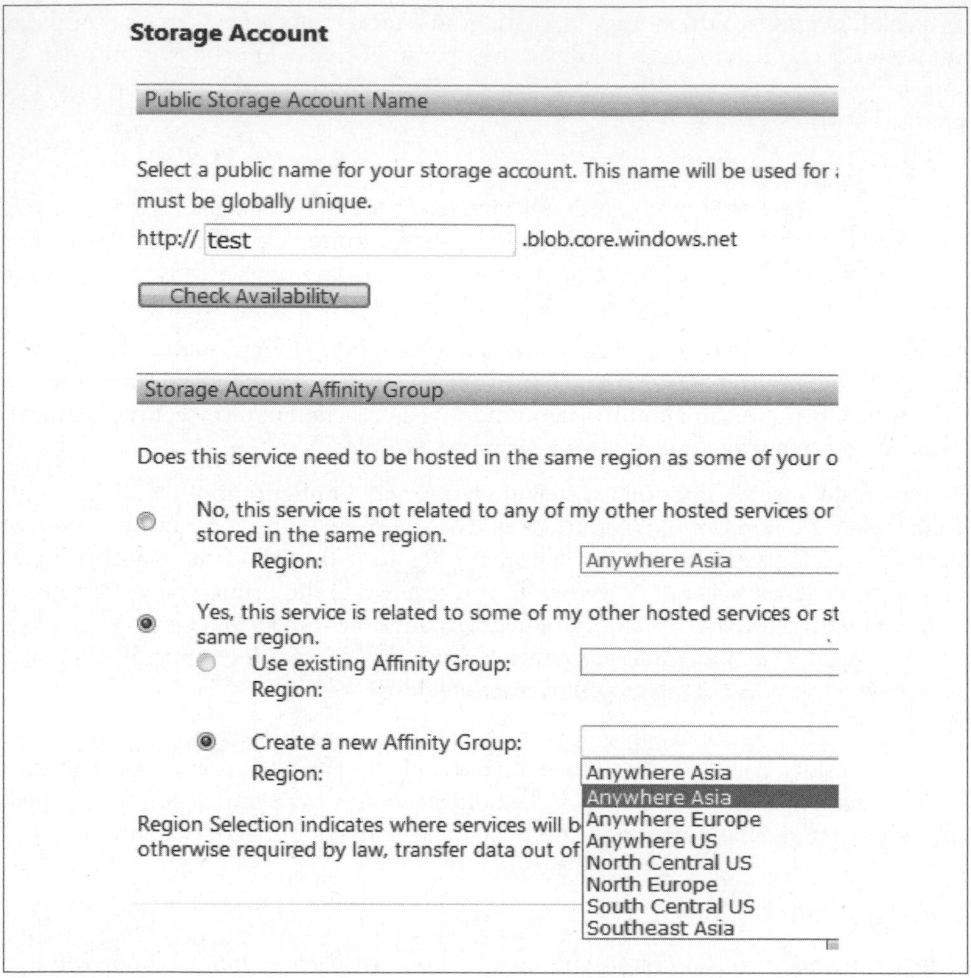

Storage Account

Public Storage Account Name

Select a public name for your storage account. This name will be used for ¦
must be globally unique.

http:// [test   ] .blob.core.windows.net

[Check Availability]

Storage Account Affinity Group

Does this service need to be hosted in the same region as some of your o

○ No, this service is not related to any of my other hosted services or
stored in the same region.
    Region: [Anywhere Asia   ]

◉ Yes, this service is related to some of my other hosted services or st
same region.
    ○ Use existing Affinity Group: [   ]
    Region:

    ◉ Create a new Affinity Group: [   ]
    Region: [   ]
                                     Anywhere Asia
                                     Anywhere Asia
Region Selection indicates where services will be Anywhere Europe
otherwise required by law, transfer data out of Anywhere US
                                     North Central US
                                     North Europe
                                     South Central US
                                     Southeast Asia

Figure 7-2. Creating an affinity group

Affinity Groups

One interesting option you have when selecting a geographic location is to place your
data in an *affinity group*. You typically want your code and your data as close together
as possible. This makes the laws of physics work on your behalf. Less distance means
less network latency between your hosted service and your storage account. By placing
your storage and hosted service accounts within an affinity group, you can tell Windows
Azure to place them as physically close together as possible.

Figure 7-2 shows a new storage account being placed in a new affinity group hosted in
Asia. When you create further hosted service or storage accounts, you can specify that
they be added to a particular affinity group, and be placed as physically close together
as possible.

With all the options available, it can be tricky to figure out what location to pick. Here are some basic rules of thumb:

- If you're creating a one-off storage account and you don't care about its location, pick Anywhere US (or Anywhere Europe/Anywhere Asia if you're based in Europe/Asia, respectively).

- If you're creating an account that is targeted at users in a specific region, or if you want to make copies in a specific region, pick the option closest to that region. For example, if you're building a site for users in Canada, it makes sense to host your data in the United States, since that will ensure lower latency than picking a data center in Europe.

- If you're creating multiple storage accounts as part of an application, create an affinity group for the first storage account you create. Add all further storage accounts to this first affinity group. Regardless of which affinity group your storage accounts/compute services are located in, remember that all storage services are always available over a public HTTP interface.

 Your geolocation decisions cannot be changed. Once you pick a location for an account or an affinity group, or decide to join an account to an affinity group, you cannot go back. In other words, Windows Azure cannot move your account once it has decided to place it somewhere. So, be careful when you make your choice. Remember that making a geolocation choice places your code/data in a specific location. Making a change would mean having to move this code/data to another location.

Pricing

Charges (pricing) for Windows Azure storage vary. The basic and straightforward method of pricing is determined through a consumption-based model. Simply put, you pay for what you use every month.

 As of this writing, Microsoft had announced that there would be other pricing models, discounts, and promotional offers, but the details hadn't been made public.

In terms of pricing for storage, here are the key details:

- Windows Azure charges $0.15 per gigabyte for each month.

- Windows Azure charges $0.01 for every 10,000 storage transactions. A "transaction" here refers to a successful authenticated request to Windows Azure storage, or a valid anonymous request in the case of public blob containers. You don't get charged for unauthenticated requests.

- Incoming bandwidth to all of Windows Azure is charged at $0.10 per gigabyte, and bandwidth flowing out of Windows Azure is charged at $0.15 per gigabyte.

Size is measured by the average daily amount of data stored (in gigabytes) over a month. For example, if you uploaded 30 GB of data and stored it on Windows Azure for a day, your monthly billed storage would be 1 GB. If you uploaded 30 GB of data and stored it on Windows Azure for an entire billing period, your monthly billed storage would be 30 GB. Depending on the length of the month, how this average is calculated varies.

Bandwidth is calculated by the total amount of data going in and out of the Windows Azure services in a given 30-day period. This means that any data access between code hosted on Windows Azure and storage is essentially free.

Pricing can get complicated when you throw in all the various promotional schemes, costs for both running code and storing data, and the calculation of what you might wind up paying for different loads. Microsoft has said that it will be building a tool to help customers calculate and project costs. However, most of this projection can be done by just playing around in a spreadsheet such as Excel.

Working with the REST API

To get a feel for how you would access your data in Windows Azure, you could run a variant of the following demo (with a different URL each time): *http://sriramkbook.blob .core.windows.net/test/helloworld.txt*. If you hit that URL in your browser, you see a nice little text file. Your browser will go all the way over to Microsoft's data centers, converse in HTTP with the Windows Azure storage service, and pull down a few bytes of awesomeness. The fact that it is a blob stored in Windows Azure blob storage really doesn't matter to the browser, since it is a plain HTTP URL that works as URLs should.

In fact, if you so choose, you can get at any piece of data you store in Windows Azure storage this way. (You'd have to make all the data publicly viewable first, of course.) But doing HTTP requests like this doesn't work if you protect the data so that only you can get access to it. It also doesn't work when you want to upload data, or if you want to access only specific subsets of your data. That's where the APIs come in.

Earlier in this chapter, you learned that the Windows Azure APIs are almost all REST-based (the exception being SQL Azure which speaks the standard SQL protocol, TDS). Don't worry if you're unfamiliar with REST APIs, or with what makes something *RESTful*. The following discussion won't make you an expert on REST, but it will tell you all you need to know as far as REST and Windows Azure are concerned. The discussions in this book barely scratch the surface of what REST entails. For more on REST, see *RESTful Web Services (http://oreilly.com/catalog/9780596529260/)* by Leonard Richardson and Sam Ruby (O'Reilly).

Understanding the RESTful API Resources

You deal with HTTP requests and responses every day. When you click a link, your web browser requests a page by sending an HTTP GET to a URL. If the page exists, the server typically sends down an HTTP 200 response code, followed by the page's contents. If the page doesn't exist, your browser gets the HTTP 404 code, and you see an error page indicating that the page could not be found.

Another way to look at this is that your browser is requesting a resource (the page) identified by the URL where it lives, and is asking the server to perform a method (GET) on it. REST takes this near-universal plumbing (every resource reachable via a URL) and uses it to build APIs. Apart from this being an elegant way to programmatically access resources over HTTP (it sticks to the nature of the Web), it is easy to code up since every language/tool set has support for HTTP. Contrast this with SOAP or CORBA where you must wield cumbersome toolkits or code generators.

To understand a RESTful API, you must first understand the resources that are being exposed. Let's illustrate with Windows Azure's blob service. Chapter 8 digs deeper into the blob service, but for now, let's just say it is a service that lets you store data (*values*) with keys associated with them. Each blob resides in a *container* (a top-level directory underneath your cloud storage endpoint).

A non-REST API would typically expose functions such as getBlobs or getContainers. The RESTful Windows Azure Blob API takes a different approach. It exposes the blobs and the containers as standard HTTP objects (known as *resources* in REST). Instead of using custom methods, you can use standard HTTP methods such as GET, POST, PUT, DELETE, and so on.

Each storage service with a REST API (blobs, tables, and queues) exposes different resources. For example, the blob service exposes containers and blobs, while the queue service exposes queues, and so on. But they all share similar patterns, so if you know how to code against one, you can easily figure out how to code against the others. The only outlier is the table service, which requires you to understand a bit of ADO.NET Data Services to do querying.

All the URLs typically fall into one of the following patterns:

- To get the default representation of the object, you send a GET to the URL. URLs are of the form *http://<account.service>.core.windows.net/<resource>*. For example, you can retrieve a test blob by making a GET request to *http://sriramk.blob.core.windows.net/test/hello.txt*.

- Operations on individual *components* are specified through a comp parameter. *Component* here is a slightly misleading term, since in practice this is used for operations such as getting lists, getting/setting access control lists (ACLs), getting metadata, and the like. For example, to get a list of blob containers, you can send an authenticated HTTP GET to *http://account.blob.core.windows.net/?comp=list*. If you try to do that with *http://sriramk.blob.core.windows.net/?comp=list* in your browser, you'll get an error page back because your browser can't add the correct storage authentication headers. (You'll learn how authentication works a bit later.)

Every resource in the Windows Azure storage world acts the same way when it comes to HTTP operations. To get an object's default representation, you send an HTTP GET request to that object's URL. Similarly, to create an object, you send a PUT request to the URL where you want it to live. And finally, to delete the object, you send a DELETE request to the URL where it exists. This is in line with what the HTTP standards specify, and behaves exactly how good RESTful APIs should.

Following is a sample interaction to create a new container. Note how simple the entire HTTP request is. You can ignore the headers related to authorization and versioning for now, since you'll learn more about them later.

```
PUT /foo HTTP/1.1
x-ms-version: 2009-07-17
x-ms-date: Sat, 09 May 2009 19:36:08 GMT
Authorization: SharedKey sriramk:I/xbJkkoKIVKDgw2zPAdRvSM1HaXsIw...
Host: sriramk.blob.core.windows.net
Content-Length: 0
```

If everything went well, you would get back a success message, as shown here:

```
HTTP/1.1 201 Created
Last-Modified: Sat, 09 May 2009 19:35:00 GMT
ETag: 0x8CB9EF4605B9470
Server: Blob Service Version 1.0 Microsoft-HTTPAPI/2.0
x-ms-request-id: 4f3b6fdb-066d-4fc5-b4e8-178c8cf571a6
Date: Sat, 09 May 2009 19:34:59 GMT
Content-Length: 0
```

 Throughout this book, you'll be seeing a lot of HTTP traffic. You can look at the HTTP traffic for your requests by using Fiddler, Netmon, Wireshark, or your network monitoring tool of choice. Another option is to construct the requests by using tools such as curl or wget. A quick web search should show you where to download them, as well as tutorials on using them.

HTTP Requests and Responses

You should now have a basic understanding of the standard HTTP operations supported by Windows Azure. Before exploring the guts of the API, here's a little refresher on the standard HTTP terms, operations, and codes, and what they mean in the Windows Azure world. If you're familiar with writing HTTP clients, you can quickly skim over this with the knowledge that Windows Azure works the way you expect it to when it comes to HTTP. This examination points out where Azure storage diverges from what other HTTP services typically do.

Let's break down a typical HTTP request and response.

URL

The URL identifies the resource that you want to get. In Windows Azure storage, this typically includes the account name in the hostname, and the resource specified by the path.

Headers

Every HTTP request and response has headers that provide information about the request. You use these headers to generate a new authentication header to let the server know that it really came from you, and then the authentication header is added to the list of headers. You'll also see some custom headers for some operations that are examined with the relevant feature. All custom headers in Windows Azure storage are prefixed with x-ms-. See the section "Understanding Authentication and Request Signing" on page 147 for details on how this works.

HTTP method

The HTTP method specifies the exact operation to be carried out. Windows Azure uses only a few of the several HTTP methods available:

GET
> This retrieves the default representation of a resource. For a blob, this is a blob's contents. For a table entity, this will be an XML version of the entity, and so on.

PUT
> This creates or updates a resource. You will typically PUT to a resource's URL with the body of the request containing the data you want to upload.

POST
> This is used to update the data in an entity. This is similar to PUT, but different in that you typically expect the resource to already exist at the URL.

DELETE
> This deletes the resource specified at the URL.

Status codes

The HTTP specification documents more than 40 different status codes. Thankfully, you have to worry about only a small subset of those 40 codes. These are used to tell you the result of the operation—whether it succeeded or failed, and if it failed, a hint as to why it failed. Here are the main classes of status codes:

2xx ("Everything's OK")
> Response codes in the 2xx range generally signify that the operation succeeded. When you successfully create a blob, you get back a 201, and when you send a GET to a blob, you get back a 200.

3xx

In the normal web world, codes in the **3xx** range are used to control caching and redirection. In the case of Azure, there is only one code you can expect to get, and that is **304**. When you get a resource, you get an `ETag` associated with it. `ETags` are also used to implement optimistic concurrency. You can think of an `ETag` as a unique identifier that specifies the current data that the server "knows" about. If the content changes, the `ETag` will change. If you specify the same `ETag` when sending a request, you'll get a **304** code if the server hasn't seen any changes since it last sent you the same resource.

4xx *("Bad request")*

Codes in the **4xx** range mean that the request failed for some reason. This could be because the headers are incorrect, the URL is incorrect, the account or resource doesn't exist, or any number of other reasons. The body of the response will contain more information on why the response failed. Two codes to note are **403** (which you get if the authentication information was invalid) and **404** (which means the resource doesn't exist).

5xx *("Something bad happened on the server")*

Of all the error codes, this is the scariest to receive. This typically means that an unknown error happened on the server, or that the server is too busy to handle requests (this almost never happens). You could see this from time to time if you request too large a dataset and the operation timed out. However, this code typically indicates a bug in Windows Azure itself. These errors are regularly logged and diagnosed by the Windows Azure team.

Building a Storage Client

You'll never have to build a storage client. You're almost always better off using one of the ones already available—be it the official one from Microsoft that ships with the Windows Azure SDK, or one of the community-supported ones for various languages.

However, there is no better way to learn the innards of how storage access works than to build a storage client. Knowing how the underlying protocols work is crucial when debugging weird errors and bugs while interacting with the storage services. You may be wondering why you are building a library when Microsoft provides a reference implementation. It is important to remember that the actual API is the REST interface, and the wrapper is just that: a "wrapper." The Microsoft implementation is just one wrapper around the storage services. You can find several other commonly used, community-written implementations, each optimized for different purposes and offering different features.

Even with the official Microsoft implementation, you'll often find yourself looking at the low-level REST interface to diagnose/debug issues. For all these reasons, knowing how the REST interface works is critical to being able to work effectively with the Windows Azure storage services.

During this examination, you will be building a trivial storage client. The code you'll be writing is for a trivial storage library meant primarily to educate. It will support the bare minimum functionality, and won't support several features such as block lists, setting metadata on containers, and the performance optimizations that have gone into the official library. It is by no means robust; at a minimum, it lacks error checking and performance optimizations. It also doesn't support anything other than creating containers and blobs.

Here, you will build this storage client piece by piece. You'll start by creating some boilerplate data structure classes. You'll add some code to construct the correct request path and headers. And finally, you'll add the authentication and signing code. You can follow along with the examples, but you won't be able to run it until the end, when all the pieces come together.

Let's start with some boilerplate code. Example 7-1 shows a skeleton C# class that brings in the right namespaces, sets up some variables and constants you'll be using, and does nothing else. You'll be using these namespaces later to perform HTTP requests and to do some cryptographic work to sign your requests. This is just skeletal infrastructure code; you can't run it at this point. You'll be using this infrastructure code and building on top of it throughout the remainder of this chapter.

Example 7-1. Skeleton code

```
using System;
using System.Collections.Generic;
using System.Collections.Specialized;
using System.Text;
using System.Net;
using System.Security.Cryptography;
using System.Security.Globalization;


namespace SimpleStorageClient
{


    public class BlobStorage
    {

        private const string CloudBlobHost = "blob.core.windows.net";

        private const string HeaderPrefixMS = "x-ms-";
        private const string HeaderPrefixProperties = "x-ms-prop-";
        private const string HeaderPrefixMetadata = "x-ms-meta-";
        private const string HeaderDate = HeaderPrefixMS + "date";


        private const string CarriageReturnLinefeed = "\r\n";
```

```
    private string AccountName { get; set; }
    private byte[] SecretKey { get; set; }
    private string Host { get; set; }

    public BlobStorage(string accountName, string base64SecretKey)
    {
        this.AccountName = accountName;
        this.SecretKey = Convert.FromBase64String(base64SecretKey);
        this.Host = CloudBlobHost; //Pick default blob storage URL
    }

    public BlobStorage(string host, string accountName, string base64SecretKey)
    {

        this.AccountName = accountName;
        this.SecretKey = Convert.FromBase64String(base64SecretKey);
        this.Host = host;
    }
  }
}
```

This code first sets up some constants specific to the Windows Azure storage service (the URL it resides at, the prefix it uses for its headers), and then sets up a simple wrapper class (`BlobStorage`) to store the storage credentials.

Next, it does something that is actually useful: it creates a *container*. Chapter 8 provides more detail about blobs and containers, so this discussion won't provide much information about them, except to say that containers can be thought of as the directories in which you store blobs and on which you set permissions.

That analogy goes only so far, because there are several differences between containers and directories. For example, you cannot nest one container within another. Typically, containers are used to set permissions—you can set whether the contents within a container are public or private. Don't worry if this sounds fuzzy at this point. Things will clear up in Chapter 8. For now, just know that this will make your small storage client library go and create your very own container.

What comes next in Example 7-2 is a little `CreateContainer` method that takes a container name and a Boolean argument specifying whether the container should be public (readable by everyone) or private (readable only by someone with access to your keys). Several operations on storage involve modifying headers. Let's make these small methods pass their own custom headers. In this case, you are setting `x-ms-prop-publicaccess` to `true`. Insert the `CreateContainer` method into the `BlobStorage` class.

Example 7-2. The CreateContainer method

```
public bool CreateContainer(string containerName, bool publicAccess)
    {
        Dictionary<string,string> headers = new Dictionary<string,string>();

        if (publicAccess)
        {
```

```
        //Public access for container. Set x-ms-prop-publicaccess
        // to true
        headers[HeaderPrefixProperties + "publicaccess"] = "true";
    }

    // To construct a container, make a PUT request to
    //http://<account>.blob.core.windows.net/mycontainer
    HttpWebResponse response = DoStorageRequest(
                                containerName ,
                            "PUT",
                            headers,
                            null /*No data*/,
                            null /* No content type*/);

    bool ret = false;

    switch (response.StatusCode)
    {
        case HttpStatusCode.Created:
            // Returned HTTP 201. Container created as expected
            ret = true;
            break;

        default:
            //Unexpected status code.
            // Throw exception with description from HTTP
            // Note that a 409 conflict WebException means that
            // the container already exists
            throw new Exception(response.StatusDescription);
            break;
    }

    return ret;

}
```

That wasn't so difficult, was it? Note the line where it called **DoStoreRequest** and specified **PUT**. This function, **DoStoreRequest**, is where the meat of the action is (but you haven't written it yet). It takes the path you want to make the request to as a parameter, along with the HTTP method to use in the request. Custom headers are passed in the form of a **Dictionary** object. It then constructs the right URL using some plain old string concatenation, and makes an HTTP request. In this case, since you are creating a container, you pass a **PUT** to specify that you want to create one. Example 7-3 shows a first cut at this method. Insert this inside the **BlobStorage** class as well.

Example 7-3. Constructing requests to storage

```
    private HttpWebResponse
DoStorageRequest(string resourcePath, string httpMethod,
            Dictionary<string,string> metadataHeaders, byte[] data, string
contentType)
        {
        // Create request object for
        //http://<accountname>.blob.core.windows.net/<resourcepath>
```

```
        string url = "http://" + this.AccountName + "." +
                     this.Host + "/" + resourcePath;

        HttpWebRequest request = (HttpWebRequest)WebRequest.Create(url);
        request.Method = httpMethod;

        request.ContentLength = (data == null? 0: data.Length);
        request.ContentType = contentType;

        //Add x-ms-date header. This should be in RFC 1123 format,i.e.,
        //of the form Sun, 28 Jan 2008 12:11:37 GMT
        //This is done by calling DateTime.ToString("R")

        request.Headers.Add(HeaderDate,
            DateTime.UtcNow.ToString("R", CultureInfo.InvariantCulture));

        //Add custom headers to request's headers
        if (metadataHeaders != null)
        {
            foreach (string key in metadataHeaders.Keys)
            {
                request.Headers.Add(
                    key,
                    metadataHeaders[key]
                    );
            }
        }

        // Get authorization header value by signing request
        string authHeader = SignRequest(request);

        //Add authorization header. This is of the form
        // Authorization:SharedKey <accountname>:<authHeader>

        request.Headers.Add("Authorization",
                            "SharedKey " + this.AccountName
                            + ":" + authHeader);

        //Write data if any. Data is only present when uploading blobs,
        //table entities or queue messages
        if (data != null)
        {
            request.GetRequestStream().Write(data, 0, data.Length);
        }




        //Make HTTP request and return response object
        return (HttpWebResponse)request.GetResponse();
    }
```

That was a bit more code than you've seen so far, so let's walk through this in sequence. First, you declare a method that accepts several arguments: a resource path, the HTTP method to use, and any custom headers and data to pass in. You must then create the right path for the resource. Thankfully, that's quite simple for containers. Just take the root account path (*accountname*.blob.core.windows.net) and append the container name/resource path after it.

Let's skip over the lines that are related to authentication for now. (You'll learn more about this in the next section.)

The last few lines make the actual request to the server. This returns a response object that contains the results of the operation. If the operation succeeds, this will contain an HTTP **2xx** code. If it fails, it will contain an error code with an XML blob containing information on why it failed.

So, what is that mysterious authentication header in the middle? If you removed those lines, you would have the right URL and all the other headers correct, but your request would fail. Let's explore that in a bit more detail.

Understanding Authentication and Request Signing

Signing the headers is arguably the most important part of writing a storage client library. Using the description of the URLs, you could make requests to your storage account. However, those requests won't succeed because they haven't been signed with either your primary or secondary key.

You might be wondering at this point why you have all these keys to manage. What's wrong with a good old username and password, and using HTTP Basic/Digest authentication like everyone else?

The answer lies in future flexibility. You may not always want to give everyone your password. For example, you may want others to access your account with your keys, but you want to limit them to a subset of all possible operations. Or you may want to give them access to your data, but charge them for each access. Another common scenario is when you want Microsoft to charge your customers directly for all the data bandwidth and storage that you handle for them. None of these features exist today, but they're possible only with the flexibility of this scheme. Another important reason is that these keys are easier to regenerate than passwords that tie into your identity on the site. So, it's somewhat safer to embed these in tools/scripts/sites, rather than having to fork over your password.

 If you're familiar with Amazon's authentication mechanisms for Amazon Web Services (AWS), a lot of this will look similar to you. There are some major differences (such as the actual algorithm used), so even if you've written code against Amazon, you should still read through this discussion.

So, how do you use these keys? Every request you make to the storage service has a URL that it acts against, and headers that get included with the request. You use the key to sign the request, and embed the signature in the request as a header. Even if the actual request were intercepted, an attacker cannot recover your private key from the request. Since the date and time is part of the request, an attacker cannot use it to make further requests as well. Of course, all this security is valid only if your private keys stay private. If someone else has access to your keys, the proverbial jig is up. She can then make requests as you, which will be charged to your credit card or method of payment for Azure services.

 Microsoft has access to your keys as well. This may scare you a bit—why does Microsoft have access to the keys to my data? This is standard practice in these cloud storage systems. As you have learned, cloud computing involves a trust relationship with the vendor. It is up to you to decide whether you're OK with this, depending on how sensitive your data is.

Using the Signing Algorithm

Let's walk through the process for creating a signature, and then examine some code that does the same thing:

1. You must construct an HTTP header of the form `Authorization="SharedKey {Account_Name}:{Signature}"` and embed the header in the final request that goes over the wire to the storage service.

2. You start with a few important components of the request:

   a. The HTTP method name (`GET`/`PUT`/`HEAD`/`POST`).

   b. The MD5 hash of the data being uploaded. (This ensures that the signature doesn't match if the data is corrupted along the way. This is an optional header; if you don't want to specify this, just insert an empty line.)

   c. The MIME type of the data and the date. (Again, this can be empty. When you create a container, no data is being uploaded, so there is no MIME type.)

3. You then must construct a *canonicalized* form of the custom headers. This is a fancy way of saying that you must consolidate all the headers that start with `x-ms-`. You do that by sorting all the custom headers lexicographically, and then consolidating repeating headers into one.

4. You finally construct something called the *canonicalized resource*, which is nothing but the account name concatenated with the path of the resource you want to access.

In short, the algorithm just described can be shortened to the following:

```
StringToSign = VERB + "\n" +
               Content-MD5 + "\n" +
               Content-Type + "\n" +
               Date + "\n" +
```

```
                CanonicalizedHeaders +
                CanonicalizedResource;
```

Once you have the string you need to sign, the actual process of signing is quite trivial. You create a base64-encoded HMAC-SHA256 hash of the string that is cryptographically secure. That is quite a bit of work. Example 7-4 shows the code required to do this. Insert this method in the BlobStorage class as well.

Example 7-4. Generating authentication header

```
    private string SignRequest(HttpWebRequest request)
    {
        StringBuilder  stringToSign = new StringBuilder();

        //First element is the HTTP method - GET/PUT/POST/etc.
        stringToSign.Append(request.Method  + "\n");

        //The second element is the MD5 hash of the data. This
        // is optional so we can insert an empty line here.
        stringToSign.Append("\n");


        //Append content type of the request
        stringToSign.Append(request.ContentType + "\n");

        //Append date. Since we always add the
        // x-ms-date header, this can be an empty string.
        stringToSign.Append("\n");

        // Construct canonicalized headers.

        // Note that this doesn't implement
        // parts of the specification like combining header fields with the
        // same name , unfolding long lines or trimming white spaces.

        // Look for header names that start with x-ms
        // Then sort them in case-insensitive manner.
        List<string> httpStorageHeaderNameArray = new List<string>();
        foreach (string key in request.Headers.Keys)
        {
            if (key.ToLowerInvariant().StartsWith(HeaderPrefixMS,
            StringComparison.Ordinal))
            {
                httpStorageHeaderNameArray.Add(key.ToLowerInvariant());
            }
        }

        httpStorageHeaderNameArray.Sort();

        // Now go through each header's values in sorted order
        // and append them to the canonicalized string.
        // At the end of this, you should have a bunch of headers of the
        // form x-ms-somekey:value
        // x-ms-someotherkey:othervalue
        foreach (string key in httpStorageHeaderNameArray)
```

```
        {
            stringToSign.Append(key + ":" + request.Headers[key] + "\n");
        }

        // Finally, add canonicalized resources
        // This is done by prepending a '/' to the
        // account name and resource path.

        stringToSign.Append("/" + this.AccountName +
        request.RequestUri.AbsolutePath);

        // We now have a constructed string to sign.
        //We now need to generate a HMAC SHA256 hash using
        // our secret key and base64 encode it.

        byte[] dataToMAC =
        System.Text.Encoding.UTF8.GetBytes(stringToSign.ToString());

        using (HMACSHA256 hmacsha256 = new HMACSHA256(this.SecretKey))
        {
            return Convert.ToBase64String(hmacsha256.ComputeHash(dataToMAC));
        }

}
```

This code essentially follows the algorithm outlined previously. It starts by adding the HTTP method, the ContentType, and an empty line for the hash, all separated by newlines.

The code then loops through all the headers, looking through header keys that start with x-ms-. When it finds them, it pulls them into a list. You now have all the custom headers you have added to the list. The code then sorts the list lexicographically through the built-in list sort function.

You then construct a long string of concatenated custom headers and their values. It is important that this be in the exact format that the server expects, but it is easy to go wrong here.

If you read the algorithm's specification, you'll find that a few shortcuts have been taken here. In real-world usage, you'll need to check for duplicate headers and for whitespace between values, and deal with them accordingly. After this, constructing the canonical resource path is quite simple. You take the account name and concatenate with the path to the resource.

Whew! You now have a string that you can sign. Just to be on the safe side, the code converts the string to UTF8 encoding. The code can then sign it. Signing involves taking the secret key and using the HMAC-SHA256 algorithm to generate a digest. This is a binary digest, and you convert it into HTTP-friendly form using base64 encoding.

If you're following along with implementing the storage client library for some new language/platform, you might get tripped up at this point. Some mainstream languages don't have support for SHA-256 (the HMAC part is trivial to implement). For example, you would have to figure out an SHA-256 implementation as well as an HMAC implementation to get an Erlang version of this library (available at *http://github .com/sriramk/winazureerl/*). Obviously, spending long nights reading and debugging through cryptographic algorithms is no fun. On the other hand, it makes your requests safer.

You now have a signed header that is good to go. On the server side, the Windows Azure storage service goes through the exact same process and generates a signature. It checks to see whether the signature you generated matches the one it computed. If it doesn't, it throws a 403 error.

Debugging these errors when writing your own storage clients can be quite painful, because several things could go wrong. When debugging the storage clients, you should step through a storage client implementation that you know is reliable, and compare intermediate values at every step of the process.

Creating and Uploading Stuff

You now have a container for uploading stuff, so let's do just that—upload stuff. After the infrastructure you've built, the act of uploading a blob is a bit of an anticlimax in its simplicity. In short, you simply must do an HTTP PUT to the right URL, and send the data you want to upload as part of the HTTP request.

Example 7-5 shows a small helper method to do that. It's interesting how small this is. The reason each additional bit of functionality you add is so small is because most of the heavy lifting is done in the core parts of signing and forming the right path to the resource. Once you have that finished, the rest of the features are quite simple to write.

Example 7-5. PUT blob

```
public bool CreateBlob(string containerName, string blobName,
                 byte[] data, string contentType)
{
    HttpWebResponse response = DoStorageRequest(
                         containerName + "/" + blobName,
                         "PUT",
                         null, /* No extra headers */
                         data,
                         contentType);

    bool ret = false;

    switch (response.StatusCode)
```

```
        {
            case HttpStatusCode.Created:
                // Returned HTTP 201. Blob created as expected
                ret = true;
                break;

            default:
                //Unexpected status code.
                // Throw exception with description from HTTP
                throw new Exception(response.StatusDescription);
                break;
        }

        return ret;

    }
```

You can now make requests to create a container and upload a sample blob. This is a small text file containing the string "Hello world!". Since it is a text file, you set the ContentType to "text/plain". Replace your blank implementation of Main with the following code. Replace the string *USERNAME* with your username, and the string *KEY* with your storage key:

```
class Program
    {
        static void Main(string[] args)
        {
            BlobStorage storage = new BlobStorage(
        "USERNAME", "KEY");
            storage.CreateContainer("testnetclient", true);
            storage.CreateBlob("testnetclient", "helloworld.txt",
                           System.Text.Encoding.UTF8.GetBytes(
                           "Hello world!"),
                           "text/plain");
        }
    }
```

 This code tries to create the container without checking whether it already exists. Windows Azure storage returns a 409 error code and a message if the container already exists. More robust code will check the list of containers to ensure that you are not attempting to re-create existing containers. You'll learn how to list containers and parse the list when we examine blobs in detail in Chapter 8. Also, note that the creation of the blob doesn't have any such checking. Windows Azure will always honor a request to create a blob, regardless of whether it exists.

You can now access this file over normal HTTP. Open a web browser and go to *http://<username>.blob.core.windows.net/test/helloworld.txt*. You should see the text file you just uploaded to blob storage. Congratulations! You've uploaded your first bits into the Microsoft cloud.

Using the SDK and Development Storage

All the storage code you've written so far has been code that works directly against the cloud. However, you'll probably not be developing your applications that way. During the development cycle, it doesn't make sense to spend money by talking to the cloud on each iteration of the edit-compile-debug cycle. It also makes development a pain from a performance perspective, because you're always going over the wire to a Microsoft data center. And finally, it blocks development if you don't have an Internet connection.

You'll probably spend most of your development time using the tools/code that ships with the SDK, and the cloud storage simulator (creatively called Development Storage) that ships as part of the SDK. In short, the Development Storage (or the Dev Storage) provides most of the features and APIs of the actual cloud services. However, it doesn't provide the performance or scalability, so you'll always need to test your final code in the cloud. There are also several minor differences between how features work in the Dev Storage and how they work in the cloud, which could lead to some gnarly debugging sessions if you weren't aware of them upfront.

 Go to *http://windows.azure.com* to find a link to the SDK download.

Installation and Prerequisites

Though installing the actual SDK is fairly straightforward, there are a couple of "gotchas" that you need to keep in mind. Some of this currently isn't very well documented, and the installer may not check for all the prerequisites.

- You'll need .NET 3.5 SP1 installed. The "SP1" part trips up a lot of people because, as of this writing, this was not widely installed. Without this, you will not be able to use ADO.NET Data Services.

- Ensure that you have a SQL Express instance installed and running with the default instance name. The Dev Storage runs backed by SQL Server and, by default, looks for a SQL Express instance. It is possible to point the Dev Storage to a normal SQL Server instance, but it's not recommended. Any version of SQL Express should do—either 2005 or 2008.

- If you plan to use Visual Studio to write code, use Visual Studio 2008 and have the latest service pack installed. As of this writing, that was SP1.

- Install IIS7 with Windows Communication Foundation (WCF) activation turned on. This is required more for the hosted services part of Windows Azure, but it is good to get all the prerequisites out of the way. This rules out Windows XP as a development platform, because IIS7 works only on Windows Vista/Windows 2003 and later.

- If possible, try to use a 64-bit operating system and the 64-bit version of the SDKs. This is a purely personal preference, and the 32-bit versions provide the same functionality. You should make your development environment as close as possible to your production environment, so you might try to spend as much time developing on an x64 box as possible.

If you're like me, you probably install an SDK and then scour through the Start menu to try to find what to launch. However, you should ensure that you unzip *samples.zip* in the SDK installation folder, as well as getting the additional samples from *http://code .msdn.microsoft.com/windowsazuresamples*. This will provide some helpful samples and Cloud Drive, an invaluable tool for debugging and interacting with storage.

Using Cloud Drive

Cloud Drive is a useful tool that Windows Azure ships as a part of its extended samples. It is a PowerShell add-in that lets you interact with blob and queue storage (sorry—not table storage) as though they were a locally mounted drive. Don't worry if you don't know PowerShell in and out; you can use a minimal set of DOS commands.

Running Cloud Drive is simple. Open a command prompt and run the *runme.cmd* file in the Cloud Drive folder. It'll build the Cloud Drive code and mount two "PowerShell providers" corresponding to blob and queue storage, respectively.

```
D:\windowsazure\v1.0\samples\CloudDrive>runme
Starting DevStore
****Starting PowerShell prompt ****
To switch to Blob drive: cd Blob:
To display the contents: dir
...

Name        Provider     Root
----        --------     ----
Blob        BlobDrive    http://blob.core.windows.net
Queue       QueueDrive   http://127.0.0.1:10001


PS D:\windowsazure\v1.0\samples\CloudDrive>
```

 By default, the drives act as a layer on top of the Dev Storage. However, you can easily switch this to point to your actual cloud storage account by modifying *MountDrive.ps1* in the *scripts* directory and switching the $Account, $Key, and $ServiceUrl variables accordingly.

Interacting with the drives is quite simple. Containers are simulated as directories, so you can cd into them as you would with normal folders. The one thing you cannot do is to view contents from directly within the `Blob/Queue` drive. To do that, you must copy the actual blob/queue message into a filesystem path, and then view it there. Example 7-6 shows how to switch into the `Blob` drive and then show a listing of all the containers. It then copies over *hello.txt* into a local drive for easy viewing.

Example 7-6. Switching into the Blob drive

```
PS Blob:\> dir


    Parent: CloudDriveSnapin\BlobDrive::http:\\blob.core.windows.net\

Type        Size        LastWriteTimeUtc            Name
----        ----        ----------------            ----
Container               5/9/2009 7:35:00 PM         foo
Container               4/19/2009 9:33:36 AM        test


PS Blob:\> cd test
PS Blob:\test> dir


    Parent: CloudDriveSnapin\BlobDrive::http:\\blob.core.windows.net\test

Type        Size        LastWriteTimeUtc            Name
----        ----        ----------------            ----
Blob        7           5/9/2009 7:21:36 PM         hello.txt


PS Blob:\test> copy-cd hello.txt d:\hello.txt
```

Using the Development Storage

The Development Storage (Dev Storage) is a local simulator of the blob, table, and queue storage services. It uses SQL Server to do the actual storing and querying. Hence, you need a SQL Server instance installed and running.

 The Dev Storage uses Windows authentication to create a database in your SQL instance. You must ensure that the user account under which you launch the Dev Storage has the right privileges set up on the SQL Server instance.

Running the Dev Storage is quite simple. You can directly launch it from the Start menu, or have it automatically launched by Visual Studio when you press F5 on a cloud project.

By default, it tries to listen on *http://127.0.0.1* and ports 10000, 10001, and 10002 for blobs, queues, and tables, respectively. If it finds the ports already in use, it'll grab the next available port.

When using the Dev Storage, there are a few differences that you should be aware of. Though it is very similar to the cloud storage service, there are a few caveats. As always, ensure that you test against the actual cloud before deploying to production.

- The Dev Storage supports only one account and key (`devstoreaccount1` found in the samples). You must use your configuration files and change which account name/credentials you use, depending on whether you're running in the cloud.

- You cannot use the Dev Storage for any sort of performance testing. Since the underlying store and implementation are completely different, performance testing against development storage is next to useless.

- The Dev Storage can be accessed only from the local machine on which it is run. You can work around this by using a port redirector so that multiple developers/ computers can get access to a shared instance of the Dev Storage for testing.

- Sizes and date ranges are different, since the underlying data store is SQL Server. For example, blobs can only be up to 2 GB in the Dev Storage.

Summary

Everyone's jumping onto the cloud storage bandwagon. Microsoft's API is similar to the others, but with a layer of tools and utilities on top. If you're a developer who likes to get your hands dirty with wire protocols and hack your own networking clients over a weekend, you'll feel right at home.

One thing conspicuously and intentionally missing from this chapter is code with the official Microsoft storage library. You'll be seeing a lot of that over the next few chapters, but it is important to understand that it is just a thin wrapper over the raw HTTP infrastructure you saw in this chapter. There are several other community-supported implementations, and it is perfectly fine to roll your own.

## CHAPTER 8

Blobs

Author William Gibson once wrote a short story titled "Johnny Mnemonic" that appeared in a 1981 issue of *Omni* magazine. The story centers on the premise that the human brain is one of nature's best storage devices. It has incredibly small seek latencies, and can store almost infinite amounts of data, meaning, of course, that you could potentially use your brain as like a giant hard disk.

In the story, Johnny Mnemonic is a "data trafficker," someone who has undergone cybernetic surgery and can carry digital data in his head. Instead of sending sensitive data over the Internet, you would send Johnny physically to the receiver, who would then pull data out of Johnny's head by using a password that only the receiver would know.

The idea of a near-infinite storage device is alluring: stick data in all the time and don't worry about running out of capacity. Even better, with Johnny Mnemonic, you would know your data is protected (in this case, by the password mechanism), and you would have the inherent physical security of Johnny not being connected to the Internet.

That is *blob storage* in a nutshell: having infinite space to store any kind of data. This chapter leaves the fictional world of Johnny Mnemonic and introduces you to the infinite possibilities associated with blob storage in the real world of Azure.

Understanding the Blob Service

Blobs by themselves are quite dumb and boring to anyone not interested in the cloud. A *blob* is a binary large object. It is any arbitrary piece of data, of any format or size, and with any content. It can be an image, a text file, a *.zip* file, a video, or just about any arbitrary sequence of ones and zeros.

The name "blob" was coined by Jim Starkey at DEC. He resisted pressure from various quarters (especially marketing) to rename the concept to something "friendlier." He claims the expansion "binary large object" was invented much later because marketing found "blob" unprofessional. Visit *http://www.cvalde.net/misc/blob_true_history.htm* for the full story.

Blobs become interesting when you look at how they're used. Similarly, the data that makes up YouTube's videos (the actual bits on disk) aren't interesting, but the funny videos they make up can be valuable. A good blob/data storage mechanism must be dumb and basic, and leave all the smartness to the application.

The Windows Azure blob service allows you to store nearly unlimited amounts of data for indefinite periods of time. All data stored in the service is replicated multiple times (to protect against hardware failure), and the service is designed to be highly scalable and available. As of this writing, the internals of how this blob service works hadn't been made public, but the principles this service follows are similar to the distributed systems that came before it. The best part is that you can pay as you go, and pay only for the data you have up in the cloud. Instead of having to sign a check for storage you may or may not use, you pay Microsoft only for what you used during the preceding billing cycle.

Using Blobs

Blobs are an important part of Windows Azure because they are just so useful. Unlike hosted services (where you have to write code), or tables and queues (where they're part of a bigger application and some code is again involved), blobs can be used for a lot of day-to-day computer tasks. Here's a short sample list:

- Performing backup/archival/storage in the cloud
- Hosting images or other website content
- Hosting videos
- Handling arbitrary storage needs
- Hosting blogs or static websites

The list could go on, but you get the idea. So, when should you think of taking the blob storage plunge? The answer to that question depends on a few candidate scenarios you should keep in mind.

Filesystem replacement

Any large data that doesn't have schema and doesn't require querying is a great candidate for blob storage. In other words, any data for which you use a filesystem today (not a database) can be moved easily to blob storage. In fact, you'll find that several filesystem concepts map almost 1:1 to blobs, and there are several tools to help you move from one to the other.

Most organizations or services have an NFS/SMB share that stores some unstructured data. Typically, databases don't play well with large unstructured data in them, so developers code up a scheme in which the database contains pointers to actual physical files lying on a share somewhere. Now, instead of having to maintain that filesystem, you can switch to using blob storage.

Heavily accessed data

Large data that is sent as is to users without modification is another type of good content to stick in blob storage. Since Windows Azure blob storage is built to be highly scalable, you can be sure that a sudden influx of users won't affect access.

Backup server

Although you may be unable to leave your current filesystem/storage system, you can still find a way to get some good use out of blob storage. Everyone needs a backup service. For example, home users often burn DVDs, and corporations often ship tapes off to a remote site to facilitate some sort of backup. Having a cheap and effective way to store backups is surprisingly tricky. Blob storage fits nicely here. Instead of using tape backups, you could store a copy of your data in blob storage (or several copies, if you're paranoid).

The fact that cloud storage is great for backups isn't lost on the multiple product vendors making backup software. Several backup applications now use either Amazon S3 or Windows Azure. For example, Live Mesh from Microsoft uses blob storage internally to store and synchronize data from users' machines.

File-share in the cloud

Employees at Microsoft often must share files, documents, or code with other employees. SharePoint is one alternative, and that is often utilized. But the easiest way to share some debug logs or some build binaries is to create a share on your local machine and open access to it. Since most Microsoft employees have reasonably powerful machines, you don't have to worry about several employees accessing the data at the same time and slowing down your machine. Since file shares can be accessed with a UNC name, you can email links around easily.

Blob storage is similar. Want to throw up something on the Web and give other people access to it? Don't know how many users will wind up accessing it, but just want something that stays up? Blob storage is great for that. Windows Azure blob storage is a great means to throw up arbitrary data and give it a permanent home on the Internet, be it large public datasets, or just a funny video.

Pricing

In Chapter 7, you learned how pricing works across the Windows Azure storage services. In short, Windows Azure charges $0.15 per gigabyte per month stored, $0.01 for every 10,000 storage transactions, and $0.10 for ingress and $0.15 for egress bandwidth.

Though this pricing model applies equally across all of Windows Azure's storage services, blobs have some interesting properties. Most importantly, blobs are the only service for which anonymous requests over public HTTP are allowed (if you choose to make your container public). Both queues and tables (which you'll learn more about in the next few chapters) must have requests authenticated at all times. Of course, without anonymous requests, a lot of the things that people use blobs for—hosting images, static websites, and arbitrary files, and exposing them to any HTTP client—won't work anymore.

However, given that anonymous requests get billed (both for transaction cost and for bandwidth cost), a potential risk is a malicious user (or a sudden surge in visitors) that results in a huge storage bill for you. There is really no good way to protect against this, and this issue generally exists with almost all cloud services.

Data Model

The data model for the Windows Azure blob service is quite simple, and a lot of the flexibility stems from this simplicity. There are essentially three kinds of "things" in the system:

- Blob
- Container
- Storage account

Figure 8-1 shows the relationship between the three.

Blob

In Windows Azure, a blob is any piece of data. Importantly, blobs have a key or a name with which they are referred to. You might think of blobs as files. Despite the fact that there are places where that analogy breaks down, it is still a useful rule of thumb. Blobs can have metadata associated with them, which are `<name,value>` pairs and are up to 8 KB in size.

Blobs come in two flavors: *block blobs* and *page blobs*. Let's look at block blobs first.

Block blobs can be split into chunks known as *blocks*, which can then be uploaded separately. The typical usage for blocks is for streaming and resuming uploads. Instead of having to restart that multigigabyte transfer from the beginning, you can just resume

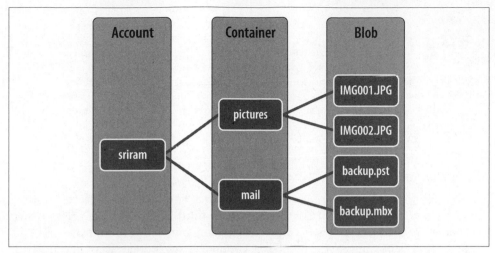

Figure 8-1. Relationship between blobs, containers, and storage accounts

from the next block. You can also upload blocks in parallel, and have the server constitute a blob out of them. Block blobs are perfect for streaming upload scenarios.

The second flavor is page blobs. Page blobs are split into an array of pages. Each page can be addressed individually, not unlike sectors on a hard disk. Page blobs are targeted at random read/write scenarios and provide the backing store for Windows Azure XDrive. You'll see more about them later.

Container

Blobs are stored in things called *containers*, which you can think of as partitions or root directories. Containers exist only to store a collection of blobs, and can have only a little metadata (8 KB) associated with them.

Apart from containing blobs, containers serve one other important task. Containers control sharing policy. You can make containers either *public* or *private*, and all blobs underneath the container will inherit that setting. When a container is public, anyone can read data from that container over public HTTP. When a container is private, only authenticated API requests can read from the container. Regardless of whether a container is public or private, any creation, modification, or deletion operations must be authenticated.

One authentication option that isn't covered in this chapter is preauthorized URIs or "signed URLs." This refers to the ability to create a special URL that allows users to perform a particular operation on a blob or a container for a specified period of time. This is useful in scenarios where you can't put the storage access key in your code—for example, client-side web apps. See *http://msdn.microsoft.com/en-us/library/ ee395415.aspx* for details on how to use this.

For users familiar with Amazon's S3, containers are not the same as S3's buckets. Containers are not a global resource; they "belong" to a single account. This means you can create containers in your code's critical path, and the storage system will be able to keep up. Deletion of a container is also instant. One "gotcha" to keep in mind is that re-creation of a container just deleted might be delayed. The reason is that the storage service must delete all the blobs that were in the container (or, more accurately, put the garbage-collection process in motion), and this takes a small amount of processing time.

Storage account

Finally, all containers are placed in a *storage account*. You saw how to create these and assign them to geolocations in Chapter 7. You can think of these as the "drives" where you place containers. A storage account can have any number of containers—as of this writing, there is no limit on the number of containers any storage account can have.

The containers also inherit the parent storage account's geolocation setting. If you specify that the storage account should be in the South Central United States, all containers under the account will show up in the same location, and by the same transitive relationship, all blobs under those containers will show up in the South Central United States as well.

Usage Considerations

Moving to using blob storage can be tricky at times. The differences between Windows Azure blob storage and a normal filesystem are significant, and though smaller, there are also significant differences between Azure blobs and other cloud blob services such as Amazon's S3.

These issues are amplified by how similar all these services are. Windows Azure blobs make every blob look like a file, but you must keep in mind that, at the bottom, they're not files, and that there are differences. Similarly, users of other cloud storage services expect similar design patterns and architecture to work unmodified, and they consequently run into "gotchas" because of underlying differences.

Let's take a look at some characteristics of blob storage that often trip up users.

Requests Could Fail

Think about a typical file server. It is sitting in a corner somewhere (or on a rack) connected by a gigabit Ethernet connection to your server running your application. Now, think about the same scenario when your application talks to Windows Azure blob storage.

First, blob storage is spread out over several hundred (if not thousand) individual nodes, and a lot more networking magic is happening. Also, if your application is not hosted on Windows Azure, you must make several networking hops to even get to the Windows Azure data centers and talk to blob storage. As anyone who has spent time in networking can tell you, requests can fail from time to time. Even if your application is hosted on Windows Azure, you might see blips if you're hosted on different data centers, or even in the same data center, because of network/software issues.

These errors can manifest in several forms. Timeout errors can show up when there is an issue between your code and the Windows Azure data centers. Errors can occur even when the request reaches Windows Azure—the service might be experiencing an outage or might experience an internal error. Your application must be resilient to such errors. The right way to deal with these errors is to back off and retry the request. When you see repeated errors and you're confident that this isn't an issue in your code, you should exponentially back off and try with longer and longer delays.

Timeout errors could show up when transferring large amounts of data in a single request. When dealing with large blobs, split interactions with them into smaller chunks. When uploading a big blob, split it into multiple blocks. When reading a large blob, use HTTP range requests, and keep track of progress so that you can resume reading a blob if you experience an error.

Finally, if you consistently see errors, contact Microsoft, since this could be caused by a bug in the blob service itself, or by an ongoing outage with Windows Azure. You can look at the status of the various Windows Azure services at *http://www.microsoft.com/windowsazure/support/status/servicedashboard.aspx*. These are extremely rare, but they do happen!

Changes Are Reflected Instantly

If you haven't used any other cloud storage service, you can safely skip this discussion. If you are familiar with other cloud storage services, you have probably dealt with some of them being eventually consistent. Essentially, changes you make take some time to propagate. The Windows Azure blob service is different in that all changes are reflected instantly. Whatever your operation—creating a blob or a container, writing data, or deleting a blob or a container—every client accessing your storage account will see those changes instantly.

This does not necessarily mean that your data is deleted from Windows Azure's disks instantly. Windows Azure reflects changes instantly, so when you delete a blob or a container, no one can access it. However, space is recovered lazily, so your data will be deleted eventually. However, this delay is very short, so you don't need to worry about your data lingering on Microsoft's servers.

Compressed Content

You may often want to compress content to reduce bandwidth costs and to improve performance. Fewer bytes sent over the wire means less time spent in the network. Typically, you do this by enabling an option on your web server. However, the Windows Azure blob service doesn't support compressing content on the fly.

In other words, you can't make it gzip-compress bytes as it serves them. One workaround you can use is to compress content before you store it in Windows Azure blob storage. Later in this chapter, you'll learn how to do this in a manner where browsers can automatically decompress this data.

Using the Blob Storage API

Like all of the Windows Azure storage services, the blob storage service is accessible over a highly available, publicly accessible REST API. Let's take a look at how this works with the blob storage API.

All API access is through HTTP operations on a storage account URI. For the Windows Azure blob storage service, that URI is of the form *http://<accountname>.blob.core.windows.net/<container-name>/<blob-name>*. For example, when accessing *http://sriramk.blob.core.windows.net/test/helloworld.txt* (you can go ahead and access that URI in your browser now), "sriramk" is the storage account, "test" is the container, and "helloworld.txt" is the name of the blob.

API access falls into two categories:

Authenticated
> Any operation that creates, modifies, or deletes anything must be authenticated. In short, you sign the request with an HMAC of your secret key, which the storage service verifies on its side by trying to construct the same signature.

Unauthenticated
> Unauthenticated requests are allowed for read operations if the container they're operating on has "full public read access" turned on or read access for blobs turned on (the other visibility option, "no public read access"). These requests can just be normal HTTP GETs, and can be issued from any dumb HTTP client (browsers are the key consumers here). Sometimes you might find yourself being forced to make a container public if your client of choice doesn't support modifying HTTP headers. An example would be early Silverlight versions that didn't support adding headers and, hence, users couldn't perform authenticated requests. Shared access signatures are useful in this case.

When you access *http://sriramk.blob.core.windows.net/test/helloworld.txt* through code, the URI goes through some DNS redirection and resolves to an IP address in a Microsoft data center; e.g., the previous example machine called *sriramk.blob.core.windows.net* currently would redirect to *blob.sn1prodc.store.core.windows.net* through a DNS CNAME, and resolve to 70.37.127.110.

> It is important to not store these directly in your code, and to always deal with only the properly formatted URIs. These DNS redirects and IP addresses are internal implementation details, and can change from time to time. In fact, the DNS redirection did change when support for multiple geolocations was added.

Using the Storage Client Library

Though you can roll your own client library using the REST API, if you're a .NET developer, you'll find yourself using the official Microsoft storage client library most of the time. Let's look at some conventions used throughout the library and some common setup you'll need to do.

The official library is a part of the SDK and is contained in the `Microsoft.WindowsAzure.StorageClient.dll` assembly. Figure 8-2 shows some of the assembly open in Visual Studio's Object Explorer and displays some of the types inside.

The type that all your code will start with is `CloudStorageAccount`. This wraps around your account name, your credentials, as well as the endpoints to find the Windows Azure storage endpoints (since you may be talking to the Microsoft cloud, or using the local Dev Storage).

> If you're developing against the Dev Storage, you might find the preinstantiated `CloudStorageAccount.DevelopmentStorageAccount` object handy. This performs the right magic to talk to the local Dev Storage instance.

A quick and easy way to set up a `CloudStorageAccount` which talks to the public code is through a code snippet such as the one shown in Example 8-1, which uses the `StorageCredentialsAccountAndKey` type to instantiate a new `CloudStorageAccount`.

Example 8-1. Creating a CloudStorageAccount

```
StorageCredentialsAccountAndKey storageCredentialsAccountAndKey =
new StorageCredentialsAccountAndKey("YourAccountName",
        "YourAccountKey");
CloudStorageAccount cloudStorageAccount =
 new CloudStorageAccount(storageCredentialsAccountAndKey, true);
```

Creating your `CloudStorageAccount` objects in this manner is quite inflexible. In a real-world application, you don't want to hardcode your credentials this way; you want them to be configurable at runtime. To do that, you need to use the storage library's support for connection strings.

Figure 8-2. Microsoft.WindowsAzure.StorageClient open in the Object Explorer

Connection strings are a short string format that lets you encode several properties for your storage account as well as for the storage library. You can specify it in a configuration file and have the storage library parse it.

A typical connection string in a configuration file looks like the following snippet. Note how it encodes not only the account name and key, but also an additional property; in this case, using Secure Sockets Layer (SSL) for all connections made to storage:

```xml
<?xml version="1.0" encoding="utf-8" ?>
<configuration>

  <appSettings>
    <add key="DataConnectionString"
```

```
value ="AccountName=YourAccountName;AccountKey=YourAccountKey;
DefaultEndpointsProtocol=https"/>
   </appSettings>
</configuration>
```

Once you have your connection string set up, you can load it to create a
CloudStorageAccount, as shown here:

```
CloudStorageAccount cloudStorageAccount =
CloudStorageAccount.Parse(ConfigurationSettings.AppSettings["DataConnectionString"]
);
```

Since development storage is used so frequently, the connection string format has a
shorthand specifier for using the Dev Storage that sets up the local endpoints, as well
as the special development storage account. All you need to do is to use the connection
string shown here:

```
"UseDevelopmentStorage=true"
```

See *http://blogs.msdn.com/partlycloudy/archive/2009/12/08/configuring-the-storage-cli
ent-with-connection-strings.aspx* for a good discussion on connection strings, and some
of the more advanced options they support.

Using Containers

As you learned previously, containers contain blobs. But containers cannot contain
other containers. Those two short statements pretty much tell you everything you need
to know about containers.

Containers are the storage-and-organization mechanism. Storage accounts contain
many containers, which in turn contain many blobs (yes, that's a lot of containin' going
on). A good rule of thumb is to think of containers as drives/partitions in your computer
or root directories. They cannot nest, and two can't share the same name. Just as two
different computers can have partitions with the same name or drive letter, containers
in two different storage accounts can have the same name.

Understanding Names and URIs

As mentioned previously, containers are typically accessed through a URI in the form
http://<accountname>.blob.core.windows.net/<container-name>. All blobs must be under a container, so any blob URI you see will include a container name in it.

A container name must be unique within the scope of a particular storage account. A
container name has the following restrictions:

- It must be a valid DNS name.
- It must start with a letter or number, and can contain only letters, numbers, and
  the dash (-) character.

- If it includes the dash character, every dash character must be immediately preceded and followed by a letter or number.
- It must appear in lowercase. Note that when you access a container, URIs can be case-insensitive.
- It must be from 3 to 63 characters long.

 You might be wondering why container names are restricted to being DNS-compatible even though they show up just in the path. The short answer is future design flexibility. By limiting the range of potential names, the storage team can change URIs in the future without breaking users, or asking people to rename their containers.

This has been an issue on other teams and products I've worked on in the past. We typically start off being very open about what names are allowed, and when we want to make a change that demands more restrictions, we suddenly have to deal with making people change names (difficult), or deal with multiple names in the system (more difficult).

At times, you may want your blobs to show up at *http://<accountname>.blob.core.windows.net/<blob-name>* instead of being preceded by the container's name. The most common use for this is for specifying cross-domain access policy files for Flash and Silverlight. Those runtimes look for specific XML files at the root of a domain.

To support this, Windows Azure blobs let you create a special container called $root. Anything you place in this container will show up at the root of the domain without being preceded by the container's name.

Creating a Container

The first step in doing anything useful with blob storage is to create a container. Since all blobs must exist within the scope of a container, you want to set up your containers beforehand.

The easiest place to put container creation code is in your application setup/initialization. You should think of it as the logical equivalent of creating directories on filesystems, or creating database instances.

Since containers aren't a global resource (as in there is no need to keep a container's name unique across storage accounts), there's no global "container lock" that Microsoft has while creating new containers. This, in turn, means that creating containers is quite fast, and if you choose to, you can create containers dynamically through your code without performance hits.

A container is created by sending an authenticated PUT request to a properly formatted storage URI for creating containers. Since all the storage services support HTTPS, you could make the same request over SSL for more security. Note that using SSL brings with it performance issues (since more cryptography is involved), so you should test before using.

The following bit of C# code creates a container. This builds on top of the simple library (instead of using the official Microsoft library) shown in Chapter 7 to show how this works under the hood. (The code to create and sign the request isn't shown here.)

```csharp
public bool CreateContainer(string containerName, bool publicAccess)
{
    Dictionary<string,string> headers = new Dictionary<string,string>();

    if (publicAccess)
    {
        //Public access for container. Set x-ms-prop-publicaccess
        // to true
        // Newer versions of the API support a
        //x-ms-blob-public-access header which lets you choose
        // from container, blob or private access.
        headers[HeaderPrefixProperties + "publicaccess"] = "true";
    }

    // To construct a container, make a PUT request to
    //http://<account>.blob.core.windows.net/mycontainer
    HttpWebResponse response = DoStorageRequest(
                                containerName ,
                                "PUT",
                                headers,
                                null /*No data*/,
                                null /* No content type*/);

    bool ret = false;

    switch (response.StatusCode)
    {
        case HttpStatusCode.Created:
            // Returned HTTP 201. Container created as expected
            ret = true;
            break;

        default:
            //Unexpected status code.
            // Throw exception with description from HTTP
            // Note that a 409 conflict WebException means that
            // the container already exists
            throw new Exception(response.StatusDescription);
            break;
    }

    return ret;

}
```

The best way to understand the storage APIs is to look at what lies under the covers and see what is happening at the HTTP layer. When debugging tricky errors, you'll often find yourself looking at the raw HTTP traffic, so it is a good idea to familiarize yourself with the actual protocol, as opposed to just the client libraries that wrap around the protocol.

 When you look at the traffic for storage requests in this and the following storage-related chapters, you might see minor differences from what is shown in this book. That is because the traffic shown here was captured with a particular version of the Windows Azure storage APIs, but these APIs evolve constantly. The storage client always tries to use the latest version of the Windows Azure storage APIs, and these have differences between versions. The core concepts remain the same, though. Always check the MSDN documentation to see what the latest version supports.

What happened under the covers in this case? There was an HTTP conversation between the client and the Windows Azure blob storage service. What follows is a partial wire capture of the underlying traffic when the **test** container was created. Note that actual hashes and values will be different if you do a wire capture with your own requests.

```
PUT /test HTTP/1.1
x-ms-date: Sat, 09 May 2009 19:36:08 GMT
Authorization: SharedKey sriramk:IqbJkkoKIVKDdRvSM1HaXsIw...
Host: sriramk.blob.core.windows.net
Content-Length: 0
```

 In newer versions of the Windows Azure blob API, this URL now needs the query string ?restype=container tagged onto it.

Let's look at this line by line.

First, you tell the server that you want to PUT to a resource at the path /test. Since this "hangs off" the root path, the server knows you are creating a container. You have an authorization header that contains an HMAC-SHA256 hash of the headers and resources. You then have a line specifying the Host. Since the server hosts multiple accounts (if not all accounts) on the same set of servers, this helps specify which account (in this case, sriramk) you are interested in. Finally, since this is a container creation operation and you are not uploading any data, the actual body of the request doesn't contain any data. You specify that by setting the Content-Length header to 0.

If everything went well (and in this case, it did), you get back a success message as follows:

```
HTTP/1.1 201 Created
Last-Modified: Sat, 09 May 2009 19:35:00 GMT
ETag: 0x8CB9EF4605B9470
Server: Blob Service Version 1.0 Microsoft-HTTPAPI/2.0
x-ms-request-id: 4f3b6fdb-066d-4fc5-b4e8-181j9asd6
Date: Sat, 09 May 2009 19:34:59 GMT
Content-Length: 0
```

Now, let's break down the success message.

First, the server sends down an HTTP 201 message to tell you that it has successfully created the resource. (Remember that any message with codes in the 2xx range means your requests were executed successfully.) Next, the server sends down two headers that both deal with when the resource was last modified. The `Last-Modified` header tells you when the resource was last touched. In this case, it is set to the current time since you are creating it for the first time.

The `ETag` header provides the "version" of the resource. Wherever you see "ETag" in this book, think to yourself, "Aha! There's the version number of the resource." You'll learn about how `ETag`s work shortly. In brief, every time you modify anything in Windows Azure storage, the server assigns it a new "version number" that you can read with the `ETag` header. When you send up a request, you can tell the server (by using the `If-Match` header), "Here's the ETag that was known when the resource was last read." The server will check the `ETag` provided in the request with the latest `ETag` it has stored internally. This ensures that, in case something has changed in the middle (such as another client making a change), the request will fail.

A lot of the HTTP traffic samples you will see have this mysterious `x-ms-request-id` tagged onto them, which doesn't get a lot of mention in the documentation. This is meant for diagnostic purposes. If you have an issue with the storage services and you contact Microsoft support, you'll use this `x-ms-request-id` identifier to help the people troubleshooting your problem see what might have gone wrong with your request.

> The request has a time that is later than the response, which is caused by a clock skew between a local machine and the Microsoft servers. All the storage services allow for up to 15 minutes of skew, so you don't have to worry about your request being rejected because of skew.

Most of you will be writing code using Microsoft's official storage library. For the rest of this chapter and the following chapters, the discussions focus a lot on that library because it is well supported and it supports all the features that the storage services do, which the previous small C# client does not.

So, let's take a look at the same container creation with Microsoft's storage client. The following code shows how to create a container using Microsoft's library:

```
        CloudStorageAccount cloudStorageAccount =
CloudStorageAccount.Parse(ConfigurationSettings.AppSettings["DataConnectionString"]
);
            CloudBlobClient cloudBlobClient =
cloudStorageAccount.CreateCloudBlobClient();

            CloudBlobContainer cloudBlobContainer =
    new CloudBlobContainer("test", cloudBlobClient);
            cloudBlobContainer.Create();
```

If you look at the HTTP traffic while executing this code (remember to switch the data connection string to not use HTTPS), you'll see that it is nearly identical to the traffic you saw with the homebrew C# code.

After executing this code, you have a container that is good to go. But right now, this is a bucket that only you can access. Let's see how to fix that.

Using an Access Policy

Blobs are unique in the Windows Azure storage universe since you can set access control policy on them. You can set three different permissions:

Full public read access
> All container and blob data can be read via anonymous requests. However, containers within the storage account cannot be enumerated.

Public read access for blobs only
> Use this to allow access to blob data, but not data on the containers themselves, or allow the ability to enumerate blobs within the container.

No public read access
> By making the container and blobs private, only authenticated API requests can access data.

If you want public access to your blob (because you want users to view your blob from within their browsers, or for any other reason) you must make your containers public. Note that access control applies only to read requests. For modification, creation, or deletion, you always need authenticated requests, regardless of whether the container is public or private.

 "HIC SVNT DRACONES," or, to use the English translation, "Here be dragons!" Remember that when anyone can access your blob, you're still footing the bill for bandwidth, storage, and transaction costs. Making your containers public is like opening a direct line to your credit card. Be sure that you know the implications first. At a minimum, check your bill regularly for signs of abuse. Microsoft also has customer support to help you in cases of abuse and fraud.

You can set access policy on a container in one of two ways.

The easiest way is to set it when you create a container. If you look at the container we created in Chapter 7, you'll notice that the access control header was added when creating the container. If you don't explicitly make a container public on creation, it defaults to being private. To make a container public on creation, add `x-ms-prop-pub` `licaccess:True` (or "container" or "blob" instead of "True" in newer versions of the API) in the header/value pair to your `PUT` request for creating the container.

The second way to set access policy is to change access policy explicitly. You do that by sending a specially formatted URI, an HTTP `PUT` request with the same `x-ms-prop-` `publicaccess` header that has the value set to `True` for a public container and `False` to make your container private. This URI is of the form *http://<account-name>.blob.core.windows.net/<container-name>?comp=acl*.

You often see the word `comp` in Windows Azure storage's query strings. The `comp` stands for "component," and is typically used on a subresource or a "meta" operation where you're not directly manipulating the object itself.

The following is a sample HTTP request to change the `test` container to private access. (Remember that you must switch the access control back to public access if you want to continue accessing its contents in a browser.)

```
PUT http://sriramk.blob.core.windows.net/test?comp=acl HTTP/1.1

x-ms-version: 2009-04-14
x-ms-date: Sat, 15 Nov 2008 00:42:49 GMT
x-ms-prop-publicaccess: True
Authorization: SharedKey sriramk:V47F2tYLS29MmHPhiR8FyiCny9zO5De3kVSFORYQHmo=
```

Like several other operations in Windows Azure, reading the access policy of a specific container is the exact inverse. You send an HTTP `GET` or `HEAD` to *http://<account-name>.blob.core.windows.net/<container-name>?comp=acl*. The server sends down the `x-ms-prop-publicaccess` header to indicate the current access control policy on that container. Following is a sample response:

```
HTTP/1.1 200 OK

Transfer-Encoding: chunked
x-ms-prop-publicaccess: False
Date: Sat, 15 May 2009 00:28:22 GMT
```

If you're using the Microsoft storage client, you can get it to do this request and parse it for you by calling `BlobContainer.GetContainerAc` `cessControl` on a `BlobContainer` object.

Listing Containers

To list the containers in an account, you send a `GET` request to a URI that specifies the storage account and a `comp=list` parameter. Over the next few chapters, you'll see that all Windows Azure storage APIs share some common idioms. Just like you create something by sending an HTTP `PUT` to a URI, you list "stuff" by appending `?comp=list` to the parent URI. In this case, to list containers in an account, you send an HTTP `GET` to *http://<accountname>.blob.core.windows.net/*. The server sends back a list of containers in the account wrapped in XML.

Following is a sample request:

```
GET http://sriramk.blob.core.windows.net/?comp=list HTTP/1.1
```

In response, the server sends down a list of all the containers. In this example account, the containers are formatted in XML. Following is the response, edited to show only one container:

```
HTTP/1.1 200 OK
Content-Type: application/xml
Server: Blob Service Version 1.0 Microsoft-HTTPAPI/2.0
x-ms-request-id: 1ef2ed0b-ab25-4ca6-b606-bd368667c2f7
Date: Sun, 19 Jul 2009 10:00:24 GMT
Content-Length: 1147

<?xml version="1.0" encoding="utf-8"?>
<EnumerationResults AccountName="http://sriramk.blob.core.windows.net/">
<MaxResults>5000</MaxResults>
<Containers>
 <Container>
  <Name>foo</Name>
  <Url>http://sriramk.blob.core.windows.net/foo</Url>
  <LastModified>Sat, 09 May 2009 19:35:00 GMT</LastModified>
  <Etag>0x8CB9EF4605B9470</Etag>
 </Container>
</Containers>
<NextMarker />
</EnumerationResults>
```

You can achieve the same thing using the storage client library, as shown in the following code:

```
CloudStorageAccount cloudStorageAccount =
    CloudStorageAccount.Parse(ConfigurationSettings.AppSettings
        ["DataConnectionString"]);
CloudBlobClient cloudBlobClient =
cloudStorageAccount.CreateCloudBlobClient();

//Returns an IEnumerable<CloudBlobContainer>

cloudBlobClient.ListContainers();
```

Earlier, you learned about `?comp=list` showing up in a lot of places in the Windows Azure storage API to list "stuff." Since this "stuff" can often be a huge list, the storage

---

API provides a way to both filter and page through results. Since this isn't often used for containers, code samples will not be presented here.

 In case you are interested (and if you're reading this book, you probably are), the official documentation has extensive code samples for all operations discussed here, as well as the rest of the APIs discussed in this book.

Filtering is simple. You add a query parameter named `prefix` to the query string with its value set to a prefix (search) string. The storage service will then return only containers that start with that prefix string. You may never need to do this, but if you wind up in a situation where you're creating thousands of containers, this might be useful.

So, let's now look at the pagination of results. If you look at the XML response from the server, you see two XML elements that were not discussed: `MaxResults` and `NextMarker`. This lets the server show results in chunks, rather than all at once. You specify a `maxresults` in the query string (the default and maximum are both 5,000), and if the number of results exceeds that, the server sends down a `NextMarker`.

You now send yet another request to the server, but this time with a new query parameter (`marker`) set to the value in `NextMarker` that the server sent down. You're essentially telling the server, "This is where you stopped last time. Start from there and continue sending results." You repeat this until you have all the results that the server intended to send you.

Once again, you may never need to use this, because this kicks in only with very large numbers of containers. In any case, most of the storage client libraries (including Microsoft's official library) take care of this under the covers for you.

Using Metadata

Some of you may remember from long ago that one of the characteristics of Visual Basic 6 was that it always provided some sort of escape hatch for you to abuse. My favorite was the `Tag` property on all controls. If you read the documentation, you couldn't have figured out what it was used for. The truth was that it was for those times when you needed to stick some data on a control, but didn't have anywhere else to put it. People would stick in everything from connection strings to fully serialized data objects. Guess what? Windows Azure has its equivalent of the `Tag` property, too.

Just like `comp=list` is the universal method used in Windows Azure to list things, you'll see several parts of the Windows Azure storage service take *metadata* requests. As the name suggests, this specifies some data about the object (in this case, a container). This is typically used as a grab bag of random things where you want to specify extra properties on the container. People have used it to store application-specific access control lists (ACLs), data hashes to protect against corruption, and so on. Let your imagination run wild, as long as it stays under 8 KB.

Metadata is made up of user-defined name/value pairs. To set/add one of them, send an HTTP PUT request with a few special headers to *http://<accountname>.blob.core.windows.net/<container-name>?comp=metadata*. These headers should be of the form x-ms-meta-*name*:*value*, where *name* and *value* are defined by your application. For example, to set the name foo to the value bar and add it to the container's metadata, you would send an HTTP request such as the following:

```
PUT http://sriramk.blob.core.windows.net/mycontainer?comp=metadata HTTP/1.1

x-ms-date: Fri, 14 May 2008 22:50:32 GMT
x-ms-meta-foo: bar
```

To view the current name/value pair headers, send an HTTP GET request to the same URI. You can do the same thing with the Microsoft storage client library using Cloud BlobContainer.Metadata.

Deleting Containers

Deleting a container is very simple. You just need to send an HTTP DELETE to the container's URI. Or in Microsoft storage library parlance, you call CloudBlobContainer.Delete. In either case, though the operation returns instantly, you won't be able to create another container of the same name for a few minutes (or longer, depending on the amount of data the storage system must delete).

 Once you delete a container, the data inside is gone forever, so don't do it unless you really don't want that data anymore. There is no Recycle Bin in the cloud on which to hit "Restore."

Using Blobs

In 1958, U.S. audiences got to see one of the all-time classic campy horror/sci-fi movies. Simply titled *The Blob*, it featured an amorphous creature from outer space that landed on Earth and, not surprisingly, started to wreak havoc (nasty things, those blobs). This movie fittingly (given its overall adherence to every movie cliché in existence) ended with the words "The End," morphing into a question mark.

Fortunately, the blobs discussed here haven't tried to conquer our planet yet. As you have seen throughout this chapter, Windows Azure blobs are quite simple. They're literally just data. They can be text files, MP3s, images, *.zip* files, movies, mapping data, and just about any arbitrary set of bytes you can conjure up.

A single block blob can be up to 200 GB in size, and a single page blob can be up to 1 TB in size. All blobs contain two types of data:

- Raw bytes that make up the blob itself
- Extraneous metadata (such as what you have seen with containers)

With blobs, metadata becomes more useful. You can use metadata to specify content headers on individual blobs, extra metadata such as creation time, and other properties.

As mentioned previously, blobs inherit the access control policy of the containers into which they're placed. To change the access policy, you change the parent container's access policy, or you copy the blob into another container with a different access control policy.

Names and Paths

Blobs are essentially *key-value pairs*, but the storage system offers you some convenient options. What is meant by a "key-value pair"? Blobs have names (the "key"). This name can be up to 1,024 characters in length. The only restriction is that they should all be valid when made part of a URI (so you need to properly escape reserved characters).

Now, a key-value naming scheme means that there is no hierarchy; one blob cannot contain other blobs or other containers. However, Windows Azure blobs let you simulate a virtual hierarchy by using a "delimiter" character. Here's how it works.

Let's say you want to mirror a filesystem using the blob service where each blob maps to a single file. And let's assume that your filesystem has paths of the form */foo/bar/ test1.file* and */foo/bar/test2.file*. When you upload that file, choose the key to be the concatenated path of the file (*/foo/bar/test.file*).

Now, let's say that, later in your application, you want to walk through your filesystem in the cloud and see the "contents" of the */foo/bar* directory. You shouldn't be able to see the "contents," since there is no container or blob actually called */foo/bar* that contains other files underneath it. Windows Azure blobs allow you to work around this by letting you specify a delimiter character with which you can split up blob keys. In this case, / is the delimiter character. You can then do a `ListBlobs` operation (described in detail later) and say that / is your delimiter character and you only want blobs with the prefix */foo/bar*. Windows Azure blobs then return everything under the */foo/bar/* prefix and give you your *test1.file* and *test2.file*.

> Scenarios in which someone actually picks a delimiter character other than / are rare. Most storage clients (including the Microsoft one) pick that as the limit. You could go wild and split up paths with other characters, but there's really no reason you would need to. One valid scenario is to use a delimiter string instead of a character. You would want to do that when you want to look for blobs with a specific substring in their names.

At this point, you might be wondering whether all this is a bit complicated. But the complexity is worth it because you get to have sensible URIs and a filesystem-like view over the namespace. For example, you can have URIs of the form *http://somedomain .com/videos/movies/matrix.mov*, instead of needing to have one long filename.

You must still remember that there is no real nesting going on, and this prefix-delimiter shenanigan provides only a virtual hierarchy when listing blobs. In reality, all blobs just have a name and don't contain any other blobs.

Creating and Deleting a Block Blob

Let's start with the most fundamental of storage operations: creating a blob. In this case, let's look at a block blob. Page blobs are similar to create and will be examined in the discussion on Windows Azure XDrives later in the chapter. The simple way to create a blob in the Windows Azure storage arena is to send an authenticated PUT request with a URI containing the blob name. The PUT request should contain, as part of its request body, the entire content of the blob—partial updates aren't supported when creating blobs this way. For example, to create a blob called `helloworld.txt` in a previously created container called `test`, you would send a PUT to *http://sriramk.blob.core .windows.net/test/helloworld.txt*.

 This is described as "the simple way." This method of creating a blob supports uploading block blobs of up to 64 MB in size. To upload larger block blobs (of up to 50 GB), as well as to do partial and out-of-order blobs, you need to deal with the individual "blocks" separately. Page blobs (which can go up to 1 TB in size) must have individual page ranges written to them.

Let's write some sample code with the Microsoft library to upload a simple blob. Following is the sample code:

```
CloudStorageAccount cloudStorageAccount =
            CloudStorageAccount.Parse(ConfigurationSettings.AppSettings
["DataConnectionString"]);
         CloudBlobClient cloudBlobClient =
cloudStorageAccount.CreateCloudBlobClient();
         CloudBlobContainer cloudBlobContainer =
cloudBlobClient.GetContainerReference("test");
         CloudBlob cloudBlob =
cloudBlobContainer.GetBlobReference("helloworld.txt");

         cloudBlob.UploadText("Hello World!");
```

What does such a request look like in terms of the actual HTTP traffic involved? The HTTP request would look as follows:

```
PUT /test/helloworld.txt?timeout=30 HTTP/1.1
x-ms-date: Wed, 22 Jul 2009 15:56:07 GMT
```

```
If-None-Match: *
Authorization: SharedKey sriramk:HLKc6rSa6LZ/g3WxEwihRD5p92lBs1r/s16T9lJLNAo=
Host: sriramk.blob.core.windows.net
Content-Length: 12
Expect: 100-continue
Connection: Keep-Alive

Hello world!
```

The request is similar to what you saw when you created a container, but let's highlight a few differences.

First, you see the optional `timeout=30` parameter. This shows up in the request, since the storage library used to generate these requests automatically inserts them. These are optional, and if you don't insert them, the storage service assumes a default value. This tells the storage service that, if the operation takes longer than 30 seconds, it should cancel it and return an error to the user. This helps your application in case you are making synchronous calls to the API, since you have a guarantee that the API will return some result in the specified time.

The second interesting header is `If-None-Match: *`. A little bit earlier, you learned about `ETag`s and how they were like version numbers. This header tells the storage service, "I don't care what version you have. Create/update the blob with the contents in this request." If you had stuck an `ETag` in here (returned by a previous request to the service), the server would have checked to see whether that `ETag` was still the latest version in the system before proceeding. This in-built concurrency mechanism protects against several bugs arising from the use of multiple clients talking to the same storage account at the same time.

And finally, you'll notice some standard HTTP headers. `Content-Length` says `12`, since that's the number of bytes in the string `"Hello world!"`. `Connection: Keep-Alive` and `Expect: 100-Continue` are optimization techniques to help with HTTP performance.

Whew! That's a lot of headers. Aren't you happy that the client libraries do all this work for you? After all the headers, you get to the most important part of the request: the actual data in the blob.

As mentioned earlier, creating blobs this way (as opposed to using blocks) means that you can have only up to 64 MB in the contents of the requests. You really shouldn't go anywhere near this limit, because a lot of HTTP clients and networking software run into issues with long-lived HTTP requests. As a rule of thumb, if your blobs go over a few megabytes, think about moving them into blocks.

That's enough about the request. What does the server send back to you?

```
HTTP/1.1 201 Created
Content-MD5: /D/5joxqDTCH1RXARz+Gdw==
Last-Modified: Wed, 22 Jul 2009 16:01:23 GMT
ETag: 0x8CBD8FCCB59A86A
Server: Blob Service Version 1.0 Microsoft-HTTPAPI/2.0
x-ms-request-id: 098d116a-eccd-4783-98b7-edf892d390cb
```

```
Date: Wed, 22 Jul 2009 16:01:15 GMT
Content-Length: 0
```

First, you get a 2xx message telling you the operation was successful. You'll learn more about Content-MD5 in a second, so let's skip over that for now. The ETag header specifies the "version" of the blob as the server sees it. On future requests, you can use this ETag as discussed before. Finally, the response wraps up with a few standard HTTP headers.

MD5 hashes

Networking is weird. You would think that with TCP, HTTP, all the handshakes, error checking, and corruption, packets sent from the sender would get over to the other side intact. As anyone who has spent time with networks can tell you, the reality is very different. Almost all large system developers will have war stories of weird network-corruption issues. The culprits are many—network drivers, routers, switches.

The only way to protect against corruption is to send a *hash* of the content you have to the other side. In this case, a hash refers to a unique signature that only that content can hash to. The receiver then computes a hash over the data it receives, and compares it with the hash in the request. If either the data or the hash got corrupted in transfer, this check will fail, and the sender will be notified.

In Windows Azure storage, hashing is done using MD5. You have two ways to use this:

- When uploading a blob, you can add a Content-MD5 header containing the MD5 hash of your blob. The blob server computes an MD5 hash over the data it receives, and returns an error (BadRequest) if they don't match.

- When you create/overwrite a blob, the server sends down an MD5 hash of the data it has received. You then verify on the client as to whether that hash matches the hash of the data.

MD5 hashing adds some performance impact, but modern CPUs are very fast at computing hashes. You should use MD5 to protect against networking failures.

Isn't MD5 Insecure?

You might have heard that MD5 is "insecure." Is this another case of Microsoft making a security mistake?

Not exactly. MD5 is insecure in the sense that researchers have shown that it is possible to produce two pieces of data that hash to the same value (a "collision"). However, this is important only if you're using MD5 as a security check. With Windows Azure, you're using MD5 only to protect against network corruption, and there's almost no chance of a networking failure producing MD5 collision. (Note that the preceding sentence says "almost," since there is always a theoretical mathematical chance.) Using MD5 hashes of data to protect against corruption is a standard practice.

The security in the Windows Azure storage protocol comes from the HMAC-SHA256 of your shared key and the request, as described in Chapter 7. That is secure, since no current research exists to produce collisions in the SHA-2 algorithms of which SHA-256 is a member. Cryptographers expect SHA-2 to remain secure for several years to come.

Content-Type and Content-Encoding

The optional headers `Content-Type` and `Content-Encoding` both are important—not for the blob service, but for future clients.

`Content-Type` should be set to a MIME type. For example, to upload a text file, set this header to `Content-Type: text/plain`. When a client retrieves the blob, this header is sent down as well. For clients such as browsers, this header is essential in figuring out what to do with the blob. For example, you would need to set JPEG images to `image/jpeg` for browsers to display the image correctly.

`Content-Encoding` is another standard HTTP header that specifies how the content is actually encoded in binary form.

You can use both of these headers for several "tricks." One such trick is to compress content and have browsers automatically decompress by using the `Content-Encoding` header. You'll see an example of how to do that later in this chapter.

Deleting a blob

To delete a blob that you created, you send an HTTP `DELETE` to its URI (or call `Cloud Blob.Delete` when using the storage client). This should make the blob instantly inaccessible to all clients. Note that you can use `ETag` matching to ensure that you're not deleting the blob if another client has made changes.

Viewing a blob

The easiest way to view and check whether your blob actually exists is to use a web browser and type in the blob's URI. However, this works only if the container is viewable to everyone.

How do you view the blobs you create? That's what you'll learn about next.

Compressed Content

If you hang around the Azure forums long enough, you'll often see questions about content compression. There are several variants to this question—from compressing content on the fly on upload/download, to compressing before upload. To understand the context of most of these questions, let's take a step back to look at how and why people use compression on the Web.

- First, you want to save bandwidth costs. Sending bytes over the Internet costs money, regardless of where you're doing it. Compressing content (along with other HTTP performance tricks) helps you keep bandwidth costs down to a minimum.
- Second, and arguably more importantly, saving the number of bytes sent over the wire can translate into much better performance, sometimes dramatically so. Modern websites are heavy on JavaScript and CSS, and both compress very well, leading to huge performance improvements on compression. Since common web servers support compression on the fly, and web browsers support decompression on the fly, this is as easy as switching on a flag in a configuration file in most cases.

This begs the question: how can you use compression on the Windows Azure blob service? Unfortunately, Windows Azure doesn't support compressing and decompressing blobs for you on the fly. However, there is nothing stopping you from uploading blobs in their compressed form. If you do that, the only thing remaining is to sprinkle some magic pixie dust (well, actually set a header) that lets browsers automatically decompress them for you.

Let's explore that pixie dust now.

Web browsers can typically decompress two kinds of compressed content: those compressed with the "deflate" algorithm (RFC 1950) or those compressed with the gzip algorithm (RFC 1952). With a quick web search, you should be able to find plenty of good reference material on gzip, so let's not spend much time on it here. Suffice it to say that gzip is a compression algorithm, originally based on LZ77 and Huffman coding. It is widely used and supported, and there are a ton of tools to help create and decompress gzipped data.

Web servers have access to the source content and can compress data on the fly. However, Windows Azure does not have this capability in its blob service. You can compress the blobs beforehand, and upload the compressed version to Windows Azure blob storage. Now, all that remains is for web browsers to decompress your compressed data.

How do web browsers know that the server is sending them gzipped data it needs to decompress on the fly? The server adds a `Content-Encoding` header (part of the HTTP 1.1 specification) with its value set to the string `gzip`. Remember that `Content-Encoding` is something you can specify when you upload a blob. Hence, all you need to do to make browsers and standards-compliant HTTP clients decompress your precompressed content is to add the right content encoding when you upload the blob.

Normal HTTP servers have access to the original source content and can choose to send a noncompressed version if the client doesn't support gzip compression. Since you're storing only the compressed version on Windows Azure blob storage, this "negotiation" doesn't take place, and clients that don't support gzip decompression will not work. However, most modern browsers have had support for gzip decompression for a long time now, and this shouldn't cause problems for you in reality.

Example 8-2 shows the code to do this. Since you want to see the results in a browser easily, let's store a JavaScript file in its compressed form.

Example 8-2. Uploading compressed content

```
public static void UploadCompressed(byte[] data, string fileName,
                                    string contentType)
    {
        var cloudStorageAccount =
                CloudStorageAccount.Parse(ConfigurationSettings.AppSettings
                    ["DataConnectionString"]);
        var cloudBlobClient = cloudStorageAccount.CreateCloudBlobClient();
        var container = cloudBlobClient.GetContainerReference("javascript");

        /*Compress the blob we're storing*/
        var compressedData = new MemoryStream();
        var gzipStream = new GZipStream(compressedData,
            CompressionMode.Compress);
        gzipStream.Write(data, 0,
            data.Length);
        gzipStream.Close();

        /* Store the compressed content to blob store
           and set the right Content-Encoding header */

        var cloudBlob = container.GetBlobReference(fileName);
        cloudBlob.UploadByteArray(compressedData.ToArray());

        cloudBlob.Properties.ContentType = contentType;
        cloudBlob.Properties.ContentEncoding = "gzip";
        cloudBlob.SetProperties();
    }}
```

The code shown in Example 8-2 takes your input data, compresses it using the GZip Stream class (which ships as part of .NET 2.0), and uploads it to blob storage using the correct ContentEncoding header.

For example, say you were to upload a 20 KB JavaScript file using this method and load it using a web browser. Figure 8-3 shows (using the popular Firebug extension to Firefox) how the 20 KB file would be compressed down to 6 KB and sent over the wire.

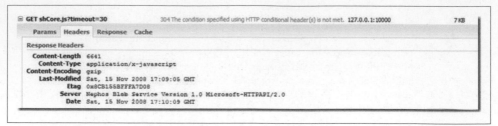

Figure 8-3. Compressed content from blob storage

Reading Blobs

The blob storage wouldn't be of much use if you couldn't read the blobs you uploaded, would it? To read a blob's data, you must send an HTTP GET request to the blob's URI. If the blob is in a private container, this request must be authenticated. On the other hand, if the blob is in a public container, unauthenticated requests will work just fine. In fact, this is how Windows Azure blobs support browsers reading blobs to render images, HTML, and so on.

For example, to easily access and view contents of the blob *http://youraccount.blob.core .windows.net/test/helloworld.txt*, enter the URL in a browser and you should be able to see its contents. What does that look like in code? Following is some C# code using the storage library to read the contents of a blob and write it to stdout:

```
CloudStorageAccount cloudStorageAccount =
        CloudStorageAccount.Parse(ConfigurationSettings.AppSettings
                    ["DataConnectionString"]);
    CloudBlobClient cloudBlobClient = cloudStorageAccount.CreateCloudBlobClient();

    CloudBlobContainer cloudBlobContainer =
  cloudBlobClient.GetContainerReference("teststorageclient");
    CloudBlob cloudBlob =
  cloudBlobContainer.GetBlobReference("helloworld.txt");
    String blobText = cloudBlob.DownloadText();
            Console.WriteLine(blobText);
```

If you've been following along with the code samples, this should look familiar to you. You get a handle to a container called teststorageclient. You then use the Download Text method to get the contents of the blob as a string. If you want a stream to read from, look at the OpenRead method of the CloudBlob type.

Let's look under the covers to see what happened over the wire with that request. Consider the following:

```
GET /teststorageclient/helloworld.txt?timeout=30 HTTP/1.1
x-ms-date: Thu, 23 Jul 2009 09:43:33 GMT
Authorization: SharedKey sriramk:QAnrJu5Qmy83YYgDvxfteKtaN7d5r366/0cKajFc7dY=
Host: sriramk.blob.core.windows.net
Connection: Keep-Alive
```

This is a straightforward GET request. The storage library likes to add authentication for all requests, so you see the authentication header fly by. The defining feature in this request is how small it is. In reality, you could have made an HTTP request with just the first line, and you still would have received the contents of your blob. That's why blob storage is so powerful. Even the dumbest of HTTP clients can work with it to read data.

Now, consider the following:

```
HTTP/1.1 200 OK
Content-Length: 12
Content-Type: application/octet-stream
Last-Modified: Thu, 16 Jul 2009 12:52:44 GMT
ETag: 0x8CBD42B725DE8D2
Server: Blob Service Version 1.0 Microsoft-HTTPAPI/2.0
x-ms-request-id: 4a55d209-6ba1-4fcd-8ed7-9a5c71a6fb26
Date: Thu, 23 Jul 2009 09:43:35 GMT

hello world!
```

The server returns plain-vanilla HTTP content. A dumb HTTP client will just read the text hello world! and process that. The server also supports standard HTTP features such as range requests and If-Modified-Since, so you can read partial content, and read it only if it has been updated since a particular time.

In fact, that header and the ETag you see in the preceding response can be used to ensure that you're reading the correct version of the blob, and reading only when you absolutely need to. How do you do that? To see that, let's look at the conditional operations open to you.

Conditional Reads

First, conditional operations are supported on almost all blob operations. They are the easiest to understand when looking at how to read blobs. If you're interested in conditional requests to operations such as creating a blob or deleting a blob, consult the MSDN documentation (*http://msdn.microsoft.com/en-us/library/dd179371.aspx*, as of this writing) to see what is supported. In almost all cases, ETag matching and If-Modi fied-Since are supported.

The following code reads a blob, simulates doing some other work for a few seconds, and then tries to read the blob again. There is a catch here. It tries to read the blob again *only if it has changed* since the last time the blob was read.

```
CloudStorageAccount cloudStorageAccount =
        CloudStorageAccount.Parse(ConfigurationSettings.AppSettings
          ["DataConnectionString"]);
        CloudBlobClient cloudBlobClient =
cloudStorageAccount.CreateCloudBlobClient();

        CloudBlobContainer cloudBlobContainer =
cloudBlobClient.GetContainerReference("test");
```

```
        CloudBlob cloudBlob =
cloudBlobContainer.GetBlobReference("helloworld.txt");
        var blobText = cloudBlob.DownloadText();
        var etag = cloudBlob.Properties.ETag;

        //Simulate doing work
        System.Threading.Thread.Sleep(1000);

        //Now read the blob again but only if has been modified
        // since the last time we read it
        try
        {
            blobText = cloudBlob.DownloadText(new BlobRequestOptions
            {
                AccessCondition = AccessCondition.IfNoneMatch(etag)
            });
        }
        catch (StorageClientException scx)
        {
            if (scx.StatusCode != System.Net.HttpStatusCode.NotModified)
            {
                // Exception wasn't caused by ETag not matching
                throw;
            }
        }
        Console.WriteLine(blobText);
```

How does this work? The first time you read the blob, the server sent down an ETag matching the version of the blob stored on its server. This was stored in your local instance of the CloudBlob class. When you tried to read the blob a second time, the client sent up a request with the ETag embedded in an If-None-Match header. The server looked at it, thought to itself, "Nope, I don't have a newer version," and sent down an empty HTTP 304 request. The storage library interpreted the request to correctly mean, "No new content," and showed you the old content again when you wrote it out to stdout.

This is clearer when you look at the underlying HTTP traffic. Let's look at the initial request and response for the first blob read:

```
Request
-------
GET /teststorageclient/helloworld.txt?timeout=30 HTTP/1.1
x-ms-date: Thu, 23 Jul 2009 17:37:59 GMT
Authorization: SharedKey sriramk:J/t9JGisn6zCHZ61dgrIObSTrz9+iZEp5CO1SXaQFig=
Host: sriramk.blob.core.windows.net
Connection: Keep-Alive

Response
--------
HTTP/1.1 200 OK
Content-Length: 12
Content-Type: application/octet-stream
Last-Modified: Thu, 16 Jul 2009 12:52:44 GMT
ETag: 0x8CBD42B725DE8D2
```

```
Server: Blob Service Version 1.0 Microsoft-HTTPAPI/2.0
x-ms-request-id: 52fb7cf4-fba1-4fa1-8ba9-689b24a7e131
Date: Thu, 23 Jul 2009 17:38:06 GMT

hello world!
```

This is pretty plain-vanilla stuff. Note the ETag line and the value in the ETag. Now, let's look at the second request and response:

```
Request
-------
GET /teststorageclient/helloworld.txt?timeout=30 HTTP/1.1
x-ms-date: Thu, 23 Jul 2009 17:38:04 GMT
If-None-Match: 0x8CBD42B725DE8D2
Authorization: SharedKey sriramk:k/BkzbxRSvEQXIzxFs8em4E5PtZ5bQ7JfReodi8S7cI=
Host: sriramk.blob.core.windows.net

Response
--------
HTTP/1.1 304 The condition specified using HTTP conditional header(s) is not met.
Content-Length: 0
Server: Blob Service Version 1.0 Microsoft-HTTPAPI/2.0
x-ms-request-id: 9ed961ad-359c-4466-81c0-dc34efbccc0a
Date: Thu, 23 Jul 2009 17:38:12 GMT
```

The magic happens in the If-None-Match header in the request. Notice how it specifies the ETag the server sent down in the first response. This is your way of telling the server of the version you know about. The server sends down an HTTP 304. It says "condition not specified," since the If-None-Match really means "give me a resource on the condition that it doesn't match this ETag". Another important aspect of this response is that it has an empty body. That is great news for you, since that means you're spending less time on the network (not to mention paying Microsoft less for bandwidth).

Always use these conditional headers whenever possible. They help with application performance by downloading resources only when they're updated. This means you have the overhead of keeping track of each resource's latest ETag, but that's a small price to pay for the benefits you get.

Listing, Filtering, and Searching for Blobs

People create a lot of blobs—lots and lots of blobs. Since blob storage isn't exactly a filesystem, you can't enumerate directories in the same way you do with a filesystem. However, you can list blobs and then search and filter them in very powerful ways.

This may be powerful, but it is slightly tricky to understand at first. The good news is that any self-respecting storage client library will hide most of these details for you.

Let's start with the basics. You want to get a listing of all blobs in a container with no fancy options. To do that, you send an HTTP GET to the container's path, followed by a ?comp=list parameter. For example, to get all the blobs in the test container, you send a normal HTTP GET request to *http://sriramk.blob.core.windows.net/test?comp=*

list. This returns a formatted XML response in the following form. (Note that this is the generic form as the specification defines it, as opposed to a specific example response in this case.)

```xml
<?xml version="1.0" encoding="utf-8"?>
<EnumerationResults ContainerName="http://sriramk.blob.core.windows.net/test">
  <Prefix>string-value</Prefix>
  <Marker>string-value</Marker>
  <MaxResults>int-value</MaxResults>
  <Delimiter>string-value</Delimiter>
  <Blobs>
    <Blob>
      <Url>blob-address</Url>
      <Name>blob-name</name>
      <LastModified>date/time-value</LastModified>
      <Etag>etag</Etag>
      <Size>size-in-bytes</Size>
      <ContentType>blob-content-type</ContentType>
      <ContentEncoding />
      <ContentLanguage />
    </Blob>
  </Blobs>
  <BlobPrefix>
    <Name>blob-prefix</Name>
  </BlobPrefix>
  <NextMarker />
</EnumerationResults>
```

Yowza! That's a lot of content for just one blob. Thankfully, most of this looks fairly straightforward. There are these mysterious entries, such as `BlobPrefix` and `Next Marker`, but you'll learn them shortly.

First, let's look at the easy parts. It contains a list of all the blobs at the "root" of the container. For each blob, it lists out the URI, name, `ETag`, and a few other properties. This might seem repetitive to you. Can't you just query the individual blob and get these properties? Yes, you can, but this saves you a bunch of calls. It also gives the server some breathing room, since all clients won't make n different calls (where n is the number of blobs) just to look up some common property on each blob.

Next, look at the tags named `<Marker>` and `<NextMarker/>`. Similar to what you learned about with containers earlier in this chapter, these are the storage service's paging mechanism.

When users have thousands of blobs, it isn't efficient to list all of them in a huge XML response. The blob service breaks these into multiple parts, with each part having 5,000 blobs. Each part has an associated "marker" that is contained in the `<NextMarker>` tag, which indicates where the server stopped. To get the next set of results, make another request to the same URI, but this time, with a tag on a marker query parameter with its value set to the contents of the `<NextMarker>` tag you just received. This tells the server from where to pick up paging results (for example, from a virtual page number).

If you want to change the number of results in each "page," add a `maxresults` query parameter and set it to any number less than 5,000 (5,000 happens to be both the default and the maximum). For example, if you wanted to enumerate containers in sets of 10, you would make an HTTP `GET` request to *http://sriramk.blob.core.windows.net/test? comp=list&maxresults=10&marker=<next-marker-from-previous-response-if-any>*. Microsoft's storage client library (as well as other client libraries) does this automatically for you, so you rarely have to deal with this yourself.

Something you do have to deal with directly is the prefix mechanism (the mysterious `BlobPrefix` tag in the XML response). This is tricky to understand, so let's start with an analogy. If you do a Unix-style `ls` on the directory such as the one used to store all materials for this book, you see something like the following:

```
D:\book>ls -l
    D:\book\*.*
d--------         0 Mon Jul 13 10:51:06 2009 [Chapter1_Overview]
d--------         0 Tue Jul 21 14:00:14 2009 [code]
--a------      4489 Tue Dec 02 09:22:03 2008 toc.txt
--a------      4701 Tue Jul 07 00:44:14 2009 toc_rev_1.txt
--a------      2546 Tue Jul 08 00:24:14 2009 random.txt
```

You see directories (such as *Chapter1_Overview*) and you see individual files (such as *toc.txt*). The `ls` tool differentiates them by putting a `d` next to the directories. If individual blobs are files inside the containers, you can think of the `BlobPrefix` tags as the equivalent of the directory listing.

Almost, that is.

That analogy isn't entirely accurate. Imagine if `ls` had an option where you could say "Hey, if any entity on the filesystem starts with the string 'toc,' show it as a directory and make all entities that start with that piece of text as files 'underneath' it." With this hypothetical `ls` tool, you would be able to get output such as the following:

```
D:\book>ls -l -magical-hypothetical-prefix=toc
    D:\book\*.*
d--------         0 Mon Jul 13 10:51:06 2009 [Chapter1_Overview]
d--------         0 Tue Jul 21 14:00:14 2009 [code]
d--------         0 Tue Dec 02 09:22:03 2009 [toc]
--a------      2546 Tue Jul 08 00:24:14 2009 random.txt
```

See the line with [toc] in it? In the case of the hypothetical `ls` and its filesystem, you should be able to drill into the "toc directory" (though it really isn't a directory) and see all the files "beneath" it. Such a mechanism would be very powerful. It essentially lets you slice through your filesystem with powerful directory enumeration, regardless of how you had laid out your files and directories.

That, in a nutshell, is the blob prefix mechanism. It lets you retrieve `BlobPrefix` objects (think directories) that you can drill into separately.

If your head is spinning because of all this, consider these two pieces of good news. The first is—you guessed it—the storage library has support for this intrinsically, so you don't have to figure out a lot of this yourself. The second is that, though this feature is quite flexible, you can just use it to simulate directories and stick to that alone.

Let's look at some code that uses this. To show off this feature, you need some blobs with hierarchical URIs. Let's create the following blobs under the container **testpath**:

```
/testpath/hello.txt
/testpath/level1-1/hello.txt
/testpath/level1-2/hello.txt
/testpath/level1-1/level2/hello.txt
```

Example 8-3 shows the storage client code to create the container and to create these blobs. The blob contents don't matter. You only care about the path for this example.

Example 8-3. Creating container and nested blobs

```
CloudStorageAccount cloudStorageAccount =
          CloudStorageAccount.Parse(ConfigurationSettings.AppSettings
            ["DataConnectionString"]);
        CloudBlobClient cloudBlobClient =
cloudStorageAccount.CreateCloudBlobClient();

        CloudBlobContainer cloudBlobContainer =
cloudBlobClient.GetContainerReference("testpath");
        cloudBlobContainer.CreateIfNotExist();

        cloudBlobContainer.GetBlobReference
        ("hello.txt").UploadText("Hello world!");
        cloudBlobContainer.GetBlobReference
        ("level1-1/hello.txt").UploadText("Hello World!");
        cloudBlobContainer.GetBlobReference
        ("level1-2/hello.txt").UploadText("Hello World!");
        cloudBlobContainer.GetBlobReference
        ("level1-1/level2/hello.txt").UploadText("Hello World!");
```

You then write some code to list contents for a few different prefix paths corresponding to the preceding hierarchy by using `CloudBlobContainer.ListBlobs`. The only tricky part here is that the enumeration code must deal with the fact that the entity returned can be either a `CloudBlockBlob` or `CloudPageBlob` (for a blob) or a `CloudBlobDirectory` (for a `BlobPrefix`). Use the following helper method to do that:

```
    private static void
    EnumerateResults(System.Collections.Generic.IEnumerable<IListBlobItem>
            enumerator)
        {
          foreach (var blobItem in enumerator)
          {
            var blob = blobItem as CloudBlockBlob;
            //Check whether it is a blob
            if (blob != null)
            {
                Console.WriteLine(blob.DownloadText());
            }
          }        }
```

Now, let's enumerate some containers. To deal with nested paths, you must use the `CloudBlobDirectory` type. Let's enumerate all blobs at the root of the container with no prefix string using `CloudBlobDirectory`, as shown here:

```
CloudBlobDirectory blobDirectory =
cloudBlobClient.GetBlobDirectoryReference("testpath");

var enumerator = blobDirectory.ListBlobs();
EnumerateResults(enumerator);
```

This translates into an authenticated HTTP GET request to /testpath??restype=con
tainer&comp=list&delimiter=%2f.

 You can use the prefix and the delimiter together to perform some very powerful queries. Since the delimiter can be any string, you can use the prefix to match blob strings from the front, and you can use delimiters to match from the other end. You should not go down this path unless you really want this power.

As a response, the storage service sends down the following XML response (which has been edited a bit to show only the parts of interest):

```
<EnumerationResults ContainerName="http://sriramk.blob.core.windows.net/testpath">
<MaxResults>100</MaxResults>
<Delimiter>/</Delimiter>
<Blobs>
  <Blob>
    <Name>hello.txt</Name>
    <Url>http://sriramk.blob.core.windows.net/testpath/hello.txt</Url>
    <LastModified>Sat, 25 Jul 2009 08:21:46 GMT</LastModified>
    <Etag>0x8CBDB1815DB96FD </Etag>
    <Size>12</Size>
    <ContentType>application/octet-stream</ContentType>
    <ContentEncoding /><ContentLanguage />
  </Blob>
  <BlobPrefix><Name>level1-1/</Name></BlobPrefix>
  <BlobPrefix><Name>level1-2/</Name></BlobPrefix>
</Blobs>
<NextMarker />
</EnumerationResults>
```

Note how the storage service returns the one blob in the root of the container, and returns two virtual "directories": the two `CloudBlobDirectory` objects for `level1-1` and `level1-2`, respectively.

What happens when you try to drill in? Following are the code, HTTP request, and response when you try to drill into `level1-1`:

```
CloudBlobDirectory blobDirectory =
cloudBlobClient.GetBlobDirectoryReference("testpath/level1-1");
```

```
var enumerator = blobDirectory.ListBlobs();
EnumerateResults(enumerator);
```

This is translated into an HTTP request to /testpath?restype=con
tainer&comp=list&prefix=level1-1%2f&delimiter=%2f. The server responds with the
following (again edited to show only the salient portions):

```
<Prefix>level1-1/</Prefix>
<Delimiter>/</Delimiter>
<Blobs>
 <Blob>
   <Name>level1-1/hello.txt</Name>
   <Url>http://sriramk.blob.core.windows.net/testpath/level1-1/hello.txt</Url>
...(ellided)
   </Blob>
   <BlobPrefix><Name>level1-1/level2/</Name></BlobPrefix>
   </Blobs>
```

This shows you the one blob you have "under" level1-1 (level1-1/hello.txt) and
shows you that you have one more virtual directory/prefix underneath with the
path /level1-1/level2. (All prefix paths start from the container.)

You can retrieve the blobs under the level1-1/level2 prefix with the following code,
which translates into a request to /testpath?restype=container&comp=list&pre
fix=level1-1%2flevel2%2f&delimiter=%2f and returns the sole helloworld.txt:

```
CloudBlobDirectory blobDirectory =
  cloudBlobClient.GetBlobDirectoryReference("testpath/level1-1/level2");

            var enumerator = blobDirectory.ListBlobs();
            EnumerateResults(enumerator);
```

If you run each of these three code samples one after the other, you get the following
output:

```
Listing of root path

level1-1/
level1-2/
http://sriramk.blob.core.windows.net/testpath/hello.txt

Listing of level1-1

level1-1/level2/
http://sriramk.blob.core.windows.net/testpath/level1-1/hello.txt

Listing of level1-1/level2

http://sriramk.blob.core.windows.net/testpath/level1-1/level2/hello.txt
```

You should now have a grasp of how you simulate a filesystem-like view on top of blob
storage, as well as how to search/filter through multiple blobs.

Copying Blob

Let's say you want to make a backup of your blob data inside the cloud storage itself. For example, you might be making manipulations to one version, and you want to ensure that you have older versions stashed away somewhere. You could manually make copies by downloading the blob and uploading it again with a new name. However, this is terribly inefficient (all the data flows from Microsoft's data centers to you and then back to Microsoft's data centers). A better way to do this (and save money in the process) is to use Windows Azure's blob copy functionality.

Using it is incredibly simple. Make a PUT request to make your backup copy of your blob. But instead of including any data, just add an x-ms-copy-source header with the path of your old blob (under the same storage account, but not necessarily under the same container). And that's it! Blob storage will initiate a copy of the entire source blob, including all metadata:

```
PUT http://sriramk.blob.core.windows.net/testbackup/backup.txt
HTTP/1.1
x-ms-date: Wed, 08 Apr 2009 00:36:19 GMT
x-ms-copy-source: /test/hello.txt
x-ms-version: 2009-04-14
Authorization: SharedKey sally:KLUKJBAn2WGPSbt8Hg61JjCRFnalLUgOw1vG9kq2/tA=
```

You can further control this process by using an x-ms-source-if-modified-since header to ensure that you initiate a copy only if the source matches your date restrictions.

Understanding Block Blobs

Scientists like to break things apart. Several decades ago, the prevailing theory was that an atom is the single smallest entity in the universe. Then, subatomic particles (or, to be specific, the physical reality of photons) were demonstrated by someone named Einstein, and it's been all downhill from there. "Quarks" were proposed in the 1960s as the fundamental constituent of matter, and have been observed in various experiments. There is no doubt that the future will bring smaller and smaller building blocks.

You probably have had a similar feeling as you waded through this chapter. First you learned how storage accounts could have many containers. Then you learned about how each container could have many blobs. You also learned that a block blob is a raw piece of data, which sounds pretty fundamental, right? Right?

Well, yes, but blobs are actually made up of these things called *blocks*. Blocks were designed because users often wanted to do things to parts of an individual blob. The most common scenario is to perform partial or parallel uploads. You might have a huge file that you want to upload to blob storage. Instead of having one long-lived connection, it makes a lot more sense to upload smaller chunks in parallel. Another benefit is with resuming uploads. For example, instead of being frustrated when uploading multigigabyte mail backups to backup services, only to have the upload fail in the middle and have to start all over again, you can use blocks to resume where you left off and not have to start from the beginning.

Using Blocks

Let's assume that you've decided to use blocks, because you want to do parallel uploads of the various pieces of a large blob, because you want to resume uploads, or just because you think the feature is cool. To do so, you follow these steps:

1. You start by breaking the input data into contiguous blocks. Each block can be up to 4 MB in size, but there is no restriction that all blocks must be of the same size. You can chop up your input data however you like. Typically, people like to chop up data into blocks of the same size.

2. Depending on how large your input data is, and how quickly your want your parallel uploads to finish, you can vary your block size. For example, if you choose 4 MB blocks and your input is image files, each around 10 MB, you can split them into three blocks each. However, if you split them into smaller blocks, you could upload them with more parallel connections. Experiment with various sizes and various numbers of parallel connections to see which gives you the best performance.

3. You upload each individual block using the `PutBlock` operation (which you'll learn about in more detail in a little bit). Each block has an associated block ID that you can use to store a block hash, a logical block name, or just about anything you want to uniquely identify the block. The size of all the block IDs (but not the blocks) must be the same across the blob. Note that `PutBlock` can be called in parallel, so you can upload several blocks at once. However, uploading the block won't make the data show up in the target blob. To do that, you need to make one final call.

4. At this point, the storage service has a bunch of blocks and block IDs, but has no idea how to compose them together into a blob. Remember that the blocks can be uploaded out of order and that the block IDs are not sequential numbers (unless you choose to name them that way). To convert the uploaded blocks into a blob, you make a call to `PutBlockList` (which you'll learn about in more detail in a second). This tells the blob service to arrange the blocks in order and *commits* the blob.

And that's it! You should now have a fully composed blob you can read using all your normal methods. If this seems like a lot of work, don't worry. Microsoft's storage client library does most of this under the covers for you. If you want to see what blocks make up the blob (or the blocks you haven't committed yet, if you haven't made a `PutBlockList` call), you have a few methods that retrieve the current committed and uncommitted blocks for each blob.

That's the process in a somewhat oversized nutshell. Let's look at the individual operations in detail.

PUT Block

To upload an individual block, make a `PUT` request to the blob's URI, followed by `?comp=block&blockid={blockid}`. For example, to upload a block with the ID 1 to *http://sriramk.blob.core.windows.net/test/helloworld.txt*, you would make an authenticated HTTP `PUT` with the base64-encoded form of the `blockID` to *http://sriramk.blob.core.windows.net/test/helloworld.txt?comp=block&blockid=MQ==*.

The body of the HTTP request contains the actual data of the block. Each block can be up to 4 MB in size, and you can combine blocks into blobs of up to 200 GB in size. If you try to upload a block of more than 4 MB, the blob service will return a `413` error (Request Entity Too Large).

Block ID

As mentioned, every block is identified by a unique block ID. You get to choose this block ID, and the system doesn't care what you choose. This ability to pick block IDs turns out to be quite useful. One good way to use this is to store hashes of the data in the block itself so that you can validate data integrity at the sub-blob level.

> You can also use this to protect the individual blocks from tampering, and use it as a security feature. To do that, use a cryptographically secure hash algorithm instead of a CRC, and store the hash as the block ID. One common way to do this is to store an SHA-256 hash (32 bytes) as the block ID. If the blob is encrypted, you could use HMAC-SHA256 with a key as the block ID. Essentially, this is a feature that can be used in a lot of interesting ways.

Put BlockList

You can `PUT` blocks until kingdom come, but the real magic happens when you make a call to `Put BlockList`. A blob could have two types of blocks associated with it:

- If it is an existing blob, the existing blocks are called *committed blocks*.
- When you're uploading new blocks either to a new blob or to an already existing blob, up until the time you make a `Put BlockList` call, these new blobs are said to be *uncommitted*.

In a `Put BlockList` call, you specify a list of block IDs in sequence. The blob service takes the blocks associated with those IDs and lays them out in sequence to make the final blob. The blocks that weren't part of the `Put BlockList` call, whether or not they were committed and part of the old blob, get garbage-collected in a week.

The actual call is very simple. You make an HTTP `PUT` request to the blob's URI, followed by `?comp=blocklist`. However, this time, you embed some XML in the request body. For example, if you wanted to commit a series of previously uploaded blocks into a huge `helloworld.txt`, you would do something like the following:

```
PUT http://sriramk.blob.core.windows.net/test/helloworld.txt?comp=blocklist
```

```xml
<?xml version="1.0" encoding="utf-8"?>
<BlockList>
   <Block>AAAAAA==</Block>
   <Block>AQAAAA==</Block>
   <Block>AGAAAA==</Block>
</BlockList>
```

The strings between the `<Block></Block>` tags are the base-64 forms of individual block IDs.

The maximum number of blocks that can be committed is 50,000. At any given point in time, you can have up to 100,000 blocks in an uncommitted state for a blob. For files with large amounts of repeating data, you can upload the data once, and refer to the block ID multiple times in the block list. The blob service is smart enough to repeat that block multiple times in the final blob.

The storage client library has support for blocks through the `CloudBlockBlob` type. Example 8-4 shows the uploading of 10 blocks to make up one complete block blob.

Example 8-4. Uploading a block blob

```
CloudStorageAccount cloudStorageAccount =
         CloudStorageAccount.Parse(ConfigurationSettings.AppSettings
["DataConnectionString"]);
         CloudBlobClient cloudBlobClient =
cloudStorageAccount.CreateCloudBlobClient();

         CloudBlobContainer cloudBlobContainer =
 cloudBlobClient.GetContainerReference("test");
         CloudBlockBlob cloudBlockBlob =
cloudBlobContainer.GetBlockBlobReference("testblockupload");

         String[] blockIds = new String[10];
         for (Int32 i = 0; i < 10; i++)
         {
           blockIds[i] =
Convert.ToBase64String(System.BitConverter.GetBytes(i)); ;
         }

         cloudBlockBlob.PutBlockList(blockIds);
```

Understanding Page Blobs

For more than a year, block blobs were the only form of blobs available in Windows Azure storage. One drawback with block blobs is random access. Think about a typical disk attached to your computer. These are random access devices where the filesystem can choose to write to any sector at any given time, without having to worry about how to chop the file into blocks even before having to write it. Launched in November 2009, *page blobs* target these random read/write scenarios. A large part of the motivation for page blobs is Windows Azure XDrive, which is discussed later in this chapter.

Pages

A page blob, like the name suggests, is made up of an array of pages. Each page is aligned on a 512-byte boundary. Unlike a block blob, page blobs can go up to 1 TB in size. Since page blobs are random access, you can write at any offset you choose, but you'll be charged for only the data you actually store.

To read and write pages, the blob service API provides a number of operations. This chapter doesn't go into these in detail, since Windows Azure XDrive takes care of these API calls under the hood for you. You can find the entire list along with documentation at *http://msdn.microsoft.com/en-us/library/ee691970.aspx*. Following are some key ones:

PutPage

> This lets you write a range of pages to a page blob. The `Range/x-ms-range` request header specifies the range of bytes to be written. The range can be up to 4 MB for an update operation. Another interesting header is `x-ms-page-write`. Depending on whether you set it to `update` or `clear`, the operation will write bytes into the blob or clear the specified range, respectively.

GetPageRegions

> This returns the list of valid page regions for a page blob. You can use the range headers as described in `PutPage` to list only a subset of page regions. The returned data is an XML blob containing the list of regions for that range. Following is a sample format:

```
<?xml version="1.0" encoding="utf-8"?>
<PageList>
   <PageRange>
      <Start>Start Byte</Start>
      <End>End Byte</End>
   </PageRange>
   <PageRange>
      <Start>Start Byte</Start>
      <End>End Byte</End>
   </PageRange>
</PageList>
```

GetBlob

> You already saw how to use `GetBlob` earlier in this chapter. One additional header that makes `GetBlob` work better with page blobs is `Range/x-ms-range`. This lets you specify the exact range of the page blob you want returned.

Example 8-5 shows you code to upload a page blob. Downloading a page blob is very similar. For further control, instead of using just a plain-vanilla `GetBlob` operation look at `CloudPageBlob.GetPageRanges` to enumerate over the list of pages.

Example 8-5. Uploading a page blob

```
CloudStorageAccount cloudStorageAccount =
        CloudStorageAccount.Parse(ConfigurationSettings.AppSettings
["DataConnectionString"]);
        CloudBlobClient cloudBlobClient =
cloudStorageAccount.CreateCloudBlobClient();

        CloudBlobContainer cloudBlobContainer =
cloudBlobClient.GetContainerReference("test");
        CloudPageBlob cloudPageBlob =
cloudBlobContainer.GetPageBlobReference("testpageupload");


        int pageSize = 512;
        int numPages = 4;
        cloudPageBlob.Create(numPages * pageSize);

        // Some random blob text which will fit into a page
        string blobText = new String('a', pageSize);

        using (MemoryStream memoryStream =
new MemoryStream(UTF8Encoding.UTF8.GetBytes(blobText)))
        {
            cloudPageBlob.WritePages(memoryStream, 0);
            memoryStream.Seek(0, SeekOrigin.Begin);
            cloudPageBlob.WritePages(memoryStream, 2 * pageSize);
        }
```

Windows Azure XDrive

One of the downsides of using the Windows Azure blob service for existing applications is to have to rewrite filesystem access code. Almost all applications access the filesystem in some way—whether via the local disk or shared network storage. Replacing all that code to use Windows Azure blob storage API calls may not be possible. In some cases, you may not even have an option to do that if you're using a third-party product or library that you can't change.

Windows Azure XDrive addresses this scenario. Windows Azure XDrive provides a durable NTFS volume for your Windows Azure application. In the previous section, you saw how page blobs simulate a disk-like interface. This similarity is deliberate. Windows Azure XDrive layers an NTFS volume on top of a page blob. For example, you would be able to mount *http://youraccount.blob.core.windows.net/container/your blob* as a local drive (say, *X:*), and then your application can use normal filesystem access code to write to it. The translation between filesystem access code and blob access code is done by a special device driver in Windows Azure.

XDrive Internals

The key to understanding XDrive is to understand that it is just a façade on top of a blob. You get all the benefits of blob storage (replication, scalability, and so on), but with an NTFS filesystem view on top.

A drive can be mounted by one virtual machine at a time for read/write access, but any number of virtual machines can mount a read-only snapshot. All NTFS nonbuffered writes and flushes/commits are made durable instantly to the underlying page blob. Reads are a bit more interesting. When you initialize XDrive, you get to pick the size of the "local cache." Reads are returned from this local cache whenever possible, or directly from the blob store whenever there is a cache miss.

The page blob contains the contents of the drive in Virtual Hard Disk (VHD) format. This is the same file format used by products such as Virtual PC and Hyper-V—you'll find a ton of utilities and documentation on working with this format. You can upload a VHD (a page blob) and have it loaded as a Windows Azure XDrive, or download the contents as a VHD anytime you choose.

Unlike other parts of Windows Azure storage, moving your application to use Windows Azure XDrive requires very little work. In most cases, you can have your existing code/libraries/applications up and running on XDrive with little or no modification. One common scenario for using XDrive is to power applications such as MySQL. In such cases, XDrive really makes your life easier because not only does it "just work," but you also get all the benefits of blob storage underneath.

CDN Access and Custom Domain Names

A big factor in storage access performance is network latency. This is usually dominated by one factor: the physical distance between the user and the data center from where the content is being served. You can use the affinity groups and georegion feature to move the content closer to some section of users, but for best performance, you need a global array of data centers—a Content Delivery Network (CDN)—that can deliver content from very close to the user.

Since building such infrastructure is beyond the ability of most companies, this is typically done by providers such as Akamai or Limelight. Microsoft has its own CDN network that it had built out for its own websites. The blob service integrates with this CDN, and lets you store blobs on Microsoft's CDN for super-fast access to your blobs.

Enabling CDN access to your blobs is quite simple. Figure 8-4 shows the CDN endpoint disabled for a storage account (its default state). You'll see this section on the storage account page in the Developer Portal. Click Enable CDN to enable CDN caching of your blobs.

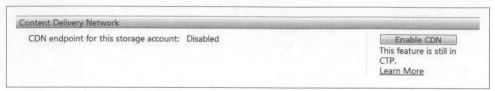

Figure 8-4. Disabled CDN endpoint

Once CDN is enabled, you'll get a URL of the form *http://<guid>.vo.msecnd.net*. This maps to your *http://<accountname>.blob.core.windows.net* URL. For example, if you had a blob at *http://foo.blob.core.windows.net/test/helloworld.jpg*, you could access it through *http://abcd.vo.msecnd.net/test/helloworld.jpg* (assuming "abcd" is the GUID assigned to you).

When a request is made to the Windows Azure CDN URL, the request is redirected to the edge location closest to the location where the request originated. If the edge location doesn't have the blob, it is retrieved from the blob service and cached at the edge. Typically, this cache has an expiry period of 72 hours (though you can modify this by setting a `Cache-Control` header on your blobs).

Using Custom Domains

You may not want to reveal the fact that you're using Windows Azure blob storage. Lots of people like to control the URLs that serve their content, and prefer to have `theirowndomain.com/some/path` instead of content being served from `account.blob.core.windows.net` or `guid.vo.msecnd.net`.

You can use Windows Azure's capability to map custom domains to your storage/CDN endpoints to make this work. This lets you map your *domain.com* to *account.blob.core.windows.net*, or your CDN URL, so that accessing `yourdomain.com/container/someblob` actually redirects to `youraccount.blob.core.windows.net/container/someblob`.

 Although this example walks through how to map a custom domain to a CDN endpoint, the process is the same for a storage endpoint. You don't need to have CDN access enabled to make this work.

The first step is to head to the Custom Domains section on the storage account's page, as shown in Figure 8-5. This shows you the endpoints for that particular storage account. Click Manage on the endpoint you want behind a custom domain. If you throw a regular storage endpoint behind a custom domain, all content will be served directly by the blob service. If you throw a CDN endpoint behind a custom domain, requests will be redirected to the CDN endpoint.

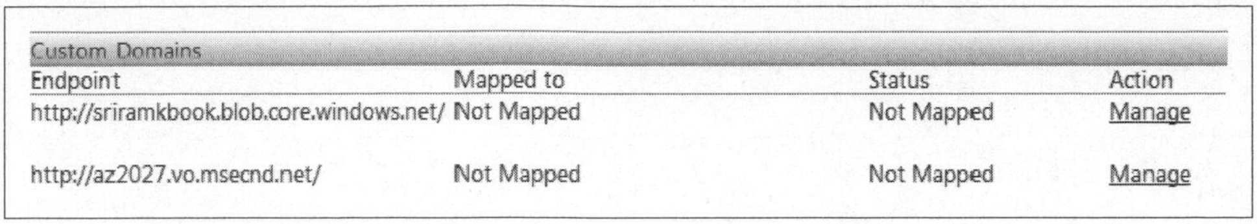

Custom Domains			
Endpoint	Mapped to	Status	Action
http://sriramkbook.blob.core.windows.net/	Not Mapped	Not Mapped	Manage
http://az2027.vo.msecnd.net/	Not Mapped	Not Mapped	Manage

Figure 8-5. Portal domain management

Before the custom domain mapping can be completed, you must verify that you actually own the domain to which you're trying to map the endpoint. To do that, the portal shows you a special GUID for which you must create a CNAME (a DNS record) entry in your domain. You can do this in your domain register, or wherever you host your DNS nameservers. Figure 8-6 shows the mapping of *cdn.sriramkrishnan.com* to *az2027.co.msecnd.net*. To validate the ownership of *sriramkrishnan.com*, the portal asks you to create a CNAME entry from that long string starting with `745....cdn.srir amkrishnan.com` to `verify.azure.com`.

Custom Domain for the CDN Endpoint

Domain Registration

In order to configure a custom domain for your storage account, you need to own a domain. If you do not already own a domain, you can register a new domain with an Internet Service Provider.

Domain Association

Associated domain name: cdn.sriramkrishnan.com

CName: 745806cc-6670-4cbd-b619-b48241379468

Copy this key and create a CName record from **745806cc-6670-4cbd-b619-b48241379468.cdn.sriramkrishnan.com** to **verify.azure.com**. You will have to perform this configuration step on your domain registrar's website.

Once you have completed this step, please click on validate to continue with the ownership verification process.

Finally, once you have validated your domain, please create a CName record from **cdn.sriramkrishnan.com** to **az2027.vo.msecnd.net** to complete this process.

Domain Ownership Validation

Once you have setup the DNS record on your domain registrar's web site, click on Validate to initiate the domain ownership validation process immediately, or click on Cancel to go back to the Storage Account property page. You will be able to validate your domain ownership at any time.

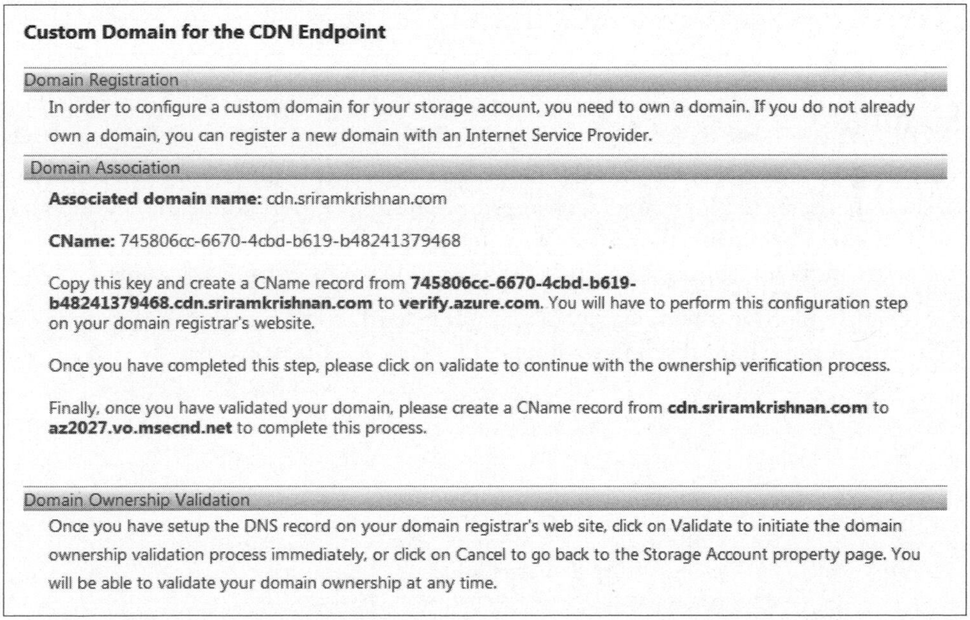

Figure 8-6. Custom domain validation

Creating CNAME entries is different from provider to provider. Figure 8-7 shows the UI in the domain registrar for *sriramkrishnan.com*. Consult your domain registrar's documentation to see how to create CNAME entries for your domain. You can see the creation of not only the verification CNAME entry, but also the *cdn.sriramk-rishnan.com* CNAME entry that will actually redirect to the CDN endpoint.

745806cc-6670-4cbd-b619-b48241379468.cdn.sriramkrishnan.com.	verify.azure.com.	CNAME	edit | delete
cdn.sriramkrishnan.com.	az2027.vo.msecnd.net.	CNAME	edit | delete

Figure 8-7. CNAME addition

Once the portal detects the CNAME entry, you should see the custom domain status change to Validated, as shown in Figure 8-8. At this point, requests to *cdn.sriramk-rishnan.com* are redirected automatically to *http://az2027.v0.mecnd.net*. This redirection happens automatically behind the scenes, so you don't need to change anything in your code to make this work. (CNAMEs are a core part of how DNS works.)

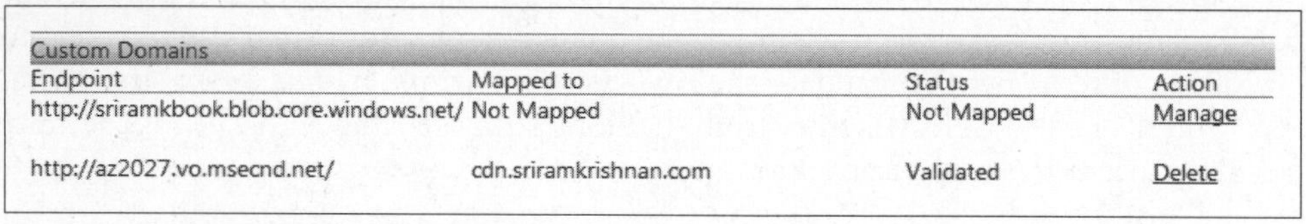

Custom Domains

Endpoint	Mapped to	Status	Action
http://sriramkbook.blob.core.windows.net/	Not Mapped	Not Mapped	Manage
http://az2027.vo.msecnd.net/	cdn.sriramkrishnan.com	Validated	Delete

Figure 8-8. Validated custom domain

Summary

This chapter provided a long look at blobs, and even then, you haven't been exposed to several aspects of blob usage, such as error handling (expect connection failures) or throttling (back off when the server asks you to). You'll see bits and pieces of that when you write individual applications using the Windows Azure storage features.

You can use blobs in a wide variety of ways. It is hard to *not* come up with a good use for a near-infinite hard disk in the cloud.

## CHAPTER 9

Queues

Elberton, Georgia, is the home of America's very own version of Stonehenge: the Georgia Guidestones. The origins of the Georgia Guidestones are shrouded in mystery. In 1979, an individual calling himself "R.C. Christian" walked into a local granite company and made a most unusual order. Claiming to represent a "small group of loyal Americans," he laid out exact specifications for the stones. When asked what it was for, he was evasive, revealing only that it needed to survive the most catastrophic of events.

Construction of the five stones made of granite, each towering 20 feet high, took almost a year. The stones are arranged in a precise astronomical pattern, aligned with the sun's solstices and equinoxes, as well as its motion through the year. Inscribed on the stones are 10 guidelines or principles, written in eight different languages. The messages themselves seem fairly benign, covering everything from keeping human population under control, to protecting people with fair laws. The only person who knew for sure what the messages meant, the mysterious R.C. Christian, disappeared, and nothing was discovered about who he really was, and what his "group" was up to.

Regardless of whether the Georgia Guidestones had their origins in paganism or were simply the product of an overzealous environmental protection group, one thing is very clear. The stones are meant to be a message, one that lasts for a long, long time, and one that humanity can decipher far into the future.

And that's exactly what this chapter addresses: sending and receiving messages. What R.C. Christian attempted to do with granite, programmers have been trying to do with various pieces of software for a long time. The problem hasn't changed: you want to send messages, typically lots of them, and you want to ensure that your receiver can get them. Your receiver may not exist when you send the message, so you use a queue mechanism (the granite stones). The queue is built to be resilient so that it doesn't lose any of the messages.

Unlike R.C. Christian, programmers tended to use techniques less wieldy than sculpting granite. Typically, you would use software such as Microsoft Message Queuing (MSMQ) or IBM's WebSphere MQ. You might use a messaging system built into the database, such as SQL Service Broker. However, all of these have limitations when you move to the cloud. In most cases, they just don't work well with the distributed nature of the storage systems that exist in the cloud.

The Windows Azure queue storage service provides a reliable queuing and message-delivery system. In short, you can queue any number of messages, and Azure will guarantee that no messages are lost and that a receiver will always be able to dequeue them. Since there is no limit on the number of messages, the sender can enqueue thousands (if not millions) of messages at a time, and whenever your application sees fit, a receiver can process these messages.

Unlike R.C. Christian, you don't have to hire a company to move around tons of granite to send reliable messages into the future.

Understanding the Value of Queues

Think about your last trip to your local, high-volume coffee shop. You walk up to a counter and place an order by paying for your drink. The barista marks a cup with your order and places it in a queue, where someone else picks it up and makes your drink. You head off to wait in a different line (or queue) while your latte is prepared.

This common, everyday exchange provides several interesting lessons:

- The coffee shop can increase the number of employees at the counter, or increase the number of employees making coffee, with neither action depending on the other, but depending on the load.

- The barista making coffee can take a quick break and customers don't have to wait for someone to take their orders. The system keeps moving, but at a slower pace.

- The barista is free to pick up different cups, and to process more complex orders first, or process multiple orders at once.

This is a significant amount of flexibility, something that a lot of software systems can be envious of. This is also a classic example of a good *queuing system*.

There are several good uses for queues, but most people wind up using queues to implement one important component of any scalable website or service: asynchronous operations. Let's illustrate this with an example most of you should be familiar with: Twitter.

Consider how Twitter works. You publish an update and it shows up in several places: your time line, the public time line, and for all the people following you. When building a prototype of Twitter, it might make sense to implement it in the simplest way possible—when you select the Update button (or submit it through the API) you publish changes into all the aforementioned places. However, this wouldn't scale.

When the site is under stress, you don't want people to lose their updates because you couldn't update the public timeline in a timely manner. However, if you take a step back, you realize that you don't need to update all these places at the exact same time. If Twitter had to prioritize, it would pick updating that specific user's time line first, and then feed to and from that user's friends, and then the public time line. This is exactly the kind of scenario in which queues can come in handy.

Using queues, Twitter can queue updates, and then publish them to the various time lines after a short delay. This helps the user experience (your update is immediately accepted), as well as the overall system performance (queues can throttle publishing when Twitter is under load).

These problems face any application running on Windows Azure. Queues in Windows Azure allow you to decouple the different parts of your application, as shown in Figure 9-1.

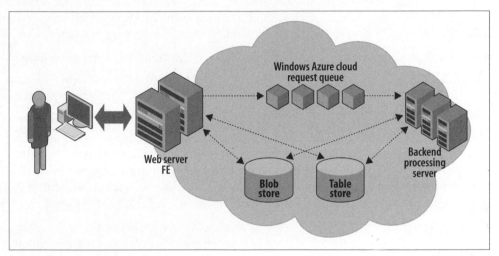

Figure 9-1. Decoupling applications with queues

In this model, a set of frontend roles process incoming requests from users (think of the user typing in Twitter updates). The frontend roles queue work requests to a set of Windows Azure queues. The backend roles implement some logic to process these work requests. They take items off the queue and do all the processing required. Since only small messages can be put on the queue, the frontends and backends share data using the blob or the table storage services in Windows Azure. (You learned about the blob storage service in Chapter 8, and will learn about the table storage service in Chapter 10.)

Video sites are a canonical, or commonly demonstrated, usage of Windows Azure queues. After you upload your videos to sites such as YouTube and Vimeo, the sites transcode your videos into a format suitable for viewing. The sites must also update their search indexes, listings, and various other parts. Accomplishing this when the user uploads the video would be impossible, because some of these tasks (especially transcoding from the user's format into H.264 or one of the other web-friendly video formats) can take a long time.

The typical way websites solve this problem is to have a bunch of worker process nodes keep reading requests off queues to pick videos to transcode. The actual video files can be quite large, so they're stored in blob storage, and deleted once the worker process has finished transcoding them (at which point, they're replaced by the transcoded versions). Since the actual work done by the frontends is quite small, the site could come under heavy upload and not suffer any noticeable performance drop, apart from videos taking longer to finish transcoding.

Since Windows Azure queues are available over public HTTP, like the rest of Windows Azure's storage services, your code doesn't have to run on Windows Azure to access them. This is a great way to make your code on Windows Azure and your code on your own hardware interoperate. Or you could use your own hardware for all your code, and just use Windows Azure queues as an endless, scalable queuing mechanism.

Let's break down some sample scenarios in which websites might want to use Windows Azure queues.

Decoupling Components

Bad things happen in services. In large services, bad things happen with alarming regularity. Machines fail. Software fails. Software gets stuck in an endless loop, or crashes and restarts, only to crash again. Talk to any developer running a large service and he will have some horror stories to tell. A good way to make your service resilient in the face of these failures is to make your components decoupled from each other.

When you split your application into several components hooked together using queues, failure in one component need not necessarily affect failure in another component. For example, consider the trivial case where a frontend server calls a backend server to carry out some operation. If the backend server crashes, the frontend server is going to hang or crash as well. At a minimum, it is going to degrade the user experience.

Now consider the same architecture, but with the frontend and backend decoupled using queues. In this case, the backend could crash, but the frontend doesn't care—it merrily goes on its way submitting jobs to the queue. Since the queue's size is virtually infinite for all practical purposes, there is no risk of the queue "filling up" or running out of disk space.

What happens if the backend crashes while it is processing a work item? It turns out that this is OK, too. Windows Azure queues have a mechanism in which items are taken off the queue only once you indicate that you're done processing them. If you crash after taking an item, but before you're done processing it, the item will automatically show up in the queue after some time. You'll learn about the details of how this mechanism works later.

Apart from tolerating failures and crashes, decoupling components gives you a ton of additional flexibility:

- It lets you deploy, upgrade, and maintain one component independently of the others. Windows Azure itself is built in such a componentized manner, and individual components are deployed and maintained separately. For example, a new release of the fabric controller is dealt with separately from a new release of the storage services. This is a boon when dealing with bug fixes and new releases, and it reduces the risk of new deployments breaking your service. You can take down one part of your service, allow requests to that service to pile up in Windows Azure queues, and work on upgrading that component without any overall system downtime.

- It provides you with implementation flexibility. For example, you can implement the various parts of your service in different languages or by using different toolkits, and have them interoperate using queues.

 Of course, this flexibility isn't unique to queues. You can get the same effect by having standardized interfaces on well-understood protocols. Queues just happen to make some of the implementation work easier.

Scaling Out

Think back to all the time you've spent in an airport security line. There's a long line of people standing in front of a few security gates. Depending on the time of day and overall airport conditions, the number of security gates actually manned might go up and down. When the line (queue) becomes longer and longer, the airport could bring more personnel in to man a few more security gates. With the load now distributed, the queue (line) moves much quicker. The same scenario plays out in your local supermarket. The bigger the crowd is, the greater the number of manned checkout counters.

You can implement the same mechanism inside your services. When load increases, add to the number of frontends and worker processes independently. You can also flexibly allocate resources by monitoring the length and nature of your queues. For example, high-priority items could be placed in a separate queue. Work items that require a large amount of resources could be placed in their own queue, and then be picked up by a dedicated set of worker nodes. The variations are endless, and unique to your application.

Load Leveling

Load leveling is similar to scaling out. Load and stress for a system vary constantly over time. If you provision for peak load, you are wasting resources, since that peak load may show up only rarely. Also, having several virtual machines in the cloud spun up and waiting for load that isn't there goes against the cloud philosophy of paying only for what you use. You also need to worry about how quickly the load increases—your system may be capable of handling higher load, but not a very quick increase.

Using queues, you can queue up all excess load and maintain your desired level of responsiveness. Since you're monitoring your queues and increasing your virtual machines (or other resources when running outside the cloud) on demand, you also don't have to worry about designing your system to always run at peak scale.

A good production example of a system that uses all of these principles is SkyNet from SmugMug.com. SmugMug is a premier photo-sharing site hosted on Amazon Web Services. Though it uses Amazon's stack, all of its principles and techniques are applicable to Windows Azure as well. It uses a bunch of queues into which the frontends upload jobs. Its system (codenamed SkyNet, after the AI entity in the *Terminator* movies) monitors the load on the job queues, and automatically spins up and spins down instances as needed.

 You can find details on SkyNet at *http://blogs.smugmug.com/don/2008/ 06/03/skynet-lives-aka-ec2-smugmug/*.

Windows Azure Queue Overview

Up to this point, the discussion has been geared toward convincing you that queues are the next best thing to sliced bread (and YouTube). Now, let's look at what Windows Azure queues are, what they provide, and how to use them.

Architecture and Data Model

The Windows Azure queue storage service is composed of two main resources in its data model:

Queues

    A queue contains many messages, and a Windows Azure storage account can contain any number of queues. There is no limit to the number of messages that can be stored in any individual queue. However, there is a time limit: messages can be stored for only a week before they are deleted. Windows Azure queues aren't meant for long-lived messages, though, so any message that sticks around for such a long period of time is probably a bug.

Message

A message is a small piece of data up to 8 KB in size. It is added to the queue using a REST API and delivered to a receiver. Note that, although you can store data in any format, the receiver will see it as base64-encoded data. Every message also has some special properties, as shown in Table 9-1.

Table 9-1. Message properties

Name	Description
MessageID	This is a GUID that uniquely identifies the message within the queue.
VisibilityTimeout	This property specifies the exact opposite of what its name suggests. This value determines for how long a message will be invisible (that is, of course, not visible) when it's removed from the queue. (You'll learn how to use this to protect from crashing servers later in this chapter.) After this time has elapsed, if the message hasn't been deleted, it'll show up in the queue again for any consumer. By default, this is 30 seconds.
PopReceipt	The server gives the receiver a unique PopReceipt when a message is retrieved. This must be used in conjunction with a MessageId to permanently delete a message.
MessageTTL	This specifies the Time to Live (TTL) in seconds for a message. Note that the default and the maximum are the same: seven days. If the message hasn't been deleted from the queue in seven days, the system will lazily garbage-collect and delete it.

The Life of a Message

The life of a message is a short (but exciting and fruitful) one. Windows Azure queues deliver *at-least-once semantics*. In other words, Windows Azure queues try really, really hard to ensure that someone reads and finishes processing a message at least once. However, they don't guarantee that someone won't see a message more than once (*no "at-most-once" semantics*), nor that the messages will appear in order.

Figure 9-2 shows the life of a message.

The typical flow is something like the following:

1. A producer adds a message to the queue, with an optional TTL.
2. The queue system waits for a consumer to take the message off the queue. Regardless of what happens, if the message is on the queue for longer than the TTL, the message gets deleted.
3. A consumer takes the message from the queue and starts processing it. When the consumer takes the message off the queue, Windows Azure queues make the message *invisible*. Note that they are not deleted. Windows Azure just flips a bit somewhere to note that it shouldn't return the message to consumers for the time being. The consumer is given a PopReceipt. This is unique for every time a consumer takes a message off the queue. If a consumer takes the message multiple times, it'll get a different PopReceipt every time. This entire step is where things get interesting. Two scenarios can play out here:

a. In the first scenario, the consumer finishes processing the message successfully. The consumer can then tell the queue to delete the message using the `PopReceipt` and `MessageId`. This is basically you telling the queue, "Hey, I'm done processing. Nuke this message."

b. In the second scenario, the consumer crashes or loses connectivity while processing the message. As noted earlier, this can happen often in distributed services. You don't want queue messages to go unprocessed. This is where the invisibility and the `iVisibilityTimeout` kick in. Windows Azure queues wait the number of seconds specified by `VisibilityTimeout`, and then say, "Hmm, this message hasn't been deleted yet. The consumer probably crashed—I'm going to make this message visible again." At this point, the message reappears on the queue, ready to be processed by another consumer or the same consumer. Note that the original crashing consumer could come back online and delete the message—Windows Azure queues are smart enough to reconcile both of these events and delete the message from the queue.

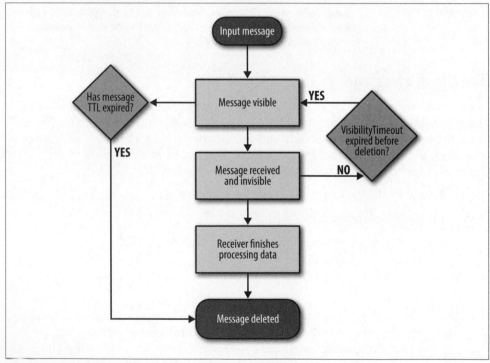

Figure 9-2. Message life cycle

Picking the right `VisibilityTimeout` value depends on your application. Pick a number that is too small and the message could show up on the queue before your consumer has had a chance to finish processing. Pick a timeout that is too large and processing the work item could take a long time in case of a failure. This is one area where you should experiment to see what number works for you.

In the real world, step 3b will see a different consumer pick up and process the message to completion, while the first crashing consumer is resurrected. Using this two-phase model to delete messages, Windows Azure queues ensure that every message gets processed at least once.

 One interesting issue that occurs when messages get redelivered on crashing receivers has to do with *poison messages*. Imagine a message that maliciously or nonmaliciously causes a bug in your code, and causes a crash. Since the message won't be deleted, it'll show up in the queue again, and cause another crash...and another crash...and over and over. Since it stays invisible for a short period of time, this effect can go unnoticed for a long period of time, and cause significant availability issues for your service. Protecting against poison messages is simple: get the security basics right, and ensure that your worker process is resilient to bad input.

Poison messages will eventually leave your system when their TTL is over. This could be an argument for making your TTLs shorter to reduce the impact of bad messages. Of course, you'll have to weigh that against the risk of losing messages if your receivers don't process messages quickly enough.

Queue Usage Considerations

Windows Azure queues trip up people because they expect the service to be just like MSMQ, SQL Service Broker, or *<insert-any-common-messaging-system>*—and it isn't. You should be aware of some common "gotchas" when using Windows Azure queues. Note that these really aren't defects in the system—they're part of the package when dealing with highly scalable and reliable distributed services. Some things just work differently in the cloud.

Messages can be repeated (idempotency)

It is important that your code be *idempotent* when it comes to processing queue messages. In other words, your code should be able to receive the same message multiple times, and the result shouldn't be any different. There are several ways to accomplish this.

One way is to just do the work over and over again—transcoding the same video a few times doesn't really matter in the big picture. In other cases, you may not want to process the same transaction repeatedly (for example, anything to do with financial transactions). Here, the right thing to do is to keep some state somewhere to indicate that the operation has been completed, and to check that state before performing that operation again. For example, if you're processing a payment, check whether that specific credit card transaction has already happened.

Messages can show up out of order

This possibility trips up people since they expect a system called a "queue" to always show first-in, first-out (FIFO) characteristics. However, this isn't easily possible in a large distributed system, so messages can show up out of order once in a while. One good way to ensure that you process messages in order is to attach an increasing ID to every message, and reject messages that skip ahead.

Time skew/late delivery

Time skew and late delivery are two different issues, but they are related because they have to do with timing. When using Windows Azure worker roles to process queue messages, you shouldn't rely on the clocks being in sync. In the cloud, clocks can drift up to a minute, and any code that relies on specific timestamps to process messages must take this into account.

Another issue is late delivery. When you place a message onto the queue, it may not show up for the receiver for some time. Your application shouldn't depend on the receiver instantly getting to view the message.

Understanding Queue Operations

Like the rest of the Windows Azure storage services, the Windows Azure queue service has a REST API. The API uses similar concepts and conventions as the other Windows Azure storage APIs you've seen thus far in this book, so a lot of this will be familiar to you.

All queue operations are through HTTP on a URI. A typical queue URI is of the form *http://<account>.queue.core.windows.net/<queuename>*. For example, if you created a queue called `testqueue` in my storage account, it would show up at *http://sriramk.queue .core.windows.net/testqueue*.

> Unlike blobs (which can be made publicly viewable), queues always need authentication. Therefore, none of the queue URIs in this chapter will work when accessed through your browser. However, you'll learn the details of how to get to queue messages later in this chapter. Authentication is through the same shared key authorization method as used by the rest of the Windows Azure storage services.

Creating a Queue

Let's start this review of queue operations with the most fundamental of operations: creating a queue. To create a queue, send an HTTP PUT signed using your storage account credentials to *http://<account>.queue.core.windows.net/<queuename>*.

The following HTTP traffic capture shows the request for the creation of a new queue called `testq1`:

```
PUT /testq1?timeout=30 HTTP/1.1
x-ms-date: Fri, 26 Jun 2009 09:59:17 GMT
Authorization: SharedKey sriramk:SAkRrcobpRnOishVIhO+4F/gLfJuFqSFLT28hxNpOlQ=
Host: sriramk.queue.core.windows.net
Content-Length: 0
Connection: Keep-Alive
```

You'll see that this is the same format you used for dealing with blobs, except that it is directed to a different HTTP endpoint. The `timeout` parameter is optional, and specifies the amount of time you want to wait before the server should time out the creation operation and return an error back to you. Queue creation is nearly instantaneous, and you generally don't have to worry about specifying this with a high value. The official Microsoft storage client library also takes care of generating a good default for timeout values for most operations.

If the queue was created successfully, you'll get back an HTTP 201. Following is an HTTP traffic capture of a successful response:

```
HTTP/1.1 201 Created
Server: Queue Service Version 1.0 Microsoft-HTTPAPI/2.0
x-ms-request-id: 15750e32-e158-4287-bf8d-297611cb2238
Date: Fri, 26 Jun 2009 09:58:01 GMT
Content-Length: 0
```

This queue can now be manipulated by sending HTTP messages to *http://sriramk.core .queue.windows.net/testq1*.

Using the Microsoft storage client library to create queues is very similar. Earlier in this book, you learned how to obtain storage account credentials and how to set up and use this library, so let's skip over that now. Example 9-1 shows the code to create a queue.

Example 9-1. Creating a queue

```
        CloudStorageAccount cloudStorageAccount =
CloudStorageAccount.Parse(ConfigurationSettings.AppSettings
        ["DataConnectionString"]);
        CloudQueueClient cloudQueueClient =
cloudStorageAccount.CreateCloudQueueClient();
        CloudQueue cloudQueue = cloudQueueClient.GetQueueReference("testq1");
        cloudQueue.CreateIfNotExist();
```

The code checks whether an existing queue with the name `testq1` exists. If it doesn't exist, the code creates it. Later, you'll see how you can add messages and manipulate this queue.

It is not directly obvious where you place the code to create queues. Do you try to create queues dynamically through code, or do you try to create them statically upfront? If you're used to the MSMQ/SQL Service Broker model, you're generally comfortable with doing your setup upfront and distinct from your application code.

In general, there are two approaches you can follow:

- The simple approach is to separate all your "creation/setup" code from your application code. Run it separately as part of your install/setup process. This code should check whether the queue exists, and create one if it doesn't. This code doesn't need to run in the cloud—it could be as simple as a script that runs as part of your build process.

- If you are running a heavyweight service, and you're using queues to manage heavy load, you might want to think about using many queues, and changing the number of queues dynamically at runtime. In this case, your queue "creation/deletion" code should form a part of the code that manages load.

Using Queue Metadata

The container entities in both the Windows Azure blob storage service and queue storage service can have metadata attached to them. These are simple name/value pairs that can be used to describe additional data about the queue itself.

As of this writing, this metadata feature hadn't been widely used by applications. Applications that do incorporate this use metadata to denote additional data about the queue—what it should be used for, data about the items it contains, and so on. For example, an application may use it to describe the priority of the work items the queue handles. For simple applications, you can use a naming convention to describe a lot of this data in the queue's name. But since names can't be changed, the data is static. Using metadata gives you a chance to change data regarding *how* and *why* your application should use that queue. For example, you can dynamically change the priority of the queue's work items.

Working with metadata is easy, in terms of both the REST API and the Microsoft storage library. To set/add a name/value pair, do an HTTP PUT to the queue's URI, followed by a `?comp=metadata`, and add a special header in the form `x-ms-meta-name:value`.

Following is a sample HTTP request that sets a name/value pair with the name `foo` and the value `bar`:

```
PUT http://sriramk.queue.core.windows.net/testq1?comp=metadata HTTP/1.1

x-ms-date: Fri, 26 Jun 2009 01:47:14 GMT
```

```
x-ms-meta-foo: bar
Authorization: SharedKey sriramk:u6PSIebDltGW5xHpO77epRpiUhcsTkWMvcM4GTmfqqA=
```

The bold lines show the changes to the URI (adding a `?comp=metadata`) and the header setting the name/value pair.

 If you plan to use metadata from outside Microsoft's data centers, test thoroughly in the code environment which talks to Windows Azure storage. Issues have been noted with proxies not sending all headers across, or mangling headers across the way, resulting in difficult-to-debug errors.

The equivalent code for this in the storage client library is simple as well. The code in Example 9-2 shows how to add the same `foo=bar` metadata using the storage library. Note that this code assumes you've already created a queue called `testq1`.

Example 9-2. Adding queue metadata

```
CloudStorageAccount cloudStorageAccount =
CloudStorageAccount.Parse(ConfigurationSettings.AppSettings
  ["DataConnectionString"]);
        CloudQueueClient cloudQueueClient =
cloudStorageAccount.CreateCloudQueueClient();
        CloudQueue cloudQueue = cloudQueueClient.GetQueueReference("testq1");
        cloudQueue.Metadata.Add("foo", "bar");
        cloudQueue.SetMetadata();
```

This code does a read on all of the queue's metadata, and then adds your metadata to it. Why do that? Setting queue metadata is a `SET/GET` call where you replace all of the queue's metadata. Using this read-response pattern ensures that you don't delete any headers already set.

This also tells you how to delete all the metadata associated with a queue—just do a `PUT` to `?comp=metadata` with no metadata headers. That will clear out all the metadata associated with the queue.

The previous code snippet also shows you the storage client API to read a queue's metadata. What does that look like in the underlying REST API? As with all good REST APIs, once you've figured out how to create a resource, reading that resource is very easy.

To read a queue's metadata, just issue an HTTP `GET` to that queue's URI, followed by `?comp=metadata`. You should get back a series of `x-ms-<name>=<value>` pairs in the HTTP headers, which contain the names and values of your metadata. The following HTTP capture shows a sample request:

```
GET /testq1?comp=metadata&timeout=30 HTTP/1.1
x-ms-date: Fri, 26 Jun 2009 17:52:30 GMT
Authorization: SharedKey sriramk:dCPWLE8dUiiaRKHFeziN5c9XzVIjxaX5s3QVSMtonYQ=
Host: sriramk.queue.core.windows.net
```

```
HTTP/1.1 200 OK
Server: Queue Service Version 1.0 Microsoft-HTTPAPI/2.0
x-ms-request-id: 24091f05-6e62-46a8-9481-dedec525f594
x-ms-approximate-messages-count: 0
x-ms-foo:bar
Date: Fri, 26 Jun 2009 17:50:46 GMT
Content-Length: 0
```

Counting Queue Messages

If you looked at the headers in the previous code, you saw a header fly by with the name `x-ms-approximate-messages-count`. As the name suggests, that header contains the approximate number of messages in the queue at any time. This is a special header automatically generated by the system.

This is useful for estimating the load on a given queue. You can use it to split work among queues and workers—assign each queue to a worker node, and then use the approximate message count to balance the load. Note the word *approximate* in the header. The value of messages is lazily refreshed, and should be used as a guideline, rather than as a hard indicator of messages in the queue.

To access this property through the storage client library, use `CloudQueue.Approximate MessageCount`.

Listing Queues

The operation to list queues returns a list of queues in your storage account. It does basically what you would expect, but has additional options to filter the result of queues you want, and a continuation marker system to deal with storage accounts that have hundreds or thousands of queues.

To get the list of queues in an account, you send an authorized HTTP GET to *http://<accountname>.queue.core.windows.net/?comp=list*. Doing so returns an XML response body containing the list of queues in your account. The following HTTP trace shows a sample request response. (The XML response has been formatted a bit for readability.)

```
GET /?comp=list&maxresults=50&timeout=30 HTTP/1.1
x-ms-date: Fri, 26 Jun 2009 18:10:23 GMT
Authorization: SharedKey sriramk:AYYja2g3eKp4getsu62Jr8JEfxDjhqVu89mKCvXjd7A=
Host: sriramk.queue.core.windows.net
Connection: Keep-Alive


HTTP/1.1 200 OK
Content-Type: application/xml
Server: Queue Service Version 1.0 Microsoft-HTTPAPI/2.0
x-ms-request-id: ee48a862-52e6-4444-b1d5-3c29f0d4871a
Date: Fri, 26 Jun 2009 18:09:14 GMT
Content-Length: 292
```

```xml
<?xml version="1.0" encoding="utf-8"?>
<EnumerationResults AccountName="http://sriramk.queue.core.windows.net/">
<MaxResults>50</MaxResults>
<Queues>
    <Queue>
    <QueueName>testq1</QueueName>
    <Url>http://sriramk.queue.core.windows.net/testq1</Url>
    </Queue>
</Queues><NextMarker />
</EnumerationResults>
```

The code to do that in the storage client library is as follows:

```
CloudStorageAccount cloudStorageAccount =
CloudStorageAccount.Parse(ConfigurationSettings.AppSettings
["DataConnectionString"]);
        CloudQueueClient cloudQueueClient =
cloudStorageAccount.CreateCloudQueueClient();

        foreach (CloudQueue q in cloudQueueClient.ListQueues())
        {
            Console.WriteLine(q.Name);
        }
```

One additional option when listing queues is limiting the results to only those that match a prefix. This is useful when building a service that creates and tears downs lots of queues—you can create a namespace of queues, and list only a certain subset of that namespace using this prefix search mechanism.

To search using a prefix, specify the **prefix** parameter in the URI (for example, *http:// <accountname>.queue.core.windows.net/?comp=list&prefix=<prefix-term>*).

The storage client library to do that is simple, and is a minor variant of the code to list all queues:

```
CloudStorageAccount cloudStorageAccount =
CloudStorageAccount.Parse(ConfigurationSettings.AppSettings
["DataConnectionString"]);
        CloudQueueClient cloudQueueClient =
cloudStorageAccount.CreateCloudQueueClient();

        foreach (CloudQueue q in cloudQueueClient.ListQueues("test"))
        {
            Console.WriteLine(q.Name);
        }
```

If you look at the XML returned for any of these queries, you'll see a **NextMarker** element. This is a continuation mechanism. By default, the server returns 5,000 queues. (Note that you can modify this using the **maxresults** option in the URI.) If you have more than 5,000 queues, the next marker contains an indicator that you must send back to the server using the **marker** URI parameter to tell the server where to resume. When using the Microsoft storage client library, this is done automatically under the covers.

Deleting Queues

The delete operation deletes a queue from your storage account. When a queue is deleted, it and its messages are instantly inaccessible. The storage system internally marks it for deletion and garbage-collects it at leisure.

 Queue deletion is not an instantaneous operation, so you must check whether the queue's deletion has completed before trying to create another queue of the same name.

To delete a queue, send an HTTP DELETE to the queue's URI. If successful, the storage service will send down an HTTP 2xx code. Following is an HTTP capture of both the request and response parts of a delete operation:

```
DELETE /testq1?timeout=30 HTTP/1.1
x-ms-date: Thu, 02 Jul 2009 11:09:33 GMT
Authorization: SharedKey sriramk:YBAGIWCXRG+d6688SXPQ2wOR/gzKL7xzux8Lhh7mfiw=
Host: sriramk.queue.core.windows.net
Content-Length: 0


HTTP/1.1 204 No Content
Content-Length: 0
Server: Queue Service Version 1.0 Microsoft-HTTPAPI/2.0
x-ms-request-id: a7a7bf21-5f61-4e4a-a508-4700d19f08ab
Date: Thu, 02 Jul 2009 11:07:35 GMT
```

Example 9-3 shows the counterpart in the storage client library.

Example 9-3. Deleting a queue

```
CloudStorageAccount cloudStorageAccount =
CloudStorageAccount.Parse(ConfigurationSettings.AppSettings
["DataConnectionString"]);
        CloudQueueClient cloudQueueClient =
cloudStorageAccount.CreateCloudQueueClient();
        CloudQueue cloudQueue = cloudQueueClient.GetQueueReference("testq1");
        cloudQueue.Clear();
        cloudQueue.Delete();
```

When you delete a queue, its messages are deleted as well. If workers are trying to remove messages of that queue, they'll immediately start seeing errors. In short, don't delete a queue unless you're really sure that you don't need the messages in it anymore. It might be safer to leave empty queues around with no messages in them. Since there's no upper limit on the number of queues you may have, there is no harm in having old queues lying around (appropriately named and ignored by your code, of course!) and cleaning them up later.

Understanding Message Operations

A *message* is an atomic piece of data stored in a queue. Each message in Windows Azure queues can be up to 8 KB in size. There is no limit on the number of messages in a queue, or the combined size of the messages you can put in the store. Messages can be in any format.

However, there is one "gotcha" here that you should be aware of. Though you typically insert messages in binary format, when you read them back out from the queue you'll get them in base64 encoding. If you're writing your own client, remember to decode them back to their binary representation.

Enqueuing a Message

Enqueuing a message adds a message to the back of the queue. To enqueue a message to a queue, send an authentic and properly formatted HTTP POST to *http://<account>.queue.core.windows.net/<queuename>/messages*. The request body must be in the following form:

```
<QueueMessage>
    <MessageText>message-content</MessageText>
</QueueMessage>
```

Most storage client libraries base64-encode the message and decode the message when reading it. The queue service itself expects the message contents to be UTF8-compatible.

Example 9-4 shows how to use the official storage client library to post a new message to the queue testq1.

Example 9-4. Adding a message

```
CloudStorageAccount cloudStorageAccount =
CloudStorageAccount.Parse(ConfigurationSettings.AppSettings
["DataConnectionString"]);
        CloudQueueClient cloudQueueClient =
cloudStorageAccount.CreateCloudQueueClient();

        CloudQueue cloudQueue = cloudQueueClient.GetQueueReference("testq1");
        CloudQueueMessage msg = new CloudQueueMessage("Sample Message");
        cloudQueue.AddMessage(msg);
```

This code gets a handle to the queue testq1 (it assumes the queue has already been created) and then inserts a small message with the contents "Sample message". Following is the HTTP traffic for creating the message. Note how the message is base64-encoded in the request body.

```
POST /testq1/messages?timeout=30 HTTP/1.1
x-ms-date: Sat, 04 Jul 2009 00:53:26 GMT
Authorization: SharedKey sriramk:26L5qqQaIX7/6ijXxvbt3x1AQW2/Zrpxku9WScYxD4U=
Host: sriramk.queue.core.windows.net
Content-Length: 76
Expect: 100-continue

<QueueMessage>
 <MessageText>U2FtcGxlIG1lc3NhZ2U=</MessageText>
</QueueMessage>
```

If the message was successfully created (which it was in this case), the server sends down an HTTP **201 Created** message as an acknowledgment:

```
HTTP/1.1 201 Created
Server: Queue Service Version 1.0 Microsoft-HTTPAPI/2.0
x-ms-request-id: adaa5b64-c737-4a36-be98-dc8b712a264e
Date: Sat, 04 Jul 2009 00:51:23 GMT
Content-Length: 0
```

Enqueuing a message adds it at the end of the queue. However, that doesn't necessarily mean you'll get the message in order, after all the messages you have inserted. Remember that one of the flipsides of using a large, distributed queue service is that the order in which the messages are delivered is almost never guaranteed.

Understanding Message TTL

Every message has a TTL that is set, by default, to seven days. This is the amount of time after which the message is automatically deleted. You can specify the TTL for the message by adding the parameter `messagettl=ttl-in-seconds` to the URI. The storage client library also has an equivalent method overload to set the TTL for the message you're inserting.

Peeking at a Message

You already saw how retrieving a message alters the visibility of the message. Peeking at a message is a quick way to view the messages at the front of the queue without having to change their visibility. It lets you see what kind of messages you're going to get before you have to deal with them.

To peek at messages in a queue, send an HTTP **GET** to *http://<account>.core.windows.net/<queue>/messages?peekonly=true*. You can control how many messages you want to peek at by setting the `numofmessages` parameter in the URI.

If the request is correct, the server sends down an XML response of the following form:

```
<QueueMessagesList>
   <QueueMessage>
      <MessageId>string-message-id</MessageId>
      <InsertionTime>insertion-time</InsertionTime>
      <ExpirationTime>expiration-time</ExpirationTime>
```

```
      <MessageText>message-body</MessageText>
    </QueueMessage>
</QueueMessagesList>
```

 There is no guarantee that the server will actually retrieve the number of messages you asked for.

The following code shows how to use the storage client library to peek at a message:

```
    CloudStorageAccount cloudStorageAccount =
CloudStorageAccount.Parse(ConfigurationSettings.AppSettings
["DataConnectionString"]);
            CloudQueueClient cloudQueueClient =
cloudStorageAccount.CreateCloudQueueClient();

            CloudQueue cloudQueue = cloudQueueClient.GetQueueReference("testq1");
            CloudQueueMessage msg = cloudQueue.PeekMessage();
            Console.WriteLine(msg.AsString);
```

This conjures up a handle to the queue, and then tries to peek at one message of the queue. Once it gets the message, it tries to write the message's contents to the console. Following is the HTTP capture of this operation that shows that one message is in the queue with the contents **"Sample Message"**, which gets base64-encoded:

```
GET /testq1/messages?numofmessages=1&peekonly=True&timeout=30 HTTP/1.1
x-ms-date: Sat, 04 Jul 2009 11:17:11 GMT
Authorization: SharedKey sriramk:JVCMBcloQQKSsOMBeZxia49MxWJ7OSASSSuVtEyEddc=
Host: sriramk.queue.core.windows.net
Connection: Keep-Alive
```

The server sends down an XML-formatted list containing the actual message contents, as well as **MessageIds**, and insertion and expiration times:

```
HTTP/1.1 200 OK
Content-Type: application/xml
Server: Queue Service Version 1.0 Microsoft-HTTPAPI/2.0
x-ms-request-id: c43f366d-88c0-4000-9c60-ba8844106fb2
Date: Sat, 04 Jul 2009 11:15:51 GMT
Content-Length: 337

<?xml version="1.0" encoding="utf-8"?>
<QueueMessagesList>
    <QueueMessage>
        <MessageId>bc5349e6-2a1c-4b39-a149-
2ef3ab60e28a</MessageId>
        <InsertionTime>Sat, 04 Jul 2009 00:54:47 GMT</InsertionTime>
        <ExpirationTime>Sat, 11 Jul 2009 00:46:52 GMT</ExpirationTime>
        <MessageText>U2FtcGxlIG1lc3NhZ2U=</MessageText>
    </QueueMessage>
</QueueMessagesList>
```

Getting Messages

Now it's time to examine one of the most critical operations: getting messages. You can get messages from a specific queue by sending an authorized HTTP GET to *http://<account>.core.windows.net/<queue>/messages*. There are two parameters you can modify here:

- The first, numofmessages, specifies the number of messages you want the queue service to return. By default, you get one message back.

 There is no guarantee that the queue service will actually return the number of messages you want, even if they exist in the queue at that time.

- The second, visibilitytimeout, specifies the visibility timeout of the messages you're retrieving. We examined this in detail in the section "The Life of a Message" on page 209. In short, when you get messages off a queue, the queue service automatically makes them invisible to give you time to process them. If you don't delete the message before the timeout expires (typically because you experienced an error), the queue service makes the message visible again so that some other queue receiver can get a chance to process the message.

The following code shows how to use the Microsoft storage client library to get a message off the queue. In this case, you use the default visibility timeout of two hours:

```
CloudStorageAccount cloudStorageAccount =
CloudStorageAccount.Parse(ConfigurationSettings.AppSettings
["DataConnectionString"]);
        CloudQueueClient cloudQueueClient =
cloudStorageAccount.CreateCloudQueueClient();

        CloudQueue cloudQueue = cloudQueueClient.GetQueueReference("testq1");
        CloudQueueMessage msg = cloudQueue.GetMessage();
        //Do something useful with the message
        cloudQueue.DeleteMessage(msg);
```

Following is the HTTP request for the same operation. Note that the numofmessages parameter is optional—if it is not specified, you'll get one message back:

```
GET /testq1/messages?numofmessages=1&timeout=30 HTTP/1.1
x-ms-date: Sat, 04 Jul 2009 00:56:52 GMT
Authorization: SharedKey sriramk:uOJs1nLfeD13a8N79TAZWvrDpK9a/AgwpwcoIS7T/BU=
Host: sriramk.queue.core.windows.net
```

Following is the HTTP response for this request. The server sends down an XML response containing the message contents, along with a few interesting properties:

```
HTTP/1.1 200 OK
Content-Type: application/xml
Server: Queue Service Version 1.0 Microsoft-HTTPAPI/2.0
```

```
x-ms-request-id: 0677a63d-fa82-476d-83e5-f206310b43a0
Date: Sat, 04 Jul 2009 00:54:51 GMT
Content-Length: 454

<?xml version="1.0" encoding="utf-8"?>
<QueueMessagesList>
   <QueueMessage>
    <MessageId>a59c9817-b54b-4b56-9480-1a40977da588</MessageId>
    <InsertionTime>Sat, 04 Jul 2009 00:55:22 GMT</InsertionTime>
    <ExpirationTime>Sat, 11 Jul 2009 00:51:23 GMT</ExpirationTime>
    <PopReceipt>AgAAAEAAAAAAAAAIPi8GoL8yQE=</PopReceipt>
    <TimeNextVisible>Sat, 04 Jul 2009 00:55:22 GMT</TimeNextVisible>
  <MessageText>U2FtcGxlIG1lc3NhZ2U=</MessageText>
  </QueueMessage>
</QueueMessagesList>
```

Apart from the usual suspects (such as expiration time, message ID, and message contents), the XML response contains two additional properties you haven't seen before.

One of them is `TimeNextVisible`, which is essentially when the visibility timeout expires and the message will show up on the queue again. The other is a `PopReceipt`. Just as a message ID uniquely identifies a message, a `PopReceipt` uniquely identifies each time you take a message off the queue.

Deleting Messages

After you've taken a message from the queue and finished processing it, you must delete it to stop it from appearing on the queue automatically again. To do so, send an HTTP `DELETE` to *http://<account>.core.windows.net/<queue>/messages/messageid?po-preceipt=<popreceipt>*.

> You need the `PopReceipt` property obtained from receiving a message to delete it. You can't delete a message just by knowing its `messageid` from a peek operation.

The following code shows how to get a message off the queue using the Microsoft storage client library and deleting it:

```
    CloudStorageAccount cloudStorageAccount =
CloudStorageAccount.Parse(ConfigurationSettings.AppSettings
["DataConnectionString"]);
            CloudQueueClient cloudQueueClient =
cloudStorageAccount.CreateCloudQueueClient();

            CloudQueue cloudQueue = cloudQueueClient.GetQueueReference("testq1");
            CloudQueueMessage msg = cloudQueue.GetMessage();
            //Do something useful with the message
            cloudQueue.DeleteMessage(msg);
```

You already saw the HTTP request-response content for getting messages. Following is the HTTP traffic for deleting a message. This assumes you already have a message and have a valid PopReceipt:

```
DELETE /testq1/messages/a59c9817-b54b-4b56-9480-1a40977da588?
popreceipt=AgAAAAEAAAAAAAAAIPi8GOL8yQE%3d&timeout=30 HTTP/1.1
x-ms-date: Sat, 04 Jul 2009 12:47:51 GMT
Authorization: SharedKey sriramk:D+xJP6G29d9z1SdQ61sb4UuJgaqiNwePYjB/pzTweS8=
Host: sriramk.queue.core.windows.net
Content-Length: 0
Connection: Keep-Alive
```

The server sends down an HTTP 204 if the delete was successful, and the message instantly disappears off the queue.

Deleting and Using PopReceipts

Why force users to get a message and use the PopReceipt to delete a message instead of the messageid? Imagine a world where you deleted a message just by specifying its ID. Now, imagine multiple queue receivers each taking different processing times. In this scenario, if a worker takes too long to process the message, the visibility timeout would kick in, make the message visible again, and hand the message to another worker. The first worker could then try to delete the message, even though some other worker has already started to work on the message.

The PopReceipt mechanism deals with this scenario. If your PopReceipt's visibility timeout has expired, your delete operation will fail, thereby ensuring that only the right worker is able to delete the message off the queue. The key point here is that a message must be deleted before its visibility timeout expires, and by the same worker/entity that dequeued that message.

Summary

It might seem like this chapter includes only a simple enumeration of what you can do with queues and messages. In a way, that might seem *too* simple. But that is all there is to queues. By themselves, they're extremely simple. Their value kicks in when you use them as glue to plug together a complex and reliable architecture. In several places in this book, you'll see how to plug together different pieces using queues to hold them together.

## CHAPTER 10

Tables

It is difficult to describe to someone what traffic in a major city in India is like. It is something that you must see for yourself. A typical road in India has a crosswalk, traffic signals, and all the other paraphernalia you expect from any self-respecting road. There are traffic laws and traffic cops, too, not so dissimilar from what you find in the United States. What *is* different is that the laws in India are more like "guidelines."

In India, crossing the road can be quite an adventure. You walk to the edge of the road, wait for a gap in the traffic, and dart across, like some human version of Frogger. You rarely find enough of a lull to get you all the way across, so you weave your way across traffic furiously signaling for folks to slow down. The key point here is that the onus is on the pedestrian to not get killed.

In the United States, pedestrians are encouraged to use the electronic button to activate a "walk" signal at a crosswalk, which, in the eyes of someone from India, magically switches on to protect walkers from oncoming traffic. What a great little system, prioritizing traffic signals on demand from pedestrians. Wouldn't it be great if India could do the same thing? This was demonstrably better than the chaos back home, right?

Actually, this system would never work in India. India has close to a billion people packed into a land mass several times smaller than the United States. It just isn't practical to build a system that changes traffic signals whenever someone wants to cross a road—traffic would never move. India is simply a different environment, with a different set of constraints.

The same type of contrast could be applied to the two kinds of storage systems that people are building services on today. On the one hand, you have the traditional relational database systems such as SQL Server and MySQL. On the other hand, you have these modern, semistructured storage systems that eschew relational capability for scale and speed, such as Bigtable, SimpleDB, and Windows Azure tables (collectively called the "NoSQL" movement). A litany of bloggers and armchair database administrators (DBAs) simply enjoy nothing better than to debate which of these systems is "better." The truth is that, like international traffic systems, the right answer depends on the environment you're in.

Windows Azure Table Overview

The Table service in Windows Azure provides highly reliable, structured storage at scale. You can use Azure's Table service in place of a traditional database to store all your data. Azure's Table service allows you to perform typical Create, Read, Update, Delete (CRUD) operations to manage your data. You don't have to install any software on your virtual machines, or even run extra virtual machines, since everything is managed by Windows Azure internally.

 Internally, the Azure Table service and the rest of the Windows Azure storage services run on the fabric, and draw the same benefits from the fabric as customer applications do.

The Table service is designed to minimize several problems that exist with traditional data management. It is highly scalable—users can store billions of entities (rows) if they choose to. It doesn't have a strict predefined schema like a typical relational database management system (RDBMS), and each row can have a different number (or different types) of properties. The service provides explicit control over how the data is partitioned, so users can choose a partitioning scheme that provides the best performance. However, it doesn't provide any relational features: you cannot enforce foreign key constraints, nor can you have queries that span multiple tables using joins.

But it does provide a query language with an HTTP REST-based API that enables you to create, modify, and query data. This REST API is compatible with Microsoft's ADO.NET Data Services (part of .NET 3.5 SP1), which means you can make use of Language Integrated Query (LINQ) and other cool features when writing .NET code. Since it is a REST API, any language/programming environment can access it.

Queries use the partitioning system to retrieve data with high performance without needing tuning from the user. Unlike other distributed storage systems, the Azure Table service is always *consistent*—any changes you make are instantly visible, and there is no propagation delay.

Azure's Table service is designed to be an adjunct to RDBMS services such as SQL, rather than a replacement. There'll be scenarios in which you need traditional database systems either hosted on-premises or hosted in the cloud. Later in this chapter, you'll learn about the difference between Azure tables and SQL Services, and how to choose between the two based on your needs.

Core Concepts

Azure's Table service incorporates a few top-level concepts:

* Tables

- Entities
- Properties

Figure 10-1 shows how these concepts relate to each other.

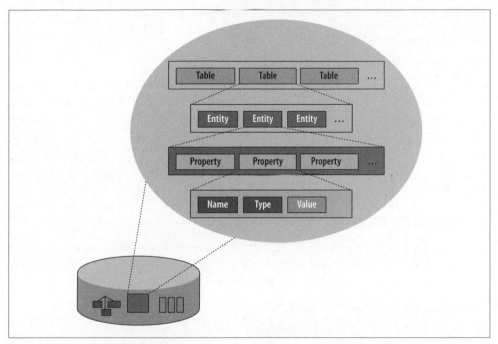

Figure 10-1. Tables, entities, and properties

Understanding tables

A *table* is a container for a related set of data. Tables are created under a storage account (as you learned in Chapter 7), and one storage account can have any number of tables. Authentication is performed at the storage account level, and you use the same authentication mechanism that you use with the other storage services. Tables are also the unit of querying—queries cannot span multiple tables.

A query against a table is through an HTTP GET against a URL and is formatted as *http://<StorageAccount>.table.core.windows.net/<TableName>?filter=<Query>*.

Understanding entities

Data is stored in tables in the form of *entities*. You can think of an entity as a row in normal database terms. A table can literally have billions of entities, if necessary. Entities are also the unit of read and write access. A successful query returns a set of entities. When you write changes back to the service, each entity is atomically written— you won't see a situation where certain parts of the entity were updated with a conflicting write. You can also specify concurrency at the entity level. You could choose to have a model where, in the case of multiple writers, only the first could succeed, or only the last could succeed.

Entities have two special properties: RowKey and PartitionKey. This controls an important aspect of Azure tables: *partitioning*. You'll learn about this in detail later in this chapter. When put together, these form the *primary key* of the entity.

Understanding properties

Properties are the equivalent of columns—they are an individual category of data in a table. An entity can have up to 255 properties. Properties do not have a fixed schema—two entities within the same table can have a different number or different types of properties.

Each property has a name, a type, and a value. The various types available in Azure tables are String (up to 64 KB), Binary (up to 64 KB), Bool, DateTime, GUID, Int, Int64, and Double.

Correlating to database terminology

It is sometimes tricky to keep track of the terminology, so Table 10-1 lists some familiar database terms and their rough equivalents in Azure's Table service. Table 10-2 lists the sizes and limits of the core resources and types.

Table 10-1. Lingo map

Database term	Azure Table service term
Table	Table
Row	Entity
Column	Property
Shard/partition	Partition
Primary key	PartitionKey + RowKey

Table 10-2. Sizes and limits

Resource/type	Size/range/limit
PartitionKey	Up to 64 KB
RowKey (String)	Up to 64 KB
String	UTF-16, up to 64 KB
Bool	True/False
DateTime	8 bytes, ranging from 1/1/1600 to 12/31/9999
GUID	16 bytes
Int	32 bits

Resource/type	Size/range/limit
Long	64 bits
Double	64 bytes
Entity	1 MB
Number of properties in an entity	255 + RowKey + PartitionKey
Property name	255 characters
Maximum entities returned from a single query	1,000
Number of tables	No limit
Number of entities	No limit
Combined size of entity	1 MB (including the property names)
Total table size	No limit (but a storage account is limited to 100 TB)

Azure Tables Versus Traditional Databases

Usually, the people who experience the least amount of trouble moving from their existing storage systems to Azure's Table service are the ones who accept that this is not a normal database system, and don't expect to find typical SQL features.

Let's take a quick look at a brief comparison of Azure tables versus traditional database tables.

Denormalized data

In a traditional database system, DBAs go to great lengths to ensure that data isn't repeated, and that data is consistent. This is done through a process called *normalization*. Depending on how much time you have and how obsessive you are, you could normalize your data to multiple levels. Normalization serves a good purpose: it ensures data integrity. On the other hand, it hurts performance.

Data stored in one Azure table does not have any relationship with data stored in another Azure table. You cannot specify foreign key constraints to ensure that data in one table is always consistent with data in another table. You must ensure that your schema is sufficiently *denormalized*.

Any user running a high-performance database system has probably denormalized parts of that system's schema, or at least experimented with it. Denormalization involves storing multiple copies of data and achieving data consistency by performing multiple writes. Though this gives the user better performance and flexibility, the onus is now on the developer to maintain data integrity. If you forget to update one table, your data could become inconsistent, and difficult-to-diagnose errors could show up at the application level. Also, all the extra writes you must do take time and can hurt performance.

In forums, in books, and on the blogosphere, you may see some "experts" recommending that people denormalize to improve performance. No one takes the trouble to explain why this can help. The reason behind it is simple: data in different tables is typically stored in different files on disk, or sometimes on different machines. Normalization implies database joins that must load multiple tables into memory. This requires reading from multiple places and, thus, hurts performance. One of the reasons Azure tables provide good performance is that the data is denormalized by default.

If you're willing to live with very short periods of inconsistency, you can do asynchronous writes or move the writes to a worker process. In some sense, this is inevitable. All major Web 2.0 sites (such as Flickr) frequently run tools that check for data consistency issues and fix them.

No schema

Several advantages come with a fixed schema for all your data. Schema can act as a safety net, trading flexibility for safety—any errors in your code where you mismatch data types can be caught early. However, this same safety net gets in your way when you have semistructured data. Changing a table's structure to add/change columns is difficult (and sometimes impossible) to do (ALTER TABLE is the stuff of nightmares).

Azure tables have no schema. Entities in the same table can have completely different properties, or a different number of properties. Like denormalization, the onus is on the developer to ensure that updates reflect the correct schema.

No distributed transactions

If you are accustomed to using transactions to maintain consistency and integrity, the idea of not having any transactions can be scary. However, in any distributed storage system, transactions across machines hurt performance. As with normalization, the onus is on the developer to maintain consistency and run scripts to ensure that.

This is not as scary or as difficult as it sounds. Large services such as Facebook and Flickr have long eschewed transactions as they scaled out. It's a fundamental trade-off that you make with cloud-based storage systems.

Though distributed transactions aren't available, Windows Azure tables have support for "entity group transactions" that allows you to batch requests together for entities in the same partition.

Black box

If you've ever run a database for a service, you've probably mucked with its configuration. The first thing a lot of developers do when setting up MySQL is dive into *my.cnf* and tune the various knobs that are available. Entire books have been written on tuning indexes, picking storage engines, and optimizing query plans.

The Azure Table service does not provide you with the individual knobs to perform that level of tuning. Since it is a large distributed system, the service itself automatically tunes based on data, workload, traffic, and various other factors. The only option you have control over is how your data is partitioned (which will be addressed shortly). This lack of knobs to turn can be a blessing, since the system takes care of tuning for you.

Row size limits

An entity can have only up to 1 MB of data, a number that includes the names of your properties. If you are used to sticking large pieces of data in each row (a questionable practice in itself), you might easily reach this limit. In cases such as this, the right thing to do is to use the blob storage service, and store a pointer to the blob in the entity. This is similar to storing large pieces of data in the filesystem, and having the database maintain a pointer to the specific file.

Lack of support for familiar tools

Like other cloud storage systems, the Azure Table service is pretty nascent. This means the ecosystem around it is nascent, too. Tools you're comfortable with for SQL Server, Oracle, or MySQL mostly won't work with Azure tables, and you might find it difficult to find replacements. This is a problem that will be solved over time as more people adopt the service.

ADO.NET Data Services Primer

The preferred mechanism to code against the Azure Table service on the Microsoft stack is through ADO.NET Data Services.

> If you're familiar with ADO.NET Data Services (you might remember it by its codename, Astoria), you can skip over this section without missing anything. Note that this is quite different from standard ADO.NET, despite the name.
>
> As of this writing, ADO.NET Data Services was being renamed to WCF Data Services. If you search the Web, you might see documentation and posts reflecting the new name. Don't worry, though, the technology is absolutely the same.

When the Red Dog team was designing what would become the Azure storage services, they knew they needed a way to let people model and query their data through an HTTP API. Instead of designing something from scratch, they found that another technology at Microsoft was designed for this specific purpose.

ADO.NET Data Services shipped along with .NET 3.5 Service Pack 1. It enables people to expose data via web services accessed over HTTP. The data is addressed through a RESTful URI. Customers can use it to both *expose* data services and *consume* data services. This discussion will deal only with the latter, since Azure's Table service takes care of exposing your data.

You can write code in .NET to consume these services, and query against the data using LINQ. Just remember that ADO.NET Data Services lets you expose data over HTTP, and on the client side it lets you write data access code (CRUD) against these services.

Exposing Data Services

In essence, you can pretend that data stored in some storage system (be it SQL Server or a file) is actually a plain Common Language Runtime (CLR) object. It may not have all the semantics of a *Plain Old CLR Object* (POCO), but most times it works just as well.

Example 10-1 shows a simple POCO class.

Example 10-1. Plain-vanilla CLR class

```
public class Cylon
{
    public int ID { get; set; }
    public String Name { get; set; }
}
```

 The choice of ID for the property isn't arbitrary. ADO.NET Data Services needs a "key" for each entity to uniquely identify it. If you have a property named ID or <Typename>ID, it automatically uses that as the key. You can use the [DataServiceKey] attribute if you want to use another property as the key.

Let's assume that you have a bunch of Employee objects, loaded from a data source somewhere. To enable people to access them as a RESTful service over HTTP, you must follow these steps:

1. Implement a web service that wraps around these objects.
2. Add code to map these objects to a JSON or XML representation.
3. Write code to perform CRUD operations.
4. Write code to perform queries. (This becomes difficult very quickly when you have to deal with arbitrary queries.)
5. Write client-side code that knows how to parse data from this service, and knows how to call such a service.

You could do all this, but it's a lot of work. A simpler approach would be to let ADO.NET Data Services take care of all this for you.

 This book touches only lightly on the server-side aspects of ADO.NET Data Services.

Let's turn this into a Cylon web service that lets you query and add Cylons. Note that this work is done for you in Windows Azure. The following examination walks you through this so that you may understand how all the pieces fit together.

 A *Cylon* (Cybernetic Lifeform Node) is a "race" of machines depicted in the television series *Battlestar Gallactica*.

1. The first step is to move the `Cylon` class shown in Example 10-1 into an ASP.NET web application or Windows Communication Foundation (WCF) web service. Any project that listens over HTTP will do.

2. You must then create a "data source" class that wraps around the `Cylon` class. Usually, ADO.NET Data Services is used to wrap around Entity Framework data, and it generates this automatically. This class needs a property that returns an `IQueryable` over the objects you want to query. The code in Example 10-2 does just that. It creates a list of Cylons, and exposes them through a property of the same name. If you want to add support for adding/removing/updating entities, you must implement `IUpdateable`, but that is not necessary in Example 10-2.

Example 10-2. Generating a list of Cylons

```
public class CylonDataModel
    {
        private List<Cylon> _emps;

        public CylonDataModel()
        {

            _emps = new List<Cylon> {
                new Cylon(){ID = 1, Name="Cavil"},
                new Cylon(){ID = 2, Name = "Leoben"},
                new Cylon(){ID = 3, Name = "D'Anna"},
                new Cylon(){ID = 4, Name = "Simon"},
                new Cylon(){ID = 5, Name ="Aaron"},
                new Cylon(){ID = 6, Name ="Six"},
                new Cylon(){ID = 7, Name = "Daniel"},
                new Cylon(){ID = 8, Name = "Sharon"}
            };
```

```
    }

    public IQueryable<Cylon> Cylons
    {
        get { return _emps.AsQueryable<Cylon>(); }
    }

}
```

3. Now you come to the meat of the operation. In Visual Studio, go to Add→New Item and add a new ADO.NET Data Service called `CylonService.svc`. This is the WCF service that clients will hit. Typically, it has very little code (most of the magic occurs under the covers). Modify the generated code so that the service inherits from `DataService<CylonDataModel>`.

 If you can't see "ADO.NET Data Service" in the New Item dialog box, ensure that you have .NET 3.5 SP1 and Visual Studio 2008 SP1 installed.

4. The final step is to specify that clients have access to all the data you are exposing and the right to call your service operations. This is always a bad idea in the real world, but it works well for this demo code. You do this by specifying a wildcard, *, for the service's configuration inside the `InitializeService` method. Example 10-3 shows the finished code.

Example 10-3. Cylon data service

```
public class CylonService : DataService<CylonDataModel>
    {
        // This method is called only once to initialize service-wide policies.
        public static void InitializeService(IDataServiceConfiguration config)
        {
            config.SetEntitySetAccessRule("*", EntitySetRights.AllRead);
            config.SetServiceOperationAccessRule("*",
                    ServiceOperationRights.All);
        }
    }
```

You now have a working ADO.NET Data Service. Let's take it for a spin. Press F5 and Visual Studio will launch the service in a browser. Visual Studio will run this on localhost and a random port. You can now query the service using any HTTP client or web browser. Example 10-4 shows the results.

Example 10-4. Querying the Cylon service

```
http://localhost:1096/CylonService.svc/Cylons
```

```
?xml version="1.0" encoding="utf-8" standalone="yes"?>
<feed xml:base=http://localhost:1096/CylonService.svc/
```

```
xmlns:d=http://schemas.microsoft.com/ado/2007/08/dataservices
xmlns:m="http://schemas.microsoft.com/ado/2007/08/dataservices/metadata"
xmlns="http://www.w3.org/2005/Atom">
 <title type="text">Cylons</title>
 <id>http://localhost:1096/CylonService.svc/Cylons</id>
 <updated>2009-04-16T08:06:17Z</updated>
 <link rel="self" title="Cylons" href="Cylons" />
 <entry>
   <id>http://localhost:1096/CylonService.svc/Cylons(1)</id>
   <title type="text"></title>
   <updated>2009-04-16T08:06:17Z</updated>
   <author>
     <name />
   </author>
   <link rel="edit" title="Cylon" href="Cylons(1)" />
   <category term="WebApplication1.Cylon"
scheme="http://schemas.microsoft.com/ado/2007/08/dataservices/scheme" />
   <content type="application/xml">
     <m:properties>
       <d:ID m:type="Edm.Int32">1</d:ID>
       <d:Name>Cavil</d:Name>
     </m:properties>
   </content>
 </entry>
 ...
```

If you look closely at the verbose XML you get back, you can see that it is an XML representation of the Cylon objects. Even better, it is a fully Atom-compliant feed. (You can also get back JSON if you choose to by sending an additional HTTP header.) Essentially, by hitting the /Cylons URL, you hit the Cylons property in your CylonDataMo del class. Since you haven't specified any sort of filtering, you get back all the items in the list.

The real power of ADO.NET Data Services shows up in automatically parsing queries and returning results. Let's walk through a few examples of that. Example 10-5 shows how you can use the $top parameter to return the first N elements (in this case, just 1).

Example 10-5. Queries through the URI

http://localhost:1096/CylonService.svc/Cylons?$top=1

```
<?xml version="1.0" encoding="utf-8" standalone="yes" ?>
 <feed xml:base="http://localhost:1096/CylonService.svc/"
xmlns:d="http://schemas.microsoft.com/ado/2007/08/dataservices"
xmlns:m="http://schemas.microsoft.com/ado/2007/08/dataservices/metadata"
xmlns="http://www.w3.org/2005/Atom">
   <title type="text">Cylons</title>
   <id>http://localhost:1096/CylonService.svc/Cylons</id>
   <updated>2009-04-16T08:43:14Z</updated>
   <link rel="self" title="Cylons" href="Cylons" />
   <entry>
   <id>http://localhost:1096/CylonService.svc/Cylons(1)</id>
   <title type="text" />
   <updated>2009-04-16T08:43:14Z</updated>
```

```
<author>
<name />
</author>
<link rel="edit" title="Cylon" href="Cylons(1)" />
<category term="WebApplication1.Cylon"
scheme="http://schemas.microsoft.com/ado/2007/08/dataservices/scheme" />
<content type="application/xml">
<m:properties>
<d:ID m:type="Edm.Int32">1</d:ID>
<d:Name>Cavil</d:Name>
</m:properties>
</content>
</entry>
</feed>
```

You can perform arbitrary filtering using the `$filter` parameter. Example 10-6 shows how to use the `$filter` parameter to retrieve only Cylons that match the filter parameters. (You can see how MSDN documents all the clauses you can use for the `$filter` clause by visiting *http://msdn.microsoft.com/en-us/library/cc668778.aspx*.)

Example 10-6. Basic filtering

```
Return entries with ID greater than 6
http://localhost:1096/CylonService.svc/Cylons?$filter=(ID gt 6)

Return entries where the Name property is 'Sharon'
http://localhost:1096/CylonService.svc/Cylons?$filter=(Name eq 'Sharon')
```

 ADO.NET Data Services supports several complex filtering operations, as well as aggregate functions (such as sum and average) and expansions. These are not examined here, primarily because Azure's Table service doesn't support any URI operations other than `$filter` and `$top`.

Awesome, isn't it? You just got a ton of querying support for free. Since the output is very web standards friendly, it is easy to build clients in any language/toolkit. This discussion showed you how ADO.NET Data Services integrates with .NET and provides rich querying capabilities over HTTP. In Windows Azure, you don't need to do any of this, since it is done by Azure's Table service. However, it is helpful to understand how the various components fit together.

Now, let's explore how to write *client-side code* for ADO.NET Data Services.

Consuming Data Services

If you chose to, you could write your own library to parse the Atom/JSON results from ADO.NET Data Services and form the right URIs for queries. For non-.NET platforms, there are various open source libraries you can use. However, if you're using .NET, you should be using the built-in support in .NET 3.5 SP1.

DataServiceContext and DataServiceQuery

`DataServiceContext` and `DataServiceQuery` form the core of ADO.NET Data Services' support on the client side. If you're familiar with the Entity Framework, you'll be pleased to learn that these perform similar functions to the Entity Framework's `Object Context` and `ObjectQuery`.

`DataServiceContext` is essentially used for state management. HTTP is stateless, and the server doesn't "remember" the status of each client between updates. `DataService Context` layers on top of the HTTP stack to support change tracking. When you make changes to data in your client, the changes are accumulated in the `DataServiceCon text`. They're committed to the server when you call `SaveChanges`. `DataServiceCon text` also controls conflict resolution and merge strategies. You can choose how to deal with conflicts when updating entities.

`DataServiceQuery` goes hand in hand with `DataServiceContext`. In fact, the only way you can get your hands on an instance of `DataServiceQuery` is through `DataServiceCon text`. If you imagine `DataServiceContext` as the local representation of a service, `Data ServiceQuery` would be analogous to a single query on that service. The two key methods on `DataServiceQuery`—`CreateQuery<T>` and `Execute<T>`—both take a URI (using the URI syntax discussed earlier) and return an `IEnumerable` to walk through the results.

Let's look at how you can take the `Cylon` service you built earlier and run queries against it from client code:

1. Add a Console project to your solution from the previous section. You can use any .NET project type. The console application is used in this examination, since that has the least amount of "cruft." Be sure to pick .NET Framework 3.5 as the framework version.

2. The client code must know to what type to deserialize the results. Add *Cylon.cs* from the other project to your console application. In a real-world application, you would put shared types in a class library that is shared by both your server-side and client-side pieces.

3. Add references to `System.Data.Services` and `System.Data.Services.Client`.

4. Add `using` statements at the top of your console app's *Main.cs* to bring in the `System.Data.Services.Client` namespace, as well as the namespace in which *Cylon.cs* resides.

5. Example 10-7 shows how you can execute a simple query that loops through all the Cylons in the service. You call up a new `DataServiceContext` instance and wrap it around the `Cylon` service. You create a `DataServiceQuery` from that instance and use it to loop through all the Cylons in the system.

Example 10-7. Client-side query

```
static void Main(string[] args)
    {
        // Replace 1096 below with the port your service is running on
        DataServiceContext ctx = new DataServiceContext(
            new Uri("http://localhost:1096/CylonService.svc"));

        DataServiceQuery<Cylon> query = ctx.CreateQuery<Cylon>("/Cylons");
        foreach (Cylon cylon in query)
        {
            Console.WriteLine(cylon.Name);
        }
    }
}
```

If you run the code shown in Example 10-7 (ensure that the service is also running!), you should see the list of Cylons you entered. In the original code, you did not add support on the server side for creating or updating entities since, frankly, that's a lot of code that you'll never need to write with Windows Azure. However, if you had implemented IUpdateable, you could write the code shown in Example 10-8 to add entities.

Example 10-8. Adding an object

```
DataServiceContext ctx = new DataServiceContext(
        new Uri("http://localhost:1096/CylonService.svc"));

ctx.AddObject("Cylons", new Cylon { ID = 9, Name = "Tyrol" });
ctx.SaveChanges();
```

Updating and deleting entities works in a similar fashion. In both cases, you get the object you want to update/delete and use the DataServiceContext to perform the operation. Example 10-9 shows both scenarios. Note how you address the entity you want to update/delete using the primary key in the URL.

Example 10-9. Update and delete

```
DataServiceContext ctx = new DataServiceContext(
    new Uri("http://localhost:1096/CylonService.svc"));
var query = ctx.Execute<Cylon>(
    new Uri("/Cylons(1)", UriKind.Relative));


//Update Cavil's name
Cylon cavil = query.FirstOrDefault<Cylon>();
cavil.Name = "Cavil is evil!";
ctx.SaveChanges();

//Now delete Cavil
ctx.DeleteObject(cavil);
ctx.SaveChanges();
```

This also highlights an issue with ADO.NET Data Services. You must load an object into the context before you can delete it. One workaround is to create an entity on the client side using the `AttachTo` method (this entity should have the same primary key as the entity you want to delete), calling `DeleteObject` and `SaveChanges`.

LINQ support

One of the biggest draws for ADO.NET Data Services is the ability to use LINQ queries. The LINQ-to-REST provider converts LINQ queries into URI requests. Note that this is only a subset of the full capabilities of LINQ. Operations such as `GroupBy` and `Count` are disallowed because these aggregate operations have no URI equivalent.

Example 10-10 shows how you could write a LINQ query to query for a specific `Cylon` differently. Note that, to make this work, you must use the Add Service Reference dialog to generate a strongly typed `DataServiceContext`.

Example 10-10. LINQ support

```
var ctx = new CylonDataModel(new Uri("http://localhost:1096/CylonService.svc"));
var query = from c in ctx.Cylons where c.ID == 4 select c;
```

Table Operations

In this section, let's look at some of the operations that are possible against individual tables using the Table service.

Creating Tables

As you have learned, Azure's Table service stores your data in one or more tables. Each table is a logically distinct domain. You cannot create queries that span tables. Currently, there is no limit on the number of tables you can create.

Every Azure table operation has a RESTful request + response with a corresponding wrapper in the storage client. All REST traffic is encoded using Atom Publishing Protocol.

The following code shows the request HTTP headers and body for creating a simple `ContactsTable` operation. Note that there is no schema specified anywhere. Properties are defined at the individual entity level, and not at the table level. The lines that specify authentication and the table name are highlighted. Authentication is performed using the `SharedKeyLite` scheme discussed in previous chapters.

```
POST /Tables HTTP/1.1
User-Agent: Microsoft ADO.NET Data Services
x-ms-date: Mon, 20 Apr 2009 17:30:08 GMT
Authorization: SharedKeyLite sriramk:mQrl9rffHDUKKPEEfUyZdLvKWTT0a8o3jvaeoS8QMIU=
Accept: application/atom+xml,application/xml
Accept-Charset: UTF-8
```

```
DataServiceVersion: 1.0;NetFx
MaxDataServiceVersion: 1.0;NetFx
Content-Type: application/atom+xml
Host: sriramk.table.core.windows.net
Content-Length: 494

<?xml version="1.0" encoding="utf-8" standalone="yes"?>
<entry xmlns:d=http://schemas.microsoft.com/ado/2007/08/dataservices
 xmlns:m="http://schemas.microsoft.com/ado/2007/08/dataservices/metadata"
xmlns="http://www.w3.org/2005/Atom">
  <title />
  <updated>2009-04-20T17:30:08.533Z</updated>
  <author>
    <name />
  </author>
  <id />
  <content type="application/xml">
    <m:properties>
      <d:TableName>ContactTable</d:TableName>
    </m:properties>
  </content>
</entry>
```

If everything went well, the server will respond with a message such as the following:

```
HTTP/1.1 201 Created
Cache-Control: no-cache
Content-Type: application/atom+xml;charset=utf-8
Location: http://sriramk.table.core.windows.net/Tables('ContactTable')
Server: Table Service Version 1.0 Microsoft-HTTPAPI/2.0
x-ms-request-id: cd54647a-140a-4085-b269-cceb86551005
Date: Mon, 20 Apr 2009 17:29:00 GMT
Content-Length: 797

<?xml version="1.0" encoding="utf-8" standalone="yes"?>
<entry xml:base=http://sriramk.table.core.windows.net/
 xmlns:d="http://schemas.microsoft.com/ado/2007/08/dataservices"
xmlns:m=http://schemas.microsoft.com/ado/2007/08/dataservices/metadata
 xmlns="http://www.w3.org/2005/Atom">
  <id>http://sriramk.table.core.windows.net/Tables('ContactTable')</id>
  <title type="text"></title>
  <updated>2009-04-20T17:29:01Z</updated>
  <author>
    <name />
  </author>
  <link rel="edit" title="Tables" href="Tables('ContactTable')" />
  <category term="sriramk.Tables"
scheme="http://schemas.microsoft.com/ado/2007/08/dataservices/scheme" />

  <content type="application/xml">
    <m:properties>
      <d:TableName>ContactTable</d:TableName>
    </m:properties>
  </content>
</entry>
```

Why use the `SharedKeyLite` authentication scheme? Why not use the same authentication scheme as blobs and queues? This stems from the way ADO.NET Data Services is implemented. In blobs and queues, signing takes place as the last step, and has access to all the headers. However, ADO.NET Data Services doesn't give access to all the headers through a "hook" that could let the same kind of signing happen. Hence, a variant of the standard authentication scheme was devised for use in the Table service.

If you're the kind of person who likes to write XML parsing code all day, you can probably skip the following discussion (and apply for a job on the Windows Azure team—a ton of XML parsing is done on that team!). However, the rest of us mortals will probably use a client library. If you're a .NET developer, the obvious choice is to use the official storage client library.

What if you're not a .NET developer? Unlike blobs and queues, not many open source libraries talk to Azure's Table service. This is partially because a lot of Atom parsing must be done. That is also why this discussion doesn't walk through a Python or Ruby sample. However, expect this situation to change as the Table service becomes more popular.

Let's build a simple `Contacts` table. If you're familiar with *Object Relational Mapping* (ORM) on .NET, the rest of this will sound familiar.

You start by creating a `Contact` class as shown in Example 10-11.

Example 10-11. Simple Contacts table

```
public class Contact : TableServiceEntity
    {
        public Contact(string partitionKey, string rowKey)
            : base(partitionKey, rowKey)
        {
        }

        public Contact()
            : base()
        {
            PartitionKey = Guid.NewGuid().ToString();
            RowKey = String.Empty;
        }

        public string Name
        {
            get;
            set;
        }

        public string Address
        {
            get;
```

```
        set;
    }
}
```

This inherits from `Microsoft.WindowsAzure.StorageClient.TableServiceEntity`, which is a class in the storage client library that takes care of a lot of the plumbing for you. You define a `PartitionKey` and a `RowKey` in this class. The partition key is always a new GUID, and you use an empty row key. This implies that every partition will have only one row that is perfectly fine. We will examine the subject of partitioning shortly, so don't worry if this sounds fuzzy now. You also define some simple properties: `Name` and `Address`.

Note that although Azure's Table service doesn't have any schema during creation of the table, you must define your schema while using the client library upfront. You must now create a wrapper `DataServiceContext`-derived type to enable you to create and execute queries.

If you are used to calling ADO.NET Data Services against the Entity Framework, you know this is automatically generated. However, in the case of Azure's Table service, the plumbing to make it automatically generated doesn't exist, and you must manually write it. However, they're very simple to author, and you can use a template from which you can copy and paste.

Example 10-12 shows a simple `ContactDataServiceContext` class that does everything required. Note that the name of the table is specified inside this class.

Example 10-12. Simple DataServiceContext-derived class

```
class ContactDataServiceContext : TableServiceContext
    {
        internal ContactDataServiceContext (string baseAddress,
                StorageCredentials credentials)
            : base(baseAddress, credentials)
        {
        }

        internal const string ContactTableName = "ContactTable";

        public IQueryable<Contact> ContactTable
        {
            get
            {
                return this.CreateQuery<Contact>(ContactTableName);
            }
        }
    }
```

With all the data-modeling table code in place, it is now time to create your tables. You typically place this code inside a startup script, or some code that is executed when your application launches. The code shown in Example 10-13 does two things. It first checks whether the table exists, and then creates a table.

Example 10-13. Creating the table

```
            var account =
                CloudStorageAccount.Parse(ConfigurationSettings.AppSettings
["DataConnectionString"]);
account.CreateCloudTableClient().CreateTableIfNotExist("ContactTable");
```

If you use Fiddler/Netmon/Wireshark to peek at the HTTP traffic, you should first see
the following HTTP request-response pair. But after that, you would see that the actual
table-creation traffic is identical to the REST messages you saw earlier in this chapter.

HTTP request for table existence check(abbreviated)

```
GET /Tables('ContactTable') HTTP/1.1
```

HTTP response (abbreviated)

```
<?xml version="1.0" encoding="utf-8" standalone="yes"?>
<error xmlns="http://schemas.microsoft.com/ado/2007/08/dataservices/metadata">
  <code>ResourceNotFound</code>
  <message xml:lang="en-US">The specified resource does not exist.</message>
</error>
```

Creating Entities

Creating entities is similar to the process for creating tables. You can create an entity
by POSTing to the URL for the table. For example, the following code shows the HTTP
request-response traffic for creating a simple contact. Note that the properties of the
entity are encoded using Atom. You annotate specific types (such as dates/times) with
the right Entity Framework attribute.

```
POST /ContactTable HTTP/1.1
x-ms-date: Tue, 21 Apr 2009 06:39:17 GMT
Authorization: SharedKeyLite sriramk:hdSwtwXUeuDrY2LTvsySw8oDOhcCwKpbqeLL4IbaBJs=
Accept: application/atom+xml,application/xml
Accept-Charset: UTF-8
Content-Type: application/atom+xml
Host: sriramk.table.core.windows.net
Content-Length: 719

<?xml version="1.0" encoding="utf-8" standalone="yes"?>
<entry xmlns:d=http://schemas.microsoft.com/ado/2007/08/dataservices
 xmlns:m=http://schemas.microsoft.com/ado/2007/08/dataservices/metadata
 xmlns="http://www.w3.org/2005/Atom">

  <title />
  <updated>2009-04-21T06:39:17.3098Z</updated>
  <author>
    <name />
  </author>
  <id />
  <content type="application/xml">
    <m:properties>
```

```
        <d:Address>One Infinite Loop</d:Address>
        <d:Name>Steve Jobs</d:Name>
        <d:PartitionKey>a844fa27-7ae2-4894-9cc6-dd0dbdcd5ec4</d:PartitionKey>
        <d:RowKey m:null="false" />
        <d:Timestamp m:type="Edm.DateTime">0001-01-01T00:00:00</d:Timestamp>
      </m:properties>
    </content>
  </entry>
```

If the entity is created successfully, the server sends down an HTTP 201 message, an ETag, and a copy of the entity.

Of course, all of this is just ADO.NET Data Services plumbing. In .NET code, you typically go through the following steps:

1. Write your data model classes. In this case, you already wrote these when you created your table.

2. Create an instance of the DataServiceContext-derived type to which to add local changes.

3. Call SaveChanges to upload changes to the cloud.

Example 10-14 shows how you can write code to add an entity to ContactTable. This produces the same HTTP traffic as shown earlier.

Example 10-14. Adding an entity

```
        var account =
CloudStorageAccount.Parse(ConfigurationSettings.AppSettings
["DataConnectionString"]);

var svc = new TestDataServiceContext(account.TableEndpoint.ToString(),
                               account.Credentials);
//We don't need to specify PartitionKey since it is generated for us in Contact
//constructor
        var contact = new Contact(){
            Name="Steve Jobs",
            Address="One Infinite Loop"
      };
      svc.AddObject("ContactTable", contact);
      svc.SaveChanges();
```

What is happening here under the covers? Think of DataServiceContext as a sync engine. It accumulates changes on the client, and sends them in one shot to the server when SaveChanges is called. In this case, you're adding an object to a table (entity set), but the same holds true when you're updating/deleting entities, too.

Querying Data

In what is probably the most famous sequence in Douglas Adams' *The Hitchhiker's Guide to the Galaxy* (Pan Books), a pan-dimensional, hyper-intelligent race of beings want to know "the ultimate answer to life, the universe, and everything." They build a supercomputer called Deep Thought that is the size of a small city, and they set it working on this problem. It calculates for seven and a half million years, and finally announces that it has the solution. The ultimate answer to life, the universe, and everything is...(drum roll)...42!

When the flabbergasted audience asks the computer whether it is sure, it answers:

> [I] checked it very thoroughly, and that quite definitely is the answer. I think the problem, to be quite honest with you, is that you've never actually known what the question was.

Regardless of whether we're talking about the ultimate answer to life, the universe, and everything, or just Azure's Table service, the key is to ask the right question. Thankfully, using LINQ and ADO.NET Data Services to query Azure tables is a lot easier than dealing with hyper-intelligent, slightly obnoxious supercomputers.

Queries are the primary mechanism for retrieving data from Azure's Table service. You can query for any entity (or a set of entities) in a table using the attributes that make up the entity. These are user-defined attributes, as well as the two "system" attributes: PartitionKey and RowKey. Queries can return a maximum of 1,000 entities as results, and there is a built-in pagination mechanism to retrieve more than 1,000 entities.

All queries get formatted into a $filter parameter that is sent as part of an HTTP GET to the Azure Table service. The service returns an Atom feed of entities formatted using the same representation as when the entities were uploaded. Example 10-15 shows a sample HTTP query to retrieve the entity that has been inserted.

Example 10-15. Sample request and response

Request
```
GET /ContactTable()?$filter=Name%20eq%20'Steve%20Jobs' HTTP/1.1
```

Response
```
<?xml version="1.0" encoding="utf-8" standalone="yes"?>
<feed xml:base="http://sriramk.table.core.windows.net/"
xmlns:d="http://schemas.microsoft.com/ado/2007/08/dataservices"
xmlns:m=http://schemas.microsoft.com/ado/2007/08/dataservices/metadata
 xmlns="http://www.w3.org/2005/Atom">
  <title type="text">ContactTable</title>
  <id>http://sriramk.table.core.windows.net/ContactTable</id>
  <updated>2009-04-21T08:29:12Z</updated>
  <link rel="self" title="ContactTable" href="ContactTable" />
  <entry m:etag="W/&quot;datetime'2009-04-21T06%3A38%3A28.242Z'&quot;">
    <id>http://sriramk.table.core.windows.net/ContactTable(
        PartitionKey='a844fa27-7ae2-4894-9cc6-dd0dbdcd5ec4',RowKey='')</id>
    <title type="text"></title>
    <updated>2009-04-21T08:29:12Z</updated>
    <author>
      <name />
    </author>
    <link rel="edit" title="ContactTable"
href="ContactTable(PartitionKey='a844fa27-7ae2-4894-9cc6-dd0dbdcd5ec4',
```

```
      RowKey='')" />
   <category term="sriramk.ContactTable"
scheme="http://schemas.microsoft.com/ado/2007/08/dataservices/scheme" />
   <content type="application/xml">
     <m:properties>
       <d:PartitionKey>a844fa27-7ae2-4894-9cc6-dd0dbdcd5ec4</d:PartitionKey>
       <d:RowKey></d:RowKey>
       <d:Timestamp m:type="Edm.DateTime">2009-04-21T06:38:28.242Z</d:Timestamp>
       <d:Address>One Infinite Loop</d:Address>
       <d:Name>Steve Jobs</d:Name>
     </m:properties>
   </content>
  </entry>
</feed>
```

If you look at the verbose XML returned from the service, you see that, apart from an Atom representation of the entities matching the query (in this case, only one), you also get back an ETag. This ETag is unique for every version of the entity, and is used to ensure that your client side updates only entities of which it has the latest copy.

Example 10-16 shows how you write the same query in LINQ. You can combine arbitrary logical operations in your query, and the "plumbing" underneath ensures that the right $filter query is generated.

Example 10-16. LINQ query

```
               var account =
CloudStorageAccount.Parse(ConfigurationSettings.AppSettings
["DataConnectionString"]);
var svc = new TestDataServiceContext(account.TableEndpoint.ToString(),
 account.Credentials);

       var query = from contact in svc.CreateQuery<Contact>("ContactTable")
                   where contact.Name == "Steve Jobs"
                   select contact;

       foreach(Contact c in query)
       {
           Console.WriteLine(c.Name);
       }
```

You can construct arbitrarily complex queries. For example, let's say you had an Employee table with a standard Employee type. You could construct queries such as that shown in Example 10-17. Consult the ADO.NET Data Services documentation on how to construct $filter queries if you're interested in constructing these by hand.

Example 10-17. Sample queries

```
//This assumes an Entity class and table with properties like ID, Salary,
//Name, Department and so on.

//Get employees with specific salary range who don't work in engineering
var query = from emp in svc.CreateQuery<Employee>("EmployeeTable">
        where emp.Salary>100000 && emp.Salary<150000
```

```
                && emp.Department != "Engineering";

//Get all lawyers. Might be useful when drawing up a list of people
// to get rid of. Just kidding!
var query = from emp.svc.CreateQuery<Employee>("EmployeeTable">
            where emp.Title=="Attorney" && emp.Department == "Legal";
```

One issue that most people run into very quickly is that Azure's Table service supports
only a subset of LINQ and the features supported by ADO.NET Data Services. If you
find an exception being thrown on query execution, check your query to ensure that
you don't have an unsupported clause.

Tables 10-3 and 10-4 document what query operations and comparison operators are
supported. If it's not in these tables, it's not supported.

Table 10-3. Supported query operators

LINQ operator	Details
From	Supported
Where	Supported
Take	Supported, but with values less than or equal to 1,000

Table 10-4. Supported comparison operators

Comparison operator	Property types supported
Equal	All
GreaterThan	All
GreaterThanOrEqual	All
LessThan	All
LessThanOrEqual	All
NotEqual	All
And	Bool
AndAlso	Bool
Not	Bool
Or	Bool

Also, you typically cannot call any method on objects in your query. For example,
calling a ToLower on an object in a query will fail.

 Though these primitives look limited, you can combine them to do some
interesting things. For example, in Chapter 11 you'll learn how you can
use these to perform prefix matching on a range of entities.

Using Partitioning

Earlier in this chapter, you were introduced to these mysterious properties called `Par titionKey` and `RowKey`, but you didn't really learn much about them. To understand partitioning, it is useful to have a mental model of how the Azure Table service works. Azure tables give developers scalable storage, which means developers should be able to dump terabytes of data if necessary. All of this data must be naturally hosted on multiple machines. The question then becomes, "How do you partition data across these nodes?"

Partitioning has a few key implications. Picking the right partitioning is critical, or you could wind up with too much data on one node (bad), or related data on different nodes (really bad). Entities with the same partition key will share the same partition, and are guaranteed to be stored together. Partitioning is the unit of distribution, and is primarily meant for scalability.

This does not mean, however, that each partition is located on a separate node. The system automatically balances your partitions based on size, traffic, and other factors. For example, several partitions might start off together on the same node, but get moved away when one partition grows in size. In any case, you should never depend on *separate partitions* being together. On the other hand, you can always depend on entities within the same partition being together.

Can I Run Out of Space in One Partition?

When users hear that entities with the same partition key are stored together, they wonder whether they'll run out of space when the actual physical machine holding the partition runs out of space. The answer is "no"—you cannot run out of space in a single partition. Without revealing some of the "secret sauce" behind the storage system, note that though terms such as *node* and *partition* are used here, they don't necessarily mean "the same machine." Some magic takes place under the covers to ensure that data in the same partition can be queried and retrieved together really, really quickly.

However, it might be useful to have a mental model of *"one partition = one machine with a disk of near infinite capacity."* It makes visualization and whiteboard drawing much easier.

Partitioning (or, to be more precise, specifying the right partition key in the query) is the biggest factor affecting query performance. The general principle behind fast queries in any storage system is to structure your data and query in such a way that the storage system must do a minimal amount of traversal.

In the database world, this typically means using indexes. Without indexes to help the query processor find the right rows, every query would result in a slow table scan across all rows. The same principle holds true for Azure tables. You must partition your data and queries to make the storage system do the least amount of traversal possible. In general, you must make your queries as specific as possible.

Consider a simple table such as the one shown in Table 10-5.

Table 10-5. Superhero table

PartitionKey (Comic universe)	RowKey (Character name)	Property 3 (Superpower)	Property N (First appeared in)
Marvel	Cyclops	Heat Ray	*The X-Men (#1)*
Marvel	Wolverine	Healing + Adamantium Skeleton	*The Incredible Hulk (#180)*
DC	Superman	Flight, super-strength, and so on	*Action Comics (#1)*
DC	Batman	None	*Detective Comics (#2)*
DC	Lex Luthor	None	*Action Comics (#24)*
DC	Flash	Super speed	*Flash Comics (#1)*

Now, with the entries in Table 10-5 in mind, let's walk through a few sample queries (specified in pseudocode) to see how partitioning can affect performance. Let's assume that each partition is hosted on a separate storage node.

First, let's find entities with the following pseudocode:

```
partition = "DC" and RowKey="Flash"
```

This is the fastest kind of query. In this case, both the partition key and the row key are specified. The system knows which partition to go to, and queries that single partition for the specified row.

 Always try to specify the partition key in your queries. This helps query performance because the storage system knows exactly which node to query. When the partition key isn't specified, the storage system must query all the partitions in the system, which obviously doesn't result in as fast a result. Whether you can specify partition keys in all your keys depends on how you partition your data.

Next, let's find entities with the following pseudocode:

```
PartitionKey="DC" and SuperPower=None
```

In this query, the partition key is specified, but a nonrow key attribute is filtered upon. This is fast (since the partition key is specified), but isn't as fast as when the row key is specified.

Finally, let's find entities with the following pseudocode:

```
SuperPower=None
```

This is the slowest kind of query. In this case, the storage system must query each of the table's partitions, and then walk through each entity in the partition. You should avoid queries such as this that don't specify any of the keys.

In a traditional RDBMS, you would specify an index to speed up such queries. However, Azure's Table service doesn't support these "secondary indexes." (The row key is considered to be the primary index.) You can emulate the behavior of these secondary indexes yourself, though, by creating another table that maps these properties to the rows that contain them. You'll see an example of how to do this later.

 Secondary indexes are part of the road map for Azure tables, and you should see them in a future release. At that time, you won't need these workarounds.

This approach has a few downsides. First, you'll wind up storing more data in the system because of the extra tables. Second, you'll be doing more I/O in the write/update code, which could affect performance.

You should keep a couple of considerations in mind that influence partitioning:

Ensuring locality of reference

In the previous query example, you saw how it is much faster to query only a single partition. Imagine a scenario in which your query must deal with different types of data. Ensuring that the data has the same partition key means the query can return results from just one partition.

Avoiding hot partitions

The storage system redistributes and load-balances traffic. However, queries and updates to a partition are served from the same partition. It might be wise to ensure that hot data is split across partitions to avoid putting a lot of stress on one node. In general, it's not necessary for you to know whether to do this. Azure's Table service can serve out data from a partition quickly, and can take quite a bit of load on one partition. This is a concern where applications have read-access rates that are very, very high. Running stress tests is a good way to identify whether your application needs this.

 You can create as many partitions as you like. In fact, the more partitions you have, the better Azure's Table service can spread out your data in case of heavy load. Like all things in life, this is a trade-off. Aggregate queries that span multiple partitions will see a drop in performance.

Picking the right partition key

Like a ritual, designing a database schema follows some set patterns. In short, you "model" the data you want to store, and then go about normalizing this schema. In the Windows Azure world, you start the same way, but you give a lot of importance to the queries that your application will be executing. In fact, it might be a good idea to begin with a list of queries that you know need good performance, and use that as the starting point to build out the table schema and partitioning scheme.

Follow these steps:

1. Start with the key queries that your system will execute. Prioritize them in order of importance and performance required. For example, a query to show the contents of your shopping cart must be much faster than a query to show a rarely generated report.

2. Using the previous key queries, create your table schema. Ensure that the partition key can be specified in performance-sensitive queries. Estimate how much data you expect in each table and each partition. If one partition winds up with too much data (for example, if it is an order of magnitude greater than any other partition), make your partitioning more granular by concatenating other properties into the partitioning key.

   For example, if you're building a web log analyzer and storing the URL as the partition key hurts you with very popular URLs, you can put date ranges in the partition key. This splits the data so that, for example, each partition contains data for a URL for only a specific day.

3. Pick a unique identifier for the RowKey. Row keys must be unique within the partition. For example, in Table 10-5, you used the Superhero's name as the RowKey, since it was unique within the partition.

Of course, hindsight is 20/20. If you find that your partitioning scheme isn't working well, you might need to change it on-the-fly. In the previous web log analyzer example, you could do that by making the size of the date range dynamic. If the data size on a particular day was huge (say, over the weekend), you could switch to using an hourly range only for weekends. Your application must be aware of this dynamic partitioning, and this should be built in from the start.

Why Have Both Partition Keys and Row Keys?

In general, partition keys are considered the unit of distribution/scalability, while row keys are meant for uniqueness. If the key for your data model has only one property, you should use that as your partition key (an empty row key would suffice) and have one row per partition. If your key has more than one property, distribute the properties between the partition key and the row key to get multiple rows per partition

---

Testing the theory

You've just seen the impact of specifying versus not specifying a partition key, or a query executing on one partition versus a query executing on multiple partitions. Now, let's build some home-grown benchmarks to prove these points.

 These benchmarks were run from a network with multiple layers of proxies in the middle (and several hundred miles) between the machine and the cloud, whereas when you run in the cloud, you'll be running in the same data center. Also, optimizations were not performed as they would have been in a production application. You should look at the relative difference between the following numbers, rather than the actual numbers themselves. Running the same unoptimized code in the cloud gives vastly different numbers—around 350 ms for retrieving 1,000 rows.

Example 10-18 shows a simple entity with a partition key and a row key (which doubles up as the **Data** member). You also write a vanilla **DataContext** to wrap around the entity. The entity isn't interesting by itself. The interesting part is how you partition the data.

Example 10-18. Test entity

```
public class TestEntity : TableServiceEntity
    {

        public TestEntity(string id, string data)
            : base(id, data)
        {
            ID = id;
            Data = data;
        }

        //Parameter-less constructor always needed for
        // ADO.NET Data Services
        public TestEntity() { }

        public string ID { get; set; }
        public string Data { get; set; }
    }

  public class TestDataServiceContext : TableServiceContext
    {
        public TestDataServiceContext (string baseAddress,
        StorageCredentials credentials): base(baseAddress, credentials)
        {}

        internal const string TestTableName = "TestTable";

        public IQueryable<TestEntity> TestTable
        {
            get
            {
```

```
            return this.CreateQuery<TestEntity>(TestTableName);
        }
    }
}
```

Though it is not shown in Example 10-18, you also create an exact copy of these two classes with the number 2 appended to the type names (TestEntity2 and TestDataSer viceContext2). You will try out two different partitioning schemes on TestEntity1 and TestEntity2.

For TestEntity, let's insert 100,000 rows, as shown in Example 10-19. Let's create them all in the same partition (with partition key 1). The storage system will place all the entities on the same storage node.

Example 10-19. Inserting 100,000 rows into the same partition

```
CloudStorageAccount.Parse(ConfigurationSettings.AppSettings
["DataConnectionString"]);
var svc = new TestDataServiceContext(account.TableEndpoint.ToString(),
                                     account.Credentials);

for (int i = 1; i < 100000; i++)
   {
            svc.AddObject("TestTable",
             new TestEntity("1", "RowKey_" + i.ToString() );
   }
```

For TestEntity2, let's insert 100,000 rows, but let's split them among 1,000 different partitions. You loop from 1 to 100,000 and modify the loop counter by 1,000 to get evenly spaced partitions. Example 10-20 shows how to do this.

Example 10-20. Inserting 100,000 rows in 1,000 partitions

```
CloudStorageAccount.Parse(ConfigurationSettings.AppSettings
["DataConnectionString"]);
var svc = new TestDataServiceContext(account.TableEndpoint.ToString(),
 account.Credentials);

for (int i = 1; i < 100000; i++)
            {
            svc.AddObject("TestTable2",
            new TestEntity2((i % 1000).ToString(), "RowKey_" + i.ToString()));
            }
```

Now, let's run three different queries. The first query will be against the 100,000 rows of TestEntity that are in the same partition. The second will be against the 100,000 rows of TestEntity2, but with no partition key specified. The third will be the same as the second, but with the partition key specified in the query. Example 10-21 shows the code for the three.

Example 10-21. Three different queries

```
// Single partition query
var query = from entity in svc.CreateQuery<TestEntity>("TestTable")
where entity.PartitionKey == "1" && entity.RowKey == "RowKey_55000"
select entity;

//Multiple partition query - no partition key specified
var query2 = from entity in svc2.CreateQuery<TestEntity2>("TestTable2")
                    where entity.RowKey == "RowKey_55553"
                    select entity;

//Multiple partition query - partition key specified in query
var query3 = from entity in svc2.CreateQuery<TestEntity2>("TestTable2")
where entity.PartitionKey == "553" && entity.RowKey == "RowKey_55553"
select entity;
```

In each of these queries, let's retrieve one entity using the `FirstOrDefault` method. Table 10-6 shows the relative numbers for 1,000 iterations of each of these queries.

Table 10-6. Query performance comparison

Query type	Time for 1,000 iterations (in seconds)
Single partition	26
Multiple partition—no partition key specified	453
Multiple partition—partition key specified	25

The results speak for themselves. Going to a single partition (either because all your data is stored in it or because you specified it in the query) is always much faster than not specifying the partition key. Of course, using only a single partition has several downsides, as discussed earlier. In general, query times are not affected by how they are partitioned as much as they are by whether the partition key is specified in the query.

If you want to do similar tests, insert the following configuration setting into your configuration file (either *App.config* or *web.config*):

```
<system.net>
  <settings>
    <servicePointManager expect100Continue="false"
useNagleAlgorithm="false" />
  </settings>
</system.net>
```

The first configuration setting deals with a bug in .NET where every request is sent with an `Expect:100-Continue`. If you're sure that your client handles errors from the server well, you can turn this off.

The second configuration setting is an issue if you do several synchronous updates close together like this benchmark program does. Since Delayed ACKs are turned on in the server, the client winds up waiting for much longer than it should when the Nagle algorithm is turned on.

Understanding Pagination

Now that you understand partition and row keys, there is one final query variant to consider. In several scenarios, Azure tables will return a subset of the entities that matched the query. This could happen if the number of entities matching the query exceeds 1,000, if it exceeds a query timeout set (by default) to 60 seconds, if it exceeds 4 MB combined, or for a few other reasons. You can also force Azure tables to return only a subset by asking for only a specific number of entities at a time.

In all of these cases, Azure tables will return two *continuation tokens*: one for the next partition and one for the next row. When you want to get the next set of results, you send these continuation tokens back to the Azure Table service. These tokens essentially tell the Table service where your query left off, and which partition/row to continue with.

For example, if you queried a hypothetical `Employee` table for 5 employees at a time (assuming the employees are partitioned by department), you would see something such as the following:

```
GET /EmployeeTable()?$top=5&NextPartitionKey=HR&NextRowKey=EmpID205
```

And as shown in the following code, you would get results that have the `x-ms-contin uation-NextPartitionKey` and `x-ms-continuation-NextRowKey` headers, the values of which are the continuation tokens:

```
HTTP/1.1 200 OK
Cache-Control: no-cache
Transfer-Encoding: chunked
Content-Type: application/atom+xml;charset=utf-8
Server: Table Service Version 1.0 Microsoft-HTTPAPI/2.0
x-ms-request-id: 91e00f79-7b87-4733-ab71-aa7b71a06c58
x-ms-continuation-NextPartitionKey: Engineering
x-ms-continuation-NextRowKey: EmpID1000
```

When writing .NET code against tables, you don't need to deal with continuation tokens if you don't want to. If you enumerate through all the results of a query, the storage client library does the right magic under the covers to get and insert continuation tokens. Look for the `AsTableServiceQuery` extension method which deals with continuation tokens automatically for you.

However, sometimes you must do this manually. The canonical scenario is when you want page output—such as several pages in a blog, and you want "back" and "next" links. Example 10-22 shows code to retrieve continuation tokens. A new class, `Data ServiceQuery`, is used here, since it gives you access to the headers of the queries you are performing.

Example 10-22. Retrieving continuation tokens

```
// Code to get continuation tokens from executing a query
//'query' below refers to a typical query created using CreateQuery
 var dsQuery = (DataServiceQuery<Contact>)query;
```

```
var res = dsQuery.Execute();

var qor = (QueryOperationResponse)res;
string partitionToken = null;
string rowToken = null;
qor.Headers.TryGetValue("x-ms-continuation-NextPartitionKey",
                out partitionToken);
qor.Headers.TryGetValue("x-ms-continuation-NextRowKey", out rowToken);
```

Once you have the continuation tokens, you must insert them into the subsequent query. Again, you use the DataServiceQuery class to do this, as shown in Example 10-23.

Example 10-23. Inserting continuation tokens

```
//Code below shows how to insert continuation tokens into a query
var dsQuery = (DataServiceQuery<Contact>)query;
query = query
    .AddQueryOption("NextPartitionKey", partitionToken)
    .AddQueryOption("NextRowKey", rowToken);
```

 This code assumes there will always be a continuation token for partitions and rows. In some cases, you might get just one (if you're on the last row or the last partition). In production code, you must add checks for that.

Updating Entities

It wouldn't be much fun if you couldn't update data once you put it in storage, would it? Thankfully, updating entities in Azure tables is pretty simple once you get the hang of the various merge/conflict options available.

Earlier, you saw how every query result returns with an ETag. This ETag corresponds to a specific version of the entity. If the entity changes, the service will ensure that it gets a new ETag. Updating an entity now becomes a simple matter of retrieving entities, making changes on the client side, and telling the server about your updates and what the ETag was when you first retrieved the entity to detect conflicts. This is similar to concurrency controls in databases.

In .NET code, this is tightly integrated with the DataServiceContext. You have several "merge" options from which you can choose, as shown in Table 10-7.

Table 10-7. Merge options

Merge option	Description
AppendOnly	Client changes for new entities are accepted, but changes to existing entities are not. This is the default value where the entity isn't loaded from the server if it is present in the client cache.
OverwriteChanges	Always update with values from the server, overwriting any client changes.
PreserveChanges	Client-side values that have changed are preserved, but other values are updated from the server. Also, when an entity instance exists on the client, it is not loaded from the server. No client-side

Merge option	Description
	changes are lost. When an object is updated, the ETag is updated as well, so this catches any errors if changes have occurred on the server without the client's knowledge.
NoTracking	There is no client-side tracking. Values are always read from the storage source, and any local changes are overwritten.

In code, to update an entity, you typically follow these steps:

1. Create a `DataServiceContext` object, and set its merge option to one of the selections from Table 10-7. You could choose to leave the default value (`AppendOnly`), because this works well in normal scenarios.

2. Query for the entity you want to update.

3. Update the object representation of your entity in code.

4. Call `DataServiceContext.UpdateObject` on the objects you updated.

5. Call `DataServiceContext.SaveChanges` to push changes back to the server.

Example 10-24 walks through a simple query-update-save pattern.

Example 10-24. Simple update

```
CloudStorageAccount.Parse(ConfigurationSettings.AppSettings
["DataConnectionString"]);
            var svc = new TestDataServiceContext
             (account.TableEndpoint.ToString(), account.Credentials);
            svc.MergeOption = MergeOption.PreserveChanges;
            var query = from contact in svc.CreateQuery<Contact>("ContactTable")
                        where contact.Name == "Steve Jobs"
                        select contact;
            var foundContact = query.FirstOrDefault<Contact>();
            foundContact.Address = "One Infinite Loop, Cupertino, CA 95014";
            svc.UpdateObject(foundContact);

            svc.SaveChanges();
```

The following HTTP traffic when `SaveChanges` is called shows this `ETag` matching mechanism clearly. You already saw how querying for an item sends down an `ETag`, which is the server's version of the object. When `SaveChanges` is called, you send out an update that says, "Update if it matches the earlier ETag." If successful, the server updates the entity and sends down a new `ETag`.

```
HTTP Request (only headers shown)

MERGE /ContactTable(PartitionKey='a844fa27-7ae2-4894-9cc6-dd0dbdcd5ec4',
    RowKey='') HTTP/1.1
User-Agent: Microsoft ADO.NET Data Services
x-ms-date: Tue, 21 Apr 2009 16:57:29 GMT
Authorization: SharedKeyLite sriramk:HVNqyS/X/AhqFxhnRKSeOSXTDSzJssFyk9JiyQvwnO4=
Accept: application/atom+xml,application/xml
Accept-Charset: UTF-8
DataServiceVersion: 1.0;NetFx
```

```
MaxDataServiceVersion: 1.0;NetFx
Content-Type: application/atom+xml
If-Match: W/"datetime'2009-04-21T06%3A38%3A28.242Z'"
Host: sriramk.table.core.windows.net
Content-Length: 864

HTTP Response
HTTP/1.1 204 No Content
Cache-Control: no-cache
Content-Length: 0
ETag: W/"datetime'2009-04-21T16%3A56%3A29.717Z'"
Server: Table Service Version 1.0 Microsoft-HTTPAPI/2.0
x-ms-request-id: 05a9f45f-bab9-417a-89b6-fc7759f31b2f
Date: Tue, 21 Apr 2009 16:56:35 GMT
```

In Chapter 11, you'll learn how this mechanism can be combined to do unconditional updates, and to simulate optimistic concurrency, as well as the pros and cons of doing so.

Deleting Tables

Deleting tables is extremely easy. A simple call to `CloudTableClient.DeleteTable` will obliterate all your tables. Note that deleting large tables can take some time. If you try to re-create a table quickly after it is deleted, you could get an error message.

Example 10-25 shows the code for deleting the `ContactsTable`. Once you delete a table, it is immediately inaccessible for operations. Unlike other distributed storage services, there is no propagation delay that lets other operations succeed.

Example 10-25. Deleting the table

```
account.CreateCloudTableClient().DeleteTable("ContactsTable");
```

The REST equivalent is just as simple. Just send an HTTP `DELETE` to the table's URL and you're done.

```
DELETE /Tables('ContactTable') HTTP/1.1
User-Agent: Microsoft ADO.NET Data Services
x-ms-date: Mon, 20 Apr 2009 18:34:37 GMT
Authorization: SharedKeyLite sriramk:vhJAA1od931iUvj8MEBu4pb1hu3fIILiA15Ndf3n+8Y=
```

Deleting Entities

Deleting entities is similar to deleting tables. You retrieve the entity you want to delete through a query, call `DataServiceContext.DeleteObject`, and save changes back. Example 10-26 shows the code to do this.

Example 10-26. Deleting entities

```
CloudStorageAccount.Parse(ConfigurationSettings.AppSettings
            ["DataConnectionString"]);
var svc = new TestDataServiceContext(account.TableEndpoint.ToString(),
```

```
                    account.Credentials);
            var item = (from contact in svc.CreateQuery<Contact>("ContactTable")
                        where contact.Name == "Steve Jobs"
                        select contact).Single();
        svc.DeleteObject(item);
        svc.SaveChanges();
```

However, this means you can delete entities only when you've already queried and retrieved them from table storage. This is inefficient when deleting large sets of entities, and it seems counterintuitive to query entities just to delete them. You can work around this by creating a dummy local entity with the right partition key and row key, attaching it to the `DataServiceContext`, and then deleting it.

Example 10-27 shows how to do this. This mandates that you already know the partition key and row key for the item you want to delete. In Example 10-27, you would replace `CorrectPartitionKey` and `CorrectRowKey` with the actual partition key and row key, respectively.

Example 10-27. Deleting entities without querying

```
            var svc =
                new TestDataServiceContext(account.TableEndpoint.ToString(),
account.Credentials);
            var item = new Contact("CorrectPartitionKey", "CorrectRowKey");
            svc.AttachTo("ContactTable", item, "*");
            svc.DeleteObject(item);
            svc.SaveChanges();
```

How does this work? Note the wildcard character passed as a parameter to the `AttachTo` method. Here, you're bringing an empty object into the `DataServiceContext`'s view of the local world, deleting it, and then using the wildcard to say that *"regardless of what changes have happened on the server, replace with changes with this version."* Since the only change here is to delete the object, the deletion is propagated to the server.

If you inspect the HTTP traffic, you'll notice one key difference between normal deletes and this variant. Normally, the delete operation specifies an `ETag` to say, "I'm trying to perform an operation on this version of the object." In this variant, you see the header `If-Match: *`, which essentially says, "Perform this operation on any version of the object."

There are trade-offs when picking either of these variants. Pick the former when you want to delete a specific version of your entity and you don't care about any intermediate updates. Use the latter version when you want to obliterate the entity, no matter what has happened since you last retrieved it.

Summary

Whew, that was a lot! However, you are still not done with tables. In Chapter 11, you'll learn how to perform modeling, optimistic concurrency, and several other common data tasks.

And speaking of common data tasks, you saw how Azure's Table service offers highly scalable and reliable storage but, in doing so, eschews some common tools and features from the RDBMS world. Some of this is because the technology is new and features will be added over time, and some of it is because this is inherently different from a traditional database. It is up to you to figure out whether this meets your needs. Like crossing roads in India, it's not an activity that is meant for everyone.

CHAPTER 11

Common Storage Tasks

Over the years, developers have built up a body of knowledge when it comes to interacting with data from storage systems. Developers know how to perform pagination, handle master-child relationships, conduct a full-text search, and perform several other tasks used in almost every website or service.

When switching to cloud storage services, it isn't immediately apparent how to do the same things. This chapter plugs that gap by walking you through the process of performing some common, day-to-day activities that you are probably extremely familiar with on a typical relational database management system (RDBMS).

Exploring Full-Text Search

Let's get something out of the way upfront. Windows Azure storage does not support full-text search out of the box. This section walks you through how you can build a trivial full-text search yourself to work around this limitation.

Understanding Full-Text Search

Imagine that you're implementing a search engine for your website. You could write some simple database queries to search your content. You might use the LIKE operator in SQL to do simple pattern matching against the search queries. However, you'll soon find out that this breaks down even in simple searches.

The terms users search for may not appear together. Users may search for variants of the term *taxes* where your database has only *tax*, or *players* where your database has only *player*. Since everyone is familiar with Google, your users will expect these search queries to work and to "do the right thing." This is way beyond what you can do with a few simple SQL queries.

Performance would be terrible, since the database would need to look through every single row to find the data you want. Unlike a numeric column, you could not create an index on which the execution engine could perform a binary search to find the right row to go to.

Though you cannot build Google, you can provide rudimentary full-text search capability. This is available out of the box with most modern RDBMSs—SQL Server has had it for a couple of versions, and MySQL added it in version 3 and enhanced it considerably in later versions. This feature examines all the words in every stored document (where "document" refers to any content you stick in the database), and attempts to match that with the user's queries.

Full-text search (FTS) engines are smart enough to recognize different versions of the same word. For example, searching for any of the words *driven*, *drove*, or *drives* should bring up *drive* as a result. FTS engines also know to detect similar phrases and perform rudimentary Boolean logic where you can search for the existence of multiple terms. They also typically contain rudimentary ranking algorithms to rank the results they find.

Another popular option is to use open source FTS projects such as Lucene that use the filesystem as a store. However, these don't typically work on Windows Azure, or don't fit into the stateless frontend model that the cloud demands, since they use the filesystem as a backend store.

 Although there are ways to change the backend store of these projects and make them store data elsewhere, they're sparsely used at this point, and in general, they don't work as well as using the filesystem. It would be quite difficult to optimize for Azure's Table service, as we will explore throughout this discussion.

Indexing

Now let's get to the fun part: what makes these FTS engines tick. No discussion on FTS engines can get far without a discussion on indexing—or, to be specific, a discussion on indexes.

You're probably familiar with the role of an index in a book. If you turn to the back of this book, you'll find one. If you look up the term *full-text search*, it should refer you back to this chapter. Now, try to imagine a book without an index. Finding a specific term in such a book would be a painful task. You would need to turn page by page, skim through the text, and try to guess in which chapter or section it appears. You may succeed quickly in a slim book, but imagine a book with several hundred pages, or even thousands of pages.

Searching through a database poses the same challenge, but on a much larger scale. Instead of having to read through thousands of pages, the computer must look through the equivalent of millions of pages (if not more). Even though databases are fast at looking through things, this is still too slow a process, and entails too much data to walk through sequentially.

The fix is simple. Create an index of the data in the database, just like the index at the back of this book, and have the computer look up the term in the index to find out where the data resides. This raises a question: what about the time it takes to look up the term in an index?

Think for a second about how you look up terms in a book's index. Since the index is alphabetically sorted, you know whether to go backward or forward, and how many pages to skip. Similarly, the index in FTS engines is stored in a sorted order. The FTS engine can perform a binary search through the index to quickly arrive at the right term.

At this point, if you were using a typical RDBMS, you probably know as much about FTS indexes as you need to. In theory, you could just ask the database to start indexing specific columns in your tables. However, as mentioned earlier, Azure storage does not come with this out of the box. That means it is up to developers to do the heavy lifting to build these indexes and write the code to look through them.

You will have help when doing this. You can use Azure storage to store the actual data, and use Azure tables to query the index. This enables you to index and query over really large datasets without having to worry about memory or storage capacity issues.

 Will Azure storage have FTS sometime in the future? At the moment, there have been no announcements from Microsoft putting FTS on the official road map. However, the Azure team knows this is something a lot of customers want, and is actively investigating adding this in a future release. If you're reading this book a few years after publication, chances are this feature may be part of the feature set, and you can skip over this entire section.

Documents and terms

Let's become familiar with two terms that are common in the FTS world:

Document
> A *document* is the unit of content that is returned in your search results. For web search engines such as Google and Bing, a document is a web page. If you're building an email search, a document is an email. You can think of it as the thing that shows up in the query results. Documents can be of any granularity. If you were indexing books, you could make an entire book one big document. Or you could drill down and make each chapter, or each section, a document to enable you to get as close as possible to the exact location of the search term. The index at the back of this book uses individual pages as its "documents," since the "result" is a page number you can turn to.

Term

A document is made up of several *terms*. Typically, for textual content, every term can be roughly approximated to a word—the previous sentence can be said to have eight terms. Note the word *approximated*, because you might be transforming the term before indexing to help with your search results.

Now let's take a look at transforming.

Case folding and stemming

Following is a famous rhyme from the book *The Lord of the Rings* by J.R.R. Tolkien (George Allen and Unwin). This will be used for the next few examples.

Three Rings for the Elven-kings under the sky,

Seven for the Dwarf-lords in their halls of stone,

Nine for Mortal Men doomed to die,

One for the Dark Lord on his dark throne

In the Land of Mordor where the Shadows lie.

One Ring to rule them all, One Ring to find them,

One Ring to bring them all and in the darkness bind them

In the Land of Mordor where the Shadows lie.

Let's assume for a moment that each word in this poem is a term, and each line is a document in itself. If a user searches for "one" (note the lack of capitalization), you would want to show all the lines starting with the text "One Ring." To put it differently, users shouldn't need to care about the case of the queries they're typing in.

To support this, you must transform your documents by *case-folding* into a standard case, either all uppercase or all lowercase. This makes life much easier when searching for this text, since you don't have to worry about the case of the actual content. For example, you would convert the first line in the poem into "three rings for the elven-kings under the sky."

Variants on terms are a trickier issue. Look at the third line in the poem. If someone searched for the term *doom*, you should be able to recognize that *doomed* is a variant of *doom*. This is almost impossible to do at query time.

The right thing to do is to convert every word into its root form through a process called *stemming*. During indexing, you convert every word into a stemmed version. For example, instead of storing *doomed*, you would store the word *doom*. Plurals, tenses, and other word variants will be converted into one standard form. At query time, you convert the terms in the query into their stemmed version as well.

There are several well-known stemming algorithms with public, open source libraries. Throughout this chapter, you will use a simple, well-known implementation called the *Porter Stemming Algorithm*. You can find implementations of Porter's algorithm for various languages (as well as information on the algorithm itself) at *http://tartarus.org/ ~martin/PorterStemmer/*.

Big search engines such as Google and Yahoo! use complex stemming and case-folding algorithms that go beyond the simple process just described. For example, the preceding algorithms can't deal with international input—most open source stemming libraries work only with English text. Even something as simple as case folding becomes tricky with some languages in which "cases" don't work in the same way they do in the English language. If you're interested in exploring these topics in detail (and exploring searching in general) you should pick up any text on information retrieval and start digging. It is a vast and rich field.

Inverted indexes

The correct term for the kind of index you'll be building here is an *inverted index* (or *reverse index*). This is not a novel computer science data structure. Religious scholars have used them for centuries, and important works have had concordances created for them manually. (A *concordance* is an alphabetical listing of key terms in a work, with the identification or citation of the passages in which they occur.)

One particular famous (but unintended) use of concordances involved the Dead Sea Scrolls, the only known surviving copies of Biblical documents made before 100 A.D. After the discovery of the Dead Sea Scrolls in the 1940s, the team that discovered and excavated the caves refused to publish most of the scrolls, but published a concordance that contained a mapping of terms to the scroll in which they appear. In 1991, a Cincinnati student entered the concordance into his computer and reconstructed the original underlying text. This caused the immediate release of the facsimile edition of the originals.

The best way to describe these indexes is with an example. They are typically made up of two data structures. One data structure contains a mapping of document IDs to the document's contents. Using the earlier poem from *The Lord of the Rings*, this mapping would look like Table 11-1 if you assume every line to be a document by itself.

Table 11-1. Document ID to document mapping

Document ID	Document
0	Three Rings for the Elven-kings under the sky,
1	Seven for the Dwarf-lords in their halls of stone,
2	Nine for Mortal Men doomed to die,
3	One for the Dark Lord on his dark throne
4	In the Land of Mordor where the Shadows lie.
5	One Ring to rule them all, One Ring to find them,
6	One Ring to bring them all and in the darkness bind them
7	In the Land of Mordor where the Shadows lie.

An inverted index contains a list of pointers of terms to the documents in which they appear. The list of terms is exhaustive—if you add up all the terms in the inverted index, you will have a lexicon of all terms that appear in all the documents that were indexed. Table 11-2 shows a snippet of an inverted index constructed from Table 11-1. (The full inverted index contains more than 45 terms.)

Table 11-2. Inverted index

Term	Document IDs
Three	0
Rings	0
for	0, 1, 2, 3
the	0, 0, 1, 3, 4, 4, 6, 7, 7
Elven-kings	0
under	0
sky,	0
Seven	1
Dwarf-lords	1
Mordor	4, 7
Ring	5, 5, 6

Looking at Table 11-2, a few things are apparent. First, you can see that a few common words dominate in occurrence (in this case, the word *the*). These are called *stop words*, and are usually eliminated from queries, since they occur so frequently and tend to pull in more search results than necessary.

You also see that two terms are very similar to each other: *Ring* and *Rings*. These appear since there was no stemming in this table. In the code samples provided in this chapter, you'll be stemming all terms to collapse every word into its root form.

At this point, you might have figured out how searching works. A query for a single term means a single look-up of the inverted index table, and a retrieval of the list of documents. A query that involves multiple terms (in which the user is looking for documents where all the terms appear) is performed by doing an *intersection* of the result sets for each term.

For example, consider the sample search "Rings the Elven-kings." Using Table 11-2, you know that the term *Rings* appears in document 0, *Elven-kings* appears in document 0, and *the* appears in quite a few documents, including document 0. The intersection of all of these is just one document (line)—0—the very first line of the poem.

Let's work through another sample query: "Ring Mordor." In this case, *Ring* maps to documents 5, 5, and 6, while *Mordor* maps to 4 and 7. Since there is no overlap, you have no results to display for this query.

This examination actually sidesteps a big part of showing search results: *ranking*. A lot of the "secret sauce" in large search engines such as Google is in ranking results. However, most users of FTS use it to display search results from a single website, or an otherwise limited source of data. Ranking results is difficult in such cases and algorithms to do so vary wildly—from examining where the search term figures in the text, to looking at page traffic for all the result pages. This also reflects the fact that ranking in FTS engines today is a bit of an unsolved problem.

Thus, this examination does not discuss ranking results. Once you have the list of results, let your imagination run wild on how to rank them.

Building an FTS Engine on Azure

That was quite a bit of theory to set up what you will do next: build your own FTS engine on Windows Azure storage.

Picking a data source

The first thing you need is some data to index and search. Feel free to use any data you have lying around. The code you are about to see should work on any set of text files.

To find a good source of sample data let's turn to an easily available and widely used source: Project Gutenberg. This amazing project provides thousands of free books online in several accessible licenses under a very liberal license. You can download your own copies from *http://www.gutenberg.org*. If you're feeling lazy, you can download the exact Gutenberg book files that have been used here from *http://www.sriramk rishnan.com/windowsazurebook/gutenberg.zip*.

Why use plain-text files and not some structured data? There is no reason, really. You can easily modify the code samples you're about to see and import some structured data, or data from a custom data source.

Setting up the project

To keep this sample as simple as possible, let's build a basic console application. This console application will perform only two tasks. First, when pointed to a set of files in a directory, it will index them and create the inverted index in Windows Azure storage. Second, when given a search query, it will search the index in Azure storage. Sounds simple, right?

As you saw in Chapter 10, setting up a .NET application to talk to Windows Azure tables requires some configuration. Let's quickly go over the steps here. For a detailed explanation of each step, refer to Chapter 10, which deals with programming tables in detail.

1. Create a .NET 3.5 Console Application project using Visual Studio. In this sample, call the project FTS, which makes the project's namespace FTS by default. If you're calling your project by a different name, remember to fix the namespace.

2. Add references to the assemblies *System.Data.Services.dll* and *System.Data.Services.Client.dll*. This brings in the assemblies you need for ADO.NET Data Services support.

3. Bring in the `Microsoft.WindowsAzure.StorageClient` library to talk to Azure storage.

4. Set up the configuration file with the right account name and shared key by adding a new *App.config* to the project and entering the following contents. Remember to fill in your account name, key, and table storage endpoint:

```
<?xml version="1.0" encoding="utf-8" ?>
<configuration>

  <appSettings>
    <add key="DataConnectionString" value
="AccountName=YourAccountName;AccountKey=YourAccountKey==;
DefaultEndpointsProtocol=https"/>
  </appSettings>
  <system.net>
    <settings>
      <servicePointManager expect100Continue="false" useNagleAlgorithm="false" />
    </settings>
  </system.net>
</configuration>
```

Modeling the data

As you learned earlier, you must create two key data structures. The first is a mapping between document IDs and documents. You will be storing that in a table in Azure storage. To do that, you use the following wrapper class inherited from `TableServi` `ceEntity`. Add the following code as *Document.cs* to your project:

```
using System;
using System.Collections.Generic;
using System.Linq;
using System.Text;
using System.Data.Services;
using System.Data.Services.Client;
using Microsoft.WindowsAzure.StorageClient;

namespace FTS
{
    public class Document:TableServiceEntity
    {
        public Document( string title, string id):base(id, id)
        {

            this.Title = title;
            this.ID = id;
        }

        public Document():base()
        {
            //Empty-constructor for ADO.NET Data Services
        }

        public string Title { get; set; }
        public string ID { get;set;}
    }
}
```

This class wraps around an "entity" (row) in a Document table. Every entity has a unique ID, and a title that corresponds to the title of the book you are storing. In this case, you are going to show only the title in the results, so you'll be storing only the title in Azure storage. If you wanted, you could choose to store the contents of the books themselves, which would let you show book snippets in the results. You use the document ID as the partition key, which will place every document in a separate partition. This provides optimum performance because you can always specify the exact partition you want to access when you write your queries.

The second key data structure you need is an inverted index. As discussed earlier, an inverted index stores a mapping between index terms and documents. To make this indexing easier, you use a small variant of the design you saw in Table 11-2.

In that table, you saw every index term being unique and mapping to a list of document IDs. Here, you have a different table entry for every index term-document ID pair. This provides a lot of flexibility. For example, if you move to a parallel indexing model, you can add term-to-document ID mappings without worrying about trampling over a concurrent update.

Save the following code as *IndexEntry.cs* and add it to your project:

```
using System;
using System.Collections.Generic;
using System.Linq;
using System.Text;
using System.Data.Services;
using System.Data.Services.Client;
using Microsoft.WindowsAzure.StorageClient;

namespace FTS
{
    public class IndexEntry:TableServiceEntity
    {
        public IndexEntry(string term, string docID)
            : base(term, docID)
        {
            this.Term = term;
            this.DocID = docID;
        }

        public IndexEntry()
            : base()
        {
            //Empty constructor for ADO.NET Data Services
        }
        public string Term { get; set; }
        public string DocID { get; set; }
    }
}
```

At this point, you might be wondering how you just get a list of documents in which a term appears easily and quickly using this design. To make that happen, note that, in the code, all entries with the same term will go into the same partition, because you use "term" as the partition key. To get a list of documents in which a term appears, you just query for all entities within the term partition.

This is easier to understand with the help of a picture. Figure 11-1 shows the index table containing the mappings for two terms, *foo* and *bar*. Since each term gets its own partition, the index table has two partitions. Each partition has several entries, each corresponding to a document in which the term appears.

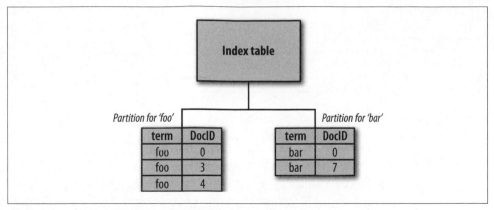

Figure 11-1. Index table with two partitions

As you saw in Chapter 10, each table entity class must be hooked up with a bit of plumbing to a `DataServiceContext` class. Add the following class as *FTSDataService-Context.cs*. This essentially wraps around the two classes you just wrote, and enables you to query them from ADO.NET Data Services:

```
using System;
using System.Collections.Generic;
using System.Linq;
using System.Text;
using Microsoft.WindowsAzure;
using Microsoft.WindowsAzure.StorageClient;
using System.Data.Services.Client;

namespace FTS
{
    public class FTSDataServiceContext:TableServiceContext
    {
        public FTSDataServiceContext(string baseAddress,
                StorageCredentials credentials)
        : base(baseAddress, credentials)
    {
    }


        public const string DocumentTableName = "DocumentTable";

        public IQueryable<Document> DocumentTable
        {
            get
            {
                return this.CreateQuery<Document>(DocumentTableName);
            }
        }

        public const string IndexTableName = "IndexTable";

        public IQueryable<IndexEntry> IndexTable
```

```
            {
                get
                {
                    return this.CreateQuery<IndexEntry>(IndexTableName);
                }
            }


        }
    }
```

Adding a mini console

The following trivial helper code enables you to test out various text files and search for various terms. Replace your *Program.cs* with the following code. This essentially lets you call out to an Index method or a Search method based on whether you enter **index** or **search** in the console. You'll be writing both very soon, so let's just leave stub implementations for now:

```
using System;
using System.Collections.Generic;
using System.Linq;
using System.Text;
using System.IO;
using Microsoft.WindowsAzure.StorageClient;
using Microsoft.WindowsAzure;
namespace FTS
{
    class Program
    {
        static void Main(string[] args)
        {
            CreateTables();
            Console.WriteLine("Enter command - 'index <directory-path>'
                or 'search <query>' or 'quit'");
            while (true)
            {

                Console.Write(">");
                var command = Console.ReadLine();
                if (command.StartsWith("index"))
                {
                    var path = command.Substring(6, command.Length - 6);
                    Index(path);
                }
                else if (command.StartsWith("search"))
                {
                    var query = command.Substring(6, command.Length - 6);
                    Search(query);
                }
                else if (command.StartsWith("quit"))
                {
                    return;
                }
```

```
                else
                {
                    Console.WriteLine("Unknown command");
                }
            }

        }
    static void Index(){}

    static void Search(){}
    }
}
```

Creating the tables

At the top of `Main`, you see a `CreateTables` method call. As the name implies, this creates your tables in Azure table storage if they don't already exist. To do that, add the following code below `Main` in *Program.cs*:

```
static void CreateTables()
        {

                var account = CloudStorageAccount.Parse(ConfigurationSettings.AppSettings
        ["DataConnectionString"]);
                var svc =
            new FTSDataServiceContext(account.TableEndpoint.ToString(),
        account.Credentials);


                account.CreateCloudTableClient().CreateTableIfNotExist
                (FTSDataServiceContext.IndexTableName);
                account.CreateCloudTableClient().CreateTableIfNotExist
                (FTSDataServiceContext.DocumentTableName);


        }
```

Stemming

You are almost ready to start indexing your literary classics. But first, you must add some stemming code. As you learned earlier, any nontrivial amount of text contains several variants of the same words: plural forms, different tenses, and so on. Users will want to search for any of these forms. (Imagine not finding a result on Google because you mistakenly searched for a plural.)

To work around this issue, you store and search the "stemmed" form of every word. Every word is converted into a root form and, since all variants share the same root, finding the root will satisfy searches for all variants. For example, the root for *Connect*, *Connection*, *Connected*, *Connecting*, and *Connections* is the same: *Connect*. By storing only the root stemmed term, users can search successfully for any of the variants.

There are several algorithms to do just this. Let's use the Porter Stemming Algorithm. Specifically, let's use the C# implementation of this algorithm, available at *http://tartarus.org/~martin/PorterStemmer/csharp2.txt*.

The implementation of this algorithm is based on Martin Porter's 1980 paper, "An algorithm for suffix stripping." You can find the original paper at *http://tartarus.org/~martin/PorterStemmer/def.txt*.

This file requires a little modification before you can use it in this project. Remove the following code from the top and add it to the project as *Stemmer.cs*:

```
using System.Windows.Forms;

[assembly: AssemblyTitle("")]
[assembly: AssemblyDescription("Porter stemmer in CSharp")]
[assembly: AssemblyConfiguration("")]
[assembly: AssemblyCompany("")]
[assembly: AssemblyProduct("")]
[assembly: AssemblyCopyright("")]
[assembly: AssemblyTrademark("")]
[assembly: AssemblyCulture("")]
[assembly: AssemblyVersion("1.4")]
[assembly: AssemblyKeyFile("keyfile.snk")]
[assembly: AssemblyDelaySign(false)]
[assembly: AssemblyKeyName("")]
```

You don't need the attributes, since Visual Studio already specifies them in *AssemblyInfo.cs* automatically for you. The `WinForms` reference is also removed, since this is a command-line interface (CLI) application.

The key method in the file is `stemTerm`. You'll be calling this to get the stemmed version of every word you index.

Indexing

You are now ready to index your content. To get the files, you asked the user in the `Main` method to enter **index** followed by the directory path containing the files to index. Let's add some code to construct a `Document` object out of every file in the directory, and pass it off to an `Indexer` class for indexing. You give every document a unique GUID to ensure that it has a unique identifier in the document table. (Remember that the document ID is also used as the partition key.)

Add the following code in *Program.cs* in the `Program` class, and replace the blank `Index` method with this implementation:

```
static void Index(string path)
{
```

```
        foreach (var file in Directory.GetFiles(path))
        {
            string title = Path.GetFileName(file);
            string content = File.ReadAllText(file);
            Indexer.AddDocument(
            new Document( title, Guid.NewGuid().ToString()), content);

        }
    }
```

The core indexing magic will happen in the `Indexer` class, which you'll see in a moment.

The algorithm for indexing a document is as follows:

1. You add the `Document` object to the `Document` table in Azure storage by adding it to an instance of `FTSDataServiceContext`.

2. You strip out all punctuation, carriage returns, line feeds, and undesirable characters in the document content. You use a simple regular expression that looks for the ASCII ranges for punctuation and special characters, as well as .NET's regular expression support, to do this.

3. You split the content into words. Since you removed all other special characters in the previous step, you can easily word-break on spaces.

4. You construct a .NET `Dictionary` object, and add every new stemmed term you see to it. You then loop over all words and, when you come across a new word, check whether it is already present in the dictionary. If it isn't present already, you add it. At the end of this process, you have a list of unique terms in the content. To stem a term, you call `stemTerm` in the `PorterStemmer` class.

5. You loop through every term collected in step 4 and construct a row for it in the inverted index table, mapping that term to the current document's ID. You save changes back to the cloud by calling `FTSDataServiceContext.SaveChangesWithRe tries`.

The following code does all of this. It follows the same set of steps as the algorithm specified. Add it as *Indexer.cs*:

```
using System;
using System.Collections.Generic;
using System.Linq;
using System.Text;
using System.Text.RegularExpressions;
using System.Configuration;
using PorterStemmerAlgorithm;
using Microsoft.WindowsAzure.StorageClient;
using Microsoft.WindowsAzure;

namespace FTS
{
    public static class Indexer
    {
        public static void AddDocument(Document doc, string docContent)
```

```
        {
            var account =
CloudStorageAccount.Parse(ConfigurationSettings.AppSettings
        ["DataConnectionString"]);
            var ctx =
            new FTSDataServiceContext(account.TableEndpoint.ToString(),
  account.Credentials);

            //Add document to documents table
            ctx.AddObject(FTSDataServiceContext.DocumentTableName, doc);

            //Now let's find all the terms
            var terms = new Dictionary<string,bool>();

            //Normalize document - strip punctuation
            var content =  Regex.Replace(docContent, @"[!-\/:-@\[-\`]", " ");
            //Strip line feeds and carriage returns
            content = content.Replace('\r', ' ');
            content = content.Replace('\n', ' ');
            var possibleTerms = content.Split(' ');

            foreach (var possibleTerm in possibleTerms)
            {

                if (possibleTerm.Trim().Length == 0)
                {
                    continue;
                }
                var stemmer = new PorterStemmer(); //Cannot reuse
                var stemmedTerm = stemmer.stemTerm(possibleTerm.Trim().ToLower());
                terms[stemmedTerm] = true;
            }

            //Loop through terms and add pointer to document
            foreach (var term in terms.Keys)
            {
                ctx.AddObject(FTSDataServiceContext.IndexTableName,
                    new IndexEntry(term, doc.ID));
                ctx.SaveChangesWithRetries();
            }


        }
    }
}
```

And that's all the indexing code you need! At this point, run the project.

In the console that pops up type in **index** followed by the path to your text files, and press Enter. The program should churn away for a while as it creates your inverted indexes, as shown in Figure 11-2. The actual time taken depends on the number of files and the size of each file. It should be on the order of several minutes, so treat yourself to a coffee. At the end, you will have a fully constructed set of inverted indexes in the cloud, mapping stemmed terms to the documents in which they appear.

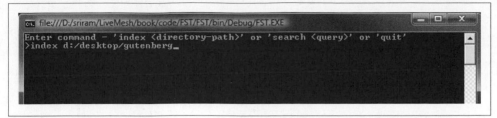

Figure 11-2. Indexer

Searching for a single term

Now that you have a fully constructed index, let's write some searching code.

In *Program.cs*, replace the blank `Search` method with the following code to pass off search queries to the helper `Searcher` class. This helper class will return a `List<Document>` that you iterate over and display as the results:

```
static void Search(string query)
    {
        var results = Searcher.Search(query);
        if (results.Count == 0)
        {
            Console.WriteLine("No results found!");
            return;
        }

        foreach (var doc in results)
        {
            Console.WriteLine(doc.Title);
        }

    }
```

Compared to the indexing code, the search code is much simpler. The first pass at your search code will support searching for only one term. Copy the following code into *Searcher.cs* and add it to the project:

```
using System;
using System.Collections.Generic;
using System.Linq;
using System.Configuration;
using System.Text;
using Microsoft.WindowsAzure;
using Microsoft.WindowsAzure.StorageClient;
using Microsoft.Samples.ServiceHosting.StorageClient;
using PorterStemmerAlgorithm;
using System.Threading;

namespace FTS
{
    public class Searcher
    {
```

```
public static List<Document> Search(string queryTerms)
    {
        var account =
CloudStorageAccount.Parse(ConfigurationSettings.AppSettings
    ["DataConnectionString"]);
        var ctx = new FTSDataServiceContext(
          account.TableEndpoint.ToString(), account.Credentials);

        //Clean up query terms
        queryTerms = queryTerms.Trim().ToLower();

        var stemmer = new PorterStemmer();
        // At this time, we support only one term in the query. Let's stem it
        var stemmedTerm = stemmer.stemTerm(queryTerms);

        // Look up all inverted index entries for the stemmed term
        var indexQuery = from indexEntry in
ctx.CreateQuery<IndexEntry>(FTSDataServiceContext.IndexTableName)
                    where indexEntry.Term == stemmedTerm
                    select indexEntry;
        var results = new List<Document>();

        // For every inverted index entry in which the stemmed
        // term exists, look up the Document
        // and add to our list of results

        foreach (IndexEntry indexEntry in indexQuery)
        {
            var docQuery = from doc in

            ctx.CreateQuery<Document>
              (FTSDataServiceContext.DocumentTableName)
                        where doc.ID == indexEntry.DocID
                        select doc;

            results.Add(docQuery.FirstOrDefault());

        }

        // Return our list of results
        return results;
    }    }
}
```

The code first creates an FTSDataServiceContext with which to perform queries later. At this time, let's deal only with single search terms—you'll add support for dealing with multiple search terms soon. Since you have only a single search term, you can directly case-fold into lowercase and stem it.

You then query the inverted index table using the stemmed term and look up all entries that have the stemmed term. This returns a list of document IDs (if the search was successful). Since displaying document IDs in the results is not useful, you look up the

`Document` entity for each of these document IDs so that you can display the title of each of these results.

At this point, you have a fully functional FTS engine that is good to go. Press F5 and run your project. Search for any term that appears in the text you've indexed by typing **search** followed by the term. Since a few classic literary works have been used in this sample, the following sample queries yield good results.

First, let's try a search that should yield only one result:

```
>search Dracula
Dracula - Bram Stoker
```

Now, let's try a common word across many books that should yield several results:

```
>search war
Count of Monte Cristo - Alexandre Dumas.txt
Art of War - Sun Tzu.txt
Dracula - Bram Stoker
Fairy Tales - The Brothers Grimm.txt
Around the World in Eighty Days - Jules Verne
On the Origin of Species - Charles Darwin
```

As you can see, basic search works well. But the key feature in an FTS engine is the ability to deal with spelling variations.

Let's try various versions of the last search. Try searching for *wars* or *warring*. You'll find that you get the same set of results, *even if the variant you typed doesn't occur verbatim in the text*. That's exactly what you want, because users rarely know the precise form that occurs in the source text or content.

Searching multiple terms

The preceding code searches for a single term only. But what about multiple terms where you want to do a Boolean `AND` and show results only where all terms are present?

To do so, you must modify the previous code to search for each individual term, and perform an intersection of all the terms. Doing so in sequence would be slow. To speed things up, you queue up all the requests in parallel using a thread queue, and wait for them to finish using a `ManualResetEvent` for each request. Therefore, the total time depends only on the slowest request, rather than being the sum of the time taken for all requests.

To perform the intersection, you use .NET 3.5's built-in `HashSet` class, as shown in the following code. Replace your earlier implementation of `Search` with the following one:

```
public static List<Document> Search(string queryTerms)
    {
        var account =
CloudStorageAccount.Parse(ConfigurationSettings.AppSettings
                    ["DataConnectionString"]);

        var terms = queryTerms.Contains(' ')?
```

```
                queryTerms.ToLower().Trim().Split(' ')                      : new
string[1]{queryTerms} /* Just one term */;


        var resetEvents = new ManualResetEvent[terms.Length];
        var allResults = new HashSet<Document>[terms.Length];
        for (int i = 0; i < terms.Length; i++)
        {
            resetEvents[i] = new ManualResetEvent(false);
            ThreadPool.QueueUserWorkItem(new WaitCallback((object index) =>
            {
                var ctx =
                new FTSDataServiceContext(account.TableEndpoint.ToString(),
                account.Credentials);


                var stemmer = new PorterStemmer();
                var stemmedTerm = stemmer.stemTerm(terms[(int)index]);
                var indexQuery = from indexEntry in
                                ctx.CreateQuery<IndexEntry>
                                (FTSDataServiceContext.IndexTableName)
                                where indexEntry.Term == stemmedTerm
                                select indexEntry;
                var results = new HashSet<Document>();

                foreach (IndexEntry indexEntry in indexQuery)
                {
                    var docQuery = from doc in
                    ctx.CreateQuery<Document>
                    (FTSDataServiceContext.DocumentTableName)
                                where doc.ID == indexEntry.DocID
                                select doc;

                    results.Add(docQuery.FirstOrDefault());

                }
                allResults[(int)index] = results;
                resetEvents[(int)index].Set();
            }), i);


        }

        //Wait for all parallel queries to finish executing
        WaitHandle.WaitAll(resetEvents);

        // Use HashSet's intersection ability. Set it to the first term's
        //results and intersect with
        // results for all other terms. Though the extension method
        // Intersect works with any IEnumerable,
        // using HashSet gives us the best search performance
        IEnumerable<Document> finalResults =
            (IEnumerable<Document>)allResults[0];
        foreach (var termResults in allResults)
        {
```

```
        finalResults = finalResults.Intersect(termResults);
    }

    return finalResults.ToList<Document>();
}
```

You can now run the project, search for multiple terms, and look for results that contain all terms. Here's a search query where each term exists in multiple books, but the combination exists in only one:

```
>search france dantes Marseilles
Count of Monte Cristo - Alexandre Dumas.txt
```

Ideas for improvement

This discussion has barely scratched the tip of the proverbial iceberg. Information retrieval is a vast field, and there is a lot of existing research and code on indexing, stemming, word breaking, ranking, and various other aspects of a search.

There is also room for improvement in how you use Windows Azure tables. For example, this examination did not include snippets of the results and where they appear inside each book. Indexing is quite slow in this current implementation, because you make a round trip to the server per term, and it will need to speed up before it can be used for interactive data entry, as opposed to a background batch job.

Depending on your scenario, there is a lot of scope for improvement on the ideas presented so far.

Modeling Data

For folks used to modeling data in an RDBMS world, not having the same tools (foreign keys, joins) in the Azure table world can be a bit of a culture shock. One area where a lot of people have trouble is basic data modeling. In Chapter 10, you saw several examples of simple data models that, in most cases, would have fit just fine into a single RDBMS table. But what about more complex data models?

Steve Marx from the Windows Azure team suggested that some of the information in this section be included in this book, and his code was the source of ideas for some of the sample code shown here.

One-to-Many

When you model data, you often have a parent-child relationship, or a one-to-many relationship. A canonical example is a customer-order data model as shown in Figure 11-3—a customer "has" many orders, and you often do lookups where you want to get all orders belonging to a single customer.

Let's turn the diagram shown in Figure 11-3 into a model in Azure tables. The following code shows a simple `Customer` data model. There's nothing fancy about it—it just represents some sample properties on the `Customer` and picks an arbitrary partitioning scheme:

```
class Customer:TableServiceEntity
{
    public Customer(string name, string id, string company,
                    string address):base(company, id)
    {
        this.Name = name;
        this.ID = id;
        this.Company = company;
        this.Address = address;

        this.PartitionKey = this.Company;
        this.RowKey = this.ID;
    }

    public Customer() { }

    public string Name { get; set; }
    public string Company { get; set; }
    public string Address { get; set; }
    public string ID { get; set; }
}
```

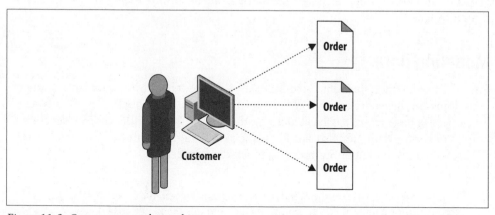

Figure 11-3. One-to-many relationship

Similarly, let's define an `Order` entity. You would want to look up a given customer's orders quickly, so a customer ID makes a natural choice of partition key, since you can always specify that in any queries you make.

The following code shows an `Order` entity that takes the customer ID it "belongs" to, as well as some other properties. For those of you who are used to specifying foreign keys, note how the "foreign key" relationship between customer and order is implicit in the fact that `CustomerID` is specified in the creation of every order. However, as mentioned previously, there is no referential integrity checking across tables. You could happily delete customer IDs and the table service won't warn you of dangling, orphaned `OrderID`s:

```
class Order : TableServiceEntity
{

    public Order(string customerID, string orderID, string orderDetails)
        : base(customerID, orderID)
    {
        this.CustomerID = customerID;
        this.OrderID = orderID;
        this.OrderDetails = orderDetails;
        this.PartitionKey = CustomerID;
        this.RowKey = OrderID;
    }


    public string CustomerID { get; set; }
    public string OrderID { get; set; }
    public string OrderDetails { get; set; }
}
```

The final piece of the puzzle is to get all orders pertaining to a given customer. There are a few ways you can do this.

The first is to store all the `OrderID`s for a given `Customer` as a property of the `Customer` object as a serialized list. This has the advantage of not having to do multiple queries—when you get back the `Customer` object, you already have the list of orders as well. However, this is suboptimal for huge numbers of orders, because you can store only a limited number of such IDs before you run into the size limits on entities.

A better model is to add a helper method to the `Customer` entity class to look up all `Order` entities associated with it. This has the overhead of adding another query, but will scale to any number of orders. The following code shows the modification to the `Customer` class code. The code assumes a data service context class that has properties corresponding to `Customer` and `Order` table name (not shown).

```
class Customer:TableServiceEntity
{
    public Customer(string name, string id, string company,
                    string address):base(company, id)
    {
        this.Name = name;
        this.ID = id;
        this.Company = company;
        this.Address = address;

        this.PartitionKey = this.Company;
        this.RowKey = this.ID;
    }

    public Customer() { }
```

```
        public string Name { get; set; }
        public string Company { get; set; }
        public string Address { get; set; }
        public string ID { get; set; }

        public IEnumerable<Order> GetOrders()
        {
            return from o in new CustomerOrderDataServiceContext().OrderTable
                   where o.PartitionKey == this.ID
                   select o;

        }
    }
```

Many-to-Many

Another common scenario in modeling data is a many-to-many relationship. This is best explained with the help of a sample model, such as the one shown in Figure 11-4. This model could form the basis of many social networking sites. It shows two entities, Friend and Group, with a many-to-many relationship with each other. There can be many friends in a single group (example groups being "School," "College," "Work," and "Ex-boyfriends"), and a friend can be in many groups ("Work" and "Ex-boyfriends").

The application may want to traverse this relationship in either direction. Given a friend, it might want to display all groups she belongs to. Similarly, given a group, it might want to list all the friends you have in it.

Let's start by creating some simple Friend and Group entity classes. They both define some simple properties, and have a simple partitioning scheme. The partitioning scheme isn't important for the discussion here:

```
class Friend : TableServiceEntity
{

    public string Name{get;set;}
    public string FriendID {get;set;}
    public string Details {get;set;}

    public Friend(string id, string name, string details):base(name, id)
    {
        this.Name = name;
        this.FriendID = id;
        this.Details = details;

        this.PartitionKey = Name;
        this.RowKey = FriendID;
    }

    public Friend(){}

}
```

```
class Group : TableStorageEntity
{
    public string Name { get; set; }
    public string GroupID {get;set;}

    public Group(string name, string id)
        : base(id, id)
    {
        this.Name = name;
        this.GroupID = id;
        this.PartitionKey = id;
        this.RowKey - id;
    }

    public Group() { }

}
```

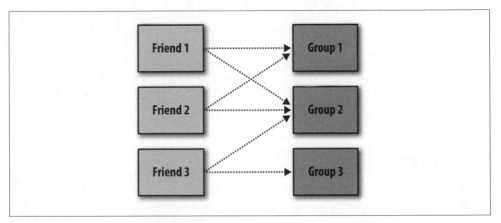

Figure 11-4. Many-to-many relationship

How do you now represent the relationship between `Friend` and `Group`? The best way
to deal with this is to create a separate "join" table that contains one entity per one
friend-group relation. To look up all friends in a group, you just need to query this table
with that specific `GroupID` (and vice versa, for all groups a friend belongs to). Following
is the code for this simple table:

```
class FriendGroupRelationship : TableServiceEntity
{
    public string FriendID { get; set; }
    public string GroupID { get; set; }

    public FriendGroupRelationship(string friendID, string groupID)
        : base(friendID, groupID)
    {
        this.FriendID = friendID;
        this.GroupID = groupID;
        this.PartitionKey = FriendID;
        this.RowKey = GroupID;
```

```
        }

        public FriendGroupRelationship() { }

    }
```

In this code, you chose to partition based on `FriendID`. This means that querying all groups to which a friend belongs will be fast, while the reverse won't be. If your application cares more about displaying all friends in a group quickly, you can pick the reverse partitioning scheme, or create two tables with two different partitioning schemes for the two scenarios.

Note that when creating a new `Friend` or `Group`, you must add an entity to the join table, and remove the entity when you delete the friend or the group. Following is a code snippet that shows how that might look:

```
var id = new Guid().ToString();
var friend = new Friend(id,
"Jean Luc Picard", "Captain, U.S.S. Enterprise");

// Add Picard to a group
var friendgrouprelation = new
  FriendGroupRelationship(id, "captains");
context.AddObject("Friend", friend);
context.AddObject("FriendGroupRelationship",
    friendgrouprelation);
```

Making Things Fast

Thus far, you've received a lot of tips for accelerating table access. The following discussion covers a few more common scenarios that are not fast out of the box with Windows Azure tables, and delves into what you can do to make them a lot zippier.

Secondary Indexes

Imagine typical tables in an RDBMS where you have multiple columns on which you want to search. Most database systems index the primary key, so queries search on the primary key. However, queries on other columns might be slow if there's no index on them. Typically, you would profile your database and add indexes to the columns on which you search frequently. This might slow down your inserts and updates (because both the table and the index must be updated), but will dramatically speed up queries that were searching on that column because the database engine just needs to do a binary search on the index to find the right rows to return.

The same scenario is tricky to achieve using Azure tables. As of this writing, Azure tables do not support having indexes on anything other than the partition key and row key. (Although the team has suggested that this is functionality that might be added at a future date.) While this makes queries on the partition/row key very fast, queries that search over individual properties might be slow because each entity in the partition must get scanned. Though you don't have the ability to create indexes on columns other than the primary/row keys, you can simulate them by creating your own home-grown secondary indexes.

How do you do that?

Let's look at what an index does in a traditional database. It stores a sorted list of all the values of the column being indexed with pointers to the original rows from which the values came. If multiple rows have the same value for a column, it stores pointers to all of them together. Table 11-3 shows a sample table schema, and Table 11-4 shows what an index for one of the columns for that table might look like.

Table 11-3. Sample table

Primary key	Col1	Col2	Col3	Col4
Key1	Value1	...	...	...
Key2	Value2	...	...	...

Table 11-4. Sample index

Col1 value	Row primary key
Value1	Key1
Value2	Key2

If you look closely, you can see that the index looks like a table. Hmm—what if you could store the index in a table? Instead of relying on the database to automatically update the index, you would add a pointer back to the entity, along with the value of the column that you want to index. That's what you'll do next.

Let's take a simple `Employee` table as shown in Example 11-1.

Example 11-1. Simple Employee table

```
public class Employee : TableServiceEntity
    {

        public Employee(string department, string employeeId,
                string firstName, string lastName)
            : base(department, employeeId)
        {
            DepartmentId = department;
            EmployeeId = employeeId;
            FirstName = firstName;
            LastName = lastName;
            PartitionKey = DepartmentId;
            RowKey = employeeId;
        }
        public Employee()
        {
            //Blank constructor for ADO.NET Data Services
```

```
    }

        public string EmployeeId { get; set; }
        public string FirstName { get; set; }
        public string LastName { get; set; }
        public string DepartmentId { get; set; }


    }
```

You saw that the most important factor in query performance is partitioning, and whether you specify the partition in the query. In Example 11-1, the `Employee` class is partitioned by department, and the `EmployeeID` is used as the row key. This typically means that several of the important queries specify the department in them (since that's how partitioning strategy is usually determined).

But let's say the requirements have changed, and now you have a few important queries that look up rows by last name. You'll find that your queries don't perform very well, since they must scan every row in every partition to return the right set of results.

To fix this, let's build a secondary index. Example 11-2 shows a secondary index class that indexes the `LastName` property. Every time you add, update, or delete an entity from the `Employee` table (the master/source data), you'll be making the same modification to the index as well. In this case, the data of the actual entity *is stored in the index entity as well*. This is similar to *clustered indexes* as used in the RDBMS world.

Example 11-2. "Clustered" secondary index

```
public class EmployeeNameIndex : TableServiceEntity
{

    public EmployeeNameIndex(string department, string employeeId,
                             string firstName, string lastName)
        : base(lastName, employeeId)
    {
        DepartmentId = department;
        EmployeeId = employeeId;
        FirstName = firstName;
        LastName = lastName;

        //Note that we now use the LastName property as
        // PartitionKey
        PartitionKey = LastName;
        RowKey = employeeId;
    }

    public EmployeeNameIndex() { }

    public string EmployeeId { get; set; }
    public string FirstName { get; set; }
    public string LastName { get; set; }
    public string DepartmentId { get; set; }
```

Another valid design is to have the index class not contain all the data, but contain only a pointer back to the original entity. This will help save costs, because less data is being stored in the cloud, but you'll incur an additional HTTP trip. Also, this saves work on updates, since you're not storing the values of the columns themselves, so updates on the master entity don't need matching updates on the index entity. Whether this works for you depends on the actual cost involved, based on the amount of data you have and the overhead of the HTTP request.

The code to update the index to keep it in "sync" with the original table is pretty simple as well. As with all storage operations, you need a data context class to take care of the plumbing for you. Example 11-3 shows a simple data service context class.

Example 11-3. Employee table and index data service context class

```
public class EmployeeDataServiceContext : TableServiceContext
    {
        public EmployeeDataServiceContext
(string baseAddress, StorageCredentials credentials)
          : base(baseAddress, credentials)              {
          }

        public const string EmployeeTableName = "Employee";

        public IQueryable<Employee> EmployeeTable
        {
            get
            {
                return this.CreateQuery<Employee>(EmployeeTableName);
            }
        }

        public const string EmployeeNameIndexTableName = "EmployeeNameIndex";

        public IQueryable<EmployeeNameIndex> EmployeeNameIndexTable
        {
            get
            {
                return
                this.CreateQuery<EmployeeNameIndex>
                (EmployeeNameIndexTableName);
            }
        }

    }
```

The key to secondary indexes is to ensure that they're in sync with the main table at all times. To do this, add an entity to the index whenever you add an entity to the original table, and update the index entity when you update the original.

There is a potential race condition here. Since the changes to the master row and the index row aren't part of one atomic transaction, a client could theoretically see an out-of-sync master and index. Normal databases don't have this problem, because the index update is done along with any modifications on the source table. One workaround for this is to add a version property to the master/source entity, and update that on every change. Clients can reject the index entity if it doesn't have the same version number as the master entity.

Example 11-4 shows two queries in action (assuming you've added some data to the Employee table already). The first makes use of the partitioning by department to quickly retrieve all employees in the Human Resources (HR) department. The second uses the index table partitioned by last name to quickly retrieve all employees with a particular last name. To retrieve a specific employee, you would add a clause looking for a particular employee ID.

Example 11-4. Querying with and without indexes

```
var account = CloudStorageAccount.Parse(ConfigurationSettings.AppSettings
            ["DataConnectionString"]);
var svc =
new EmployeeDataServiceContext(account.TableEndpoint.ToString(),
account.Credentials);

// Searches using department ID on table
// partitioned by department
var employeeQuery = from employee in
svc.CreateQuery<Employee>
(EmployeeDataServiceContext.EmployeeTableName)
            where employee.DepartmentId == "HR"
            select employee;

//Searches using last name on index table
//partitioned by last name
var indexQuery = from indexEntry in
svc.CreateQuery<EmployeeNameIndex>
(EmployeeDataServiceContext.EmployeeNameIndexTableName)
            where indexEntry.LastName == "Wozniak"
            select indexEntry;
```

Entity Group Transactions

Though the Windows Azure Table service doesn't support full-featured transactions like a normal RDBMS, it does support a limited form that helps batch request performance, and provides all-or-nothing semantics under certain conditions.

Entity group transactions in Windows Azure table storage let you perform up to 100 operations in a batch against a given partition. (It might be helpful to think of them as "per-partition transactions.") Two key properties are useful.

First, all operations are executed as a single atomic unit. If one fails, the entire set of changes is rolled back, just as you would expect in a normal transaction. Second, the entire set of operations is embedded in a single POST request, instead of doing multiple HTTP requests. When you're doing a lot of small updates, this can really help with performance.

As mentioned previously, this works under only certain conditions. So, what are they?

- All operations must act against a single partition. This is the easiest requirement to trip over. When constructing your partitioning strategy, this is something to think about.

- There can only be a maximum of 100 operations (either create/update/delete) in a single change set.

- All the operations must be of the same "type." In other words, the transaction must comprise all create operations or all delete operations. They all must share the same query.

- The total size of the payload cannot exceed 4 MB.

- Every entity can have only one operation in the payload. You cannot make multiple changes to the same entity as part of the same transaction.

- All requests with entity group transactions in them must specify the versioning header (x-ms-version) and set that to 2009-04-14 or later.

Using entity group transactions

The best part about using these transactions with ADO.NET Data Services is that you have very few code changes to make. In all the code samples presented thus far, you've called SaveChanges on the DataServiceContext class to upload all the accumulated changes to cloud storage. To change to using batch transactions (provided that all your accumulated requests meet the constraints previously described), you just need to change that call to SaveChanges(SaveChangesOptions.Batch). That's it!

Utilizing Concurrent Updates

For any nontrivial application, you will have multiple clients talking to the Azure Table service at the same time. Concurrency becomes critical, since multiple clients could easily wind up trampling all over each other's changes. Windows Azure Table service uses optimistic concurrency to deal with this issue.

1. Each entity has an associated version number that is modified by the Azure Table service on every update.

2. When an entity is retrieved, the server sends this version to the client as an HTTP ETag.

3. When the client sends an update request to the Table service, it sends this ETag to the server as an If-Match header. This happens automatically with ADO.NET Data Services under the hood.

4. If the version of the entity on the server is the same as the ETag in the If-Match header, the change is accepted, and the entity stored gets a new version on the server. The new version is returned to the client as an ETag header.

5. If the version of the entity on the server is different from the ETag in the If-Match header, the change is rejected, and a "precondition failed" HTTP error is returned to the client.

Figure 11-5 shows an example in which two clients are trying to update the same entity.

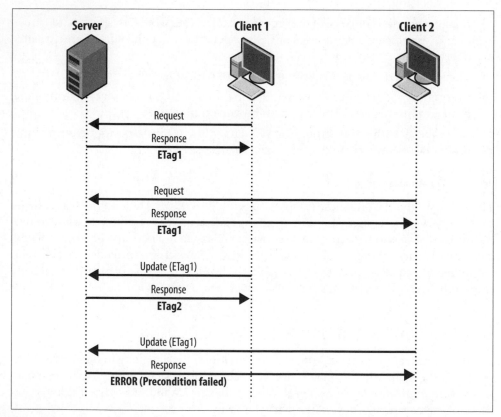

Figure 11-5. Concurrent updates

Client 1 updates the entity after Client 2 has retrieved a copy, so Client 2's update fails because it doesn't match the newest ETag.

How do you deal with this error? Well, the good news is that ADO.NET Data Services sends the right ETag headers if you set DataServiceContext.MergeOption to

MergeOption.PreserveChanges. When the server sends down a "precondition failed" error, it gets wrapped in a DataServiceRequestException, which you can catch and check for by using DataServiceRequestException.Response.First().StatusCode.

What if you don't care if you have the latest update on the client side, and you just want your last write to succeed? This is common in performance-critical scenarios where some data loss is tolerated. In these cases, you don't want to retrieve the latest version of the object before updating the entity.

Doing so is slightly obtuse using ADO.NET Data Services because this support isn't as well "baked in" and, frankly, feels slightly weird. You essentially must send a "*" as the ETag from the client to the server. This basically tells the server, "Hey, I don't care what version you have, just accept these changes." Doing so with ADO.NET Data Services involves detaching the object from the data context, attaching it back with the wildcard "*" ETag, and then calling UpdateObject.

The following code snippet shows this:

```
// set the merge option to overwrite to allow the tracked entity to be updated
context.Detach(entity);

// Attach the entity to the context using the table name, the entity to
// update, and "*" as the ETag value to use.
context.AttachTo("MyTable", entity, "*");
entity.Details = "This write will always succeed";
try
{
    context.UpdateObject(entity);
    DataServiceResponse response = context.SaveChanges();
}
catch (DataServiceRequestException e)
{
    // Error handling - but it cannot throw a PreCondition failure
}
```

Summary

At one point, this chapter was in danger of exploding in page count. The reality is that people normally do several things with databases that require some rethinking in the world of Azure tables. This chapter should have provided you with an idea of what that rethinking encompasses for some common scenarios so that even if you encounter a scenario that isn't covered here, you have a feel for how to tackle the problem.

## CHAPTER 12

Building a Secure Backup System

When using cloud services, you often have to worry about security, and resort to cryptographic techniques such as digital signatures and encryption. There are many reasons for doing this. You may be storing sensitive data (for example, people's health reports) and you are mandated by law to provide extra protection. You may be protecting sensitive data regarding your business that you don't want in the wrong hands. Or you could simply be paranoid and not trust Microsoft or any other cloud provider. Whatever your reason, you can take several steps to add further levels of protection to your data.

All of this has very little to do with your trust for Microsoft or any other cloud provider. All cloud providers (and Microsoft is no different) have multiple levels of security and several checks to ensure that unauthorized personnel cannot access customer applications or data. However, you often have little choice of whether you want to trust a cloud provider. You might be mandated to add further security levels by anything from internal IT policy to financial regulations and compliance laws.

This chapter is slightly different from all the others in that a majority of the discussion here is devoted to looking at security and cryptography. Frankly, the code and techniques used in this chapter could just as easily be used for data on a file server as for data in the cloud. Why does it show up in a book on cloud computing, then?

The decision to include an examination of security and cryptography resulted from two key motivations. First, this is useful to a lot of people when they have to build applications with highly sensitive data. More importantly, it is *so difficult* to get this stuff right that any time invested in examining good security and cryptographic techniques is well worth it.

The danger of having an insecure system is known to everyone.

This chapter shows you how to build a secure backup system for your files. It will cover how to use the right kinds of cryptographic practices and blob storage features to ensure some security properties.

 This chapter is not meant as a comprehensive introduction to cryptography. If you're interested in that, *Practical Cryptography* by Niels Ferguson and Bruce Schneier (Wiley) is a good place to start. A quick web search brings up a lot of good references as well.

Developing a Secure Backup System

In this chapter, you will learn how to build a secure system that should satisfy even the most "paranoid" conspiracy theorist. You will discover how a real-world application (hopefully, a useful one) will use the blob service, as well as the challenges and trade-offs involved. Finally, you will learn how to code to a nontrivial application.

 Don't infer that the word *paranoid* suggests that these techniques aren't relevant to normal users. Mentally insert "highly conservative from a security perspective" whenever you see the word *paranoid* throughout the ensuing discussions.

The application has a highly creative name, Azure Backup (`azbackup`), and it is quite simple to use. It mimics the `tar` utility that ships with most modern Unix systems. Instead of compressing and making a single backup out of multiple files and directories to disk, `azbackup` lets you compress files and make backups to Windows Azure blob storage instead. The tool `tar`s multiple files and directories together into one big file (in exactly the same manner as the Unix `tar` command). This `tar` file is then compressed using the popular `gzip` algorithm.

Why `tar` and then compress? Why not compress each file individually? By combining multiple files in one large file, you gain higher compression rates. Compression algorithms compress data by finding redundancy. They have a better chance of finding redundancy in one large file, rather than in several small files individually. Having one large file is also easier for you to manage when it comes to moving around, copying, and managing any operation.

The entire code for this sample is available at *http://github.com/sriramk/azbackup*. You'll be seeing snippets of code as this chapter progresses, but you can always look at the entire source code. It is also very easy to set up and run, and should work on Windows as well as any modern Unix system that has Python support.

The sample takes inspiration from the excellent tarsnap (*http://www.tarsnap.com/*) service. If you're really paranoid and want to delve into a real, production backup service, tarsnap's design makes for great reading. Colin Percival, tarsnap's creator, also helped with some of the cryptography in this chapter.

Understanding Security

A primary challenge developers face is deciding how secure to make an application. When you ask most people how secure they want their data or their application, you're going to hear superlative terms such as *impenetrable*, *totally secure*, and so on. When you hear someone say that, you should run as quickly as you can in the opposite direction.

Unfortunately (or fortunately, for security consultants), there is no completely secure system. In theory, you can imagine an application running on an isolated computer with no network connections in an underground bunker surrounded by thick concrete, protected by a small army. And even that can't be completely secure.

Security, like other things, is a spectrum in which you get to pick where you want to be. If you're building a small social bookmarking service, your security needs are different than if you're working for the government building a system for the National Security Agency (NSA).

For the sample backup application you'll see in this chapter, you will be as paranoid as possible. The goal is that your data should be secure even if three-letter government agencies wanted to get to it. This is overkill for applications you'll be building, so you can look at the security techniques used in this chapter and pick which ones you want to keep, and which ones you don't care about.

Before you figure out how to secure something, you must know what you are securing it from, and what *secure* even means. For the application in this chapter, let's define a few security properties that should hold at all times.

The first property is *secrecy*. The data that you back up using this application should not be in the clear either in motion or at rest. No one should be able to get data in plain form apart from you. Importantly, this data should not be in the clear with your cloud provider of choice here, Microsoft.

The second property is *integrity*. You must instantly verify whether the data you backed up has been tampered with in any way. As a bonus, it would be nice if this verification were done with something bound to your identity (also known as a *digital signature*).

The third property is the *ability to verify your tools*. Essentially, you will be so paranoid that you don't trust code you can't see in any layer charged with enforcing the previous two properties. This means you will force yourself to stick to open source tools only. Note that the fact that Microsoft is running some code in the data center is irrelevant here, because the data is protected "outside" the data center, and the blob service is used only as a very efficient byte storage-and-transfer mechanism.

We will discuss the first two properties throughout the course of this chapter. For the third property, you will stick with open source tools that will work just as well on a non-Windows open source platform.

To run the code in this chapter, you need two pieces of software. The first is Python 2.5 or later, which you can download from *http://www.python.org* if you don't already have it.

 Almost all modern *nix operating systems ship with some version of Python. As of this writing, most did not ship with Python 2.5 or later. To check the version of Python you have, run `python --version` at a command line.

Unfortunately, Python lacks some of the core cryptographic functionality that is used in this chapter, so the second piece of required software is an additional Python package called M2Crypto. You can find prebuilt versions for your operating system of choice at *http://chandlerproject.org/Projects/MeTooCrypto*. This is a popular Python library maintained by Heikki Toivonen that wraps around the OpenSSL tool set to provide several cryptographic and security features.

 M2Crypto doesn't have the greatest documentation in the world, but since it is a thin wrapper around OpenSSL, you can often look up documentation for the OpenSSL function of the same name. *Network Security with OpenSSL (http://oreilly.com/catalog/9780596002701/)* by John Viega et al. (O'Reilly) is a great place to read more on OpenSSL development. That and *Practical Cryptography* were two books that were invaluable while writing this chapter.

Protecting Data in Motion

Any sort of cloud backup solution obviously must transfer bits to the cloud and back. An attacker shouldn't be able to peek at your data as it is flowing through the Internet. Note that, although an attacker can't look at your data, there is no easy protection from attackers detecting that some data transfer is happening in the first place, or guessing at the amount of data being sent. Size and timing over any communication protocol is difficult to keep secret.

Thankfully, you need to do very little to actually protect your data in motion. In Chapter 7, you learned that all the Windows Azure storage APIs have an HTTPS variant that is protected using Secure Sockets Layer (SSL)/Transport Layer Security (TLS). You can perform the same API operations, but with an https:// URI instead of an http:// URI. This will give you a great deal of security with only a small drop in performance. Most people would stop with this. But as mentioned, paranoia will reign in this chapter. This means you must ensure that the way you do SSL is actually secure in itself.

This looks easy on the surface, but it actually requires some work from the client side. The common mistake developers make is to replace all http:// URIs with https:// URIs in their code. Though this will let the application continue working, it is actually insecure. To understand the right way to do this and why just making calls to https:// URIs isn't sufficient, let's first take a quick peek at how SSL works.

SSL (or TLS, to use its more modern reference) is a way for client/server applications to communicate securely over a network without risk of eavesdropping, tampering, or message forgery. Most everyone has probably interacted with an SSL-based website (for example, when shopping online), and a lot of programmers have probably built web services or websites secured using SSL.

SSL is built on two core concepts: certificates and certification authorities.

A *certificate* (an X.509v3 certificate, to be specific) is a wrapper around a public key and a private key, installed together on the web server. When the browser contacts the web server, it gets the public key, and uses some standard cryptographic techniques to set up a secure connection with data that only the server can decrypt. That is sufficient to ensure that you are securely talking to the server, but how do you tell that the server itself can be trusted? How do you know that *https://www.paypal.com* is actually the company PayPal?

 To understand what happens under the covers with certificates, see a great blog post that goes into excruciating detail at *http://www.moser ware.com/2009/06/first-few-milliseconds-of-https.html*.

This is where a *certification authority* (*CA*) comes in. CAs are a few specialized companies, trusted by your browser and/or your operating system, whose only purpose is to verify the authenticity of certificates. They do this through various offline mechanisms—anything from a phone call to requiring a fax. Once they've verified that the person asking for a certificate to, say, *https://www.paypal.com* is actually the company PayPal and not some scammer, they sign PayPal's certificate with their own.

Figure 12-1 shows PayPal's certificate. You can see that it has been authenticated by VeriSign, which is a trusted CA.

Similarly, Figure 12-2 shows the certificate Microsoft uses for Windows Azure blob storage. In this figure, you can see the "certification chain." CAs often sign certifications of other CAs, who in turn can validate individual certificates or sign yet another CA, thereby constructing a chain. In this case, you see at the bottom that **.blob.core.windows.net* is signed by Microsoft Secure Server Authority. If you follow the chain, you wind up at GTE CyberTrust, which is a well-known CA that is trusted on most browsers and operating systems and is now owned by Verizon.

This certificate has been verified for the following uses:

SSL Server Certificate

Issued To

Common Name (CN)	www.paypal.com
Organization (O)	PayPal, Inc.
Organizational Unit (OU)	Information Systems
Serial Number	5F:4D:90:B8:00:C3:07:B0:95:8D:97:68:A1:58:1E:FB

Issued By

Common Name (CN)	VeriSign Class 3 Extended Validation SSL CA
Organization (O)	VeriSign, Inc.
Organizational Unit (OU)	VeriSign Trust Network

Validity

Issued On	4/27/2009
Expires On	4/1/2010

Fingerprints

SHA1 Fingerprint	DC:5A:CB:8B:9E:B9:B5:DE:71:17:C5:36:8C:15:0E:75:BA:88:70:2E
MD5 Fingerprint	C5:B8:7D:DD:CC:C7:53:7F:88:61:B4:76:07:8D:E8:FD

Figure 12-1. PayPal certificate

When you make a storage request to *https://*.blob.core.windows.net*, your connection should be secured by the certificate shown in Figure 12-2. As you might have figured by now, the connection is insecure if the server is actually using some other certificate. But how is that possible? Unfortunately, the answer is that it is quite easy.

One attack would be to redirect your request to a server that has a certificate chaining to a valid CA, but not for *blob.core.windows.net*. The attacker would use a man-in-the-middle (MITM) attack where he redirects your request to a server of his choosing. If your code only asks for an SSL connection, but doesn't check that the certificate it is getting matches the domain/host it is connecting to, it can get fooled by the server presenting any certificate.

Another attack is equally easy to execute. The attacker generates a special kind of certificate called a *self-signed certificate* where, instead of getting it validated by a CA, it is validated by itself. In the real world, that's like asking people for a proof of identity and they hand you a piece of paper signed by them and certifying them to be who they say they are. Just like you wouldn't trust that piece of paper, you shouldn't trust self-signed certificates either.

 This is not to say that self-signed certificates are insecure. They are very useful in various other scenarios, and are even used in other parts of Windows Azure for perfectly valid, secure reasons.

This certificate has been verified for the following uses:

SSL Server Certificate

Issued To

Common Name (CN)	*.blob.core.windows.net
Organization (O)	<Not Part Of Certificate>
Organizational Unit (OU)	<Not Part Of Certificate>
Serial Number	56:E6:3B:1A:00:05:00:00:E8:28

Issued By

Common Name (CN)	Microsoft Secure Server Authority
Organization (O)	Microsoft Secure Server Authority
Organizational Unit (OU)	<Not Part Of Certificate>

Validity

Issued On	10/6/2008
Expires On	10/6/2009

Fingerprints

SHA1 Fingerprint	5C:D2:59:43:BF:ED:2A:6B:84:F2:C7:C0:B5:E1:9A:9C:84:B7:21:32
MD5 Fingerprint	68:42:AB:E0:25:90:2D:F3:18:AF:BE:FA:F5:2C:AF:B6

Certificate Hierarchy

⊿ GTE CyberTrust Global Root
  ⊿ Microsoft Internet Authority
    ⊿ Microsoft Secure Server Authority
      *.blob.core.windows.net

Figure 12-2. The blob.core.windows.net certificate

Figure 12-3 shows a self-signed certificate generated for **.blob.core.windows.net*. Apart from the fact that it is "signed" by itself, note how it looks like a legitimate certificate in every other aspect.

There is another way to fool SSL clients that is more difficult to protect against. CAs are not equal, and some are more lax in how they verify a request than others are. In several cases, attackers have fooled CAs into issuing certificates for well-known domains. Not only should you check for the presence of a CA, but you should also check for the presence of the right CA!

The first thing we need is a Python version of the simple storage client you saw back in Chapter 7. You can find this at *http://github.com/sriramk/azbackup/blob/master/stor age.py*. This is essentially a line-by-line translation of the C# code in Chapter 7 to Python. This also contains some code to protect against these attacks which you'll see next.

Python up to version 2.5 doesn't have any good mechanism to do these checks. Python 2.6 added an SSL module that included some, but not all, of this functionality. Let's use the OpenSSL library to do the heavy lifting in terms of verifying SSL certificates.

Issued To	
Common Name (CN)	*.blob.core.windows.net
Organization (O)	<Not Part Of Certificate>
Organizational Unit (OU)	<Not Part Of Certificate>
Serial Number	30:B7:F1:59:BC:7D:B1:85:46:8B:E3:BC:B6:C6:3F:BA
Issued By	
Common Name (CN)	*.blob.core.windows.net
Organization (O)	*.blob.core.windows.net
Organizational Unit (OU)	<Not Part Of Certificate>
Validity	
Issued On	8/15/2009
Expires On	5/11/2012
Fingerprints	
SHA1 Fingerprint	B4:1E:1B:D6:66:E1:7D:E6:26:11:9A:67:B4:F3:38:4F:D2:D9:D8:51
MD5 Fingerprint	DA:7B:DF:E3:34:74:EB:13:0A:ED:35:BD:17:0B:2A:13

Figure 12-3. Fake blob.core.windows.net certificate

OpenSSL is a native library that can't be accessed directly from Python. The M2Crypto package provides a nice Pythonic wrapper around OpenSSL.

 It is easy to implement the same using .NET, Java, or pretty much any modern programming platform. In .NET, look at `System.Net.Service PointManager`'s `ServerCertificateValidationCallback`. In Java, look at `javax.net.ssl.TrustManager`. Both .NET and Java do some of this validation (checking a certificate's validity, whether the certificate's Common Name matches the hostname) by default, but not all of it. For example, neither can actually check whether the certificate chains to the right CA.

You can find the entire source code for this in the *storage.py* file as part of the `azbackup` source tree. `USE_HTTPS` is a useful variable that you'll use to toggle whether the storage library should use HTTPS. HTTPS can be quite painful when debugging, and having the ability to turn it off with a configuration option is useful.

```
from M2Crypto import httpslib, SSL

USE_HTTPS= False
```

The first task is to switch over from using an HTTP connection to an HTTPS connection. Doing so provides an unexpected bonus. M2Crypto (or, to be specific, OpenSSL) checks whether the hostname matches the certificate's Common Name (CN), and takes care of the first of the two attacks previously described. Example 12-1 shows how to make `_do_store_request` use an SSL connection if required. The actual SSL connection is made using M2Crypto's `httpslib`, which is a drop-in, interface-compatible SSL version of Python's `httplib`.

Example 12-1. Using an HTTPS connection

```
# Create a connection object
        if USE_HTTPS:
            ctx = SSL.Context()
            # The line below automatically checks whether cert matches host
            connection = httpslib.HTTPSConnection(account_url,ssl_context=ctx)
        else:
            connection = httplib.HTTPConnection(account_url)
```

The next step toward protecting your SSL connection is to ensure that it comes from the right CA. This is a tricky proposition. There are several well-known CAs, and depending on your programming platform and operating system, you might trust any number of them. Windows has a default list of CAs it trusts (which you can find by running `certmgr.msc`). OS X has a default list that you can find in KeyChain, and Firefox maintains a huge list of CAs that it trusts. .NET trusts everything that Windows trusts by default. OpenSSL and M2Crypto trust no CA by default, and expect you to tell them which ones to trust. All in all, this is quite messy and confusing.

You solve this by using the "let's be paranoid" principle. Instead of trusting several CAs, you trust only *one* CA: the CA that issues the certificate for **.blob.core.windows.net*, namely, GTE CyberTrust. To make M2Crypto/OpenSSL trust this CA, you need GTE CyberTrust's certificate in a specific format: PEM-encoded. (PEM actually stands for "Privacy Enhanced Email," though its common uses have nothing to do with "privacy" or "email," or any form of "enhancement." It is a simple technique for representing arbitrary bytes in ASCII-compatible text. The best reason to use it is that it is widely supported.) There are multiple ways to do this.

 This paranoid approach means your application could break if Microsoft appoints someone else to issue its SSL certificate. After all, nowhere does Microsoft promise that it will stick to the same SSL provider.

The easiest way to do this is to export the certificate from Firefox or Internet Explorer. Add that to your source as the file *cacerts.pem* and place it in the same directory as the rest of the source code.

You can now check whether the certificate for the HTTPS connection is signed by a chain that ends in "GTE CyberTrust." Example 12-2 shows the code to do that. This is a modification of `_do_store_request` and builds on the code shown in the previous example. Example 12-2 uses the `SSL.Context` class from M2Crypto, and sets it to verify that the endpoint you are connecting to has a certificate and that it is a certificate you trust. The code then adds a list of trusted root certificates by looking for a file called *cacerts.pem*, in which you place GTE CyberTrust's certificate.

Example 12-2. HTTPS checking for a specific CA

```
# Create a connection object
if USE_HTTPS:
    ctx = SSL.Context()

    # Verify that the server chains to a known CA.
    # We hardcode cacerts.pem in the source directory
    # with GTE CyberTrust's certs which is what
    # Windows Azure chains to currently.
    ctx.set_verify(SSL.verify_peer | SSL.verify_fail_if_no_peer_cert, 9)

    # GTE's certs are kept in cacerts.pem in the same directory
    # as source. sys.path[0] always
    # contains the directory in which the source file exists
    if ctx.load_verify_locations(sys.path[0] + "/cacerts.pem")!=1:
        raise Exception("No CA certs")

    # The line below automatically checks whether cert matches host
    connection = httpslib.HTTPSConnection(account_url,ssl_context=ctx)
else:
    connection = httplib.HTTPConnection(account_url)

# Perform the request and read the response
connection.request(http_method, path , data, headers)
response = connection.getresponse()
```

You now have some secure SSL code that you can rely on to only talk over an encrypted channel to the Windows Azure blob storage service. How much performance overhead does it add? Surprisingly little. During performance tests, several thousand iterations were run before any perceptible performance difference could be measured by using SSL. Your results may vary, and you should always test before making a change like this.

Note that you can go further if you want. There are always more things to check and enforce—such as certificate validity, the cipher suite picked by the SSL connection, dealing with proxy servers along the way, and so on.

Protecting Data at Rest

Now that the transfer of data over the wire is secure, the next step is to secure the data when it has reached Microsoft's servers. A reasonable question is, why bother? SSL protects against anyone snooping or modifying traffic over the wire. Microsoft implements various security practices (from physical to technological) to protect your data once it has reached its data centers. Isn't this sufficient security?

For most cases, the answer is "yes." This isn't sufficient *only* when you have highly sensitive data (health data, for example) that has regulations and laws surrounding how it is stored. Though you may be secure enough in practice, you might still need to encrypt your data to comply with some regulation.

Once you've decided that your having data in the clear in Microsoft's data centers isn't acceptable (and you've taken into account the performance overhead of doing so), what do you do?

When Crypto Attacks

Cryptography is very dangerous. It is the technological equivalent of getting someone drunk on tequila and then giving him a loaded bazooka that can fire forward and backward. It (cryptography, not the fictitious bazooka) is fiendishly difficult to get right, and most blog posts/book samples get it wrong in some small, but nevertheless devastating, way.

The only known ways to ensure that some application is cryptographically sound is to do a thorough analysis of the cryptographic techniques it uses, and to let experts review/ attack the application for a long time (sometimes years on end). Some of the widespread cryptographic products (be it the Windows crypto stack or OpenSSL) are so good because of the attention and analysis they've received.

With this in mind, you should reuse some well-known code/library for all your cryptographic needs. For example, GPGME is a great library for encrypting files. If you're rolling your own implementation, ensure that you have professional cryptographers validate what you're doing.

The code and techniques shown in this chapter should be sound. You can use them as a starting point for your own implementation, or to help you understand how other implementations work. However, you shouldn't trust and reuse the code presented here directly in a production application for the simple reason that it hasn't undergone thorough scrutiny from a legion of experts.

The goal here will be to achieve two things with any data you back up with the service presented in this chapter. The first is to encrypt data so that only the original user can decrypt it. The second is to digitally sign the encrypted data so that any modification is automatically detected.

Understanding the Basics of Cryptography

To thoroughly understand how this will be accomplished, you must first become familiar with some basics of cryptography. Entire books have been written on cryptography, so this is nothing more than the most fleeting of introductions, meant more to jog your memory than anything else.

If you've never heard of these terms, you should spend a leisurely evening (or two...or several) reading up on them before writing any cryptography code. Unlike a lot of programming where a coder can explore and copy/paste code from the Web and get away with it, cryptography and security are places where not having a solid understanding of the fundamentals can bite you when you least expect it. To quote the old G.I. Joe advertising slogan, "Knowing is half the battle." The other half is probably reusing other people's tried-and-tested crypto code whenever you can.

Encryption/decryption

When the term *encryption* is used in this chapter, it refers to the process of converting data (*plaintext*) using an algorithm into a form (*ciphertext*) in which it is unreadable without possession of a *key*. *Decryption* is the reverse of this operation, in which a key is used to convert ciphertext back into plaintext.

Symmetric key algorithms

A *symmetric key algorithm* is one that uses the same key for both encryption and decryption. Popular examples are the Advanced Encryption Standard (AES, also known as Rijndael), Twofish, Serpent, and Blowfish. A major advantage of using symmetric algorithms is that they're quite fast. However, this gets tempered with the disadvantage that both parties (the one doing the encryption and the one doing the decryption) need to know the same key.

Asymmetric key algorithms (public key cryptography)

An *asymmetric key algorithm* is one in which the key used for encryption is different from the one used for decryption. The major advantage is, of course, that the party doing the encryption doesn't need to have access to the same key as the party doing the decryption.

Typically, each user has a pair of cryptographic keys: a *public key* and a *private key*. The public key may be widely distributed, but the private key is kept secret. Though the keys are related mathematically, the security of these algorithms depends on the fact that by knowing only one key, it is impossible (or at least infeasible) to derive the other.

Messages are encrypted with the recipient's public key, and can be decrypted only with the associated private key. You can use this process in reverse to digitally sign data. The sender encrypts a hash of the data with his private key, and the recipient can decrypt the hash using the public key, and verify whether it matches a hash the recipient computes.

The major disadvantage of public key cryptography is that it is typically highly computationally intensive, and it is often impractical to encrypt large amounts of data this way. One common cryptographic technique is to use a symmetric key for quickly encrypting data, and then encrypting the symmetric key (which is quite small) with an asymmetric key algorithm. Popular asymmetric key algorithms include RSA, ElGamal, and others.

Cryptographic hash

A *cryptographic hash* function is one that takes an arbitrary block of data and returns a fixed set of bytes. This sounds just like a normal hash function such as the one you would use in a `HashTable`, correct? Not quite.

To be considered a cryptographically strong hash function, the algorithm must have a few key properties. It should be infeasible to find two messages with the same hash, or to change a message without changing its hash, or to determine contents of the message given its hash. Several of these algorithms are in wide use today. As of this writing, the current state-of-the-art algorithms are those in the SHA-2 family, and older algorithms such as MD5 and SHA-1 should be considered insecure.

With that short introduction to cryptography terminology, let's get to the real meat of what you will do with `azbackup`: encrypt data.

Determining the Encryption Technique

The first criterion in picking an encryption technique is to ensure that someone getting access to the raw data on the cloud can't decrypt. This means not only do you need a strong algorithm, but also you must keep the key you use to encrypt data away from the cloud. Actual encryption and decryption won't happen in the cloud—it'll happen in whichever machine talks to the cloud using your code. By keeping the key in a physically different location, you ensure that an attack on the cloud alone can't compromise your data.

The second criterion in picking a design is to have different levels of access. In short, you can have machines that are trusted to back up data, but aren't trusted to read backups.

A common scenario is to have a web server backing up logfiles, so it must have access to a key to encrypt data. However, you don't trust the web server with the ability to decrypt all your data. To do this, you will use public key cryptography. The public key portion of the key will be used to encrypt data, and the private key will be used to decrypt backups. You can now have the public key on potentially insecure machines doing backups, but keep your private key (which is essentially the keys to the kingdom) close to your chest.

You'll be using RSA with 2,048-bit keys as the asymmetric key algorithm. There are several other options to choose from (such as ElGamal), but RSA is as good an option as any other, as long as you are careful to use it in the way it was intended. As of this writing, 2,048 bits is the recommended length for keys given current computational power.

 Cryptographers claim that 2,048-bit keys are secure until 2030. In comparison, 1,024-bit keys are expected to be cracked by 2011.

Since the archives `azbackup` works on are typically very large in size, you can't directly encrypt them using RSA. You'll be generating a symmetric key unique to every archive (typically called the *session key*, though there is no session involved here), and using a block cipher to encrypt the actual data using that symmetric key. To do this, you'll be using AES with 256-bit keys. Again, there are several choices, but AES is widely used, and as of this writing, 256 bits is the optimum key length.

Since you will use RSA to encrypt the per-archive key, you might as well use the same algorithm to sign the archives. Signing essentially takes the cryptographic hash of the encrypted data, and then encrypts the hash using the key you generated. Cryptographers frown on using the same key for both encryption and signing, so you'll generate another RSA key pair to do this.

Don't worry if all of this sounds a bit heavy. The actual code to do all this is quite simple and, more importantly, small.

 You might have noticed that the Windows Azure storage account key hasn't been mentioned anywhere here. Many believe that public key cryptography is actually better for super-sensitive, government-regulated data because no one but you (not even Microsoft) has the key to get at the plaintext version of your data. However, the storage account key does add another layer of defense to your security. If others can't get access to it, they can't get your data.

Generating Keys

Let's take a look at some code. Earlier, you learned that for the sample application you will be using two RSA keys: one for encrypting session keys for each archive, and one for signing the encrypted data. These keys will be stored in one file, and will be passed in the command line to `azbackup`. Since you can't expect the users to have a couple of RSA keys lying around, you will need to provide a utility to generate it for them.

Since there's a fair bit of crypto implementation in `azbackup`, they're bundled together in a module called `crypto` with its implementation in *crypto.py*. You'll learn about key pieces of code in this module as this discussion progresses.

Example 12-3 shows the code for the key-generation utility (creatively titled *azbackup-keygen.py*). By itself, it isn't very interesting. All it does is to take in a command-line

---

parameter (`keyfile`) for the path to generate the key to, and then calls the `crypto` module to do the actual key generation.

Example 12-3. The azbackup-gen-key.py utility

```
#!/usr/bin/env python
"""
azbackup-keygen

Generates two 2048 bit RSA keys and stores it in keyfile

Call it like this
azbackup -k keyfile
"""
import sys
import optparse
import crypto

def main():
    # parse command line options

    optp = optparse.OptionParser(__doc__)
    optp.add_option("-k","--keyfile",action="store",\
                    type="string", dest ="keyfile", default=None)
    (options, args) = optp.parse_args()


    if options.keyfile == None:
        optp.print_help()
        return

    crypto.generate_rsa_keys(options.keyfile)



if __name__== '__main__':
    main()
```

The real work is done by `crypto.generate_rsa_keys`. The implementation for that method lies in the `crypto` module. Let's first see the code in Example 12-4, and then examine how it works.

Example 12-4. Crypto generation of RSA keys

```
try:
    import M2Crypto
    from M2Crypto import EVP, RSA, BIO
except:
    print "Couldn't import M2Crypto. Make sure it is installed."
    sys.exit(-1)

def generate_rsa_keys(keyfile):
    """ Generates two 2048 bit RSA keys and stores them sequentially
    (encryption key first,signing key second) in keyfile
    """
```

```
    # Generate the encryption key and store it in bio
    bio = BIO.MemoryBuffer()
    generate_rsa_key_bio(bio)

    #Generate the signing key and store it in bio
    generate_rsa_key_bio(bio)

    key_output = open(keyfile, 'wb')
    key_output.write(bio.read())


def generate_rsa_key_bio(bio, bits=2048, exponent = 65537):
    """ Generates a 2048 RSA key to the file.
     Use 65537 as default since the use of 3 might have some weaknesses"""
    def callback(*args):
        pass
    keypair = RSA.gen_key(bits, exponent, callback)
    keypair.save_key_bio(bio, None)
```

If you aren't familiar with M2Crypto or OpenSSL programming, the code shown in Example 12-4 probably looks like gobbledygook. The first few lines import the M2Crypto module and import a few specific public classes inside that module. This is wrapped in a **try/catch** exception handler so that you can print a nice error message in case the import fails. This is the best way to check whether M2Crypto is correctly installed on the machine.

The three classes you are importing are **EVP**, **RSA**, and **BIO**. **EVP** (which is actually an acronym formed from the words "Digital EnVeloPe") is a high-level interface to all the cipher suites supported by OpenSSL. It essentially provides support for encrypting and decrypting data using a wide range of algorithms. **RSA**, as the name suggests, is a wrapper around the OpenSSL RSA implementation. This provides support for generating RSA keys and encryption/decryption using RSA. Finally, **BIO** (which actually stands for "Binary Input Output") is an I/O abstraction used by OpenSSL. Think of it as the means by which you can send and get byte arrays from OpenSSL.

The action kicks off in **generate_rsa_keys**. This calls out to **generate_rsa_key_bio** to generate the actual RSA public/private key pair, and then writes them into the key file. Two **BIO.MemoryBuffer** objects are allocated. These are the byte arrays into which **generate_rsa_key_bio** will write the RSA keys.

The key file's format is fairly trivial. It contains the RSA key pair used for encryption, followed by the RSA key pair used for decryption. There is no particular reason to use this order or format. You could just as easily design a file format or, if you are feeling really evil, you could put the contents in an XML file. Doing it this way keeps things simple and makes it easy to read out the keys again. If you ever need keys of different sizes or types, you will need to revisit this format.

The actual work of generating an RSA public/private key pair is done by **generate_rsa_key_bio**. This makes a call to **RSA.gen_key** and specifies a bit length of 2,048 and a public exponent of 65,537. (This is an internal parameter used by the RSA algorithm typically set to either 3 or 65,537. Note that using 3 here is considered just as secure.)

The call to `RSA.gen_key` takes a long time to complete. In fact, the callback function passed in is empty, but the `RSA.gen_key` calls it with a progress number that can be used to visually indicate progress.

Why does this take so long? Though this has a bit to do with the complex math involved, most of the time goes into gathering entropy to ensure that the key is sufficiently random. Surprisingly, this process is sped up if there's activity in the system. The OpenSSL command-line tool asks people to generate keyboard/mouse/disk activity. The key generation needs a source of random data (based on pure entropy), and hardware events are a good source of entropy.

Once the key pair has been generated, it is written out in a special encoded form into the `BIO` object passed in.

 If you plan to do this in a language other than Python, you don't have to worry. Everything discussed here is typically a standard part of any mainstream framework.

For .NET, to generate RSA keys use the `RSACryptoServiceProvider` class. Generating the PEM format from .NET is a bit trickier because it isn't supported out of the box. Of course, you can choose to use some other format, or invent one of your own. If you want to persist with PEM, a quick web search shows up a lot of sample code to export keys in the PEM format. You can also `P/Invoke` the `CryptExportPKCS8Ex` function in *Crypt32.dll*.

Thankfully, all of this work is hidden under the covers. Generating a key file is quite simple. The following command generates a key file containing the two RSA key pairs at *d:\foo.key*:

```
d:\book\code\azbackup>python azbackup-gen-key.py --keyfile d:\foo.key
```

 Remember to keep this key file safely tucked away. If you lose this key file, you can never decrypt your archives, and there is no way to recover the data inside them.

Compressing Backup Data

Now that the key generation part is out of the way, let's write the tool that generates the backup itself. You'll be writing the code for this in a file called *azbackup.py*.

Users will pass in directories to back up to this little tool. You have several ways of dealing with this input. One valid technique is to encrypt every file separately. However, this quickly becomes a hassle, especially if you have thousands of files to deal with.

Thankfully, the Unix world has had experience in doing this sort of thing for a few decades.

 One of the earliest references to `tar` is from Seventh Edition Unix in 1979. This is a descendant of the `tap` program that shipped with First Edition Unix in 1971.

Backups are typically done in a two-step process. The first step is to gather all the input files into a single file, typically with the extension *.tar*. The actual file format is very straightforward: the files are concatenated together with a short header before each one.

Managing a single file makes your life easier because it enables you to manipulate this with a slew of standard tools. Authoring scripts becomes a lot easier. Compressing the file gives much better results (because the compression algorithm has a much better chance of finding patterns and redundancies). The canonical way to create a tar file out of a directory and then compress the output using the gzip algorithm is with the following command:

```
tar -cvf output.tar inputdirectory|gzip >output.tar.gz
```

Or you could use the shortcut version:

```
tar -cvzf output.tar.gz inputdirectory
```

To get back the original contents, the same process is done in reverse. The tarred, gzipped file is decompressed, and then split apart into its constituent files.

Example 12-5 shows the code to do all of this inside *azbackup.py*. There are two symmetric functions: `generate_tar_gzip` and `extract_tar_gzip`. The former takes a directory or a file to compress, and writes out a tarred, gzipped archive to a specified output filename. The latter does the reverse—it takes an input archive and extracts its content to a specified directory. The code takes advantage of the `tarfile` module that ships with Python, and adds support for all this.

Example 12-5. Compressing and extracting archives

```python
import tarfile

def generate_tar_gzip(directory_or_file, output_file_name):
    if directory_or_file.endswith("/"):
        directory_or_file = directory_or_file.rstrip("/")
    # We open a handle to an output tarfile. The 'w:gz'
    # specifies that we're writing to it and that gzip
    # compression should be used
    out = tarfile.TarFile.open(output_file_name, "w:gz")

    # Add the input directory to the tarfile. Arcname is the
    # name of the directory 'inside' the archive. We'll just reuse the name
    # of the file/directory here
    out.add(directory_or_file, arcname = os.path.basename(directory_or_file))
```

```
    out.close()

def extract_tar_gzip(archive_file_name, output_directory):
    # Open the tar file and extract all contents to the
    # output directory
    extract = tarfile.TarFile.open(archive_file_name)
    extract.extractall(output_directory)
    extract.close()
```

Encrypting Data

azbackup will use the following three-step process to encrypt data (with "data" here being the compressed archives generated from the previous step):

1. For every archive, it'll generate a unique 256 key. Let's call this key K_{sym}.

2. K_{sym} is used to encrypt the archive using AES-256 in CBC mode. (You'll learn what "CBC" means in just a bit.)

3. K_{sym} is encrypted by the user's RSA encryption key (K_{enc}) and attached to the encrypted data from the previous step.

Example 12-6 shows the code in the crypto module corresponding to the previously described three steps.

Example 12-6. Encrypting data

```
def generate_rand_bits(bits=32*8):
    """SystemRandom is a cryptographically strong source of randomness
     Get n bits of randomness"""

    import random
    sys_random = random.SystemRandom()
    return long_as_bytes(sys_random.getrandbits(bits), bits/8)

def long_as_bytes(lvalue, width):
    """This rather dense piece of code takes a long and splits it apart into a
    byte array containing its constituent bytes with least significant byte
    first"""

    fmt = '%%.%dx' % (2*width)
    return unhexlify(fmt % (lvalue & ((1L<<8*width)-1)))


def block_encrypt(data, key):
    """ High level function which takes data and key as parameters
        and turns it into
        IV + CipherText after padding. Note that this still needs a sig added
        At the end"""
    iv = generate_rand_bits(32 * 8)
    ciphertext = aes256_encrypt_data(data, key, iv)

    return iv + ciphertext
```

```python
def aes256_encrypt_data(data, key, iv):
    """ Takes data, a 256-bit key and a IV and
    encrypts it. Encryption is done
    with AES 256 in CBC mode. Note that OpenSSL is doing
    the padding for us"""
    enc =1
    cipher = EVP.Cipher('aes_256_cbc', key,iv , enc,0)

    pbuf = cStringIO.StringIO(data)
    cbuf = cStringIO.StringIO()

    ciphertext = aes256_stream_helper(cipher, pbuf, cbuf)
    pbuf.close()
    cbuf.close()
    return ciphertext


def aes256_stream_helper(cipher, input_stream, output_stream):

    while True:
        buf = input_stream.read()
        if not buf:
            break
        output_stream.write(cipher.update(buf))
    output_stream.write(cipher.final())
    return output_stream.getvalue()

def encrypt_rsa(rsa_key, data):
    return rsa_key.public_encrypt(data, RSA.pkcs1_padding)
```

That was quite a bit of code, so let's break down what this code does.

Generating a unique K_{sym}

The work of generating a random, unique key is done by `generate_rand_bits`. This takes the number of bits to generate as a parameter. In this case, it'll be called with 256 because you are using AES-256. You call through to Python's `random.SystemRandom` to get a cryptographically strong random number.

> It is important to use this rather than the built-in random-number generator—cryptographically strong random-number generators have a number of important security properties that make them difficult to predict. Using Python's built-in random-number generator will cause an instant security vulnerability because an attacker can predict the key and decrypt data. As you can imagine, this is a common mistake, made even by reputable software vendors.

Where does this cryptographically strong random-number generator come from? In this case, Python lets the operating system do the heavy lifting. On Unix this will call /dev/urandom, while on Windows this will call CryptGenRandom. These are both valid (and, in fact, the recommended) means of getting good random numbers.

Encrypting using AES-256

After generating a unique K_{sym}, the next step is to encrypt data using AES-256. The "256" here refers to the block size. AES is a block cipher—it takes a block of size n (256, in this case) and a key of length n, and then converts into ciphertext of length n. The obvious problem here is that the data is somewhat longer than 256 bits.

Not surprisingly, there are several mechanisms to deal with this, and they are called *modes of operation*. In this particular case, the chosen mode is *cipherblock chaining* (CBC). Figure 12-4 shows how this mode works. The incoming data (plaintext) is split into block-size chunks. Each block of plaintext is XORed with the previous ciphertext block before being encrypted.

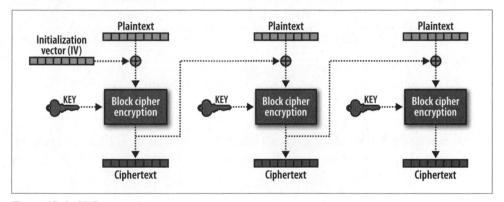

Figure 12-4. CBC encryption

Why not just encrypt every block separately and concatenate all the ciphertext?

This is what the *Electronic Codebook (ECB)* mode does, and it is very insecure. Typically, input data will have lots of well-known structures (file format headers, whitespace, and so on). Since each block encrypts to the same output ciphertext, the attacker can look for repeating forms (the encrypted versions of the aforementioned structure) and glean information about the data. CBC (the technique used here) prevents this attack because the encrypted form of every block also depends on the blocks that come before it.

This still leaves some vulnerability. Since the first few blocks of data can be the same, the attacker can spot patterns in the beginning of the data stream. To avoid this, the block cipher takes an *initialization vector (IV)*. This is a block filled with random data that the cipher will use as the "starting block." This ensures that any pattern in the beginning input data is undetectable.

This data doesn't need to be secret and, in fact, is usually added to the encrypted data in some form so that the receiver knows what IV was used. However, it does need to be different for each archive, and it can never be reused with the same key. In this sample code, you generate IVs the same way you generate random keys: by making a call to `generate_rand_bits`.

 Reusing the same IV is typically a "no-no." Bad usage of IVs is the core reason Wireless Encryption Protocol (WEP) is considered insecure.

The core of the encryption work is done in `aes256_encrypt_data`. This takes the input plaintext, K_{sym}, and a unique IV. It creates an instance of the `EVP.Cipher` class and specifies that it wants to use AES-256 in CBC mode. The `EVP.Cipher` class is best used in a streaming mode. The little helper method `aes256_stream_helper` does exactly this. It takes the cipher, the input data stream, and an output stream as parameters. It writes data into the cipher object, and reads the ciphertext into the output stream.

 Again, these techniques can be used on any major programming platform. In .NET, AES is supported through the `System.Security.Cryptography.Rijndael` class.

All this is wrapped up by `block_encrypt`, which makes the actual call to generate the IV, encrypts the incoming data, and then returns a concatenated version of the encrypted data and the IV.

Encrypting K_{sym} using K_{enc}

The final step is to encrypt K_{sym} using K_{enc}. Since this is an RSA key pair, this encryption is done with the public key portion. RSA is sensitive to the size and structure of the input data, so the encryption is done using a well-known padding scheme supported by OpenSSL.

The actual encryption is done by `encrypt_rsa`. This takes an RSA key pair as a parameter (which, in this case, is a type in the M2Crypto package) and calls a method on that object to encrypt the input data.

 The fact that you're using only the public key portion to encrypt is significant. Though no support for this was added as of this writing, a different key format can be implemented that separates the public key from the private key, and puts them in different files. The encryption code must have access only to the public key, and thus can run from insecure machines.

At the end of this process, you now have encrypted data and an encrypted key in a large byte array that can then be uploaded to the cloud.

Decrypting Data

Decrypting is the exact inverse of the encryption process, and the code is very similar to that used for encryption. In short, the following are the two steps for decryption:

1. Separate K_{sym} in the encrypted archive and decrypt K_{sym} using K_{enc}.
2. Decrypt data by using AES-256 in CBC mode and using K_{sym} as the key.

Example 12-7 shows the code to do this.

Example 12-7. Decrypting data

```
def aes256_decrypt_data(ciphertext, key, iv):
    """ Decryption and unpadding using AES256-CBC and
    the specified key and IV."""

    dec =0

    cipher = EVP.Cipher('aes_256_cbc', key, iv, dec, 0)
    pbuf = cStringIO.StringIO()
    cbuf = cStringIO.StringIO(ciphertext)

    plaintext = aes256_stream_helper(cipher, cbuf, pbuf)
    pbuf.close()
    cbuf.close()
    return plaintext


def block_decrypt(ciphertext, key):
    """ High level decryption function. Assumes IV is of block size and
    precedes the actual ciphertext"""
    iv = ciphertext[:32]
    ciphertext = ciphertext[32:]


def decrypt_rsa(rsa_key, ciphertext):
    return rsa_key.private_decrypt(ciphertext, RSA.pkcs1_padding)
```

Signing and Validating Data

You now have encrypted data. The only cryptographic piece that is missing is the ability to sign the archive and validate this signature to catch tampering of any form.

In ancient days, this was done with a wax seal. The sender would pour molten wax over the letter, affix his emblem on the molten wax, and let it cool. The idea here was that no one else had access to the same seal (authenticity), and that any tampering could be easily detected (integrity).

It is difficult to believe that some enterprising craftsman couldn't replicate the seal of the King of England or other such royalty. But then, secrecy and cryptography in the Middle Ages worked in mysterious ways, and the real security might have come from the messenger carrying the letter, rather than the unbroken seal itself.

The signing RSA key (K_{sign}) can be used to achieve the exact same goals.

This is different from the key pair you used for encryption (K_{enc}). Though an actual attack would be difficult, reusing the encryption key is considered a bad practice in RSA, since the math for encryption is the exact inverse of what happens when signing, effectively killing security.

Signing is very simple. The data to be signed is hashed using a cryptographically strong hash algorithm, and the hash is then encrypted with the private key to create the signature. The receiver computes a hash using the same algorithm, decrypts the signature using the public key of the sender, and checks whether the hashes compute.

In this case, the receiver is the user trying to restore a backup in the future. Any changes to the data would cause a change in the hash, and could be used to detect integrity failure. Since only the user knows the private key, an attacker cannot attach a signature, thus providing authenticity.

Example 12-8 shows the code for signing and verification. The code is straightforward because M2Crypto/OpenSSL does all the heavy lifting for you.

Example 12-8. Signing and verifying data

```
def sign_rsa(rsa_key, data):
    """ Expects an RSA key pair. Signs with SHA-256.
    Would like to use RSASSA-PSS but only dev
    versions of M2Crypto support that"""

    digest = hashlib.sha256(data).digest()
    return rsa_key.sign(digest, 'sha256')

def verify_rsa(rsa_key, data, sig):
    """ Verifies a signature"""

    digest = hashlib.sha256(data).digest()
    return rsa_key.verify(digest, sig, 'sha256')==1
```

The only tricky bit is that M2Crypto expects the caller to hash the data before calling it. Though a `type` parameter is passed in with the hash algorithm used (`SHA256`, in this case), this parameter is not used by OpenSSL to hash the data, but rather to determine digest information before padding is added.

Putting the Cryptography Together

Now you need some "glue" code to put all the pieces together. Example 12-9 shows the code to create an encrypted archive given an input directory or file. It uses all the code you've seen so far to create a tar+gzip file, encrypt that file using a temporary session key, and then encrypt and append the session key itself. A signature is added at the end, and the encrypted archive is ready to be pushed to the cloud.

Example 12-9. Decrypting an encrypted archive

```
def extract_encrypted_archive(archive_name, keys):


    #Load archive. Separate into encrypted AES key, plaintext sig of
    # encrypted data and encrypted archive itself

    enc_file = open(archive_name, "rb")
    enc_file_bytes = enc_file.read()
    enc_file.close()


    enc_aes_key = enc_file_bytes[0:256]
    rsa_sig = enc_file_bytes[256:512]
    enc_data = enc_file_bytes[512:]

    rsa_sign_key = keys[crypto.SIGNING_KEY]
    rsa_enc_key = keys[crypto.ENCRYPTION_KEY]

    # Check the signature in the file to see whether it matches the
    # encrypted data. We do Encrypt-Then-Mac here so that
    # we avoid decryption
    if not crypto.verify_rsa(rsa_sign_key, enc_data, rsa_sig):
        print "Signature verification failure. Corrupt or tampered archive!"
        return

    # Decrypt the AES key and then decrypt the
    # encrypted archive using the decrypted AES key
    aes_key = crypto.decrypt_rsa(rsa_enc_key, enc_aes_key)
    decrypted_archive_bytes = crypto.block_decrypt(enc_data, aes_key)

    # Write a temporary file and then extract the contents to the
    # current directory

    [os_handle,temp_file] = tempfile.mkstemp()
    temp_file_handle = os.fdopen(os_handle, 'wb')
    temp_file_handle.write(decrypted_archive_bytes)
    temp_file_handle.close()
    extract_tar_gzip(temp_file, ".")
    os.remove(temp_file)
```

Encrypt-Then-MAC Versus MAC-Then-Encrypt

The code shown in Example 12-9 takes the encrypted archive data and appends a signature (a *MAC*, in cryptographic parlance) computed over the encrypted data, as opposed to the plaintext version. In the cryptographic world, opinion is split on whether this is a better way of doing this, as opposed to computing a signature over the plaintext and encrypting both the signature and the plaintext.

In reality, both techniques are valid, and it comes down to an individual preference. The book *Practical Cryptography* leans toward computing a signature over plaintext. Doing it the other way enables you to instantly detect whether an archive is valid without having to decrypt anything. You can find a summary of the arguments for doing encrypt-then-MAC at *http://www.daemonology.net/blog/2009-06-24-encrypt-then-mac .html*.

The code in Example 12-9 is a bit longer than it needs to be, since a bug in Python's `tarfile` module prevents you from dealing with tar+gzip files completely in memory. The data must be temporarily written to disk, and then read back into memory, where it is then encrypted and signed using the code already seen:

```
def create_encrypted_archive(directory_or_file, archive_name, keys):
    # First, let's tar and gzip the file/folder we're given to
    # the temp directory. This is a roundabout way of getting the tar+gzipped
    # data into memory due to a bug in tarfile with dealing with StringIO

    tempdir = tempfile.gettempdir() + "/"
    temp_file = tempdir  + archive_name + ".tar.gz"

    generate_tar_gzip(directory_or_file, temp_file)


    gzip_file_handle = open(temp_file,"rb")
    gzip_data = gzip_file_handle.read()
    gzip_file_handle.close()
    os.remove(temp_file) #We don't need source tar gzip file


    #Generate a session AES-256 key and encrypt gzipped archive with it

    aes_key = crypto.generate_rand_bits(256)
    encrypted_archive = crypto.block_encrypt( gzip_data, aes_key)

    # Encrypt Ksym (session key) with RSA key (Kenc)
    rsa_enc_key = keys[crypto.ENCRYPTION_KEY]
    aes_key_enc = crypto.encrypt_rsa(rsa_enc_key, aes_key) #256 bytes

    # Sign encrypted data
    # There's much debate regarding in which order you encrypt and sign/mac.
    # I prefer this way since this lets us not have to decrypt anything
    # when the signature is invalid
    # See http://www.daemonology.net/blog/2009-06-24-encrypt-then-mac.html
```

```
rsa_sign_key = keys[crypto.SIGNING_KEY]
rsa_sig = crypto.sign_rsa(rsa_sign_key, encrypted_archive) #256 bytes

# Append encrypted aes key, signature and archive in that order
return aes_key_enc + rsa_sig + encrypted_archive
```

Extracting an encrypted archive is the exact reverse. The code first splits apart the encrypted AES session key (K_{sym}) and the signature from the encrypted data. This code relies on the fact that the lengths of these are well known. If different sizes were used in the future, this trivial method of parsing out the various parts of the file wouldn't work.

The code then checks and verifies the signature and exits if the signature isn't valid. If the signature is valid, the encrypted data is decrypted after decrypting the AES session key. Since the decrypted data is nothing but a gzipped, tarred archive, you wrap up by extracting the archive to the current working directory.

Uploading Efficiently Using Blocks

azbackup isn't only about cryptography and security—it is also about providing a good backup experience (after all, it has the word *backup* in its name). The straightforward way to back up encrypted data to the cloud is to initiate a "Create blob" operation and start uploading data.

However, there are two downsides to doing things this way. First, uploads are limited to 64 MB with a single request. Backups of huge directories will often be larger than 64 MB. Second, making one long request means not only that you're not making use of all the bandwidth available to you, but also that you'll have to restart from the beginning in case a request fails.

During the discussion of blob storage in Chapter 8, you learned about the answer to this problem: blocks. To do a quick recap, blocks let you upload data to blob storage in small chunks, which are then concatenated together to form the final blob. However, the mini storage client implementation you did in C# in Chapter 7 didn't have support for blocks.

The first order of business is to add support in *storage.py* for adding a block and committing a block list. Example 12-10 shows the code to do this.

Example 12-10. Block support in storage.py

```
def put_block(self, container_name, blob_name, block_id, data):

        # Take a block id and construct a URL-safe, base64 version
        base64_blockid = base64.encodestring(str(block_id)).strip()
        urlencoded_base64_blockid = urllib.quote(base64_blockid)

        # Make a PUT request with the block data to blob URI followed by
        # ?comp=block&blockid=<blockid>
        return self._do_store_request("/" + container_name + "/" + \
```

```
                            blob_name + \
                                "?comp=block&blockid=" + \
                                urlencoded_base64_blockid, \
                                'PUT', {}, data)

    def put_block_list(self, container_name, blob_name, \
                        block_list, content_type):
        headers = {}
        if content_type is not None:
            headers["Content-Type"] = content_type

        # Begin XML content
        xml_request = "<?xml version=\"1.0\" encoding=\"utf-8\"?><BlockList>"

        # Concatenate block ids into block list
        for block_id in block_list:
            xml_request += "<Block>" + \
            base64.encodestring(str(block_id)).strip() + "</Block>"

        xml_request += "</BlockList>"

        # Make a PUT request to blob URI followed by ?comp=blocklist
        return self._do_store_request("/" + container_name + \
                            "/" + blob_name + \
                                "?comp=blocklist", 'PUT',\
                            headers, xml_request)
```

We covered the XML and the URI format in detail earlier in this chapter. Since the XML constructed is fairly trivial and with well-defined character ranges, the code can hand-construct it instead of using Python's XML support.

With this support in place, azbackup can now chop up the encrypted archive into small blocks, and call the previous two functions to upload them. Instead of uploading the blocks in sequence, they can be uploaded in parallel, speeding up the process. Example 12-11 shows the entire code.

Example 12-11. The azbackup block upload code

```
def upload_archive(data, filename, account, key):
    conn = storage.Storage("blob.core.windows.net",account, key)

    # Try and create container. Will harmlessly fail if already exists
    conn.create_container("enc", False)

    # Heuristics for blocks
    # We're pretty hardcoded at the moment. We don't bother using blocks
    # for files less than 4MB.
    if len(data) < 0:# 4 * 1024 * 1024:
        resp = conn.put_blob("enc", filename, data,"application/octet-stream")
    else:
        resp = upload_archive_using_blocks(data, filename, conn)

    if not (resp.status >=200 and resp.status < 400):
        # Error! No error handling at the moment
```

```
            print resp.status, resp.reason, resp.read()
            sys.exit(1)


def upload_archive_using_blocks(data, filename, conn):

    blocklist=[]

    queue = Queue.Queue()
    if parallel_upload:
        # parallel_upload specifies whether blocks should be uploaded
        # in parallel and is set from the command line.
        for i in range(num_threads):
            t = task.ThreadTask(queue)
            t.setDaemon(True) # Run even without workitems
            t.start()

    offset =0

    # Block uploader function used in thread queue
    def block_uploader(connection, block_id_to_upload,\
                    block_data_to_upload):
        resp = connection.put_block("enc", filename, block_id_to_upload,\
                                        block_data_to_upload)
        if not( resp.status>=200 and resp.status <400):
            print resp.status, resp.reason, resp.read()
            sys.exit(1) # Need retry logic on error

    while True:

        if offset>= len(data):
            break

        # Get size of next block. Process in 4MB chunks
        data_to_process = min( 4*1024*1024, len(data)-offset)

        # Slice off next block. Generate an SHA-256 block id
        # In the future, we could use it to see whether a block
        # already exists to avoid re-uploading it

        block_data = data[offset: offset+data_to_process]
        block_id =  hashlib.sha256(block_data).hexdigest()
        blocklist.append(block_id)

        if parallel_upload:
            # Add work item to the queue.
            queue.put([block_uploader, [conn, block_id, block_data]])
        else:

            block_uploader(conn, block_id, block_data)

        # Move i forward
        offset+= data_to_process

    # Wait for all block uploads to finish
```

```
queue.join()

# Now upload block list
resp = conn.put_block_list("enc", filename, \
        blocklist, "application/octet-stream")
return resp
```

The action kicks off in `upload_archive`. If the input data is less than 4 MB, the code makes one long sequential request. If it is greater than 4 MB, the code calls a helper function to split and upload the data into blocks. These numbers are chosen somewhat arbitrarily. In a real application, you should test on your target hardware and network to see what sizes and block splits work best for you.

The `upload_archive_using_blocks` function takes care of splitting the input data into 4 MB blocks (again, another arbitrary size chosen after minimal testing). For block IDs, an SHA-256 hash of the data in the block is used. Though the code doesn't support it as of this writing, it would be easy to add a feature that checks whether a block of data already exists in the cloud (using the SHA-256 hash and the `GetBlockIds` operation) before uploading it.

Each block is added into a queue that a pool of threads process. Since Python doesn't have a built-in thread pool implementation, a simple one that lives in *task.py* is included in the source code. (The source isn't shown here, since it isn't directly relevant to this discussion.) This manages a set of threads that read work items of a queue and process them. Tweaking the number of threads for your specific environment is imperative for good upload performance.

In this case, the "work item" is a function reference (the inner function `block_uploader`) and a Python tuple containing arguments to that function. When it is time to be processed, `block_uploader` gets called with the arguments contained in the tuple (a storage connection object, a block ID, and the data associated with that block ID). `block_updater` calls `put_block` in the storage module to upload that specific block.

Uploading block uploads in parallel not only provides better performance, but also provides the flexibility to change this code later to support retries on error scenarios, complex back-off strategies, and several other features.

Usage

All of this work wouldn't be much fun if it weren't useful and easy to use, would it? Using `azbackup` is actually quite simple. It has a few basic options (parsed using code not shown here), and the workflow is fairly straightforward.

From start to finish, here are all the steps you take to back up data to the cloud and restore encrypted backups:

1. Set the environment variables `AZURE_STORAGE_ACCOUNT` and `AZURE_STORAGE_KEY` to your Windows Azure storage account name and key, respectively. For example, if your blog storage account was at *foo.blob.core.windows.net*, your `AZURE_STOR AGE_ACCOUNT` should be set to `foo`. The tool automatically looks for these environment variables to connect to blob storage.

2. Run `python azbackup-gen-key -k` *keyfilepath*, where *keyfilepath* is the path and filename where your RSA key pairs will be stored.

 Do not lose this file. If you do, you will lose access to data backed up with this tool, and there's no way to get back the data.

3. To create a new backup, run `python azbackup.py -c -k` *keyfilepath* `-f` *archive_name directory_to_be_backed_up*, where *keyfilepath* is the key file from the previous step, *archive* is the name of the archive that the tool will generate, and *directory_to_be_backed_up* is the path of the directory you want backed up. Depending on the size of the directory, this might take some time because this tool isn't really optimized for speed at the moment. If no errors are shown, the tool will exit silently when the upload is finished.

4. To extract an existing backup, run `python azbackup.py -x -k` *keyfilepath* `-f` *archive_name*. This will extract the contents of the backup to the current directory.

   All tools take an `-h` parameter to show you usage information.

Summary

There are two ways to think about blob storage. You can think of it as a dumb container for a lot of bytes, or you can think of it as a smart platform with complex, sophisticated features. This chapter definitely takes the former approach.

A legitimate argument can be made that encryption should be a feature provided by the platform. However, regardless of whether the Windows Azure team adds it in a future release, you can use the techniques in this chapter as a starting point for building your own solution. Just be careful, though. *"I'll use cryptography to solve that"* have been the famous last words in many a programmer's career.

## CHAPTER 13

SQL Azure

Think about how you deal with a traditional database such as SQL Server or Oracle. You typically set up hardware (computation plus storage) to install it on. Based on your needs, this may range from very cheap (think box in a closet) to very expensive (think multimillion-dollar Storage Area Networks or SANs). Either way, you have work to do. After that comes installing the software itself, starting with the license fee (or no license fee, if you're using something like MySQL). Pretty soon, you have a nice service humming along, accessing data from your database. That is, until scaling problems kick in. You start to think about partitioning data, replication, sharding, and so on. And pretty soon you have a lot of rearchitecting and modifications to worry about.

SQL Azure is meant to tackle exactly these types of problems. It provides you with a logical view of SQL Server, with all the SQL tools and language support you expect, but it does a lot of magic under the covers to scale with usage.

SQL Azure is Microsoft's *database in the cloud*. So far, you've seen how Windows Azure storage provides you with scalable blob storage, queue storage, and semistructured table storage. SQL Azure extends that concept to a database, and in this case, to the familiar world of SQL Server.

SQL Azure is *SQL Server as a service*. The "SQL Server" part means you get to create a database, connect to it using SQL Server Management Studio (SSMS), write code using familiar libraries such as ADO.NET, and in general, do a lot of the things you can do with traditional SQL Server. The "service" part means Microsoft manages the hardware it runs on for you. Apart from just managing hardware, the service also replicates your data, and scales up and down based on your usage. So, instead of worrying about hardware failures or repartitioning data, you can spend more time writing code.

A big selling point for SQL Azure is that it is *just SQL Server* in the sense that, if you have existing code and tools written against SQL Server, it is an easy (and natural) migration path. Apart from that, you get to use any expertise you might have built up. For example, note the length of this chapter. This chapter is rather short, since SQL Server programming has been covered in innumerable books already. The only major difference with SQL Azure is how you connect to it and manage it.

Creating and Using a SQL Azure Database

Let's start by creating a SQL Azure database and playing with it a bit. SQL Azure's signup process and development experience are slightly different from the rest of the Windows Azure storage services.

Creating a Database

The first step is to go to *http://sql.azure.com* and provision an account. Note that this is not the same URL as the one for the rest of the Windows Azure services (which fall under *http://windows.azure.com*). During the process, you'll be asked to provide an administrator username and a password to log on to your SQL Azure database instances. After creating an account, you should see something similar to Figure 13-1.

There are several key elements to note in Figure 13-1. The DNS name `fhdb1swfkd.data base.windows.net` (easy to pronounce, isn't it?) is unique to your account. You can think of it as the equivalent of a "server," and use it where you traditionally use SQL Server's "server" names—in connection strings, SSMS, and other tools. However, remember that in this case, this DNS entry is just a façade, and in reality your service stems from multiple machines, rather than just one "server." This façade is required to make the existing tools and frameworks work against the cloud.

Figure 13-1 also shows a list of databases. By default, you are allocated a `master` database. This plays a similar role as in the SQL Server world. The next step is to create a

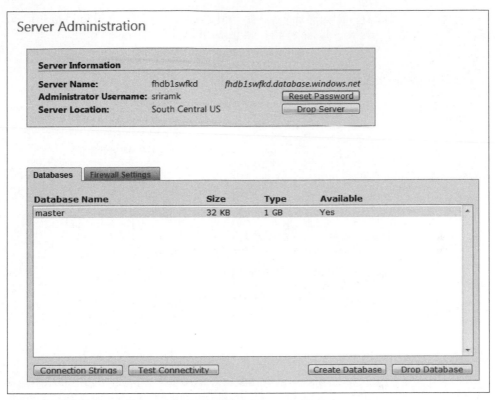

Figure 13-1. SQL Azure Server Administration page

database that you can use to create tables and store actual data. To do that, click the Create Database button. This brings up the dialog shown in Figure 13-2. This sample database is called booktest, but you can obviously call it whatever you want.

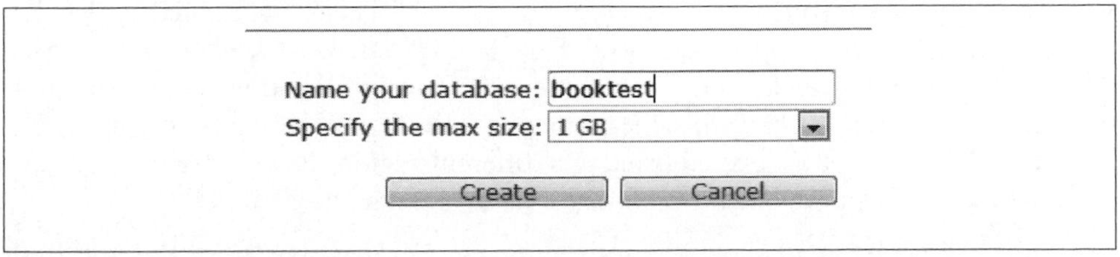

Figure 13-2. New database dialog

You can use this to create a new database and specify the size limit of that database. Currently, SQL Azure supports databases of up to 10 GB in size. Note that the two sizes offered in the drop-down box (1 GB and 10 GB) differ in pricing, so be sure to check the prices for each. The idea here is that, if you have larger data, you shard it by creating multiple databases and spreading the data over them.

Once you've created the new database, it should show up as indicated in Figure 13-3. This screen also shows you the size of all your databases at any given time.

Databases	Firewall Settings			
Database Name		**Size**	**Type**	**Available**
booktest		0 B	1 GB	Yes
master		64 KB	1 GB	Yes

Figure 13-3. Database listing

 You can also create databases through code or through the command line at any time. For example, you can use the `sqlcmd` utility to create a database through a command such as the following:

```
SQLCMD -U [MyUsername]@[MyServername]
-P [MyPassword] -S
[MyServername].database.windows.net -d master
CREATE DATABASE [MyDatabaseName]
GO
```

Adding Firewall Rules

By default, SQL Azure blocks access to your services from any incoming IP address. To change this, you must manually add firewall rules for all the IP addresses from which you plan to access the service.

To look at the current set of firewall rules and to add/modify rules, switch to the Firewall Settings tab, as shown in Figure 13-4. This lists all the rules you currently have.

One important thing to note here is the checkbox at the top, which asks whether you want to "Allow Microsoft Services access to this server." This is unchecked by default, which means that any application hosted on Windows Azure *cannot* talk to your database on SQL Azure. If you plan to host applications on Windows Azure that talk to SQL Azure, you must have this checkbox checked. Don't worry about your application on Windows Azure being hosted in a different region/data center—SQL Azure does the right networking magic to allow packets through.

Let's add a firewall rule to allow access from the current machine. Click the Add Rule button to bring up the dialog shown in Figure 13-5. If you already know the IP address range of the machines from which you will access SQL Azure, you can enter them here.

If you want to allow access from your current machine, use the IP address displayed at the bottom as the range you want to open. This is the external-facing IP address of your current machine, and is typically dynamically assigned by your ISP. Note that, if this IP address changes, you must modify this rule as well. Unfortunately, there's no good way to know when your ISP will throw you behind a different IP address. You must

Figure 13-4. Firewall rules

Add Firewall Rule

Name: work
IP Range: 98.247.244.14
to
98.247.244.14

Your IP address: 98.247.244.14

Submit   Cancel

Note: Firewall rules may take up to 5 minutes before they come into effect.

Figure 13-5. Add Firewall Rule dialog

constantly monitor access to SQL Azure, or use a website such as *http://whatismyipad dress.com* to figure this out.

At this point, you're all set. You have a server and a database provisioned. Let's connect to it!

Using SQL Server Management Studio

The primary tool every user of SQL Server uses to connect to and play with a database is SQL Server Management Studio (SSMS). Support for SQL Azure is built into SSMS 2008 R2 (which was available as a CTP as of this writing). Earlier versions will work against SQL Azure, but you must enter queries manually, and most of the GUI integration won't work.

Open SSMS 2008 R2 to see the dialog shown in Figure 13-6.

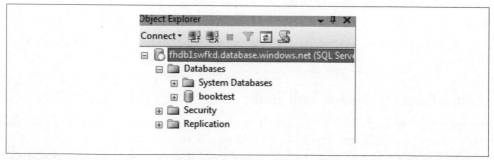

Figure 13-6. SSMS connection

Enter the DNS name from Figure 13-1. Switch the authentication type to SQL Server Authentication and use the username and password you picked when creating your SQL Azure account.

SSMS will connect to your database and open the Object Explorer, as shown in Figure 13-7. You can see both the `master` and the `booktest` databases you created earlier. If you get a connection error at this stage, check that you've set up the right firewall rules in SQL Azure to allow access to your external IP address.

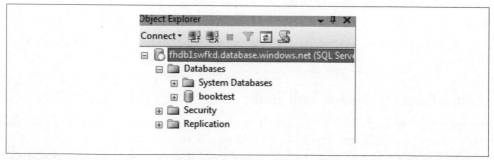

Figure 13-7. Object Explorer with SQL Azure

At this point, you can create tables as you normally would. Let's create a simple table. Execute the code shown in Example 13-1 using the query editor.

Example 13-1. Simple table creation

```
CREATE TABLE Employees(EmpID int primary key, Name varchar(30))
GO
```

If the query executes successfully, you should see the table displayed in the Object Explorer, as shown in Figure 13-8.

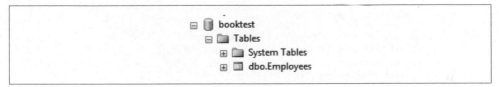

Figure 13-8. Employee table

You can now insert rows into the table and query from it, as shown in Example 13-2 and Figure 13-9.

Example 13-2. Inserting and querying

```
INSERT INTO Employees (EmpID, Name) VALUES
 (1, 'Michael Scott'),
 (2, 'Jim Halpert'),
 (3, 'Dwight Schrute'),
 (4, 'Pam Halpert'),
 (5, 'Andy Bernard')
GO

SELECT * FROM Employees
GO
```

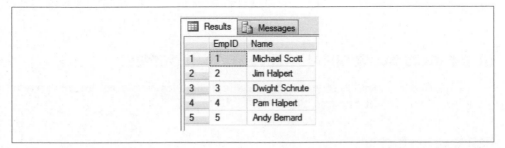

Figure 13-9. Simple query results

This is obviously a trivial example, but it does show that standard SQL concepts and tools work as you would expect with SQL Azure.

Using ADO.NET

Coding against SQL Azure is the same as coding against normal SQL Server. The same ODBC/ADO.NET idioms work out of the box. The only difference you should be mindful of here is that SQL Azure doesn't support switching database contexts. Your sessions must query against objects in the same database for the lifetime of the connection.

Example 13-3 shows the same listing from Figure 13-9, but querying through ADO.NET using a C# application.

Example 13-3. Query table using ADO.NET

```
var connectionBuilder = new SqlConnectionStringBuilder();
        connectionBuilder.DataSource = "fhdb1swfkd.database.windows.net";
        connectionBuilder.InitialCatalog = "booktest";
        connectionBuilder.Encrypt = true;
        connectionBuilder.UserID = "sriramk";
        connectionBuilder.Password = "<MyPassword>";

        using(var con = new SqlConnection(connectionBuilder.ToString()))
        {
            con.Open();
            using(var command = con.CreateCommand())
            {
                command.CommandText = "SELECT * FROM Employees";
                using (var reader = command.ExecuteReader())
                {
                    while (reader.Read())
                    {
                        Console.WriteLine("EmpID: {0}, Name:{1}",
                                        reader["EmpID"].ToString(),
                                        reader["Name"].ToString());

                    }
                }
            }
        }
```

Differences Between SQL Azure and SQL Server

Since SQL Azure is a shared service, there are some considerations to be aware of when moving code from SQL Server to SQL Azure.

Resource Restrictions

Because SQL Azure is a service built on top of shared resources, it takes precautions to maintain the same level of service for all users. You might see connections to the service terminated for some of the following reasons:

Excessive resource usage

Your connections can be terminated when your database or your usage of the service uses excessive resources. For example, when you hit the database size limit on your database (either 1 GB or 10 GB), you'll get an error code when you try to insert/update data, rebuild indexes, or create new objects.

Long-running transactions

Long-running transactions will be canceled. Typically, this is after five minutes of execution, though this limit might change.

Idle connections

Idle connections to the service (since SQL is inherently session-based) will be terminated.

Language/Feature Differences

SQL Azure provides a unified virtual view over a set of physical resources. You'll generally find that T-SQL features that are meant to manipulate direct physical resources (such as file groups) aren't supported. Apart from that, several features from the desktop SQL Server aren't currently available, but will be made available in a future release. These include support for profiling, data synchronization, full-text search, and so on.

 A good list of differences is available at *http://msdn.microsoft.com/en-us/ library/ee336245.aspx*.

Tips and Tricks

Since SQL Azure is a remote service, you might need to tweak the way you call SQL in your code to ensure that you're not affected by latency or network failures. Also, given the size limitations (1 GB/10 GB), you must partition data differently. Following are some tips and tricks for moving to SQL Azure:

- Connections could drop when talking to SQL Azure more often than when talking to SQL Server. When you detect a closed connection, reconnect immediately. If you still get a connection failure, back off (10–15 seconds would be a good period of time) and then try again. If you continue getting failures, check the portal to see the health of the service and your database.

- Use pooled connections. By reusing connections as much as possible, you avoid expensive re-login logic.

- Make communication with SQL Azure as "chunky" as possible, as opposed to "chatty." Since SQL Azure is a remote service, network latency plays a huge part in query performance time. Using stored procedures and limiting round trips to the server can greatly aid in performance.

- Partition your data into small pieces. This lets you fit them into SQL Azure's database sizes easily, and also, it lets the service load-balance you effectively. It is easier to do this upfront, rather than having to do this after hitting size limits.

Summary

SQL Azure is the logical migration path if you have a significant investment in SQL Server or in RDBMS services in general. However, the fact that this is a remote service as opposed to a box sitting on the local network makes performance characteristics very different. You must modify your code and architecture accordingly to reap the benefits. The same network latency works in your favor when hosting applications on Windows Azure that talk to SQL Azure. If they're in the same georegion, they're in the same data center and on the same network backbone, so network performance tends to be very zippy indeed.

Index

Symbols
/ (forward slash)1, 177

A
Access Control, 10
access policies, 172
account keys, Microsoft access to, 148
ADO.NET and SQL Azure, 334
ADO.NET Data Services, 231–239
   client-side code, 236–239
   LINQ support, 239
   querying, 234
      filtering query results, 236
   supported query operators, 247
   updating and deleting entities, 238
AES algorithm, 306, 308
   AES-256, encryption with, 315
affinity groups, 58, 136
Amazon Web Services), authentication, 147
API access keys, 134
API call operation IDs, 100
API requests, 96–98
AssemblyInfo.cs, 274
AsTableServiceQuery method, 255
asymmetric key algorithms, 306
at-least-once versus at-most-once semantics,
     209
authentication, 147
azbackup, 296
   cryptography, implementation in, 308
   data encryption, 313
     key generation, 314
   data encryption with AES-256, 315
   encryption with RSA key pairs, 316
   uploading data in blocks, 321
   usage, 324
azbackup block upload code, 322
azbackup-gen-key.py, 309
azbackup.py, 312
Azure (see Windows Azure)
Azure AppFabric services, 9
Azure Backup (see azbackup)
Azure FTS engine, building, 267–281
   adding a mini console, 272
   console application, 268
   creating tables, 273
   data modeling, 268
   data source, choosing, 267
   indexing, 274
   partition key, 270
   searching multiple terms, 279
   searching on a term, 277
   stemming, 273
Azure Platform stack, 9

B
base VHD, 41
Bemer, Bob, 2
blob storage, 17, 132, 157
   as backup storage, 159
   blob storage API, 164
   blobs (see blobs)
   block blobs (see block blobs)
   compression of content, 164
   containers (see containers)
   data model, 160
   file sharing, 159
   filesystems, replacement with, 158

We'd like to hear your suggestions for improving our indexes. Send email to *index@oreilly.com*.

instantaneous changes to stored content, 163
page blobs (see page blobs)
pricing, 160
requests, potential for failure, 162
storage accounts, 162
storage client library, 165
uses, 158
BlobPrefix tag, 189
blobs, 176–193
access policies and, 172
block blobs (see block blobs)
caching on Windows Azure CDN, 200
compressed content, 181
delimiter characters in blob keys, 177
listing, 187
names and paths, 177
page blobs (see page blobs)
reading blobs, 184
conditional reads, 185
block blobs, 193–196
block IDs, 195
creating, 178–181
container creation, compared to, 179
deleting, 181
Put BlockList, 195
PUT requests, uploading with, 195
size limits, 176
using, 194
viewing, 181
block support in storage.py, 321

C

cacerts.pem, 303
CAs (certificate authorities), 299
importance of verification, 301
trusted by Windows, 303
case-folding, 264
CBC (cipherblock chaining), 315
CDNs (Content Delivery Networks), 199
certificates, 299
certification chain, 299
CGI (Common Gateway Interface), 118
ciphertext, 306
client certificates, 92
cloud computing, 1–8
characteristics, 7
cloud services, 8
developing applications, 50–62

Hello World!, 50
packaging code, 55
grid computing, contrasted with, 5
history, 2–6
hyped aspects of, xiii
pitfalls, 18
capacity planning, 20
custom infrastructure requirements, 19
migration and interoperability, 21
security, confidentiality, and audits, 19
unpredictable performance, 20
service availability, 18
Cloud Drive, 154
cloud operating systems, 24
Cloud Service project, 63
cloud service solutions, 63
cloud storage simulator, 153
cloudapp.net URL, 58
CloudStorageAccount, 165
CLR (Common Language Runtime), 232
clustered indexes, 288
CNAMEs, 201
Codd, E.F., 4
command shell operations, 109–116
building a command shell proxy, 110
enabling native code execution, 113
running a command shell proxy, 114
committed blocks, 195
Common Gateway Interface (CGI), 118
"comp" in query strings, 173
comp=list parameter, 174, 187
Compatible Time Sharing System (CTSS), 2
components, 139
concordance, 265
ContactsTable, 239–243
containers, 139, 144, 161, 167–176
blobs, setting access policies to, 172
creating, 168
deleting, 176
listing, 174
metadata requests to, 175
naming requirements, 167
content compression, 181–183
Content-Encoding header, 181, 182
Content-Type header, 181
continuation tokens, 255
CreateContainer method, 144
CreateQuery<T> method, 237
crypto generation of RSA keys, 309

cryptography, 305–311
   cryptographic hash functions, 307
   drawbacks, 305
   encryption and decryption, 306
   encryption techniques, choosing, 307
   key generation, 308
   keys, public and private, 306
   symmetric and asymmetric key algorithms,
      306
csmanage.exe, 99–101
   API call operation IDs, 100
CSPack, 52
CSPack binary, 46
CTSS (Compatible Time Sharing System), 2
Custom Domains, 200
Customer data model, 282
Cutler, Dave, 11, 30
Cylon web service, 233–236

D

data centers, 25
   compliance, 26
   security, 26
data security in storage, 304–324
   backup data, compressing, 311
   cryptography (see cryptography)
   data upload in blocks, 321–324
   decrypting data, 317
   encrypting data, 313–317
   signing and validation of data, 317
data security on the web, 298–304
database lingo map, 228
databases (see Table service; tables)
DataServiceContext, 237, 244
   entity updates and merge options, 256
DataServiceQuery, 237, 255
debugging support, 62
decryption, 306, 317
   decrypting an encrypted archive, 319
DELETE method, 141
denormalization, 229
deployment labels, 60
deployment slots, 59
Dev Fabric (Development Fabric), 47
   packaging of application code, 52
   running application code, 54
Dev Storage (Development Storage), 49, 153–
      156, 155
Developer Portal, 43

blob storage, versus, 60
   hosted service projects, creating, 56
   service management, uses and limitations,
      90
differencing disk, 41
DNS CNAME redirection, 58
document-to-document mapping, 265
Document.cs, 269
documents, 263
DoStoreRequest function, 145

E

ECB (Electronic Codebook), 315
enableNativeCodeExecution attribute, 109
encrypt-then-MAC versus MAC-then-encrypt,
      320
encryption, 306
encrypt_rsa function, 316
endpoints, 78
   InternalEndpoint, 81
enlightened kernels, 30
entities, 227
   creating, 243–244
   deleting, 258
   size limits, 231
   updating, 256–258
entity group transactions, 230, 290
ETag headers, 171, 179, 181, 185
   entities and, 256
eventual consistency, 130
Exetcute<T> method, 237
extract_tar_gzip function, 312

F

fabric, 24, 35–42
fabric controllers, 11, 15, 35
   management and monitoring, 41
   provisioning and deployment, 40
   service models, 37
FastCGI, 118–120
   on Windows Azure, 119
      PHP example, 120–125
fault domains, 39
Ferguson, Niels, 296
Friend entity class, 284
FTSDataServiceContext.cs, 271
full trust, 109
full-text search, 261–281

case-folding and stemming, 264
document-to-document mapping, 265
documents, 263
FTS (full-text search) engines, 262
    Azure, building on (see Azure FTS
        engine, building)
indexing, 262–267
intersection, 267
inverted indexes, 265
terms, 264

G

generate_rand_bits function, 314
generate_rsa_keys, 310
generate_tar_gzip function, 312
GET method, 141
GET requests, 184, 187
    listing of queues, 216
    table queries, 227
GetBlob operation, 197
GetPageRegions operation, 197
Globus toolkit, 6
Gray, Jim, 5
grid computing, 5
Group entity class, 284
GTE CyberTrust, 299, 303
Guardian OS, 5
guest operating systems, 27
guest partitions, 32
gzip, 296
gzip algorithm, 182

H

hardware virtualization, 14
hashes, 180
    cryptographic hashes, 307
HashSet class, 279
headers, 141
    signing of headers, 147
Hello World! application, 50–62
    application code, 50–52
    code packaging for the Dev Fabric, 52–53
    running the application, 54–62
        in Dev Fabric, 54
        in the cloud, 55–62
host operating systems, 27
host partition, 32
hosted service projects, 56

HPC (Windows High Performance
        Computing) servers, 6
HTTP methods and operations, 140
HTTP status codes, 141
HTTPS, 298
    toggling during debugging, 302
Hyper-V, 14
    Windows Azure Hypervisor and, 31
hypercalls, 30
hypervisors, 11, 14, 23, 27–34
    architecture, 28
    image-based deployment model, 34

I

IaaS (Infrastructure-as-a-Service), 8
idempotency, 211
IIS, runtime integration (see non-native code in
        Windows Azure)
image-based deployment model, 34
IMS (Information Management System), 4
in-place upgrade mechanism, 102
in-process module, 118
Index method, 274
IndexEntry.cs, 269
Indexer.cs, 275
indexing, 262
    clustered indexes, 288
    inverted indexes, 265
    secondary indexes, 286–290
Information Management System (IMS), 4
Infrastructure-as-a-Service (IaaS), 8
InitializeService method, 234
instant consistency, 130
integrity, 297
InternalEndpoint, 81
IVs (initialization vectors), 315

K

key-value pairs, 177

L

LINQ, 239
    LINQ queries, 246
load leveling of queues, 208

M

M2Crypto, 298

M2Crypto module
    imported classes, 310
mainframe computing, 3
maintenance os, 40
makecert.exe tool, 93
man-in-the-middle attack, 300
many-to-many relationships, 284–286
<Marker tag>, 188
MaxResults element, 175
McCarthy, John, 2
MD5 hashes, 180
merge options, 256
MessageID, 209
messages, 209, 219–224
    binary and base64 formats, 219
    deleting messages, 223
    enqueuing messages, 219
    getting messages, 222
    message life cycle, 209
    message order, 212
    peeking at messages, 220
    time skew/late deliver, 212
MessageTTL, 209, 220
metadata
    queue metadata, 214
metadata requests, 175
Microsoft Web Platform installer, 45
Microsoft.WindowsAzure.ServiceRuntime.dll,
        76
modeling data, 281–286
    many-to-many relationships, 284–286
    one-to-many relationships, 281–283

N

name/value pairs, 214
native code in Windows Azure, 107–116
    command shell operations, 109
        building a proxy shell, 110–113
        running a command shell proxy, 114–
            116
    enabling native code execution, 113
    full trust, 109
    standard user privileges, 107
    Windows Azure partial trust, 108
.NET
    running .NET code in Windows Azure (see
            native code in Windows Azure)
.NET 3.5 SP1, 153
netstat command, 116

networking
    between roles, 80
NextMarker element, 175
<NextMarker/> tag, 188
non-native code in Windows Azure, 117
    FastCGI and PHP, 117
normalization, 229
NoSQL movement, 225

O

one-to-many relationships, 281–283
OpenSSL, 298
optimistic concurrency, 17, 291
Order entity, 282
Ozzie, Ray, 10

P

PaaS (Platform-as-a-Service, 8
packages
    staging and production versions, 56
    uploading, 59–62
page blobs, 161, 196–198
    size limits, 176
    Windows Azure XDrive and, 198
pages, 197
pagination, 255
partial trust restrictions, 108
partitioning, 248–254
    entity group transactions and, 291
    key considerations in design, 250
    query performance comparison, 254
    querying benchmarks affected by, 252
PartitionKey, 245, 248
    choosing correctly, 251
PartitionKeys
    versus RowKeys, 251
partitions, 32
Paxos algorithm, 36
PayPal certificate, 299
PHP on Windows Azure, 120–125
plaintext, 306
Platform-as-a-Service (PaaS), 8
POCO (Plain Old CLR Object), 232
PopReceipts, 209, 224
port listening, 78
    declaring an endpoint, 79
POST method, 141
Preboot Execution Environment (PXE), 40

preconfig.cer file, 93
prefix parameter in listing of queues, 217
prefix query parameter, 175
Primary Access Key, 134
privilege levels, 28
privileges, 107
problem state, 3
process pairs, 5
production slot, 59
Program.cs, 272
project, 133
Project Gutenberg, 267
projects, 56
properties, 228
public key cryptography, 306
Put BlockList, 195
PUT method, 141
PUT requests
    block blobs, creating with, 178
PutBlock operation, 194
PutPage operation, 197
PXE (Preboot Execution Environment), 40
Python, 298
    differences in versions, 301
    storage client, 301
    tarfile module, 312

Q

queries, 244–247, 245
queue service, 17
queue storage, 132
queues, 204–208
    counting messages, 216
    creating, 213
        coding approaches, 214
    decoupling applications using, 206
    deleting, 218
    listing, 216
    load leveling, 208
    queue operations, 212–218
    scaling out, 207
    utilizing queue metadata, 214
    Windows Azure queues, 208–218
        other message systems , compared to, 211

R

Red Dog, 11

replicas, 36
request signing, 147
resources, 139
REST APIs, 91
RESTful APIs, 131, 138–142
    blob storage API, 164
    HTTP requests and responses, 140
    resources, 139
        URL patterns, 139
reverse indexes, 265
Rings, 28
RoleEnvironment properties, 77
RoleEnvironmentChanging and
        RoleEnvironmentChanged events,
        83
roles, 52, 67–72
    inter-role communication, 80–82
    port listening, configuration for, 78
    role instances, 69–71
        instance number, 70
        load balancing and, 69
    role size, 71
    role templates, 68
    worker roles (see worker roles1)
root partition, 32
RowKey, 245
    unique identifiers, 251
RowKeys
    versus PartitionKeys, 251
rows
    size limits, 231
RSA
    key generation, 309
RSA cryptographic algorithm, 307

S

SaaS (Software-as-a-Service), 8
scalable storage, 12
scaling out of queues, 207
schemas, 230
Schneier, Bruce, 296
SDK (Software Development Kit), 46–50, 153–
        156
    installation and prerequisites, 153
    prerequisites for installation, 44
    storage client library, 165
searching text (see full-text search)
Second Level Address Translation (SLAT), 33
Secondary Access key, 134

secondary indexes, 286–290
    syncing code, 289
secrecy, 297
security, 295, 297–298
    backup systems, 296
    data backup and compression, 311
    data security on the web, 298–304
    properties, 297
    secure storage, 304–324
        code for decrypting an encrypted
                archive, 319–321
        cryptography (see cryptography)
        data compression, 311
        data signing and validation, 317
        decryption, 317
        encrypting compressed data, 313–317
self-signed certificates, 300
ServicDefinition.csdef, 73
Service Bus, 9
service configuration, 51, 74
service configuration files, 38
service configuration settings, accessing, 78
service definition, 51, 72, 73
service hosting and management, 12
Service Level Agreement (SLA), 7
Service Management API, 76, 91–101
    API call operation IDs, 100
    API requests, 96–98
    authentication, 92
        X.509 certificates, 92–95
    calling from Cygwin/OS X/Linux, 101
    csmanage.exe, 99–101
    supported operations, 92
service models, 15, 37
service names, 57
Service Runtime API, 75–78
    update subscriptions, 83
ServiceConfiguration.cscfg, 74, 78
ServiceDefinition.csdef, 78
ServiceDefinition.rd files, 38
services
    management (see Service Management API)
    upgrades, 102–104
        in-place upgrades, 102
        VIP swap, 104
    Windows Azure services characteristics, 89
session keys, 308
Seti@home, 5
shadow page tables, 33

SharedKeyLite authentication, 241
SLA (Service Level Agreement), 7
SLAT (Second Level Address Translation), 33
Software-as-a-Service (SaaS), 8
SQL Azure, 10, 133, 327–336
    ADO.NET, 334
    creating a database, 328
        firewall rules, 330
    partitioning, 335
    resource restrictions, 334
    SQL Server compared to, 334
    SQL Server Management Studio, 331
    SQL Server, migration from, 327
    Table service, compared to, 328
    tips for using, 335
Srivastava, Amitabh, 11
SSL (Secure Sockets Layer), 92, 299
stack, 23
staging slot, 59
standard user privileges, 107
Starkey, Jim, 158
Stemmer.cs, 274
stemming, 264, 273
stop words, 266
storage accounts, 133, 162
    affinity groups, 136
    geographic location, choice of, 135
    pricing, 137
    signing up, 133
storage clients, 142–152
    authentication and request signing, 147
    boilerplate code, 143
    data creation and uploading, 151
    requests to storage, constructing, 145
    signing algorithm, 148
storage services, 128
    Cloud Drive, 154
    consistency, 130
    Dev Storage and the SDK, 153
    distribution of services, 129
    geographical location, 131
    replication, 130
    RESTful HTTP APIs (see RESTful APIs)
    scalability, 129
    space availability, 129
    Windows Azure storage services, 131–133
        storage accounts (see storage accounts)
storage.py, 302, 321
strong consistency, 130

superhero table, 249
supervisor state, 3
symmetric key algorithm, 306
System R, 4

T

table service, 226–231
Table service
  absence of need for tuning, 230
  accelerating table access, 286–291
    entity group transactions, 290
    secondary indexes, 286–290
  concurrent updates, 291–293
  core concepts, 226
  creating entities, 243–244
  creating tables, 239–243
  deleting entities, 258
  deleting tables, 258
  evolution of tools, 231
  lingo map, 228
  operations, 239–259
  pagination, 255
  partitioning, 248–254
  querying data, 244–247
  REST API for, 226
  sizes and limits, 228
  SQL Azure, compared to, 328
  traditional databases, compared to, 229
  types, 228
  updating entities, 256–258
table storage, 17, 132
tables, 227
  creating for a full-text search engine, 273
  Windows Azure table service (see table
    service)
Tandem Computers, 4
tar, 312
tar utility, 296
tarsnap service, 297
tasklist command, 115
TEMP folder, 115
terms, 264
time-sharing systems, 2
TLB (Translation Lookaside Buffer), 33
TLS (Transport Layer Security), 299
Toivonen, Heikki, 298
transactional computing, 4
transactions, 4, 230
Translation Lookaside Buffer (TLB), 33

Tymshare, 2

U

uncommitted blocks, 195
update domains, 39
upgrade domains, 102
upgrades, 102–104
  in-place upgrades, 102
  VIP swap, 104
upload_archive function, 324
upload_archive_using_blocks function, 324
URIs
  as container names, 167
URLs, 141
USE_HTTPS variable, 302
utility fabric controller, 37

V

verification, 297
VHD (Virtual Hard Disk), 34, 199
Viega, John, 298
VIP swap, 104
Virtual Hard Disk (VHD), 34
Virtual Machine Bus (VMB), 32
Virtual Machine Monitor (VMM), 28
virtual machines, 27
  sizes, 71
virtualization, 3, 13, 27
virtualization stack, 32
VisibilityTimeout, 209
VisibilityTimeouts, 210
Visual Studio Tools, 44, 62–64
  prerequisites for installation, 44
VMB (Virtual Machine Bus), 32
VMM (Virtual Machine Monitor), 28
vmsize attribute, 71

W

Watts, Vern, 4
web roles, 52, 68, 84
Windows Azure, 10–18
  data centers, 25
  fabric controller, 15
  features, 12
  origins, 10
  REST APIs, 91
  stack, 23
  storage, 16

storage on (see storage services)
virtualization, 13
Windows Azure Developer Portal (see
        Developer Portal)
Windows Azure hypervisor, 30
   guest operating system, 32
   hypervisor architecture, 30
   hypervisor features, 33
   image-based deployment model, 34
   standard user privileges, 107
   Windows Azure Hypervisor and Hyper-V,
       31
Windows Azure partial trust, 108
Windows Azure platform, 9
Windows Azure queues (see queues)
Windows Azure sandbox, 107
Windows Azure SDK (see SDK)
Windows Azure Service Management API
   Service Management API (see Service
       Management API)
Windows Azure Tools for Visual Studio (see
       Visual Studio Tools)
Windows Azure XDrive (see XDrive)
Windows High Performance Computing
       (HPC) servers, 6
Windows Hyper-V, 14
Windows Server Core, 41
Wolski, Rick, 5
worker roles, 68, 84–87
   caching layer, 87
   common patterns, 86
   creating, 84
   life cycles, 85
   port listening on an external endpoint, 79
   queue-based, asynchronous processing, 86
   UDP traffic and, 78

X

x-ms-approximate-messages-count headers,
       216
X.509 certificates, 92–95
   creating, 93
   uploading, 95
X509 certificates
   X.509v3 certificates, 299
x86/x64 processor hypervisor extensions, 28
XDrive, 198–199

About the Author

Sriram Krishnan works on the Windows Azure program management team. He has been involved with the product since before its public launch and has worked on several of the features covered in this book. Previously, Sriram worked on several Microsoft products, ranging from Web 2.0 sites to developer tools. Sriram is a frequent speaker at Microsoft events, and he blogs at *http://www.sriramkrishnan.com*.

Colophon

The animal on the cover of *Programming Windows Azure* is a dhole (*Cuon alpinus*). Nicknamed "red dog" by Rudyard Kipling in *The Second Jungle Book*, this canine species is also known as an Asiatic wild dog or Indian wild dog. Dholes are found in forests in India, southern Asia, Sumatra, and parts of Russia, but are classified as endangered animals. Disease, habitat loss, and the subsequent depletion of prey have all caused the population to decline. Humans also commonly hunt them, as dholes will attack livestock if they cannot find another food source. Presently, it is estimated that only 2,500 adult dholes remain in the wild, primarily in wildlife sanctuaries.

The dhole is a medium-size canine with rusty red fur (though regional variations of yellow and gray exist), a white chest and belly, and a bushy black tail. They are known for their extensive range of vocal calls—hisses, high-pitched screams, mews, squeaks, barks, clucks, yelps—and a strange whistle that is distinctive enough to identify the individual dhole making the sound.

Like wolves and other canids, dholes are a very social animal, living in packs with a strict hierarchy. There are more males than females within a pack, and usually only one dominant breeding pair. Dhole packs engage in activities like playing, grooming, mock-fighting, and of course, hunting. As a group, dholes can successfully attack and subdue much larger prey. They primarily feed on deer, but will also hunt hare, wild boar, or water buffalo. There is little aggression between adult dholes—they do not fight over a kill, but rather will compete by eating as quickly (and as much) as they can.

The cover image is from Wood's *Animate Creatures*. The cover font is Adobe ITC Garamond. The text font is Linotype Birka; the heading font is Adobe Myriad Condensed; and the code font is LucasFont's TheSansMonoCondensed.

Buy this book and get access to the online edition for 45 days—for free!

Programming Windows Azure

By Sriram Krishnan
May 2010, $49.99
ISBN 9780596801977

With Safari Books Online, you can:

Access the contents of thousands of technology and business books

- Quickly search over 7000 books and certification guides
- Download whole books or chapters in PDF format, at no extra cost, to print or read on the go
- Copy and paste code
- Save up to 35% on O'Reilly print books
- **New!** Access mobile-friendly books directly from cell phones and mobile devices

Stay up-to-date on emerging topics before the books are published

- Get on-demand access to evolving manuscripts.
- Interact directly with authors of upcoming books

Explore thousands of hours of video on technology and design topics

- Learn from expert video tutorials
- Watch and replay recorded conference sessions

To try out Safari and the online edition of this book FREE for 45 days, go to *www.oreilly.com/go/safarienabled* and enter the coupon code EKCEGDB. To see the complete Safari Library, visit safari.oreilly.com.

Spreading the knowledge of innovators   safari.oreilly.com